REVOLUTION
DOWNEAST

```
973.309741 L474r
Leamon, James S.
Revolution downeast
```

REVOLUTION
DOWNEAST

The War for American Independence in Maine

James S. Leamon

THE UNIVERSITY OF MASSACHUSETTS PRESS *Amherst*
Published in cooperation with the Maine Historical Society

Copyright © 1993 by
The Maine Historical Society
All rights reserved
Printed in the United States of America
LC 92-17757
ISBN 0-87023-959-7
Designed by Mary Mendell
Set in Janson Text
Printed and bound by Thomson Shore
Library of Congress Cataloging-in-Publication Data
Leamon, James S.
Revolution downeast :
the war for American independence in Maine /
James S. Leamon.
p. cm.
Includes bibliographical references and index.
ISBN 0-87023-959-7 (pbk.: alk. paper)
1. Maine — History — Revolution, 1775–1783. I. Title.
E263.M4L3   1992
973.3'09741 — dc20   92-17757
CIP
British Library Cataloguing in Publication
data are available.

For my parents
John H. and Clarice P. Leamon

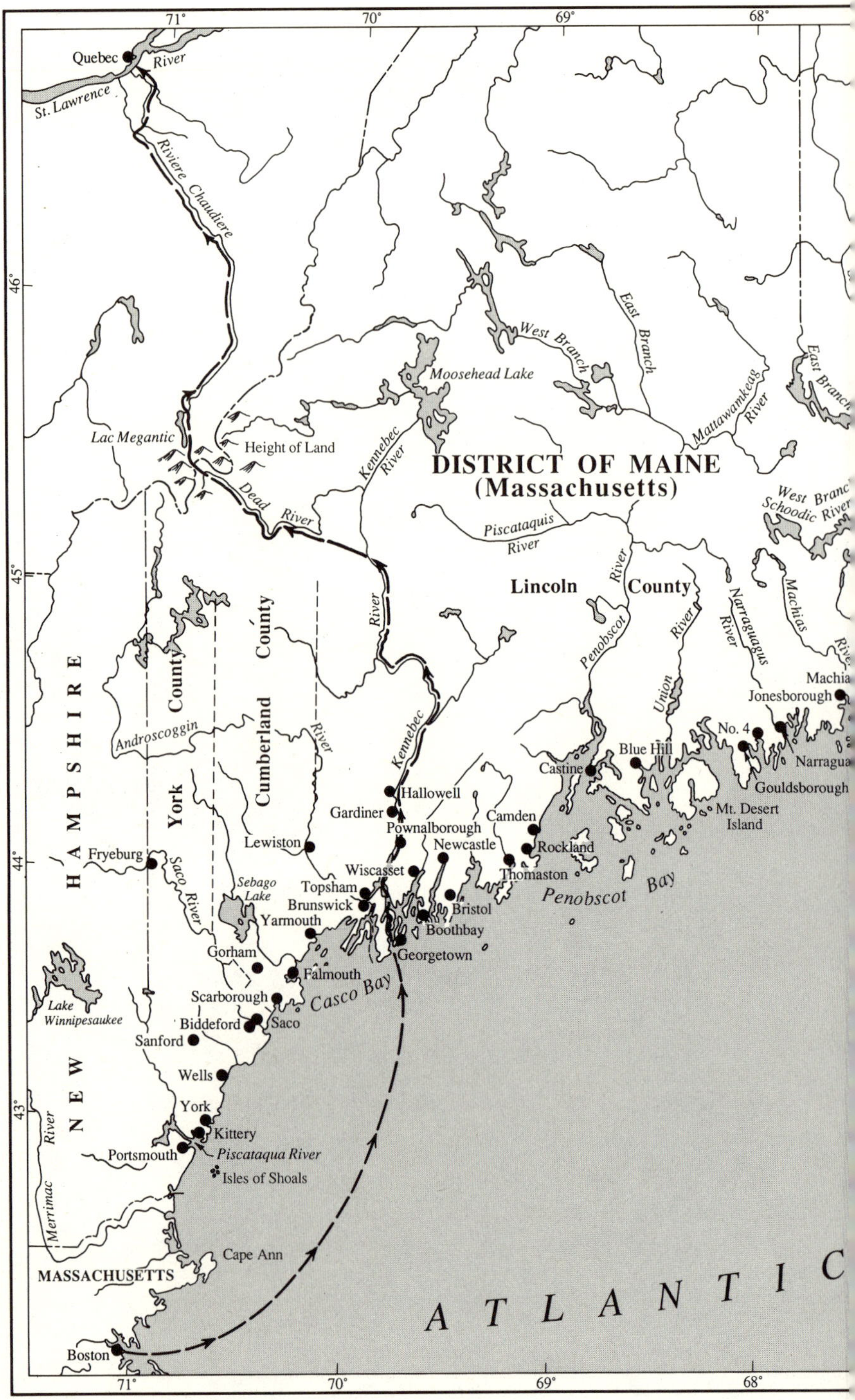

DISTRICT OF MAINE
(Massachusetts)
Lincoln County
Cumberland County
York County
NEW HAMPSHIRE
MASSACHUSETTS
ATLANTIC
Quebec
St. Lawrence River
Riviere Chaudiere
Lac Megantic
Height of Land
Dead River
Kennebec River
Moosehead Lake
West Branch
East Branch
Mattawamkeag River
Piscataquis River
Penobscot River
Union River
Narraguagus River
Machias River
West Branch Schoodic River
Androscoggin
Saco River
Sebago Lake
Lake Winnipesaukee
Merrimac River
Piscataqua River
Isles of Shoals
Cape Ann
Boston
Portsmouth
Kittery
York
Wells
Sanford
Biddeford
Saco
Scarborough
Casco Bay
Falmouth
Gorham
Yarmouth
Brunswick
Topsham
Wiscasset
Lewiston
Fryeburg
Hallowell
Gardiner
Pownalborough
Newcastle
Bristol
Boothbay
Georgetown
Camden
Rockland
Thomaston
Penobscot Bay
Castine
Blue Hill
Mt. Desert Island
No. 4
Gouldsborough
Jonesborough
Machias
Narraguagus
71°
70°
69°
68°
46°
45°
44°
43°

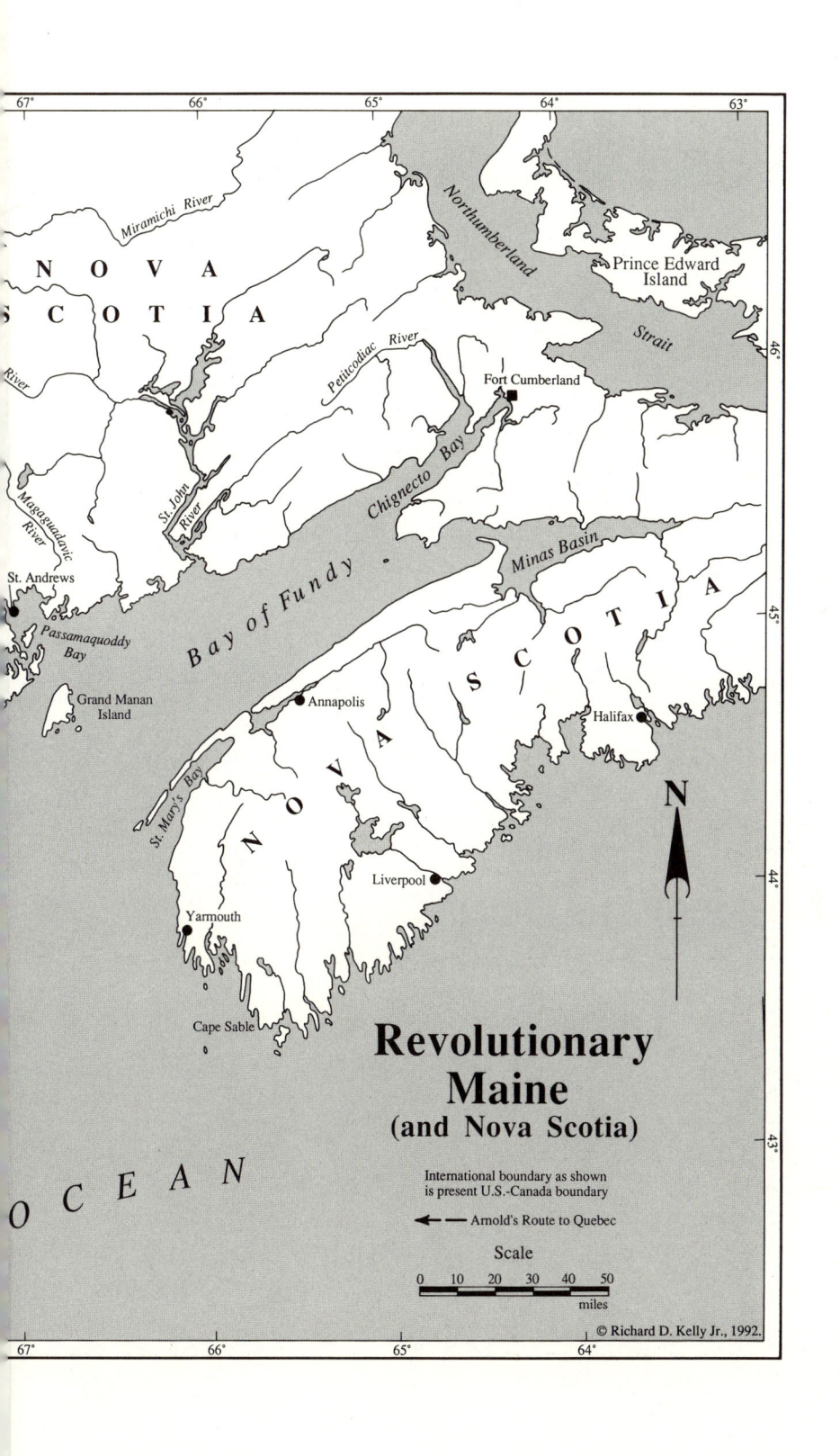

Revolutionary Maine
(and Nova Scotia)

International boundary as shown is present U.S.-Canada boundary

← — Arnold's Route to Quebec

Scale
0 10 20 30 40 50
miles

© Richard D. Kelly Jr., 1992

CONTENTS

Illustrations xi

Preface xiii

1 Maine: The Colony of a Province in an Empire 3

2 The Revolution Comes to Maine 40

3 Protective Insignificance 74

4 Crisis on the Penobscot 104

5 A People Divided: The Economic and Social Costs of Revolution 135

6 State Making and State Breaking 166

7 The Legacy of Revolution 188

Abbreviations 224

Notes 225

Bibliography 269

Index 291

ILLUSTRATIONS

1   Village of Machias, 1776   10

2   Double Sawmill, Machias, 1776   11

3   Map of Falmouth (Portland), 1775   16

4   The Reverend Samuel Deane   22

5   Lincoln County Courthouse   26

6   Attorney John Adams   28

7   Falmouth Being Burned, October 1775   71

8   H.M.S. *Canceaux*   72

9   Map of American Defeat on the Penobscot River   115

10   British Pursuit of American Vessels up Penobscot Bay   116

11   Map of Penobscot Bay   124

PREFACE

In the late eighteenth century, a disgruntled resident of Maine complained that Maine was nothing but "an insignificant colony to Massachusetts." That remark has a validity for both the history *of* Maine and history *about* Maine. Since the middle of the seventeenth century, the powerful Massachusetts Bay Colony had exercised an increasing hegemony over the settlements downeast—a hegemony legalized in the Massachusetts royal charter of 1691. From then until 1820, when it became a state, Maine remained an integral part of Massachusetts. Geographically isolated from the Bay Colony by the province of New Hampshire, and dependent on Massachusetts for its very existence, Maine was indeed a colony, in every sense of the word.

The significance of this dependency extends to the writing of Maine's early history. The larger Massachusetts context has tended to obscure Maine as a legitimate object of study, nowhere more than in the period of the American Revolution. Studies of the Revolution in Massachusetts focus on famous leaders and the "inarticulate" crowd, on towns large and small, on revolutionary agitation, on constitutions, political parties, and on Shays' Rebellion in western Massachusetts—but not on Maine. Maine has remained a colony to Massachusetts historiographically much as it was politically and economically.

Even historians of Maine have slighted the period of the American Revolution. Where appropriate, town historians devote a chapter or so to the event, but only in the context of a particular community. Surprisingly, the basic historical surveys of Maine offer little better treatment of the Revolution. James Sullivan was a resident of Maine at the time of the Revolution and even a participant, yet his *History of the District of Maine*

(1795) ends at the very point where the Revolution begins. William Williamson, who published a two-volume history of Maine in 1832, certainly did not ignore the topic. He took no less than seven chapters to cover the revolutionary period, and today his work is still a valuable source. Yet Williamson's style is deadly for modern readers. His book, a vast compendium of data arranged in strict chronological fashion, leaves out *nothing* and explains *nothing*.

More readable is *Maine: A History*, edited by Louis C. Hatch and published in 1919. Hatch had already distinguished himself with a book on the administration of the American revolutionary army, but unfortunately his interest in the Revolution did not include Maine. In his three-volume history of the state, Hatch allocated to the Revolution a mere ten pages sandwiched between chapters dealing with the colonial period, on the one side, and the Indians of Maine on the other.

Modern studies of the Revolution in Maine tend to highlight specific areas and groups rather than the movement as a whole. John Ahlin's *Maine Rubicon: Downeast Settlers during the American Revolution* (1966) concentrates on the dramatic events in eastern Maine along the Penobscot River and farther east around Machias. Alan Taylor, in his doctoral dissertation, several articles, and recently published book, *Liberty Men and Great Proprietors: The Revolutionary Settlement on the Maine Frontier, 1760–1820* (1990), examines the struggle of settlers on the frontier against the great landowners and the government that supported them. Ahlin and Taylor contribute much to an understanding of revolutionary Maine, but their special interests are focused on particular regional experiences. There still exists no general history of the Revolution in Maine.

This present work is intended to meet that deficiency by drawing together town and general histories, specialized studies, and primary sources, both published and unpublished. It examines why and how Maine fought the Revolution and the changes that occurred in Maine during and after the war.

The history of the Revolution in Maine is the story of a people who did not really want a revolution — at least at first. Most of Maine's residents were too isolated and too preoccupied with surviving in a grudging environment to be much concerned over imperial issues. Maine's leading commercial centers felt tremors of agitation as early as 1765, but

Maine paid little heed to political radicals until Parliament's heavy-handed response to the Tea Party in 1774. Only then did Maine join the movement to resist Britain's policies.

Leaders and spokesmen of the Revolution in Maine were generally the local elite with close ties to Boston — merchants, lawyers, preachers, judicial officers — who carefully preserved their own local leadership while defying the authority of king and Parliament. Revolutionary leaders in Maine and elsewhere had no intention of encouraging social revolution. Despite the spread of revolutionary enthusiasm, Maine's traditional leaders maintained control of an essentially conservative revolution with remarkable success.

They were less successful in protecting Maine from the enemy. The constant threat of the British in Nova Scotia shaped Maine's response to the war. Since Massachusetts could not protect so extended a frontier, Mainers relied on nearby Indians — whom they had always exploited — and on their own obscurity and insignificance in the hope that the British might pass them by. But neither Indians nor obscurity could save Maine. Enemy privateers plundered Maine shipping and coastal settlements almost at will, and in 1779 the British established a base at the mouth of the Penobscot River. The British presence aroused local loyalists to action and transformed a revolution into a bitter civil war. Pessimism and exhaustion induced some of the more vulnerable settlements in far eastern Maine to propose an early peace, but Maine's towns rejected such temptations and persevered in the patriotic cause to the end.

The war physically devastated Maine and polarized its people, accentuating differences between rich and poor, between interior and coastal communities, between revolutionaries and loyalists, between the establishment and dissenters, and eventually if not immediately, between Massachusetts and Maine. Liberty, rather than an objective goal, turned out to be a disruptive, divisive process that different groups and sections interpreted differently and achieved imperfectly, if at all. Unexpectedly, the experience of revolution had unleashed demands for change.

The refusal of the state's revolutionary leaders to introduce social and political reforms alienated and eventually inspired dissidents in the District to initiate their own revolution — statehood. In short, Maine experienced two revolutions, not one. Maine participated in the first, independence from Britain, as a colony to Massachusetts. In *Maine Becomes a State* (1970), Ronald F. Banks examined what is really the second, independence from Massachusetts. It is the first of these two revolutions that is the topic of this book.

Significant for Maine as its history of the Revolution may be, the topic possesses an importance beyond that of Maine itself. Recent historical interest has focused on the revolutionary experience of frontier or "conflicted" societies, such as Maryland's Delmarva Peninsula or, more particularly, the Carolinas and Georgia. In some respects, the Maine experience replicates that of the lower South in the Revolution. Like Georgia, for example, its settlements lay isolated and exposed to the enemy with few economic and military resources. Such conditions whether in the North or the South tended at first to dampen revolutionary ardor and, as much as ideology, helped to shape political loyalties.

When the Revolution came to these outlying areas, it did so with devastating impact. Both Maine and Georgia had to contend with an Indian threat, plundering raids by enemy privateers, invasion and territorial occupation by British regulars—all of which brought the struggle between loyalists and Whigs to a new level of intensity. The brutality of guerrilla warfare, which characterized the Revolution in the backcountry of Georgia and the Carolinas once the British occupied Savannah and Charleston, had its counterpart along the coast of eastern Maine after the British occupation of Castine in 1779. Exercising a weak and precarious authority, revolutionary leaders north and south struggled to find strategies to preserve order in a disintegrating society and to create from the chaos of war a stable republic. Surprisingly enough, they succeeded.

Significant differences make the revolutionary history of Maine unique, but the similarities are sufficient to warrant the examination of Maine's revolutionary experience within the larger context of other conflicted regions contending with poorly defined loyalties, disrupted economies, enemy incursions, and internecine violence. Currently, Maine is not on the list of such regions, but clearly it ought to be, and its history can thereby contribute to an understanding of how such underdeveloped and dependent areas responded to the challenges of revolution.

Several geographical terms need clarification. At the time of the Revolution, three Massachusetts counties, York, Cumberland, and Lincoln, composed all of Maine. In 1778 the United States Congress divided the country's entire coastline into customs districts, one of which included the three Maine counties, so the region was often referred to as the District of Maine until it became a state. The District's coastline curves sharply northeastward, and so the Maine counties were the easternmost in Massachusetts. Because the prevailing direction of the wind is easterly, vessels sail *down* east and *up* to Boston. Mainers are, therefore, "downeasterners."

When we refer to the state of Massachusetts alone, however, the more conventional terms apply. The *western* counties, Berkshire, Hampshire, and Worcester, are farthest from the coast. The eastern counties are those along the coast, such as Suffolk, Essex, and Middlesex. This may seem simple enough, but the possibility of confusion arises when we refer to the *eastern* towns of Boston, Gloucester, and Newburyport, for example, and the coastal towns in *western* Maine of York and Kittery. Obviously, the difference lies in the points of reference. Town names present another problem, for many names have changed since the eighteenth century. In this study, the eighteenth-century names are given, but when they first appear in the text their modern names are given in parentheses.

Throughout this undertaking, the help of friends and colleagues has been indispensable. Both Joan Morrison and Silver Leamon, despite the burdens of farm and family, assisted in researching newspapers and local histories. Fred Grant shared with me his research on Paul Revere and on the movement for legal reform in postwar Massachusetts. I learned much about merchants in eighteenth-century Falmouth from Edwin Churchill, chief curator of the Maine State Museum, who also contributed his broad bibliographical knowledge of early Maine. Alice Stewart, Professor Emeritus, University of Maine at Orono, gave me the benefit of her research materials on John Allan. Thomas Gaffney brought to my attention many valuable collections in the Maine Historical Society when he was curator of manuscripts there.

Indeed, there is a vast army of librarians and archivists whose skill and patience have been crucial. To those at the following institutions, I am especially grateful: Library of Congress, Public Archives of Nova Scotia, Massachusetts Historical Society, Massachusetts State Archives, Maine State Archives, Museum, and Public Library, the Lincoln County Cultural and Historical Association, Wiscasset Public Library,

Hawthorne-Longfellow Library at Bowdoin College, and the Ladd Library at Bates College.

Many colleagues took the time to read versions of the manuscript and to contribute critical insights: At Bates, Steve Crow and Ernest P. Muller; Richard Beeman of the University of Pennsylvania; Jere Daniell, Dartmouth College; Alan Taylor, Boston University; and at the University of Maine at Orono, Jerome Nadelhaft, and especially Richard Judd. The late Ronald F. Banks had a special relationship to this project from the very start—as he did for so many such undertakings. As chairman of the Maine State Revolutionary Bicentennial Commission, he invited me to assume this task back in 1974. Now, eighteen years and countless interruptions later, it is finally complete.

Generous financial help made the long task easier—if not quicker. I am grateful for assistance from the Maine State Revolutionary Bicentennial Commission and also from the National Endowment for the Humanities. Bates College has been particularly supportive in granting me a special leave of absence, financial assistance from the President's Discretionary Fund for Faculty Publication, a Schmutz Faculty Research Grant, as well as help in manuscript preparation. In addition, the continuing interest of the Maine Historical Society has been a constant source of encouragement; I derive special pride and pleasure from the Society's sponsorship of the manuscript for publication.

Finally, I must recognize five young people who grew to maturity in the Leamon household along with this manuscript. To Ann, Sue, Becky, John, and Tom, my gratitude and love for your humor, support, and constant reminder to an occasionally grumpy academic that there are some things more important than academic pursuits. That lesson endures, thanks to Nicci, my wife, and another young person, Sander, whose understanding and support helped bring the task to completion.

REVOLUTION
DOWNEAST

ONE

*Maine: The Colony of a Province
in an Empire*

🌲

Throughout the colonial period, Maine existed as a colony of Massachusetts, quite as much as Massachusetts itself was an imperial province of Great Britain. During the latter half of the seventeenth century, Massachusetts had slowly extended its authority over the territory to the east. New Hampshire escaped annexation, but the scattered settlements and feudal jurisdictions east of the Piscataqua River gradually surrendered to the power of the Bay Colony. When the British crown issued Massachusetts a new charter in 1691, Maine officially became a possession of Massachusetts.[1] Geographically isolated and thinly settled, the communities of Maine looked to the Bay Colony for protection from the French and Indians, for economic support, and for government sufficient to maintain order over an expanding, restless society.

I

English settlement of Maine occurred in the face of stubborn resistance from the aboriginal inhabitants. From the early seventeenth century, Maine's Indians had been drawn into the French orbit through trade and conversion to the Roman Catholic faith. In the imperial struggle between England and France for control of North America, the Indians remained faithful and active allies to the French. But disease and five major wars between 1675 and 1763 culminating in the defeat of France left Maine Indians isolated and decimated. By 1775 the Indians in Nova Scotia and eastern Maine numbered about 3,000. In western and southern Maine, those who had once occupied the Saco, Kennebec, and Androscoggin river valleys barely existed as organized tribes. East of the

Penobscot River, the Indians, although badly weakened, still preserved their tribal identities. The Penobscots, living along the river of that name, were reduced to 250 people and could muster but 50 warriors. The total strength of the Passamaquoddy–Saint John or Malecite Indians did not exceed 600, from which they could raise 150 warriors at the most. East of the Saint John River, in what is now New Brunswick but was then part of Nova Scotia, lived the Micmacs, who could supply about 500 fighting men from their population of 2,000. At the most, the combined military strength of Maine and Nova Scotian Indians numbered only between 700 and 800 warriors.[2] Even this figure is more apparent than real, for never were the eastern Indians able to combine their strength despite a common cultural background.

The collapse of French power in North America left the Indians at the mercy of their ancient enemies, the British. The royal governor of Massachusetts declared that since the Indians had repeatedly broken their peace treaties with the British to assist the French, the Indians were traitors to the British crown and their lands forfeit by right of conquest. To the British, therefore, the Indians were "tenants at will," living on their lands only at the sufferance of the crown. In 1769 representatives from the Penobscots and Passamaquoddies acknowledged their dependent status by pleading with the British king "to extend his pity to us and grant us so much Land as will give us and our Families subsistence in the way of life which we have been used to."[3] Neither the crown nor the Massachusetts provincial government heeded the pleas of the Indians, who remained virtual squatters on what had once been their ancestral land, subject to constant encroachment by an expanding English population.

Cultural disintegration proved as devastating to the Indians as the impact of war and disease. Once the Indians became dependent on English manufactured goods, they were twice the losers; they lost their skill to produce their own articles, and they had to rely upon a declining supply of fur-bearing animals to obtain manufactured goods from the English. In addition, white settlement steadily reduced the Indians' capacity to range widely over the countryside according to the seasons for planting, hunting, and fishing. Indians, therefore, came to rely on government trading posts, or truck houses, for food as well as for manufactured articles. The provincial government, keenly aware of the situation, used the truck house as a means of regulating Indian activities.[4]

Sporadically, the Massachusetts government tried to protect the Indians from unscrupulous traders by prohibiting unregulated commerce between the races. However, the government control was weak, not only among the whites but among the Indians as well. Indian sachems held positions of leadership by force of personality alone, so that there were few restraints to hinder Indians who had a thirst for rum and Europeans with a lust for land. Poorly regulated trade constituted a constant source of friction, friction exacerbated by the lack of clearly defined boundaries separating Indian-occupied territory from land open to white settlement. On the eve of the Revolution, conditions among the Penobscots moved one English visitor to lament,

> Oh Penobscot! Into what a sink of filth,
> folly & beastly nastiness & intemperance are
> thy original warlike inhbs. [inhabitants]
> fallen! Oh! my soul pities all those who are
> never to know the pleasures of Men & wise men
> —May those Remains be treated justly &
> Temperately by all the English that now dwell
> on their borders.[5]

II

The decline of Indian power and the expulsion of the French from North America permitted English settlement of the Maine frontier to surge ahead. Prior to 1760, English settlement in Maine followed a wavelike motion, sweeping forward during times of peace and falling back under the fury of war. At the opening of the eighteenth century, the towns of Berwick, Scarborough, Falmouth (Portland), and all the settlements farther east had to be repopulated and built anew after the ravages of King William's War. Kittery, York, and Wells had just barely managed to withstand ferocious assaults by the French and their Indian allies. During Queen Anne's War, which erupted in 1702, the enemy again laid waste Maine's communities. Kittery, York, Wells, and Biddeford survived the raids, but to the eastward most of the settlements were either abandoned or destroyed. Saco, Scarborough, and Falmouth remained, but only as fortified posts defending a desolated region. Peace came in 1713, and during the next thirty years or so the frontier recovered and pushed ahead. The midcoast communities bore the brunt of the next war, named after King George, which broke out in 1745. Although attacked, Scarborough, Falmouth, North Yarmouth, Topsham, Brunswick, Georgetown, and Saint George all managed to survive, in part because the Massachusetts legislature provided a bounty for families who defended their homes rather than join the flood of refugees in York, Portsmouth, or Boston. Only six years of peace separated the end of King George's War in 1748 from the opening of the final struggle for North American supremacy. But as soon as the British seized Quebec in 1759, population from Massachusetts began to flow unchecked into the eastern frontier.

In 1690 Maine's estimated population was about 2,000; it was 12,000 in 1743, and 23,000 twenty years later. With the end of the colonial wars, Maine's population literally exploded. It doubled to 47,000 in the decade prior to the Revolution, 14 percent of the Bay Colony's total population of 333,400. Much of this increase occurred in easternmost Lincoln County, which experienced a phenomenal growth rate of 500 percent, from 2,600 to 15,546 inhabitants in just ten years. Twenty-one townships had been established in Maine during the bloody first half of the eighteenth century, but in the next twenty-five years between 1750 and 1775 no less than 120 townships were settled.[6] The point needs emphasis, for this booming population accounts for many of the region's problems, such as disputes over land titles, the exploitation of natural resources, and the difficulties faced by towns trying to absorb new settlers and diverse religions. Such problems plagued — and shaped — Maine during and after the Revolution.

The government of Massachusetts encouraged immigration into Maine. Frontier settlements supposedly created a barrier against the enemy during times of war; in between the wars, land grants provided an inexpensive way to reward soldiers. In addition, eastern settlement helped to relieve overcrowding within the older towns around Boston where good land was becoming scarce. Even the British government stimulated immigration to Maine. After 1763 Indian unrest in the Ohio valley led Parliament to extend a line down the Appalachian Mountains west of which English settlement was prohibited. This Proclamation Line diverted land-hungry settlers to newly won Florida, Canada, Nova Scotia, and also to Maine.[7]

In the normal process of settlement, the provincial government approved a petition from a group of proprietors for a grant of land. Government approval required that a certain number of people had to settle on the grant within a limited number of years, that they had to construct dwellings of a specified minimum size and clear a stipulated number of acres. For their part, proprietors had to provide a meetinghouse, a school, and an educated, orthodox minister. The proprietors themselves seldom took up residence in the new towns, intending simply to profit from the rising land prices generated by the increased settlement.[8] However, New Boston (Gray), New Marblehead (Windham), and New Gloucester still testify to the community origins of many of Maine's eighteenth-century towns.

Successful land speculation was expensive, risky, and time-consuming. Even the most powerful of the land companies, the Kennebec Proprietors, found it difficult. Acquiring a seventeenth-century title to 3,000 square miles along the Kennebec River, these developers built two forts, a courthouse, and settled hundreds of families in a dozen towns, some still bearing names honoring the proprietors: Bowdoinham, Gardiner, Pittston, Hallowell, Vassalborough, and Winslow.[9]

Such accomplishments came in the face of constant opposition from competing companies, such as the Pejepscot Proprietors and the heirs to Clarke and Lake, busy developing their own settlements on the lower Kennebec and Androscoggin rivers.

The Kennebec Company survived through the economic and political power of its leading proprietors. These included the elite of the mercantile families in and around Boston: Thomas Hancock, Charles Apthorp, William and James Bowdoin, Benjamin Hallowell, James Pitts, and Dr. Silvester Gardiner. As members of the Governor's Council or provincial legislature, these proprietors skillfully manipulated public policy to corporate advantage by enmeshing royal governors in company affairs. At public expense, Governor William Shirley built and garrisoned Fort Halifax on the Kennebec River, which protected company land. He received a proprietary share from the grateful company. His successor, Governor Thomas Pownall, constructed another fort on the lower Penobscot River and approved the assembly's creation of Cumberland and Lincoln counties in Maine. Lincoln County included Kennebec Company lands and the company town of Frankfort, which became the county seat, appropriately renamed Pownalborough. The proprietors bestowed a gift of land in Pownalborough on the next royal governor, Francis Bernard, and in the legislature members of the Kennebec Company helped to pass a land grant making Bernard the sole proprietor of Mount Desert Island. Thus, Governor Bernard, too, was indebted to the Kennebec Company and became a land speculator in his own right. The next governor of Massachusetts, Thomas Hutchinson, was less obliging to the Kennebec Proprietors, not through any sense of conflict of interest but simply because he was already a leading member of the Pejepscot Proprietors, the Kennebec Company's chief competitor.[10]

Proprietors great and small found it difficult to entice settlers to their lands during the period of the colonial wars. Between 1720 and 1750, however, several enterprising speculators lured unsuspecting Scots-Irish and German immigrants to Maine. One group of Scots-Irish accepted the invitation of Captain Robert Temple to settle near present-day Bath, only to be scattered by Indian attacks. The Lincolnshire Company had more success in establishing a community of Scots-Irish near Warren on the Saint Georges River. Another promoter, Samuel Waldo, recruited German and Swiss immigrants to come to Waldoboro on Broad Bay around 1740 to farm, produce limestone, and manufacture iron. The Kennebec Proprietors followed suit. Typically, they helped to persuade the provincial assembly to undertake an extensive recruiting campaign in Germany at public expense and then settled on company lands the Germans and Swiss immigrants who arrived.[11]

These non-English European immigrants created pockets of cultural diversity in Maine. The first federal census of 1790 identifies 4.5 percent Scots, 8 percent Scots-Irish, 3.7 percent Irish, and 1.3 percent Germans amid an English majority of only 60 percent of the total — a significant contrast to the rest of Massachusetts where, according to the census, the English constituted 82 percent of the population. Even if a part of Maine's surprisingly large 21 percent "unassigned" nationality is counted as English, the ethnic contrast between Maine and the rest of the Bay Colony is obvious.[12]

Once the wars were over, settlement moved so rapidly that frequently it reversed the normal pattern of petition, grant, and settlement. In 1763 a group from the Maine town of Scarborough discovered the advantageous location of Machias while searching the coast for wild grass to feed their livestock. Sixteen of them occupied the land as squatters. Jurisdiction over the region was so vague that the settlers first petitioned Nova Scotia for a grant before turning to Massachusetts. The Bay Colony approved the request with the condition that the grant receive royal approbation. Despite this uncertainty and the settlement's isolation, Machias grew rapidly. By 1776 it had attained a population of 626 and served as the regional metropolis for other new communities nearby, which were as anonymous as Number Four and as minute as Jones Plantation with a total population of forty-nine.[13]

To the south and west of Machias, settlements were not only more numerous and populous but began to stretch up the rivers into the interior. At the start of the Revolution, Georgetown, at the mouth of the Kennebec River, had 1,700 white residents, and twenty-five miles upriver, Pownalborough, Lincoln County's shire town, had over 1,400. The county seat for Cumberland County was Falmouth with a county jurisdiction extending forty miles inland along the Androscoggin River to the frontier towns of Sylvester (Turner), Raymondtown, and Lewiston. Falmouth was also Maine's leading seaport with about 3,800 inhabitants. Despite Falmouth's prominence, the most thickly settled region of all was York County in southwestern Maine. Here the old seventeenth-century towns of Kittery, York, Berwick, and Wells were all in close proximity one to another, constituting a population center of their own. Berwick, with 3,315 whites, led its neighboring communities, which had populations ranging between 2,600 and 2,900.[14] Fryeburg, eighty miles north of Kittery, marked the county's frontier. In effect, the population pattern for Maine resembled a great wedge, the base of which was the eighty-mile line between Kittery and Fryeburg with Machias as its apex more than 250 miles by sea from Kittery.

III

Whether Mainers lived in the more densely settled regions of southwestern Maine or in an eastern outpost like Machias, most of them made their living by some combination of agriculture, fishing, and lumbering. The emphasis varied according to location, but the three activities remained constant. The newer the community, the more the residents tended to exploit the most readily available natural resources, timber and fish. One of the first structures erected in any settlement was a sawmill. In 1774 a traveler downeast counted forty-six sawmills between Narraguagus (Cherryfield) and Union River, and nearly as many more from Union River to the west side of Penobscot Bay. Within a

10 Maine

1. "Mechios River near the Mills," the village of Machias, 1776. Detail from *Atlantic Neptune* III, no. 49, by Joseph F. W. Des Barres. London, 1780, reprinted, New York: Barre Publishing, 1970. Courtesy of Maine State Museum.

year of its settlement, Machias produced a million and a half board feet of lumber. In addition, Maine communities exported building timber, shingles, clapboards, barrel staves, and quantities of firewood. Masts, yards, and bowsprits were more difficult to produce. Suitable trees were protected by law, and the legal cutting of them required a license as well as laborers, hewers, teams of oxen, and special vessels to carry them. Wiscasset, Georgetown, and Falmouth all exported masts, as did many other communities, but most of the newer settlers preferred the more immediate income from lumber and firewood.[15]

The alternative to lumbering was to fish for the cod, mackerel, hake, and haddock that had drawn Europeans to the Maine coast since the sixteenth century. By the middle of the eighteenth, the fishermen had expanded their endeavors beyond the Gulf of Maine to the fishing banks off Nova Scotia and then to the fabulous wealth of the Grand Banks east of Newfoundland. Indeed, one factor in the rivalry between Britain and France was the control of these rich fishing grounds. The imperial wars seriously disrupted colonial fishing, but once the French were expelled from Canada, New England fishing regained its importance. Fleets of little sloops and schooners once again exploited the deep-sea fishing grounds, and fishermen cured their catch on deserted shores unmolested by the enemy. In the decades prior to the Revolution, Maine averaged about sixty vessels and about 300 men a year in the fishing business.[16]

In new communities, fishing and lumbering tended to be exhausting, full-time occupations, leaving little opportunity for agriculture. Most families maintained a garden and cut hay for the family cow, but they

2. "A Sketch of Mechios Mills," the sawmills at Machias. From *Atlantic Neptune* III, no. 49, by Joseph F. W. Des Barres. Courtesy of Maine State Museum.

depended on the proceeds from fishing or lumbering to pay for imported food—as well as their rum. One observer of this situation grumbled, "Hence we see the fatal consequences of living in the way of lumber to the neglect of husbandry—And not only as to their outward support, but their intemperance, especially in Rum drinking." However, Maine's leading seaport, Falmouth, also remained precariously dependent on imported food. In 1763, 1765, and again in 1772, only the timely arrival of vessels importing corn and flour saved the town from severe shortages or even famine.[17]

In general, the older communities in southwestern Maine were better off than those downeast. They had progressed beyond the primitive stage of depending solely on the sale of fish or lumber and had developed more diversified economies. Farmers in York, Kittery, and Berwick had long ago cleared their land, pulled the stumps and some of the rocks, and now raised enough grains and livestock to supply the region. Indeed, with sufficient hay, pasturage, and access to markets, they exported agricultural produce beyond New England to Nova Scotia, Newfoundland, and the Caribbean. The farmers in Berwick and Kittery enjoyed a level of prosperity that placed them among the ten most prosperous agricultural-commercial towns in the entire province—let alone Maine. In both communities, a majority of the farmers invested their profits in merchandise for retail, money at loan, and shipping. The nearby towns of Sanford and Gorham, on the other hand, like communities downeast, were among provincial towns noted for poverty and propertylessness—evidence of their newness and isolation.[18]

Regardless of whether Maine communities were new or old, poor or prosperous, ocean-borne trade was essential to their existence. To be sure, land roads linked the coastal communities, Pownalborough to North Yarmouth to Falmouth to York to Portsmouth and eventually to Boston. By 1760 a weekly postal service initiated by the innovative editor of the *New-Hampshire Gazette* ran from Portsmouth to Falmouth. A light horse-drawn vehicle could make the trip from North Yarmouth to Boston in six days, including a day of rest for the Sabbath. The overland route, however, could be exhausting and dangerous. In 1766 the bridge at York over the Cape Neddick River had become "ruinous rotten and decayed—haveing Divers large holes therein," endangering travelers along the King's Highway.[19] To John Adams, traveling on horseback through Maine on legal business, the route around Saco was "vastly disagreeable," with many steep hills and roads deeply rutted and filled with rocks. Conditions got worse between Falmouth and Pownalborough. Adams described a veritable wilderness, "So great a Weight of Wood and timber, has never fallen in my Way. . . . The Roads, where a Wheel has never rolled from the Creation, were miry and founderous," marked by fresh-cut stumps, roots, and fallen trees, one of which measured seven feet in diameter. Adams finally reached his destination, but the mere report of such road conditions was sufficient to turn back another, less intrepid traveler. Beyond the Kennebec River, overland travel was so unusual that ownership of a horse was rare.[20] The nature of the coastline, combined with the primitive conditions of overland travel, meant that transportation was cheapest, quickest, and most reliable by water.

Large ships, especially constructed for cargoes of masts, bowsprits, and spars, sailed straight from England for the Maine coast. Usually, however, little vessels built along the rivers and inlets carried Maine's fish, lumber, and wood. The Caribbean sugar islands were an essential market where traders from Maine exchanged their cargoes for island products, which they carried to England and to all the American provinces as far east as Halifax. In this way Mainers procured a means of exchange with which to obtain food and manufactures. But Maine's most vital economic link lay by sea with Boston. Despite a population that had leveled off at about 15,000 and an economy disrupted by war and depression, mid-eighteenth-century Boston was still the metropolis that attracted the newly built vessels from downeast with their cargoes of firewood, timber, and fish. The urbanites had long ago outstripped their own supplies of food, shelter, and fuel, and Maine communities readily helped to fill those needs, thereby obtaining money and credit for their own wants.[21]

Boston was more than a market; it was also a source of the investment capital and credit vital to Maine's economic development. Boston merchants did much more than merely speculate in Maine lands; often they financed the initial expense of transporting settlers to their new communities and of setting up the first saw and grist mills. Their credit and shipping services kept new settlements alive. In the decade prior to the Revolution, several Boston area merchants, Ichabod Jones, Francis Shaw, and Robert Gould, actively developed the lumber trade with Machias and with the nearby towns of Gouldsborough and Chandler's

River (Jonesborough). Ichabod Jones headed a family firm that included his son, John Coffin Jones, a merchant and speculator after whom Jonesborough and Jonesport were named, and his nephew, Stephen Jones, who ran the family store in Machias from which he oversaw his uncle's investments in sawmills and land. Ichabod's brother, Nathan, joined with Francis Shaw and Robert Gould as leading proprietors for the new settlement of Gouldsborough. Shaw's son, Francis Shaw, Jr., and Nathan Jones conducted the company's business at Gouldsborough, selling goods, exporting lumber, and investing in land.[22]

Silvester Gardiner performed a similar function for the people whom the Kennebec Proprietors settled on company lands. A Boston physician, Gardiner was also a merchant who imported and retailed medical supplies. One of the most aggressive of the Kennebec Proprietors, he supervised company affairs and his own personal interests with such vigor that he repeatedly clashed with settlers and company colleagues alike. He quickly saw the advantages of obtaining a vessel, with which he supplied the residents of Pownalborough. He built the first sawmills there and in general provided goods and services essential to the new community.[23]

Numerous other merchants provided the same crucial link between the frontier communities and the metropolis. Nathan Phillips of Boston was involved in the lumber business in the town of Majabigwaduce (Castine) on Penobscot Bay. Like Silvester Gardiner and Ichabod Jones, he operated a store there in partnership with several local men. On Deer Isle, Nathaniel Kent, another Bostonian, was the entrepreneur who supplied the settlers and financed their improvements.[24]

In some of the older towns, such as Falmouth, Scarborough, and York, economic development had reached the point where resident merchants could assume the functions that outsiders performed in newer communities. Enoch Freeman in Falmouth, Richard King in Scarborough, and Jonathan Sayward in York were all either native or long-term residents of their towns. Primarily they exported lumber, masts, fish, sometimes newly built vessels, and occasionally furs and skins to Boston. They did business with other mainland ports as well as the Caribbean islands and sometimes England. King and Sayward frequently sent livestock to Halifax and Newfoundland. They imported molasses, rum, wine, sugar, tea, corn, various sorts of cloth, and a wide variety of manufactured articles, which they wholesaled to smaller merchants and retailed through their stores to individual customers.

In payment, merchants frequently had to accept from their currency-poor customers a means of exchange called "country rate," labor, lumber, livestock, and agricultural produce at fixed value.[25] The system required astonishing versatility on the part of the merchants, who cleared profits only by constant and diligent attention to business and books. Despite a 35 percent average mark-up at which Enoch Freeman sold most of his goods, historian Edwin Churchill figures that considering Freeman's own costs of credit, plus transportation, warehousing, and wages, he probably secured only a 10 percent profit.[26] Like most of his commercial colleagues, Freeman improved his earnings by profitable investments in shipping, insurance, money at loan, mortgages, mills, and land.

Possibly, in a commercial center like Falmouth, competition among merchants tended to limit mark-ups and profits. But downeast merchants who faced little competition exercised little restraint. The Reverend Jacob Bailey, speaking on behalf of the poor settlers along the Kennebec River, vehemently condemned "petty traders and coasters" for charging extravagant prices for necessities, while taking in return shingles, staves, and timber at the lowest possible rates.[27] In correspondence among themselves, downeast merchants admitted to a 200 percent mark-up for rum and to charging four times the legal maximum for credit.[28] Little wonder that merchants, even in the best of times, had the reputation of being a hard, grasping class of men. These were precisely the qualities needed to survive in the uncertain, competitive commercial world of the eighteenth century.

Maine's economic relationship to Massachusetts was a colonial one, much like the connection between all the provinces and Great Britain. Maine depended on the Bay Colony for goods and even for food, yet the value of exports from Maine did not cover the costs of what Maine had to procure from the metropolis. Boston firms, such as Thomas and John Hancock, sold their goods on credit to their counterparts downeast, who in turn did the same for their customers on the local level. A delicate web of credit relationships extended from the lowest to the highest level of society. A war, a storm, a depression, or a glutted market could spell disaster for merchants, their debtors, and their creditors. Jonathan Sayward surely spoke for merchants everywhere in the little prayer with which he concluded each annual reckoning: "I have had a general Blessing on all my Concerns this year past blessed be God."[29]

Maine's merchants formed the apex of a social pyramid which, in the

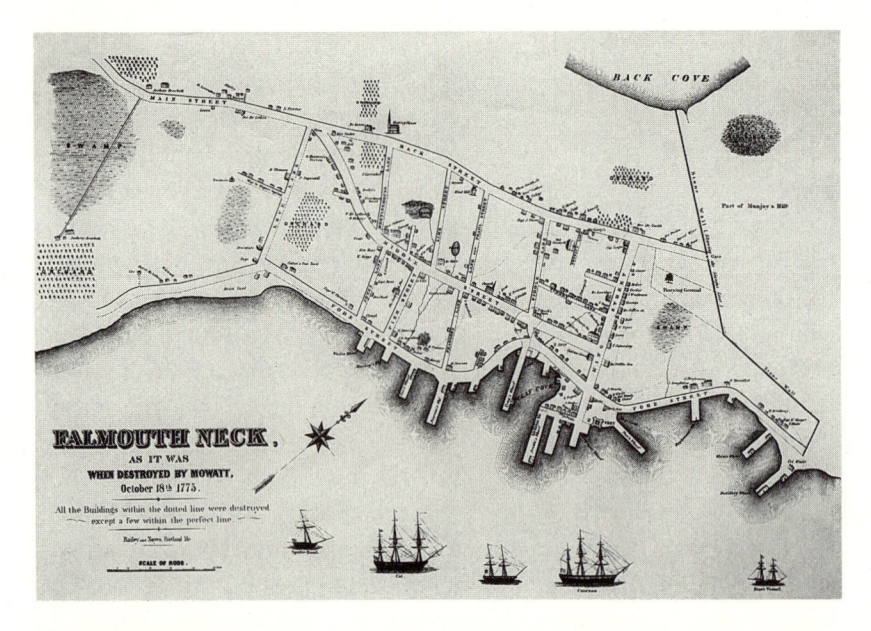

3. Falmouth Neck (Portland), 1775. From William Willis, *The History of Portland* (Portland, Me.: Charles Day, 1833), vol. 2. Courtesy of the Maine Historical Society.

more highly developed commercial towns, was a close approximation of the social order in other seaports of Massachusetts. Maine's merchants could not rival the ostentatious wealth of the Boston elite, but their economic preeminence enabled them to dominate judicial and political activities in their respective communities as effectively as their colleagues in the provincial capital. In the thirty years before the Revolution, Enoch Freeman, for example, held the positions of selectman for the town of Falmouth, town treasurer, notary public, justice of the peace, representative to the General Court, naval officer for the port, deputy collector of customs, register of deeds, judge of the Court of Common Pleas, judge of probate, and colonel of militia.[30] Leading merchants, such as Freeman, Richard King, Jonathan Sayward, Ichabod Jones, and their colleagues, were the "better sort," the gentlemen who, despite some very humble origins, had acquired enough worldly success to expect and generally receive deference from the rest of the community. Together with lawyers, doctors, and the Congregational clergy, these local leaders distinguished themselves from the rest of society by their education, the possession of two-story, occasionally three-story, houses, fine clothes, wigs, lace hats, and especially their ability to avoid working with their hands in an age of manual labor.

Beneath the "better sort" on the social-economic scale extended a hierarchy of smaller merchants, shopkeepers, artisans, craftsmen, and farmers, some of whom had achieved sufficient social stature to warrant the title of "yeoman." The term implied that the recipient possessed the personal competence, wisdom, even virtue to accumulate property enough to free him from dependence on the will of others. The ambition to attain such a condition was "perhaps the most powerful drive in the British-American colonizing process from the seventeenth century through much of the nineteenth century."[31]

Despite its significance, the title "yeoman" was very imprecise and bestowed informally by the community. William Rouse, a hatter of Falmouth, had achieved the status of yeoman by the time he died, although his estate was valued at only ninety-six pounds—half of it in felt hats. So too Edward Bowman, a shopkeeper who died with an equally modest estate. Illustrating the other end of the spectrum, a Falmouth fisherman named John Mariner owned enough land, livestock, agricultural implements, and standing timber to place him in the upper levels of yeomanry with an estate assessed at 2,430 pounds.[32]

Farming, however, was the traditional yeoman's occupation. To possess and improve sufficient agricultural land to provide the necessities of life for this generation and the next was a goal that lured many an immigrant to the Maine frontier. Clarence Day, historian of Maine agriculture, describes Hugh McLellan of Gorham as the typical frontier farmer, representative of countless Maine farmers well into the nineteenth century. Like him, they conquered the wilderness with axe and fire, planted corn, potatoes, peas, and pumpkins on the new burn. Like him, they pastured their livestock amid the stumps or cut the sparse "volunteer" hay crop—the harvest of which helped to determine the number of livestock they could winter over. Like McLellan, Maine farmers suffered hardship and privation to attain their goal of real independence. They lived in hewn timber cabins built with their own hands and farmed with the crudest of tools and techniques. Like him, they turned lumbermen whenever the opportunity offered. Depending on their ability to produce a surplus and the availability of markets, Maine farmers, with their wives and children, either prospered or else suffered the grim gnawings of hunger. Property ownership alone did not guarantee prosperity or a comfortable living and real independence, but property was an essential first step.[33]

Individuals who owned no property lacked that essential sense of freedom from the arbitrary will of others. They were tenants or day laborers associated with work on farms, on the docks, in shipyards, and occasionally in activities less legal. Unskilled laborers constituted a growing class of transients who traveled from one community to the next looking for work. Poor, rootless, and exploited, they readily turned to petty crime, leaving their mark chiefly in court records, newspaper accounts, and in one remarkable autobiography. The author, Henry Tufts, wandered through towns in New Hampshire and southern Maine searching for opportunities where he could find them. He discovered them, not as a laborer but as a thief, horse stealer, "con artist," jailbreaker, bigamist — and eventually as a military deserter and counterfeiter. Tufts's account makes it clear that his life was not exceptional; wherever he traveled, he found men and women who shared his delight in defying social conventions while seeking their own pleasure — and other people's property.[34]

Growing seaport towns tended to attract the more systematic illicit activities. In 1765 the *New-Hampshire Gazette* implied the existence of organized prostitution in the town of York with the report that a group of six women were convicted there of fornication. Two novices escaped physical punishment, but the other four, "Veterans in the Service" who could not pay their fines, received ten lashes each on the naked back at the public whipping post. For "additional faults," probably stealing, two of the women were then committed to the local house of correction where, "by way of Entrance," each had to submit to ten stripes more.[35]

Below the shifting segment of the near poor and the poor were the unfree elements of the population, apprentices, indentured servants, and slaves. The first two groups were bound for only a limited number of years, and there is little data on their numbers or condition in Maine. Slaves, however, were property for life and constituted a status symbol among the wealthier segment of the population, for whom slaves served as household servants and farm laborers. Enoch Freeman occasionally imported slaves; Jonathan Sayward, Richard King, and other merchants owned them, as did the Reverend Thomas Smith of Falmouth and the Reverend James Lyon of Machias. Slaveholding in Maine was most prevalent in the older, more commercial regions, and though the practice was not economically significant in 1765, it was even less so by 1776. Negroes, probably slaves, totaled 334 in 1765 and 468 in 1776.[36] This increase of about 40 percent in over a decade occurred when the total population in Maine more than doubled, an indication of slavery's declining importance downeast. Yet the very existence of slavery and its gradual spread to small towns like Pittston, Bristol, and Machias indicate widespread acquiescence in the institution's contradictions and inherent cruelties.

A sampling of thirteen prerevolutionary towns in Maine leads a modern scholar to describe society as polarized between the privileged few and the many poor, who in turn divided equally between those who possessed property sufficient only to enjoy few comforts and those living in poverty without any taxable property.[37] In an overwhelmingly agricultural society, a remarkably high proportion of 48 percent of taxpayers in the sample towns owned no cultivated land at all; 47 percent possessed only one to five cultivated acres, and only the remaining 5 percent of the taxpaying population owned more. The ownership of livestock followed the same pattern: The number of taxpayers who possessed no sheep, goats, hogs, or cattle about equaled those owning only one to five — in contrast to a very small number of persons claiming significantly more. The same situation prevailed in the ownership of a dwelling; 46 percent of the taxpayers in the sample did not own a house, while 53 percent owned one — in many cases a log structure. A mere 0.8 percent owned two or more dwellings. Similarly, among the sample towns only 8 percent of the taxpayers owned all the listed commercial property, 6 percent possessed lumber or grist mills, 2 percent owned slaves, and a minute 1 percent loaned money at interest.[38]

The distribution of taxable property confirms the economic polarization. In seaports and coastal communities such as Falmouth and Scarborough, the top decile owned well over 40 percent, while in both communities the upper 20 percent of taxpayers owned 64 percent of the property. Even in inland Gorham, distinguished for its propertylessness and its lack of commercialization, the upper 10 percent owned 38 percent of the wealth, and the upper 20 percent of the taxpayers possessed about 60 percent. In Brunswick, Falmouth, Gorham, and Scarborough alike, despite differences in size, locality, and economic development, the lower half of the taxpayers owned only 4 to 6 percent of the taxable property.[39] In communities farther downeast and in the interior, such as Jonesborough or Gouldsborough, isolation and newness presumably truncated the social pyramid. Merchants, money, and professional men were scarce, and a correspondingly large segment of the residents owned little or no property, sharing an equality near to poverty. Even so, stratification persisted; 16 percent of the taxpayers in Boothbay owned half the community's real estate, in Pownalborough it was 13 percent, and in Georgetown a mere 11 percent of the taxpayers possessed half the town's real property.[40]

Such contrasts in the distribution of property and the corresponding social structure could produce deep resentments and tensions among individuals, rival towns, and geographical sections. Until the Revolution, however, the institutions of church and government, as well as the realities of a mobile society, helped to mute such antagonisms, or at least keep them in check. Social and economic inequities were not static; many of those who constituted the propertyless poor were young adults still living with parents or were young men, single or heads of new families, just starting their careers. Many could reasonably hope for an improvement in their condition in time, for economic and social progress was partly a matter of age. Even in the seaports, a laborer who remained single and developed a skill could look to the future with anticipation rather than dread.[41] For Maine's poor, the promise of the future helped to mitigate the frustrations of the present.

IV

More directly, the institutions of church and government exercised a restraining influence upon Maine's dynamic, potentially restless population. The most immediate was town government. In town meeting the adult white males who met the property qualification of a twenty-pound estate — and many who did not — expressed the corporate will of the majority. In terms of the eighteenth century, the qualification was remarkably inclusive in an effort to achieve a town consensus rather than a polarized, fractionalized community. The large number of offices that the town filled each spring illustrates another way the community tried to form and enforce the local consensus. Each year, an average of anywhere from 5 to 13 percent of the adult males assumed official responsibilities in town government. The young, untried men received the humbler posts of pound keeper, hog reeve, and viewer of the roads and fences. The local elite, noted for their probity and prosperity, occupied the more prestigious positions as moderator, selectman, treasurer, assessor, and clerk. These men did not constitute an oligarchy in any rigid sense — few held office more than three or four years at a time — yet their wealth, education, and experience gave them the obligation and "right" to speak out on important issues and to define alternatives in reaching the consensus.[42]

In most towns the established church provided another kind of social control. By law, each town had to provide for a learned and orthodox minister, which meant that the town supported by public taxation a Congregational church and a university-trained minister, usually from Harvard or Yale. Although elected by their parishioners and ultimately answerable to them, ministers occupied a social station and religious vocation above and apart from their congregations. Their special training and calling enabled them to set the prosaic events of daily life within the larger moral world view shaped by Calvinism. By word and example, Congregational preachers expounded the ideal Christian life which, in addition to love and charity, included the traditional values needed to restrain sinful man, sobriety, industry, thrift, moral virtue, deference, and order. It was no accident that in the aftermath of a riot in far-off Machias, the provincial government not only appointed another justice of the peace but authorized the town, although still unincorporated, to raise taxes for the support of a Congregational minister — a spiritual benefit, obviously, but one "which may likewise tend to the ... support of Civil order."[43]

Maine's growing and diverse communities found it increasingly difficult to agree on suitable ministers and on the number and location of meetinghouses within towns. In Arundel (Kennebunkport) and also in Bristol, feelings became so intense over the location of the meetinghouse that rival factions literally tore down the structure of their opponents. The citizens of Newcastle took ten bitter years before they could finally agree on a pastoral candidate willing to accept the call — and then only with serious misgivings about "a People among whom a party Spirit prevailed."[44] The religious excitement of the 1740s, called the Great Awakening, divided many communities between New Light supporters of the revival and the Old Light opposition. In Falmouth, the conservative Old Lights not only withdrew from the New Lights but

4. Cosmopolitan Congregationalist: The Reverend Samuel Deane of Falmouth's First Parish Church. Portrait by John Brewster, Jr. (1766–1854). Courtesy of the Maine Historical Society.

proceeded to establish an Anglican church. In Gorham, on the other hand, the New Lights split from the established Congregational church to form a parish of their own under the inspired leadership of an illiterate shoemaker.[45]

New religious sects, such as Baptists and Quakers, offered additional alternatives to the established church and demanded exemption from the tax supporting the Congregational minister. Town authorities tried to protect the status quo by jailing dissidents and by confiscating their property when they publicly denounced the minister and refused to pay their taxes. Rather than a means of social control, religion had become a source of discord in both church and town.[46]

In addition to challenges by dissidents and sectarians, a more subtle threat confronted the Congregational establishment in its failure to provide ministers to the rapidly expanding population downeast and in the interior. In 1780 Ezra Stiles, president of Yale, expressed concern over the number of vacant pulpits throughout northern New England.[47] Not only had demand outstripped supply, but many of the towns most in need had the least resources with which to attract the few preachers available. In such a religious vacuum, settlers, deprived of the social and religious benefits of the established church, either remained unchurched or sought the religious alternatives offered by dissenting sects, such as the Baptists.

Recognizing the challenge and its implications as early as 1772, an association of Congregational ministers in York County petitioned the provincial government, pointing out that "many of the new settlements in the Eastern Parts of this Province are without the Preaching of the Gospel" and "That unless some Provision be made for their Instruction, they must remain . . . destitute of the Means of Religion; and in danger of loosing [sic] the Knowledge and Sense of their Duty to God, and their King, and one another; and sinking into Ignorance, Irreligion, and all Manner of Disorder." To prevent such an eventuality, the government agreed to support at public expense "One Missionary of sober life & conversation for promoting Christian Knowledge in the Eastern Parts of this Province in such Places as are destitute of the Preaching of the Gospel, and are unable to support the same."[48]

So inadequate a response to a problem of such dimensions only meant that conditions in the backcountry and downeast did not improve. And with the coming of the Revolution, political and religious leaders had little time to spend on the religious state of the frontier. Impoverished communities remained "destitute" of orthodox preachers and continued their slide into "Ignorance, Irreligion, and all Manner of Disorder."

With traditional religious institutions increasingly inadequate as instruments of social control, the provincial court system remained as the essential means of preserving order and stability. No other organ of provincial government so intruded on local life as did the hierarchy of judicial officials appointed by the royal governor. At the bottom were justices of the peace who exercised jurisdiction over petty civil and criminal cases. In the twenty-five years prior to the Revolution, Maine's three counties received 154 appointments as justice — 13 percent of the provincial total — heavily weighted toward towns of wealth and prominence. The town of York received twenty-seven commissions as justice of the peace, Falmouth had thirty-four, whereas Pownalborough, shire town for Lincoln County but much newer and poorer than the other county seats, had only six.[49]

The record book of Nathaniel Thwing of Pownalborough reveals the matters that came to his official attention: defamation of character, cursing ("God Damn" was a favorite even then), Sabbath breaking, theft, bodily assault, and debt.[50] Although fines could not exceed twenty shillings, most of the guilty appealed to the next system of courts where the principals could enjoy their English right to a trial by a jury drawn from fellow townsmen.

Depending on whether the issues were civil or criminal in nature, the case would go before one of the two county courts, both of which sat quarterly. The Inferior Court of Common Pleas dealt chiefly with civil issues involving debt and property ownership. Criminal cases went before the county's justices sitting as the Court of General Sessions of the Peace. In addition to hearing cases concerning physical violence, theft, bastardy, and fornication, the sessions court exercised broad administrative functions for the county, overseeing county roads and buildings such as jails and courthouses, administering county taxes, levying fines upon towns that lacked schools, licensing taverns, and supervising the operation of the poor law.[51]

The most important civil and criminal cases, appeals from the county courts, as well as cases involving the king, all came before the five justices of the Supreme Judicial Court, from which a litigant, if he were wealthy, might appeal to the Privy Council in England. The Supreme Court rode a circuit touching all fourteen counties in the province. At Falmouth in Maine, however, the justices heard cases for Lincoln County as well as for Cumberland, so they were spared the rigors of travel to Pownalborough. Wherever it went, the Supreme Court performed its functions with color and ceremony, attended by a flock of lawyers anxious for business. As they approached the county seat, the justices formed into a procession preceded by the sheriff and his deputies, all in their finery. They entered town to the thunder of cannon fire and opened each session with the beat of a drum. Justices and barristers then appeared in the full regalia of their professions, wigs and long robes, to consider the judicial business before them.[52] Such pomp and ceremony underlined the awesome authority of the law and the officials who expounded it.

The entire legal system favored those with money, time, and political connections. Judges of the Court of Common Pleas often held commissions as justices of the peace and so could sit as judges of the sessions court as well. Many of the judges and justices served as delegates to the provincial assembly and helped to make the laws that they themselves enforced in their judicial capacities. For the common people, the judicial system was expensive and inconvenient. Most courts met only quarterly, so that prisoners and key witnesses had to be detained for long periods at their own expense. Travel to attend court at the county seat could be long and arduous. The residents of Machias or Boothbay in Lincoln County, for example, had to travel all the way to their shire town of Pownalborough, and sometimes even to Falmouth.[53]

Litigants had to contend with fees for every step in the legal process: for drawing up and serving a writ, for entering the action in court, and then, if the judge did not quash the action on a triviality, for recording judgment. In addition, there was always the lawyer and his expenses. The loser in an action faced damages as well as court costs, and having gone so far, most appealed from the inferior to the superior courts, where the entire process began anew. Even after the Supreme Court rendered a judgment, a litigant might obtain an entirely new trial through a practice called a "writ of review." It is little wonder that those with limited means regarded the courts as potential tools of oppression and lawyers as parasites who lived off the troubles of others.[54]

The image was not entirely misplaced. Provincial lawyers were just beginning to express a sense of corporate identity by trying to exclude from legal practice those who had not been admitted formally to the bar.[55] This threatened a widespread practice of paraprofessionals who supplemented their incomes as schoolteachers, storekeepers, or minor officeholders by drawing up writs, bills of sale, and deeds quite as effectively and far less expensively than a professional lawyer. The professional exclusiveness of the legal fraternity prompted a bitter rebuke by one writer who accused lawyers of a diabolical plot to monopolize business. Referring to a recent example of violent protest in the Carolina backcountry known as the Regulator Movement, this writer warned the legal profession that their "vile avarice" could provoke a similar response in the province of Massachusetts.[56]

The provincial legislature, called the General Court, reflected the same elitist, conservative character as did the legal profession and the court system—indeed, they were generally composed of the same per-

26 Maine

5. Lincoln County's first courthouse, in Pownalborough (Dresden), built in 1761. Property of Lincoln County Cultural and Historical Association.

sonnel merely performing different functions. The lower house of the General Court, the assembly or House of Representatives, served as the "popular" institution of provincial government, which also included a royally appointed governor and a council as an upper house. Besides electing the council, the Massachusetts assembly generally fulfilled the same role as did the House of Commons in the British Parliament; it levied taxes and passed legislation with the approval of the council and governor. Each incorporated town in the province with forty voters or more had the privilege — and the obligation — of sending a representative to the assembly. If a town had less than forty voters, representation was voluntary. With 120 voters or more, a town had the option of adding one additional delegate. Boston, the metropolis, could send four. A provincial voter was a white, adult male possessing property worth forty pounds or an estate providing an annual income of forty shillings. The discriminatory nature of this franchise has stimulated much more controversy among modern professional historians than among those who lived under the system. Prior to the Revolution, there were few complaints about the franchise except from royal officials who felt it was too democratic.[57]

The towns of Massachusetts found representation a mixed blessing.

All valued the cherished principle, but many sought to escape the burdens of paying the delegates' subsistence while attending the legislature. Small towns either pleaded their poverty to be excused from the obligation or else accepted the fine imposed by law as the least burdensome alternative. Between 1765 and 1770, the number of towns listed in the House journals as eligible for representation expanded from 178 to 240, yet the towns defaulting also increased from about 30 to 40 percent. Many of these towns were new and poor, especially in Maine. Throughout the entire period, towns in Lincoln County failed to send a single delegate although the number of eligible towns grew from four to eight. Similarly, newly eligible towns in Cumberland and York counties regularly defaulted. The number of towns qualified to send delegates expanded from four to nine in Cumberland County and from five to ten in York, but only four or five of the older towns in each of those two counties generally sent representatives. In the assembly of 1770, however, only a single delegate from Cumberland County attended, and since Lincoln County towns continued to default, Maine's total representation was a mere six in an assembly composed of 126 delegates. Twenty-seven Maine towns could have sent delegates, many more than one, had they wished to do so.[58] But the financial burden, combined with the absence of disciplined political parties and the lack of modern concepts of representation, created political apathy that overrode whatever benefits representation may have brought.

The few towns in Maine that did send delegates were generally coastal commercial communities. They elected one of their local elite — a man in his forties, possibly a college graduate, who had acquired significant wealth in the legal profession, as a merchant, as a prosperous farmer, or in some combination of these activities. He frequently had prior political experience as selectman or in some county office such as justice of the peace, and he usually served as representative from three to four terms. At age fifty-six, Jonathan Sayward was somewhat older than the profile when in 1766 he began the first of three terms as representative to the General Court from the town of York. Otherwise, he fits the profile well. A wealthy merchant, shipowner, and landowner, he first served his town as constable, clerk, moderator, and justice of the peace before being elected as representative. Afterward, the governor rewarded Sayward for his loyal support not only by reappointing him justice but by commissioning him judge of probate and of the Court of Common Pleas. Iron-

6. John Adams about the time he attended court at the Pownalborough courthouse. Portrait by Benjamin Blyth (1737?–1803?). Courtesy of the Massachusetts Historical Society.

ically, this profile accurately describes delegates whom even the inland and agricultural communities occasionally sent as delegates.[59]

Since towns rarely instructed their delegates, Maine's representatives in the assembly were free to follow their own inclinations. These led them to support the so-called court faction, a loose confederation of delegates from the coastal commercial centers and the Connecticut River valley who rallied to the patronage and conservative policies of chief justice and lieutenant governor Thomas Hutchinson.[60] In 74 percent of the roll-call votes between 1760 and 1789, Maine delegates deferred to the leadership of the court faction, readily acquiescing in a provincial fiscal policy that favored commercial property and discriminated against farmers throughout the province—and of course in

Maine. Such loyalty was more pragmatic than ideological. Similar economic interests linked most Maine delegates to the provincial administration, but in addition, Maine's representatives could hardly ignore their dependence on the governor's favor for their commissions as sheriffs, justices of the peace, as judges of the courts of probate, common pleas, and general sessions, and for commissions in the militia as well.[61] In effect, the assembly represented only those regions and segments of society with sufficient wealth, interest, and expertise to manipulate the system in their own behalf.

Those whose interests and grievances were ignored by the established institutions of government had only one recourse—violence. Several historians have pointed out recently that in the eighteenth century a riot, or crowd action, constituted a semilegitimate means of social protest.[62] Different kinds of violence existed, but frequently a community arose to protest an affront to established values or institutions. In such a case, the mob's objectives differed little from those of the courts: the preservation of traditional mores and standards. In Boston, mobs repeatedly prevented the export of food during times of scarcity; on other occasions, they pulled down houses of ill repute when the law seemed powerless. The actions of a press gang forcibly enlisting sailors into the Royal Navy provoked rioting in Boston during which even the militia joined the mob.[63]

During the 1760s, groups of settlers along the Sheepscot River in Maine donned Indian disguises and took collective action to protect their land. They so terrified one unpopular proprietor that he fled the region in terror of his life. In the town of Woolwich, "White Indians" burned down the houses and drove out tenants who were the willing tools of another proprietor.[64] On the eve of the Revolution the hostile actions of a crowd in Falmouth, Maine's leading seaport, prevented the capture of several pressed seamen who had escaped from a British naval vessel in the harbor.[65]

Downeast in far-off Machias occurred a riot in 1770 with the avowed objective of curbing the excesses of a public official. A mob, whose principal participants included Jeremiah O'Brien, one of the community leaders, set upon Justice of the Peace Stephen Longfellow and severely beat him. To obtain further information, the General Court sent several commissioners to Machias, for whom merchant Ichabod Jones provided transportation and housing. The commission's report tacitly justified the riot by noting that Longfellow had "misconducted in his office" and, in effect, had gotten what he deserved. However, rather than remove him from office and thereby justify the violence, the commissioners recommended the establishment of a Congregational minister and the appointment of an additional justice. Not surprisingly, Stephen Jones, Ichabod's nephew and resident agent in Machias, received the new commission as justice.[66]

Few of the provincial elite were comfortable with mob violence — or crowd action — as an expression of popular protest. To be sure, mobs had their occasional utility if kept in control, but they could be dangerously unpredictable. After a particularly violent mobbing in Scarborough that left the victim's home in shambles, John Adams responded by drawing a distinction between legitimate and illegitimate mobs when he wrote, "These private Mobs, I do and will detest. If Popular Commotions can be justified, . . . it can be only when Fundamentals are invaded, nor then unless for absolute Necessity and with great Caution." But violence "by rude and insolent Rabbles, in Resentment for private Wrongs or in pursuance of private Prejudices and Passions, must be discountenanced, cannot be even excused upon any Principle which can be entertained by a good Citizen."[67] Mob violence against property and persons was to Adams a breach of the social covenant, an infringement upon English liberty that declared every man's home was his castle. To deprive a man of security and liberty was to treat him "not like an Englishman not like a Freeman but like a Slave — like a miserable Turk, or Tartar."[68] Surely Adams spoke for many others in his privileged station when he condemned the "rude and insolent Rabbles" as a threat to social order. Against such a threat stood the church, the courts, and the government — both local and provincial. In the hands of the elite these institutions preserved life and property and thereby liberty itself.

V

The reference by John Adams to the glories of English liberty illustrates the larger imperial context linking all the American provinces to Great Britain. As part of the British Empire, Americans rejoiced in the empire's strength and exulted in its liberty. Once again, John Adams clearly articulated this sentiment when he described the English government as "the most perfect combination of human powers in society which finite wisdom has yet contrived and reduced to practice for the preservation of liberty and the production of happiness."[69] The key to Britain's liberty and power, eighteenth-century theorists argued, lay in the precious balance of its mixed government, which incorporated the principles of monarchy, aristocracy, and democracy. The concepts of a balanced and a limited government were enshrined in British constitutional thought, and Americans were convinced the same principles extended to America through their common British heritage and their own provincial governments.[70]

British Americans gloried in the empire's physical power as well as in its liberty. In 1763 British subjects on both sides of the Atlantic had just won their greatest test of strength against their age-old nemesis, absolutist France. The incredible year, 1759, when Niagara, Ticonderoga, Crown Point, and finally Quebec all fell to British arms inspired Enoch Freeman of Falmouth to record eighteen stanzas of atrocious verse glorifying the empire and its monarch. He entitled the work "A New Song on the Success of 1759."

> Fame let thy Trumpet Sound,
> Tell all ye world around
>   Great George is King
>
>   . . . .
>
> While Amherst and Wolfe command,
> None can the power withstand
>   of George our King
>
>   . . . .
>
> Canada's boasted Strength
> They have reduc'd at Length
>   for George our King
>
>   . . . .
>
> No more shall Savages
> Commit vile Ravages
>   George is their King
>
>   . . . .
>
> May he defend our Laws
> And ever give us Cause
> To say with Heart and Voice
>   God Save ye King[71]

Americans cherished the empire as a source of military protection and of political liberty. But the provincials were uncomfortably aware that they held an ideal view. Behind that ideal stood the reality of teeming cities, antiquated franchises, rotten boroughs, and venal parliamentary factions whose greed enabled the king's ministers to manipulate legislation. This, in turn, jeopardized the constitutional balance between the organs of government and thereby threatened liberty itself. By contrast, Americans regarded themselves as simple, pure, and as yet untainted by Old World corruptions. From Falmouth, Samuel Freeman conveyed this sense in a letter to a brother who was preparing to leave parents and friends to go, as Samuel described it, "to a strange Land where corruption dwells & all sorts of Vices have a Habitation."[72]

A similar dualism characterized the manner in which provincials regarded the mercantile aspects of the British Empire. Americans generally acquiesced in the ideal of an economically self-sufficient empire. Like all ideals, this was an impossibility, but by regulating the empire's economic life, the British government sought to come as close to it as possible. By reducing dependence on foreign goods and by selling surpluses, Britain could improve the flow of capital to its own advantage. The object was to benefit the mother country. The provinces might share in the advantages, as they did in the expulsion of the French from North America, but from the British government's point of view, the intended beneficiary was Britain itself.

Since the seventeenth century, the British government had developed a complicated series of regulations concerning trade and manufacturing throughout the empire that reflected this mercantilist outlook. In general, imperial policy envisioned the American provinces as perpetual consumers of British manufactured articles while being sources of agricultural goods, such as rice and tobacco, and of products, like naval stores and pig iron, derived from primitive extractive industries. The static role assigned the provinces was perhaps the greatest weakness of Britain's imperial system. Britain never imagined the Americans as anything more than producers of raw materials and consumers of British manufactured goods despite the doubling of the American population every twenty-five years, so that by 1775 it had reached two and a half million, and Philadelphia, less than a century old, had 30,000 inhabitants.[73]

For Maine, in particular, the imperial connection posed several serious problems. One difficulty concerned imperial regulation of the mast business. This, in turn, involved a second issue, the legalization of land grants. The third problem had nothing to do with either land or masts; it concerned the startling growth of the Anglican church, or the Church of England, throughout New England and especially in Maine. Maine's rapidly increasing population was a common element in all three issues.

To supply masts for its ships, Britain depended heavily on the countries around the Baltic Sea, but the mercantile ideal called for the production of masts from America, reducing Britain's reliance on foreign supplies. When the king granted to Massachusetts its new charter in 1691, the crown reserved for the use of the Royal Navy all white pines that were of sufficient size and on lands not yet granted to private persons.[74] But in Maine the distinction between privately owned lands and those owned by the crown was not clear. Since the seventeenth century, Maine had been a mosaic of conflicting land grants as kings of England and of France, provinces of Massachusetts and New York, proprietors as groups and as individuals all made grants that conflicted one with another. Private claims based on original Indian purchase added to the confusion. Many of these patents were speculative in nature, merely titles to unimproved wild land, yet their owners insisted that they were private property and exempt from the royal prohibition on cutting white pines. The pressure of population made the distinction important as land and timber became increasingly valuable resources.

In an effort to clarify the situation, Parliament passed a series of acts that actually had the opposite effect. By 1729 the government had extended the prohibition on cutting pines geographically throughout New England and as far south as New Jersey. At the same time, it expanded the definition of mast trees to include literally *all* white pines not on private property. Included in the sweeping prohibition were all unsettled lands granted after 1691. Parliament's legislation claimed for the Royal Navy all the white pines, large and small, that stood on unoccupied land between Nova Scotia and New Jersey—a situation so patently ridiculous as to undermine the effectiveness of the law. Nonetheless, the surveyor general of the king's woods, who was also the governor of New Hampshire, and his deputies granted licenses to cut masts and prosecuted offenders according to the broad interpretation of the law. In 1763, for example, they seized over 6,000 trees cut illegally throughout New England. The Kennebec Proprietors successfully fought the matter in the courts and managed to exempt their lands from the royal regulation because the company could prove title prior to 1691.[75] Few others could afford the time and the costs of a legal suit that reached all the way to England.

A particularly complicating factor in Britain's regulation of the mast trade was that it became enmeshed in land policy. In an effort to protect the mast trees, Parliament seemed to be moving toward a policy of effective occupation as the test of private property, an obvious challenge to the speculative urge that characterized so much of Maine's land settlement. It was increasingly evident that the imperial government was anxious to discourage settlement that threatened stands of mast trees, and this brought the royal government into direct opposition with Massachusetts and with many of the settlers themselves. After the fall of Quebec, settlers streamed into Maine, encouraged by Massachusetts, which readily granted twelve townships in the area east of the Penobscot River. Whether this territory lay within the jurisdiction of Massachusetts or Nova Scotia was not clear, and in any case the charter required the General Court to make its grants there conditional on the recipients' gaining royal approbation within eighteen months.[76] Undoubtedly, the General Court hoped to force the royal government to legitimize occupation of the region by Massachusetts. Although Massachusetts repeatedly extended the time limit for obtaining the crown's approval, it never came.

The crown's reluctance seemed to be based on the conviction that beyond the Penobscot stood great tracts of trees suitable for masts and that promoting settlement in the area would simply invite the destruction of that timber. Repeatedly, the governor of Massachusetts, Thomas Hutchinson, warned the assembly that the king would never approve the grants. He urged the assembly to take the initiative in removing the settlers or risk incurring the king's displeasure.[77] The legislature, however, refused to act and merely suggested that the royal surveyors were the proper persons to protect the king's woods against trespassers.[78] Meanwhile, settlers beyond the Penobscot had no legal basis for their lands, no security for their improvements, and few buyers for property without a secure title. They existed in a legal limbo, never knowing from one moment to the next if they might be evicted. When Governor Hutchinson sent a surveyor to report on the condition of the lands beyond the Penobscot, settlers at first regarded him with fear as the vanguard of an armed force to be sent to dispossess them.[79] Another alarm occurred when speculators in England resurrected a seventeenth-century claim to 100,000 acres beyond the Penobscot. Nothing came from their efforts, yet settlers in that region lived in a stage of nervous expectation, hoping for the best but always fearing the worst because of the crown's determination to protect its mast trees. Making it all the more ironic were reports from special commissioners indicating that beyond the Penobscot the supply of trees suitable for masts was disappointingly thin.[80]

A somewhat similar situation prevailed between the Kennebec and the Penobscot rivers, around Boothbay. Here, too, the crown withheld its approval for the lands that settlers had occupied since 1731. Once the danger of war with France had ended, agents of various land companies and even those who possessed only Indian deeds plagued the settlers with competing claims to their lands. Threats of law suits and of ejectments pressured settlers into purchasing their own lands over and over again from claimants who then left the harassed settlers defenseless before the next onslaught. Newspapers carried accounts of roving bands of men thinly disguised as Indians burning houses and barns in disputes over land.[81] Violence, confusion, and anxiety attended Britain's efforts to preserve its mast supply in Maine. Not only was the imperial policy disruptive to the orderly process of settlements, but at the same time it challenged the traditional concept of private property and the widespread practice of speculation.

The religious imperialism of the Anglican church as it spread through New England and into Maine presented another source of growing concern. It was bad enough that New England Congregationalists had to battle Baptists, Quakers, and even other disgruntled Congregationalists from time to time; they at least all shared the dissenting religious tradition. Congregationalists had left England and its state church in the seventeenth century for New England where they intended to establish a community based on their own Calvinist version of God's truth. The ideal had dimmed over the years, but New Englanders never surrendered the sense of superiority and purity that had accompanied the ideal. Now their old nemesis, the Church of England, was on the march in New England, newly aggressive under the auspices of its well-financed missionary agency, the Society for the Propagation of the Gospel (SPG).

By 1760, Massachusetts alone contained seven SPG preachers, eight Society churches, and at least eight more congregations without churches.[82] Even more alarming was the success of the Anglicans in recruiting converts, not just laymen but even clergy, from the Congregationalists. The Great Awakening, with its religious enthusiasm and denominational bickering, drove many into the Church of England.[83] Furthermore, Anglican missionary preachers were particularly welcome in struggling frontier communities because not only were preachers of any kind scarce but those from the SPG came with subsidized salaries. Without success, Congregationalists tried to set up a competing organization called the Society for Propagating Christian Knowledge.[84] Sectarian resentment reached a high point in 1758 when rumors circulated that British authorities would soon establish an American bishopric centered in Massachusetts. It came to nothing, but the rumor aroused a flurry of excitement and a bitter pamphlet debate in which Congregationalists denounced a bishopric as a plot against their own religious liberty, a mere disguise for the extension of imperial power into America.[85]

Maine was an area where the Anglicans seemed to be enjoying some of their most remarkable success and arousing some of the most bitter rivalry. In Georgetown, at the mouth of the Kennebec River, a converted Presbyterian preacher, William MacClenachan, served as missionary for the SPG. When some of the Kennebec Proprietors persuaded him to minister to their own settlers upriver at Pownalborough, the Congregationalists in the company resolutely denied him the use of lands set aside for religious purposes.[86] But the Anglicans were not to be denied. They succeeded in filling the vacancy created by MacClenachan's departure with yet another Anglican, the Reverend Jacob Bailey. A Harvard graduate, Bailey had preached and taught in several towns as a Congregationalist before turning to the Church of England. Through the patronage of Silvester Gardiner, the wealthy Boston merchant-physician and member of the Kennebec Proprietors, Bailey readily obtained holy orders in England. He returned to accept the parish in Pownalborough where Gardiner helped to finance the construction of an Anglican church and parsonage on lands the company had reserved for ecclesiastical use — presumably by the Congregationalists.[87]

The Congregational faction within the Kennebec Proprietors was furious with Gardiner and his Anglican supporters for their successful coup. In Pownalborough, their wrath fell upon Parson Bailey, who endured personal abuse and legal harassment instigated by Judge Jonathan Bowman and Sheriff Charles Cushing.[88] James Bowdoin, another of the proprietors, tried to achieve for the Pownalborough Congregationalists what Gardiner had done for the Anglicans, but despite his efforts Congregationalists there remained without a church or a minister with which to compete with the Anglicans. Nonetheless, Pownalborough officials tried to exclude Anglicans from town meeting and to tax them for the support of the nonexistent Congregationalist establishment.[89]

The religious quarrel in Pownalborough aggravated the town's pre-existing ethnic and social divisions. Bailey's congregation was composed mainly of the German, Dutch, and French immigrants whom the company had imported, along with a scattering of Irish, Scots-Irish, and a few English. Religiously, they represented a bewildering array of denominations: Lutherans, Dutch Reformed Calvinists, French Huguenots, Presbyterians, a few Catholics, and some Anglicans. Most were poor, and many had little mastery of the English language. They clustered around their pastor, Jacob Bailey, who, despite his college education, had known poverty in his own youth. By contrast, opponents to Anglicanism included Pownalborough's officials, ambitious, well-educated, with powerful friends and relatives among the proprietors in Boston. Bailey too had his supporters among the proprietors, especially Silvester Gardiner, and the growing schism in Pownalborough reflected a deepening rift within the company.[90]

Jacob Bailey was soon joined by another Anglican preacher, William Wheeler, who took the vacant pulpit at Georgetown. Like Bailey, he too was a Harvard graduate, a former dissenting minister who had converted to the Church of England. Bailey had been trying to serve the religious needs of Georgetown as well as Pownalborough, and hearing of Wheeler's availability, he alerted Dr. Henry Caner, rector of King's Chapel in Boston. Through Caner's influence, Wheeler came to Georgetown as yet another SPG missionary preacher in the Kennebec valley.[91]

The growth of Anglicanism in Maine was not confined to the Kennebec River towns. The Church of England also made impressive gains in Maine's leading town of Falmouth. There it attracted not the poor immigrants but those at the opposite end of the social-economic scale.

It all began as a typical quarrel among the members of Falmouth's first Congregational parish where a demand developed for a second meetinghouse. Popular dissatisfaction with the elderly pastor, Thomas Smith, and the decision merely to hire an assistant rather than to replace Smith spurred on a separation movement. At this point, a strong faction evolved among the dissidents urging that the new church adopt the order of the Church of England. Tempers became so inflamed that two of the leading separationists, men of wealth and standing in the community, came to blows in the street over whether the new church should be Congregationalist or Anglican.

The Anglicans not only won out but found a ready candidate for their preacher in John Wiswall, Congregational pastor of the nearby New Casco (now Falmouth) church. Like Jacob Bailey and William Wheeler, Wiswall was a Harvard graduate who had taught school and then entered the ministry, taking the parish in 1755. In 1764, without formalities, he withdrew from his position and declared for the Church of England. It was a timely conversion, for the cornerstone of the new Anglican church in Falmouth was just being laid. Wiswall took passage to England in a convenient mast ship, obtained holy orders, and returned in the spring of 1765 to minister to the Falmouth Anglicans. His congregation included some of the wealthiest, most prestigious families in town, as well as most of the imperial customs officers. They provided their new pastor with a handsome salary of 100 pounds yearly, to which the SPG contributed an additional twenty pounds.[92] An article in the *Boston Gazette* took notice of the religious events in Falmouth and tried to dismiss them as merely the activities of disgruntled Congregationalists who resorted to Anglicanism because of an unpopular preacher.[93] However, the impressive gains made by the Church of England in New England and in Maine reveal the inadequacy of that argument; Congregationalists had good cause to be concerned. In the 1760s the rejuvenated Church of England was providing a doctrinal and emotional satisfaction that New England orthodoxy no longer offered — and could not combat.

Tensions over Anglicanism, over land policy, and over the imperial government's white pine policy were some of the more burdensome costs of empire for Maine. Yet, for all its limitations, the empire had some distinct advantages. It was one vast protected market that all provincials, as British subjects, could exploit without fear of foreign competition. The exclusion of foreign shipping stimulated shipbuilding in America. By the time of the Revolution, one-third of all British-owned merchant vessels were American-built, a situation that benefited Maine. Maine also shared in the British government's bounty policy designed to stimulate the production of valuable goods, such as naval stores and especially masts. One final advantage for Maine in the mercantile system was that most of the provincial goods restricted to the markets of the British Empire were southern in origin, tobacco, rice, and indigo, for example. The goods Maine produced for export, except for furs, naval stores, and masts, could be shipped legally direct to foreign ports. For Maine, as well as for the American provinces in general, inclusion in the British Empire had its difficulties but was not an intolerable burden. Americans generally accepted the premise of mercantilism and learned to live with, or around, the regulations. Overall, membership in the British Empire meant markets, military protection, and a wide degree of autonomy in town and in province.

In the 1760s the advantages of empire far outweighed the disadvantages. For Maine, a mere colony of Massachusetts, existence outside the British Empire was inconceivable. In the dozen years following the end of the Seven Years' War, however, the benefits of empire faded to such a degree that the inconceivable became a reality—war erupted between Great Britain and its American colonies, who then declared their independence. By contrast, the collapse of imperial authority in America only strengthened Maine's connection to Massachusetts. During the Revolution, Maine looked to its "mother province" as a source of protection against the British and also for help in preserving order in a potentially volatile society.

TWO

The Revolution Comes to Maine

Britain's white pine policy, the crown's reluctance to validate land grants, and aggressive Anglicanism were all irritants but not sources of revolution. Towns of Maine became converts to the revolutionary cause through the efforts of Boston's radicals who "educated" the backcountry and goaded Great Britain into actions that seemed to justify the radicals' accusations of tyranny. But in Maine and throughout America, patriotic defiance of imperial authority provided the occasion and the logic for those discontented with the domestic status quo to express their hostility in ways that appeared to threaten social order and, indeed, the very nature of the Revolution.

I

In general, Maine was oblivious to the dangers inherent in Parliament's reorganization of the empire following the end of the French and Indian War. From its defeated enemies, Britain acquired land in India, islands in the Caribbean, as well as Florida and the vast territory of Canada, including the region east of the Mississippi River and north of the Ohio. To protect and administer the American acquisitions alone would require 10,000 troops and 220,000 pounds at a time when the British national debt stood at an all-time high of 130 million pounds.[1] As part of a broad program of imperial reorganization, Parliament agreed that Americans ought to contribute to the expense of maintaining royal troops in America through a stamp tax placed on all legal documents, business and shipping papers, college diplomas, newspapers, and playing cards.

To colonists struggling with a postwar depression, the stamp tax came at a very inopportune time, but it was the underlying assumptions of the act that aroused legislatures from Virginia to New Hampshire and, in October 1765, produced the Stamp Act Congress in New York. The common concern was the obvious fact that Parliament 3,000 miles away had extended its power to tax Americans who were not represented in that body. Furthermore, legal cases arising under the act were not to be tried by jury in common law courts but in admiralty courts where decisions were made by a single royally appointed judge.[2]

When constitutional protests made no impact on king, ministry, or Parliament, many provincials placed their faith in more forceful means of persuasion, such as nonimportation and intimidation. As the fateful date of November 1, 1765, approached when the act would go into force, there were neither stamps nor persons to distribute them anywhere in the colonies. Gradually, seaports and courts of law resumed normal operations as if the Stamp Act never existed. The absence of stamps and distributors resulted from mob action. Throughout most of the provinces, crowds numbering in the thousands and calling themselves Sons of Liberty terrorized stamp officials into resigning their offices and prevented stamps and stamped paper from being circulated. During August, Boston experienced two violent riots in which mobs pillaged and destroyed the houses of the stamp distributor-designate, Andrew Oliver, as well as the homes of two customs officers and even the mansion owned by Lieutenant Governor Thomas Hutchinson.[3]

In Maine, Falmouth was the only town to get caught up in the constitutional concerns posed by the Stamp Act. Although the town voted to instruct its delegate to the assembly to "use his utmost efforts to prevent the Stamp Act taking place in the Province," the leaders resorted to direct action rather than mere legislative remedies. On January 1, 1766, the justices of the Inferior Court of Common Pleas for Cumberland County met at Falmouth and, in contrast to their more conservative counterparts in York, decided to continue their legal business as usual without stamps. Possibly to persuade the customs officials to follow suit and to open the ports without stamped clearances, a mob gathered and threatened the customs house one week later.[4]

The Falmouth people then made certain no stamps would be available for distribution. When a vessel arrived from Halifax at the end of January carrying a parcel of stamp paper, a well-organized crowd marched to the customs house and forced the officers to surrender the package, "declaring that an Article so *odious* to all America, they would not suffer to be kept there." They paraded the bundle on the end of a pole through the town to a bonfire, where they burned it "amidst the Acclamations of a great Concourse of People." The newspaper account then concluded approvingly, "They then dispersed without offering the least injury to any Person."[5]

The newspaper's obvious relief that the Falmouth mob had refrained from personal injury revealed a nervousness over such unpredictable methods of nullification and nonimportation. Yet they all seemed to pay off when news of Parliament's repeal of the Stamp Act arrived in mid-May 1766. Falmouth received the news with wild excitement. Bells pealed, drums beat, cannon boomed from the fort and from ships in the harbor. Vessels broke out their colors, and everywhere loyal toasts were drunk to the king, the queen, and to members of Parliament friendly to the American cause. "A deluge of drunkenness" is how the Reverend Thomas Smith described it.[6] By ignoring the Declaratory Act, by which Parliament asserted its claim to legislate for the colonies in any matter whatsoever, Americans convinced themselves that they had won the constitutional debate and that Parliament's repeal was admission that it could not tax those whom it did not physically represent. Americans were soon to discover how wrong they were.

Americans were also to discover that a mob was easier to raise than to control; indeed, patriotic violence offered an irresistible opportunity for securing personal advantage. According to rumor, the instigators of the second of Boston's Stamp Act riots directed the mob against Hutchinson's mansion, not just to protest British policy but to destroy important legal papers relating to a land dispute in Maine, which the lieutenant governor had in his possession.[7] The constitutional issue over taxation simply offered the occasion and the excuse.

About two weeks after the destruction of Hutchinson's house in Boston, a similar sort of riot occurred in Falmouth, Maine, but without any redeeming constitutional implications whatsoever. On the night of September 10, 1765, a mob armed with axes, clubs, and sticks broke into the house of William Bennet, an innkeeper and creditor to numerous persons. The rioters bound Bennet hand and foot and smashed his furniture and utensils, cut up his clothing and bedding, tore out paneling, and then departed carrying Bennet's petty cash, his notes of indebtedness, and account books. It took several years before two of the rioters were convicted and imprisoned, but even then they were soon rescued by a mob, which broke open the jail and released them.[8]

A "rescue" of a different sort took place in Falmouth one evening early in August 1766. A crowd carried away to safety a cargo of smuggled sugar and rum belonging to merchant Enoch Ilsley, which customs officers had seized. Once again constitutional issues were somewhat muted but not resistance to unpopular authority. The customs officers had made their seizure at Ilsley's store, but with night coming on they left the confiscated cargo in the charge of a deputy sheriff while they retired to their lodgings. That evening a crowd surrounded the house where the two officers were staying and pelted it with sticks and stones for several hours. In the morning the customs men discovered the reason behind the crowd's odd behavior. While one crowd was diverting the officials, another had been busy removing and hiding the sugar and rum from Ilsley's store. Ilsley vowed he had been ill that evening and confined to his house; the deputy sheriff claimed that the mob had forcibly carried him away from the scene, thus preventing him from performing his duty.[9] When Governor Francis Bernard reported the incident to the Board of Trade in England, he observed that "Formerly a rescue was an accidental or occasional Affair; now it is the natural & certain Consequences of a seizure, & the Effect of a predetermined Resolution that the Laws of Trade shall not be executed."[10]

It was in the town of Scarborough, however, where occurred the most blatant effort to convert the patriotic violence of the times into private gain. Richard King, the town's wealthiest merchant and leading creditor, fell victim to his own debtors and personal enemies who spread the rumor that King not only supported the Stamp Act but even had stamped paper in his home.[11] To give such a man a "rally," or a mobbing, would obviously be a patriotic duty. Moreover, it would benefit Scarborough by punishing a person whose path to wealth had flouted the traditional community standards of economic morality. Indeed, some of the rioters were of the opinion that the riot might help King mend his ways and reform his character. In recruiting members for the mob, one leader declared that King was a "bad man, and will ruin us all if he goes on at this rate; . . . if he is not humbled." Another instigator asked, "Has not the Potter Power over the Clay[?] We built him up and why Shant we pull him down[?]"[12]

Thus fortified, thirty face-blackened men descended upon Richard King's house and store on the night of March 19, 1766. In the now familiar manner, they harmed neither King nor his family, but they gutted the interior of his house, tore out the doors, the woodwork, and paneling, hurled furniture and furnishings through the windows, and then made off with their victim's financial records. In retiring, the mob attached to the gatepost a crude note to intimidate King and to claim a patriotic legitimacy for their acts. Signed by the "Suns of liburty," the note warned King that if he took legal action against any one of them, "he ma Depend onit that he not onley will have houses and barnes burnt and Consumed but him Self Cut in Peses and burnt TO ASHES."[13]

King's persistent efforts to obtain legal redress despite the warning only encouraged his enemies to make good their threats. Over the next several years, they forced King's tenant to flee and destroyed the house he had leased from King. They burned King's barns, mutilated his livestock, stole his implements, broke windows, defiled his door with human excrement, and assaulted him physically. King eventually did obtain some legal satisfaction in the superior court, but it was a moral victory at best. The court awarded him a mere fraction of the damages he claimed, and even these were uncollected when he died in 1775.[14]

Such threats of social disorder haunted the leaders of colonial society as they tried to define and defend the position of the colonies within the empire. They were discovering that the atmosphere of nullification and defiance to traditional authority could not be confined to imperial issues alone. Various forms of social discontent were also released, not in the backcountry, which for the time being remained aloof from imperial issues, but in the coastal commercial communities where social and economic differences could fuse with patriotic violence in a tradition of crowd action. Frequently, pent-up hostility within a commercial community took form against persons regarded as economic oppressors, such as William Bennet and Richard King. Since the victims were leaders within their communities, the violence raised the specter of anarchy and social revolution. Colonial leaders of the resistance movement against Britain were keenly aware that their task was a dual one of directing a disciplined opposition to imperial policy while maintaining order and stability at home. But with the repeal of the Stamp Act, most Americans regarded such problems as part of the past, not the future.

II

Parliament's passage of the Townshend Acts ended such complacency and resumed the process of Maine's political education. A new ministry in England had inherited the problems of the old, imperial reform and colonial taxation. In the spring of 1767, Parliament agreed to raise new revenues in America by customs duties on paper, paint, lead, glass, and tea. The funds raised would contribute toward paying salaries of royal officials in America and relieve them from depending on annual grants voted by provincial assemblies. In addition, a new American Board of Customs Commissioners, aided by the Royal Navy, would provide vigorous enforcement of all customs regulations, new and old.[15]

America's initial response was largely institutional and constitutional. John Dickinson published his immensely popular series, "Letters from a Farmer in Pennsylvania," reproduced in newspapers throughout the land, wherein he denied any distinction between stamp duties and custom duties. If both were designed to raise a revenue, both were unconstitutional taxes levied by a body in which the colonies had no representation.[16]

Massachusetts officially responded to the Townshend program on February 11, 1768, when the legislature approved a circular letter to all the other colonies. Not only were the new duties unconstitutional, argued the letter, but to have salaries of governors and judges paid out of these duties threatened the popular control of government. Although the Massachusetts circular letter contained nothing particularly radical and carried expressions of loyalty to the king, the British secretary of state for the colonies, the earl of Hillsborough, reacted vehemently. He retaliated with a circular letter of his own ordering all colonies to ignore the communication from Massachusetts. To that province in particular, he sent special instructions requiring the legislature to rescind its circular letter on threat of dissolution. By a vote of 92 to 17, the Massachusetts legislature defied Hillsborough and refused to retract its letter. Governor Bernard, following his orders, dissolved the assembly amid public acclaim for the ninety-two defenders of liberty and condemnation for the pusillanimous seventeen.[17]

Jonathan Sayward, representative from the town of York, was one of the seventeen who had voted to rescind the controversial circular letter. Typically, the delegates from most of the other Maine towns were absent from the assembly on the day of the crucial vote, and during the following month newspapers were filled with their public assurances that had they only been present they would have voted with the glorious ninety-two. Jonathan Sayward, on the other hand, had stoutly voted his conservative conscience. He was as ardent a friend to natural rights and English liberties as any flaming Whig, but he feared the Americans would lose the very rights they were seeking to defend by antagonizing the ministry and bringing its vengeance upon the province. Through the summer of 1768, patriot newspapers poured a constant stream of vituperation upon the rescinders to discredit them with their constituents. The *Boston Gazette* described Sayward as the "Sooth-Sayer of York," pronouncing curses and prophesying plagues upon those who were virtuous and honest. The town of York soon performed what was expected of it. A town meeting voted its appreciation of those delegates who opposed rescinding and "who were for maintaining our just Rights & Liberties" and then removed the unrepentant Sayward as York's representative.[18]

Other Maine towns were drawn into the excitement when Massachusetts Governor Bernard decided not to convene a new General Assembly for fear its presence would merely escalate tensions over the circular letter and the imminent arrival of British soldiers sent to protect the newly arrived customs commissioners. However, Boston radicals were not to be denied their forum. Under the direction of Sam Adams and Thomas Cushing, the Boston town meeting invited all the provincial towns to send delegates to a convention to be held in Boston on September 22, 1768. The precise purpose of the meeting was never very clear; after a week of discussing the current threats to the province, the convention presented an address to the governor and a petition to the king and then dispersed. The real significance of the convention lay in that over 100 of the 250 towns and districts in the province of Massachusetts sent delegates to what was potentially a dangerous extralegal gathering.[19] The convention represented a major broadening of resistance to British policy.

For some Maine towns, the election of delegates to the convention was their first official participation in the movement to protect constitutional rights. Arundel, Scarborough, Gorham, Brunswick, North Yarmouth, and even Newcastle in far-off Lincoln County sent representatives.[20] Their willingness to undergo the effort and expense of sending delegates reveals an expanding concern in Maine with the constitutional issues of the day.

Falmouth, responsive as ever to events in Boston, not only sent off its delegate to the convention but was the only Maine town to participate in the nonimportation movement against Britain. No sooner did the Townshend Acts go into effect than Boston began to initiate efforts to promote home manufacturing, frugality, and even boycott agreements against British goods. Mutual suspicion and jealousy among leading seaports in America delayed intercolonial cooperation until well into 1769. Even the towns of Massachusetts proved reluctant to undertake the self-sacrifice of nonimportation and the dangers of enforcement by local Sons of Liberty. It was far easier to demonstrate patriotism by encouraging home manufacturing and discouraging luxury, as did a number of towns in Maine. Falmouth alone, as Maine's leading seaport, participated in the boycott but did it grudgingly. The town adopted a nonimportation agreement some ten months after Boston and resolved it would remain in effect only six months, until January 1, 1770.[21] Resistance to the Townshend duties, however, continued well past the first of the year and into the spring. By that time, Falmouth's merchants began to relax their restrictions on hearing rumors that Parliament had repealed all customs duties except those on tea. A rebuke by Boston merchants published in the *Boston Gazette* quickly brought the delinquents back into line. Merchants in Falmouth promptly adopted a new nonimportation agreement to remain in force until all obnoxious duties were removed, including those on tea. The *Boston Gazette* responded approvingly that, despite reports to the contrary, Falmouth's merchants were determined to adhere strictly to nonimportation.[22] Like York, Falmouth marched to the tune that Boston played. The Boston merchants held out until early October, and then they too caved in and resumed normal trade relations with Great Britain despite Parliament's refusal to repeal the tea tax.

The most serious result of the Townshend Acts was not merely the renewal and intensification of the constitutional dispute but the escalation of violence. The enforcement of nonimportation agreements, the arrival of royal troops, and the expanded, aggressive customs service all increased the points of friction and the occasions for violence. In Boston a riot over the seizure of a sloop belonging to John Hancock resulted in a severe beating for two customs officers. Secretary Hillsborough sent yet more troops to Boston, and this, in turn, multiplied chances for conflict between the military and civilians, culminating in the Boston Massacre of March 5, 1770.

Falmouth had no soldiers to contend with but had its share of conflict with the vigorous, sometimes unscrupulous customs service. The Townshend Acts had created an autonomous American Board of Customs Commissioners whose officers and agents developed customs racketeering into a fine art. Enoch Freeman, one of Falmouth's leading merchants, sued one official for charging exorbitant clearance fees.[23] One of the most furious of all Falmouth's riots occurred in an effort to discover the identity of a customs informer whose knowledge had led to the seizure of a sloop belonging to merchant William Tyng. Tyng was no popular hero; he was a prerogative man and a sheriff. For the moment, however, his cause became that of mercantile Falmouth as the town sought out the culprit. On the night of November 12, 1771, a crowd seized the deputy comptroller of customs and marched him about the town, stopping periodically to demand the informer's name. Terrified and exhausted, the officer finally gave in when the mob leader presented a loaded pistol and swore "That by the living God [he] must now lett them know, or take the consequences."[24] After making him swear several times to the truth of his information, the mob released the official with a warning of dire results if he took legal action against them.

The customs officer was unable to initiate legal proceedings in Falmouth in any case; not one of the justices of the peace was willing to accept his sworn testimony required for warrants. Only in Boston was he successful, and eventually three persons were arrested and held for trial. They were not laborers, sailors, or apprentices but masters of vessels then lying in Falmouth Harbor.[25]

No evidence exists concerning the informer's name or fate, but the punishment society inflicted on such a person is best revealed in the complaint of one who sued for defamation of character when accused publicly of being a customs informer. The accusation alone caused acquaintances to withdraw from his company and to refuse to do business with him. Furthermore, argued the plaintiff, it put him "in Danger of being mobb'd and evilly intreated by sundry of the Kings disorderly subjects who have at all Times heretofore been used to mobb & otherwise evilly intreat all Persons supposed or known to be informers to any of the King's Officers ... appointed to collect the customs."[26]

Without doubt, the customs officer who did the most to arouse the coastal communities east of Boston was John Malcom, a former resident of Georgetown at the mouth of the Kennebec River and brother to Captain Daniel Malcom, one of Boston's leading Whigs. Malcom became comptroller of customs for Falmouth in 1773 after an already turbulent career in the British customs service in Rhode Island and North Carolina. His exploits in the latter province provoked even the royal governor there to refer to him as "this hairbrained Comptroller."[27] By the time Malcom returned to Maine, most of the Townshend duties had been repealed, and in any case the effects of the Townshend Acts had not made much of an impression east of Falmouth. John Malcom, however, brought to the inhabitants of downeast Maine the full impact of the new American Board of Customs Commissioners and became a symbol of their arrogance and greed.

In October 1773 Malcom seized a vessel at Wiscasset for possessing improper papers and thereby precipitated the first of several riots in which he was the victim. With encouragement from merchant Abiel Wood, a part owner of the vessel's cargo, and even from Justice of the Peace Thomas Rice, a crowd of sailors seized Malcom, broke his sword—his symbol of authority—and doused the obnoxious official with tar and feathers. For an hour or so, they paraded him about town and finally let him go after extracting a promise to conduct no more seizures in the area. A letter reporting the incident in the newspaper observed that the rioters regarded Malcom as "an Epitome of the whole Board of Worshipful Com-s [customs commissioners]; that they may see what special regard would be paid them, even in a remote part of the Province, were they personally present."[28]

The Townshend program, with its duties, customs commissioners, and the royal forces to assist them, reactivated, expanded, and deepened the imperial crisis throughout America. In Maine, Falmouth continued to lead the way in the constitutional struggle and in resisting the depredations of the customs officers. But the presence of several easterly towns at the Boston convention of 1768 and the far-ranging eccentricities of John Malcom meant that Maine's political detachment was coming to an end.

III

A new issue, that of judicial salaries, continued this process of political enlightenment. Parliament's repeal of most of the Townshend duties in

1770 still left royal officials dependent on colonial assemblies for their salaries. In the fall of 1772, Boston's Whig leaders discovered that in the province of Massachusetts, at least, the crown already had begun to pay the governor's salary and that it would soon assume support for the leading judicial figures as well. From the imperial point of view, this was a badly needed reform designed to free the royal executive and judiciary from control by the legislature. To Sam Adams and his fellow Whigs, independent salaries meant that the ministry in England was destroying popular control of government—a crucial aspect of liberty.

To meet this new crisis, the Boston Whigs formed a Committee of Correspondence to reaffirm the rights of the colonists, to enumerate Britain's violation of those rights, and then to communicate these matters to all provincial towns with a request for their reaction. It was an ingenious scheme for educating the towns of Massachusetts and for coordinating their opposition to British policy. The activities were legal and effective; letters and pamphlets went out virtually to every town in the province, providing each with an occasion to discuss the issues in public. In addition, Boston's request for advice flattered many towns, dispelling the distrust some may have felt for the metropolis.[29]

Replies from Maine ran the spectrum from embarrassed self-consciousness to reasoned concern to belligerent outrage. Woolwich requested the Boston committee to correct its spelling and grammar if its resolves were to be published.[30] Gorham's reply suggests the town had not even been conscious of any grievances until Boston pointed them out. But, now aroused, Gorham hinted it was ready to seek redress by force if necessary: "many of our Women had been used to handle the Cartridge, and load the Musquet, and the Swords which we whet and brightened for our Enemies are not yet grown rusty." York and Falmouth placed their faith in the ultimate good will of the king, and North Yarmouth expressed hope that Parliament would be willing to recognize and rectify American complaints.[31] Pownalborough, however, despite its isolated location, produced the most sophisticated and original of Maine's replies.

The Pownalborough letter presented a remarkable interpretation of colonial history, conceiving Massachusetts, and presumably other colonies as well, as existing originally in a state of nature. It was not the vague, mythical condition envisioned by philosophers but a definite period in historical time to which a return was entirely possible. English settlers in America had emerged from this state of nature to form their own autonomous political societies. Later, each colony joined in a separate, voluntary association, a charter, or a "Solemn Covenant and Agreement," with the king of England. Parliament had no role in this process; it was merely England's representative body without any authority beyond the boundaries of Britain. The king, therefore, was the sovereign over a federated empire of autonomous states, each with its own legislature. Should the monarch transgress the limits of the compact with any portions of the empire, he would destroy the foundations of allegiance; his subjects would be justified in declaring the "Solemn Covenant and Agreement" at an end and once again resuming their original independent status.[32] The Pownalborough reply did not recommend so extreme a step. For the present it urged a restoration of the harmonious relationship that once supposedly existed in the empire. If that proved impossible, however, this theory offered a logical alternative.

Collectively, the town responses demonstrated an expanding and deepening awareness of the constitutional struggle. Whereas Falmouth alone had been alert to such issues in 1765, the furor over judges' salaries seven years later elicited reasoned responses from towns in all three of Maine's counties, some of which had never been heard from before. An increasingly large number of people were thinking about the origins of government and of the empire, the nature and source of political rights, and how they might be protected. Town meetings, which formerly had been preoccupied with laying out roads and voting bounties on wolves, were now becoming forums for constitutional debate. The results of these debates varied widely, yet they all emphasized, consciously or not, that the people were the sovereign source of political power, that governments existed to serve the people, and that when government failed to do so people had a right to alter that situation.[33] The Boston Committee of Correspondence did not create these concepts in the minds of the Massachusetts townspeople; they evolved from their English heritage and from the colonial experience. The Boston committee merely stimulated this political consciousness and encouraged the towns to articulate it.

The dispute over tea that erupted late in 1773 added further refinements to American constitutional thought. Parliament had permitted the financially troubled East India Company to ship tea directly to the colonies tax-free, except for the last vestige of the Townshend duties, which Parliament refused to repeal. Most provincials viewed the Tea Act of 1773 not as an opportunity to obtain cheaper tea but rather as an insidious challenge to their constitutional scruples. Increasingly, they adopted the argument already expressed in the Pownalborough letter of 1773, that Parliament had no constitutional power over Americans in any way; allegiance lay to the king alone. North Yarmouth described parliamentary authority over the colonies as "worse than Egyptian Bondage." York pointed out that "the several Colonies and Provinces in America have ever recognized the Protestant Kings of Great Britain as their lawful Sovereign; and it doth not appear that any Parliament have been parties to any Contract with the American Settlers in this howling Wilderness."[34] Each colony therefore possessed its own representative institution as a miniature parliament and owed allegiance only to the crown.

In addition to popularizing this federal view of empire, the tea crisis, following as it did in rapid succession the disputes over salaries, the Townshend Acts, and the Stamp Act, seemed to offer proof of some diabolical plot in England directed against American liberties and rights. The king was still above suspicion but not his ministers. They were the ones whom Americans professed to see behind the series of crises since 1765. The town of Falmouth exclaimed,

> A corrupt & disaffected ministry, have hitherto attempted to enslave us, by endeavouring to bring us to submit to acts of parliament, which they, and some of our enemies, adders in our bosom, had unjustly planned; and of which the late formidable stamp-act, was a manifest instance. . . . [Now] they have let loose the monstrous East-india company upon us to devour us; who have begun their baneful *commission*, by endeavouring to wash down the fatal pill, with the bewitching, the unsalutary BOHEA TEA.[35]

Gorham also saw a conscious plot against American liberties and repeated the conviction that the Tea Act was a "deep laid scheme to betray the unwary & careless into the snare laid to catch & enslave them." These plots had destroyed a veritable golden age wherein, formerly, every individual had sat under his own "Vine and Figtree," a smile on his face and joy in his heart, savoring the fruits of his own toil in perfect harmony and love with the mother country. But now mother love had turned to hatred as "Tools of Power" appointed by "Egyptian Taskmasters" extorted revenue from the colonists so that villains in England "may Wallow in Luxury on our spoil."[36]

Once more, opposition went beyond constitutional arguments and involved boycotts against the use of tea and occasionally its physical destruction. The use of violence to enforce boycotts again raised the threat of social disorder. Some towns did not seem much concerned; Gorham and Kittery both rejoiced in Boston's notorious Tea Party. Kittery voted its approval that Boston had not permitted the tea to be landed. More explicitly, Gorham declared, "we are particularly charm'd with the conduct of the Indians of which we had accot in the Publick prints." York, on the other hand, where the conservative influence of Jonathan Sayward still prevailed, coolly voted its thanks to the town of Boston, "so far as they have Constitutionally exerted themselves in support of their Just liberties and priviledges."[37]

York, in fact, experienced its own peculiar tea party in its own typically restrained manner. In mid-September 1774, a vessel arrived at York carrying a cargo of tea consigned to none other than Jonathan Sayward. By this time, even York had adopted an embargo against tea, and so a committee confiscated the tea and locked it up in a nearby storehouse. The evening following, the *New-Hampshire Gazette* reported, "a Number of Pickwacket Indians came into Town and broke open said Store, and carried it [the tea] off; which has not been heard of since."[38] Patriotic accounts make it appear that the tea was somehow destroyed and that the York tea party, modeled on that of Boston, upheld the town's patriotic reputation. The account of this affair, which Jonathan Sayward recorded in his diary, had a significantly different conclusion, however. He described the disappearance of his tea from the storehouse but then added, "two days after[,] the tea was replaced I know not by whome."[39] It is hard to believe that Sayward could make a mistake or deliberately misrepresent the facts in his personal journal. His comments raise the suspicion that York may have found a way of "destroying" its tea publicly while drinking it privately — a painless sort of radicalism.

In Falmouth, where there existed considerable skepticism as to whether the merchants would honor the town's boycott, a paper circulated early in 1774 that assured the townspeople, "you need not doubt of your Resolutions being carried into Execution," for the subscribers promised that "no Person in this Town, Great or Small, Rich or Poor, shall dare to counteract your laudable Designs." The real thrust of the paper lay in the overt symbolism in the aliases of those who signed it: "Thomas Tarbucket, Peter Pitch, Abraham Wildfowl, David Plaister, Benjamin Brush, Oliver Scarecrow, and Henry Hand-Cart," collectively styled the "Committee for Tarring and Feathering." The solid citizens of Falmouth responded with a universal shudder at this crude threat. The next town meeting voted unanimously to "detest and abhor" the threatening paper and resolved "that the said Town of Falmouth will at all Times discourage and discountenance Riots & Mobs, let their Pretence be what it will."[40] The good people of Falmouth had seen enough of mobs and violence; yet the time for peaceful protest was rapidly drawing to a close as Parliament responded to Boston's Tea Party.

London received the news of Boston's outrageous behavior regarding the tea early in 1774. From March to June, an exasperated Parliament readily consented to a series of acts collectively known in America as the "Intolerables" and in England as the "Coercives." As the name implies, the acts had punitive purpose: to punish Boston for its destruction of the tea and to chastise Massachusetts in general for its resistance to the mother country. The Port Act declared Boston Harbor closed after June 1, 1774, until the town restored peace and stability and compensated the East India Company for the lost tea. The Massachusetts Government Act and the Administration of Justice Act strengthened the royal prerogative in the province by altering the charter. The former act replaced the elective council with one appointed by the crown. The act confirmed the governor's power to appoint judges, justices, and sheriffs and extended his authority yet further to approve all town meetings, save for the annual one at which the towns elected their officials. Finally, the act changed the manner of jury selection, giving the sheriff, an appointee of the governor, power to make the final determination rather than leaving the choice up to the towns as before. The Administration of Justice Act, called the "Murder Act" in Massachusetts, enabled a royal official charged with a capital crime in pursuit of his duty to stand trial outside the province if, in the governor's opinion, the official could not otherwise obtain an impartial trial.[41]

Two other acts did not apply to Massachusetts alone. The Quartering Act, however, fell most heavily on the Bay Colony owing to the number of troops quartered in Boston. It allowed military commanders to quarter their troops in vacant houses, empty barns, and sheds if a town made no provision for them. The last bill in the series, the Quebec Act, was not intended as one of the Coercives, although colonists viewed it as such. On the contrary, it was surprisingly liberal in its intent but poorly timed. The Quebec Act restored civilian government to an enlarged Canada by placing the entire region north of the Ohio River under the administration of a royal governor in Quebec and his royally appointed council. The act did not provide for an elective assembly in Canada, for the French majority had no experience with that sort of institution. Yet Americans found the omission ominous. Equally disturbing to suspicious Americans, the British government legitimized such tools of despotism as French civil law and the Roman Catholic church throughout the vast territory of Quebec.[42]

IV

It is impossible to overemphasize the importance of the Coercive Acts in unifying the towns of Massachusetts and in intensifying their sense of alienation from the empire. The British government could have done nothing more calculated to convince the townsmen of Maine that there was indeed a conscious plot afoot in the British government to deprive them of their constitutional liberties. For the very first time, imperial policy directly and adversely affected government, justice, and the economy at the local rather than on the provincial level. Towns, even those in the backcountry and downeast, could not ignore these acts even had they wished to do so. The result was nothing less than a political "Great Awakening."

Maine towns felt the effects of the Port Act almost at once for, great or small, they all depended for survival on the carrying trade and on Boston as their chief market. The act allowed for the continued importation of firewood and food under close supervision, but the concession made little economic sense since vessels were not allowed to take cargo out of Boston in exchange for what was imported.[43] Numerous Maine towns not only passed resolves expressing indignation at Parliament and sympathy with the Bostonians but also joined an intercolonial movement sending relief to the beleaguered town. Rice came from South Carolina, grain from Pennsylvania; Connecticut sent livestock, and the communities throughout Massachusetts did what they could to help. Firewood was the most common contribution from Maine, in addition to fish, potatoes, and a few sheep. Instead of isolating Boston, the Port Act had evoked a widespread sense of unity. The York County town of Buxton expressed a widespread sentiment when it resolved that the closing of Boston Harbor was an "Attack upon Us which tends utterly to destroy our civil Liberties—For the same Power may at pleasure destroy the Trade And Shut up the Harbors of any other Colonies in Their Turne."[44]

Parliament's constitutional assault on the charter of Massachusetts elicited equally great concern. To Americans, charters were fundamental law guaranteeing their traditional rights as Englishmen and the institutions of government to protect those rights. The Massachusetts Government Act and the Administration of Justice Act clearly reflected the British conviction that colonial charters were nothing more than common legislation, which Parliament in its supremacy might alter at will. The permanence of every charter in America and the constitutional rights they embodied thus became subject to the whim of Parliament, a body physically representing Britain alone. The practical impact touched virtually every American.

Pondering the implications of all this, merchant Enoch Freeman, a prominent Falmouth Whig, mused in his journal on the relationship between a government and its people. From John Locke he quoted at length passages declaring that popular consent was the true basis of political authority. But, asked Freeman, what did this mean? In business, the employer could evaluate and dismiss his employee; yet in public affairs, where the welfare of millions of people was at stake, "*Who shall be Judge*, whether the Prince or Legislature, act contrary to their Trust?" Still quoting Locke, Freeman concluded, "the People shall be Judge," and if they judged the political compact void, they were still bound together by a social compact and could act as the supreme authority, reforming the old government or erecting a new one.[45]

Throughout Massachusetts, the people did judge. The conviction was widespread that Parliament had acted unconstitutionally, that the provincial government as modified by the Coercive Acts was illegal and deserved no obedience. Through 1774 and 1775, royal government in Massachusetts crumbled, and in its place evolved a series of institutions based on popular sovereignty. The provincial courts, already under fire because of the salary dispute, were the first to go. The superior court completed its eastern circuit through Maine before the Massachusetts Government Act with its provision for the selection of juries became known. Once public, the act completed the discrediting of the judicial system. Demonstrations in most of the counties prevented the courts — inferior as well as superior — from sitting and forced judges to act no further.

In the three Maine counties, the inferior courts continued to meet through 1774, although with a notable decline in the amount of judicial business. Most of them suspended their activity in the year following. Late in 1774, a mob at Pownalborough forced the Lincoln County justices sitting in court to disavow the new parliamentary arrangements.[46] In York County, the threat of popular violence forced the Court of Common Pleas to dismiss a jury selected in the new manner in favor of one drawn by the towns as before. It was only a theoretical victory, however; no cases were referred to the jury, and after July the civil court in York failed to meet. The criminal court continued sitting but only in its administrative capacity.[47] By occasional threats of violence and by the withdrawal of legal actions, the courts in Maine, like those throughout the entire province, virtually disappeared by 1775.

Considering the importance of the legal system in the everyday life of the colonists, society's ability to survive without courts for a year or more is nothing short of phenomenal. Little information exists concerning judicial alternatives; probably most towns met the problem as did Cape Elizabeth, which urged would-be litigants to submit to arbitration. Those who insisted on resorting to the courts, thereby acknowledging the legitimacy of the altered provincial government, were to be termed "Enemies," their names posted on the meetinghouse, and, declared the town resolve, "we will withdraw all connections with them."[48]

People such as sheriffs, justices, and members of the provincial council, who held public offices under the newly altered charter government, came under similar pressure to disavow the authority granting them their commissions. The *Boston Gazette* vilified Sir William Pepperell of York County for agreeing to serve on the new provincial council. Later, a county convention urged that all Pepperell's tenants allow their leases with him to lapse and that all persons "withdraw all connection, commerce, and dealing from him." The convention even suggested that those who refused this recommendation be subjected to the same sort of notoriety and ostracism. Before a county convention in Falmouth in September 1774, Cumberland County sheriff William Tyng publicly swore he would refuse to act in conformity with the remodeled government. About the same time, in the woods near Pownalborough, a surly crowd extracted a similar promise from Charles Cushing, high sheriff for Lincoln County.[49]

Popular action against political institutions and officers aimed only at nullifying the unconstitutional authority embodied in the Coercive Acts. Sheriffs Tyng and Cushing continued to exercise their offices as long as they acknowledged the traditional source of authority in the old charter rather than in the one revised by the Massachusetts Government Act. But since the old charter no longer existed as a legal entity, this actually meant the recognition of popular sovereignty as the ultimate source of political power. What had formerly been either a philosophical statement of faith without practical application or a pragmatic expedient without theoretical basis now became a deliberate plan of political action. Throughout Massachusetts, at all levels, provincial, county, and local, popular forms of government began to evolve without any legitimacy except general acceptance. Inexorably, they absorbed the functions of government from the legal institutions that no longer had the power to command allegiance.

The new royal governor of Massachusetts, General Thomas Gage, inadvertently initiated the events leading to the formation of an extralegal provincial government when he tried to cancel a General Court scheduled to meet at Salem on October 5, 1774. Ninety representatives met anyway, waited in vain several days for the governor to appear, and then organized themselves into a Provincial Congress. From October 1774 to July 1775, three successive congresses met variously at Cambridge, Watertown, and Concord. Finally, on July 19, 1775, the last Provincial Congress gave way to a House of Representatives and a council based on the old charter, without, of course, the royal governor or any royal sanction. From Maine, five towns each in York and Cumberland counties sent delegates to the first session of the Provincial Congress; at the second, representatives were also present from no less than six towns in Lincoln County. Several towns, too poor to send delegates on a regular basis, took pains to explain that their lack of representation did not imply disapproval. On the contrary, declared Bowdoinham, "we heartily Concur with ye Measures you have propos[d]

And heartily Beg the Almighty Will not only Bless them but Direct you further."⁵⁰

Well might Bowdoinham call for the Almighty's blessing on the Provincial Congress, for it appeared to be heading directly for a military confrontation with the "illegal" authority established by Parliament's Coercive Acts. The Provincial Congress, in coordinating the opposition, was assuming the functions of government by appointing public officials, sending delegates to the Continental Congress in Philadelphia, diverting public funds to its own treasurer, stockpiling military supplies, taking command of the provincial militia, and concerting action among county and town organizations. Conflict seemed inevitable.

County conventions and town committees evolved simultaneously with, or even preceded, the Provincial Congress. Conventions first appeared in western and central Massachusetts in the summer of 1774 and then spread rapidly throughout the province.⁵¹ They were regional responses from the towns to the constitutional threat posed by the Coercive Acts and to the power vacuum that was developing with the nullification of those acts. Conventions provided individual towns with additional support and force in opposing the Coercives and at the same time in maintaining order and stability on the local level. More than ever, local leaders feared that resistance to imperial authority might turn into a repudiation of all authority. Conventions therefore directed their energies in both directions, encouraging popular contempt for one level of government while encouraging obedience for another.

In Maine the convention movement emerged relatively late. The towns of Cumberland County moved first by meeting in county convention at the end of September 1774. York County waited until November, and the towns in the county of Lincoln, small, isolated, and poor, took no action at all. In many respects the Cumberland and York conventions were similar. Both passed resolves declaring their loyalty to the crown but condemning Parliament for its dangerous acts. It was before the Cumberland County Convention that Sheriff William Tyng publicly repudiated the authority of the remodeled provincial government. Sir William Pepperell declined to appear before the York County Convention, so its members condemned him *in absentia*. The conventions also urged their respective towns to prepare militarily and to withhold public money from the provincial treasurer appointed by the governor. Understandably, both conventions advocated measures to preserve public order amid all this defiance of imperial government. The Cumberland delegates admonished their constituents to remember that they were always "in the presence of the great *God*, who loveth order, and not confusion." The York convention, with equal emphasis, declared that riots, disorders, and tumults were "subversive of all Civil Government" and "destructive to the very end and design of the present struggle for Liberty."[52]

V

The conventions had good reason to be concerned about tumults and confusion. The enforcement of trading restrictions against Britain was again becoming a major point of contention. Throughout Massachusetts there was widespread support for some sort of economic pressure against Great Britain but equally widespread disagreement on what form it should take. Most towns insisted that economic sanctions, to be effective, would have to be intercolonial in scope and looked for direction to the Continental Congress, which did not meet until September 1774. In Boston, however, the Committee of Correspondence proposed a "Solemn League and Covenant" as early as June 1774, which bound subscribers to suspend all economic contact with Britain by the end of August and to refrain from the use of any British goods whatsoever after October 17.[53] Controversial even in Boston, the Solemn League and Covenant won few supporters in Maine, except for Gorham and Brunswick, towns that now began to challenge Falmouth's leadership of the resistance movement.

Coastal towns, such as Falmouth, were naturally reluctant to sacrifice their economies once again after the boycotts against tea, against the Townshend duties, and before that, against the Stamp Act, all enforced with the threat of mob violence. Furthermore, as opposition to Britain escalated into rebellion, seaports became uncomfortably aware of their exposed positions. The less commercial towns farther inland, like Gorham and Brunswick, were now thoroughly aroused politically and tended to view hesitation in adopting a new boycott as a lack of commitment to the patriot cause.

Disagreement over the boycott fed on a preexisting relationship between Falmouth and its satellite towns—a relationship epitomized by Falmouth's merchants who were suppliers and creditors to the surrounding communities. It is significant that when historian Edward M. Cook evaluated the degree of commercialization in various Massachusetts towns based on the number of professional men, hard currency in circulation, stock in trade, vessels and wharfs owned, and so forth, he assigned to Falmouth a relatively high figure of 13.5, to Brunswick a modest 3.9, and to the town of Gorham a mere 1.5. Other historians as well have noted Gorham's relative poverty and lack of commercial development on the eve of the Revolution.[54]

Debtor and dependent towns readily saw in Falmouth a role similar to the one that Scarborough imposed on Richard King—ultimately with the same result. By 1774 these interior, inferior inland towns, now thoroughly aroused, assumed positions of moral and political superiority over their effete, luxury-loving entrepôt. Gorham, annoyed at Falmouth's halfhearted support for the boycott, bluntly informed the other towns in the county that "The Covenant signed by the Inhabitants of Falmouth is not satisfactory to this Town."[55]

Besides criticizing Falmouth, Gorham embarked on a policy of political hegemony by sending its militia into several neighboring towns to enforce the prohibition against trading with the British at Boston, apparently on the assumption that local town governments were incapable or unwilling to do it. In both Pepperellborough and Scarborough, the Gorham militia publicly humiliated suspect merchants by mounting them on upturned barrels from which they had to expound patriotic sentiments to bemused townsfolk. In Scarborough, one of the victims was the hapless Richard King who, in his public address, made the blunder of expressing doubts that a few scattered colonists could resist the might of the British Empire. According to one account, such apprehensions enraged the militia, whose commander forced King to kneel and to beg forgiveness for such a lack of confidence in the American cause.[56]

Even inland communities were not immune to the violence and confusion accompanying the spread of the boycott movement. Towns divided sharply over the issue; a few townsmen demanded immediate action; others urged delay until the Continental Congress acted; Tories tried to prevent any action at all. During July 1774, a Solemn League and Covenant being circulated among the residents of Pownalborough polarized the community. "A Number who have Signed, Refuse to have any Connection with those that have not, and would Distroy them that have not, both root and Branch, if in their Power," wrote one observer. He went on to describe conditions in neighboring Woolwich where opponents of a boycott burned one covenant. The proponents then drew up another version which, however, differed from the original, so that many who had signed the first refused to sign the second. Downriver at Georgetown, a clergyman signed a covenant but then, fearing the consequences, returned and destroyed the entire document. In Pownalborough, the Reverend Jacob Bailey, the Anglican missionary, stiffened Tory sentiment by continuing to preach "Loyalty to our King and Due Obedience to the Laws."[57]

Sometimes resistance arose from towns that simply resented outside interference in their internal affairs. The town of Bowdoinham unanimously rejected several different boycott agreements, but for fear the royal governor might misconstrue the motive, a local official carefully explained to him that the town's refusal to sign did not signify any indifference regarding its liberties: "No Sir we Value Them as our Lives. But we would faine have them Continued to us By Some more Reagular [sic] Stream than what We think these Covenants or any thing of that Nature is like to do."[58]

But resistance in Pownalborough, Bowdoinham, and elsewhere simply stimulated radicals to greater efforts. During the fall of 1774, armed mobs crisscrossed the lower Kennebec valley enforcing nonimportation and terrorizing suspected Tories. No one gained a greater — or more notorious — reputation than Samuel Thompson of Brunswick, just embarking on a career as revolutionary agitator and professional republican that would ultimately lead him to the state Senate.

Thompson was a man of importance to the 876 residents of Brunswick. He had steadily accumulated property in real estate, but his influence probably evolved from the tavern he operated and the roughhewn republicanism he vigorously espoused. The relationship between Thompson's political views and his religious convictions is impossible to determine, but it may be significant that he rejected orthodox Calvinism in favor of the spiritual equality of Universalism. Despite his contentious personality and a marked tendency to stutter when excited, Thompson acquired a local political following. By the time of the Revolution, he had served his town as selectman, moderator, militia officer, and delegate to the Provincial Congress and the Cumberland County Convention. Admirers described this short, stocky, opinionated leader as "running over with zeal and patriotism." Thompson's enemies would have agreed with one who called him "a violent highflying Stuttering foolish fellow."[59]

Thompson set about earning both of these reputations in the late summer and fall of 1774. Under his direction, an armed mob visited Wiscasset and Pownalborough and, later, Georgetown and even Falmouth itself. Some Tories, like Parson Jacob Bailey, fled before his approach; others tried to defy him, but for refusing to sign the covenant they suffered severe physical abuse. One was almost drowned; another was forced to dig his own grave and prepare for death when, at the very last moment, the mob released him.[60] When the mob reached Pownalborough, the inferior court was in session. The justices appeared before the intruders, signed a document, probably the covenant, and gave public assurances that none of them had accepted a commission under the new provincial government. Then, after harassing the local Tories and humiliating them publicly, the mob dispersed.[61]

It is doubtful that Thompson and his crowd won many converts to their boycott, but that may not have been Thompson's objective. The Solemn League and Covenant provided an admirable excuse to intimidate and humiliate the known supporters of the Coercive Acts. Thompson's "parade" clearly demonstrated the absolute inability of the royal government to protect those who were its most outspoken defenders. There were no royal troops to disperse the mob; the justices of the peace made no effort to call up the militia or even to reprimand the rioters. Tories could hardly escape the conclusion that, along the Kennebec, royal government was at an end. Confronted by Thompson and his armed followers, even local governments seemed powerless to provide protection and order.

Samuel Thompson reappeared next spring at Georgetown near the mouth of the Kennebec. This time his role was to enforce not the Solemn League and Covenant but the Association, the embargo, which the Continental Congress had urged the states to impose against Britain. The Massachusetts Provincial Congress consequently ordered Thompson to the Kennebec area early in April 1775 to prevent a British mast agent, Edward Parry, from sending a valuable cargo of masts to England. Shortly after Thompson arrived at Georgetown, rumors of fighting at Lexington and Concord reached there on April 23, heightening yet further a potentially dangerous jurisdictional dispute between the town and the authority of the Provincial Congress, represented by Samuel Thompson.[62] Town authorities quickly took mast agent Parry into custody, but Thompson felt that the situation required more dramatic action.

Heedless of Georgetown's jurisdiction in the matter, Thompson devised his own plans for Parry. They involved a British naval vessel, the *Canceaux*, anchored close by in Falmouth Harbor protecting a Tory shipbuilder who refused to be bound by the Continental embargo. Parry was friendly with the *Canceaux*'s commanding officer, Lieutenant Henry Mowat, and this friendship offered Thompson a scheme by which to seize the British vessel. Using Parry as an involuntary decoy, Thompson planned to come alongside the *Canceaux* in his own sloop. At the crucial moment, Thompson's crew would board and take the British vessel by surprise.[63]

An unforeseen obstacle arose, however, when the Georgetown authorities, resenting Thompson's intrusion into their own jurisdiction, refused to surrender Parry without instructions from the Provincial Congress.[64] Thompson departed in a fury but soon returned leading fifty armed militiamen accompanied by fife and drum. The Georgetown officials refused to be intimidated by this martial array. Thompson had to be satisfied with placing Parry under bond to appear before the Provincial Congress and with obtaining payment from the town for the cost of "entertaining" his troops.

Thompson did not forget the *Canceaux*; he simply modified his plan for seizing it. A crisis had been building in Falmouth since March 1775, when a vessel from England arrived carrying sails, rigging, and equipment for a ship that merchant Thomas Coulson was completing. The Continental Association was in force, and the situation became a test of Falmouth's patriotic zeal. The town's Committee of Inspection, headed by Enoch Freeman, ordered Coulson to send the cargo back to England at once.[65] Representatives of Falmouth's mercantile community, however, pleaded for leniency on Coulson's behalf. Coulson himself argued that the vessel that brought the cargo could not return without first unloading and undergoing extensive repairs. At Coulson's request, the royal authorities in Boston sent H.M.S. *Canceaux* to Falmouth to protect him and to maintain order.[66] At the same time, there came a sharp communication from the Boston Committee of Inspection to the committee at Falmouth reminding them that "the eyes of the whole Continent" were upon them. "The tools of power wish for an opportunity to charge us with negligence, and are watching for it, to make a division between this Province and the other Colonies." The Boston committee exhorted its Falmouth counterparts "that you conform strictly and religiously to the Association of the Continental Congress in every respect, without favour or affection to any person whatever."[67]

In this tension-filled atmosphere, the Committee of Inspection tried to deter violence with a resolve that it would exert all its efforts to prevent "riots, tumults, and insurrections, or attacks on the private property of any persons . . . as injurious to the liberty of *America* in general, and that [it] will, as far as lies in [its] power, promote peace and good order, as absolutely necessary to the existence of society."[68] Coulson, meanwhile, protected by the *Canceaux*'s guns, defied the embargo by transferring the cargo directly to his new vessel. Despite the exhortations from Boston, Falmouth's leaders refused to resort to whatever means were required to prevent him. As at Georgetown, a tense situation became yet more volatile when news of Lexington and Concord reached Falmouth on April 20. Fearing the worst, customs officials began to seek refuge aboard the *Canceaux*, and some of Falmouth's inhabitants began to move their possessions into the interior.

Samuel Thompson took it upon himself to end Falmouth's indecision by removing its most immediate cause, H.M.S. *Canceaux*. He had assured the town's nervous leaders that he had no plans to intrude in their affairs, yet, with a small detachment of militia, he quietly arrived in Falmouth and on May 9 succeeded in capturing the *Canceaux*'s commander, Lieutenant Henry Mowat, and one of his officers while they were ashore visiting with Falmouth's Anglican preacher, John Wiswall.[69]

Thompson's rash behavior horrified the town. Panic-stricken inhabitants fled, carrying their possessions in every conceivable sort of conveyance. Leading citizens beseeched Thompson to release his prisoners before Mowat's second-in-command made good his threat to bombard the town. Some few even considered calling up Falmouth's militia, not to attack the *Canceaux* but to force Thompson into releasing Mowat.[70] But Falmouth escaped the incongruity of American militia fighting each other for possession of a British naval officer by the simple fact that Falmouth's militia was nowhere to be found. Some detachments were already on their way to join the American army forming at Cambridge. Remaining men either were enlisting in a new provincial regiment—

still without order and discipline — or were preoccupied with saving their own possessions and families from the destruction expected momentarily.

Throughout the chaos, known as "Thompson's War," the Falmouth militia never appeared as an organized force. But others did; militia from the nearby communities of Cape Elizabeth, Scarborough, Windham, and Gorham began to pour into Falmouth. By the morning of May 10, 600 truculent militiamen ended any pretense to civilian government in the town. In desperation Enoch Freeman wrote to the Provincial Congress, "We are in confusion. . . . Pray let Congress be informed of this affair, and let us know whether *Thompson* had such orders; and pray Congress to give us some direction, for we are in such confusion nobody seems to be rational."[71]

As confused as anyone was Samuel Thompson, who did not know what to do with Mowat now that he finally had him. According to one report, Thompson had originally intended to use Mowat in the forefront of a party to board the *Canceaux*, a variation of the scheme involving Parry.[72] Lacking support for his plan, especially in Falmouth, Thompson had no alternative when it fell through. He grudgingly agreed to release his prisoners on condition that Mowat promise to return the next day and that two prominent Falmouth merchants and leading Whigs, Enoch Freeman and Jedediah Preble, stand surety in Mowat's behalf.[73] Very likely, Thompson hoped that Mowat would *not* return, a desire that Mowat readily fulfilled. This allowed Thompson to shift attention and blame to the perfidious British commander and to Freeman and Preble, for whose caution and lack of resolve Thompson had nothing but contempt. The militia shared their leader's resentment. One worried resident wrote, "The soldiery thought nothing too bad to say of the *Falmouth* gentry. Some of them were heard to say as they walked the streets yesterday, 'this Town ought to be laid in Ashes.'" The writer suspected a concerted plan to do so — "to humble *Falmouth*."[74] Such was not yet to be the town's fate; the metropolis had been humbled sufficiently for the time being. After harassing local Tories and pillaging several of their homes, the militiamen returned to their own towns.

By May 13 Falmouth was free of its uninvited guests. The town quickly made apologies to Mowat for the disturbance caused by outside agitators. The British commander seemed to understand, and so the townsmen feared no retribution at his hands. Almost forgotten was the cause of all the trouble. Thomas Coulson succeeded in defying the Continental Association; he completed the work of fitting out his new ship and sailed off in convoy with the *Canceaux*, carrying Falmouth's first group of Tory refugees.

Falmouth was left to consider its brief traumatic experience. The local Committee of Correspondence remonstrated with the Provincial Congress that Thompson, without any authority, had exposed the defenseless town to the threat of bombardment, civil war, and anarchy. As Falmouth's Committee of Correspondence phrased it, "We are afraid that if any number of men at any time, and in any manner, may collect together, and attack any thing, or any person they please, every body may be in danger."[75] Fearing destruction, war, and anarchy, Falmouth's merchant leaders had refused to take the last violent steps in defense of the Association. They had lost face, and now the initiative shifted to the less commercial, more aggressive rural towns of the interior and those downeast.

VI

Falmouth finally suffered the devastation it had tried so desperately to avoid when Lieutenant Henry Mowat, commanding a small fleet, returned on October 18 and bombarded the town, leveling two-thirds of its buildings and destroying the town's shipping. Oddly enough, one of the primary causes for this shocking event occurred in the remote lumbering town of Machias. There too, as at Falmouth, the trade embargo created a violent confrontation involving the British navy.

Ichabod Jones, Machias's leading entrepreneur, was not one to turn down a business opportunity. When the Port Act closed Boston Harbor, he remained at Machias. From there he worked out an arrangement with the British in Boston to exchange firewood and lumber from Machias for provisions that were desperately needed downeast. Jones's business transactions aroused the ire of Machias Whigs, who threatened to destroy his vessels for trading with the enemy. When Jones's critics began salvaging cannon from a wrecked schooner, he realized they soon might have the means to carry out their threat. Inside Boston, the British were reduced to dismantling fences and church pews to obtain firewood. Vice Admiral Samuel Graves therefore agreed to send a naval vessel to protect Jones from interference when he traded at Machias.[76]

On June 2, 1775, Jones's two sloops, *Unity* and *Polly*, accompanied by the armed sloop, H.M.S. *Margaretta*, commanded by Midshipman James Moore, sailed upriver to the village of Machias.

Jones at once set about circulating a document by which he agreed to exchange provisions for lumber and firewood, provided the signers promised to protect him and his property from retaliation. A segment of Machias's population bitterly opposed this effort to bribe the village into surrendering its constitutional scruples for a "mess of pottage," but economic necessity won out: A town meeting agreed to trade on Jones's terms.[77] The entire situation was strikingly similar to recent events in Falmouth. In both cases, a merchant, protected by the Royal Navy, defied the Continental Association with the consent of the town. Furthermore, the radicals in both towns responded with plans that closely resembled each other's. Benjamin Foster, colonel of militia in Machias, justice of the peace, and one of Jones's business partners, gathered some militia from nearby communities and devised a plan to seize Ichabod Jones, his nephew Stephen Jones, and the naval officers while they were at church on Sunday morning. As at Falmouth, the plan miscarried and precipitated a crisis. The militiamen revealed their presence as they were surrounding the church building, and they captured only Stephen Jones. Ichabod momentarily escaped the inevitable by fleeing into the woods. The officers of the *Margaretta* managed to reach their vessel, which drew out into the river; from there Midshipman Moore threatened to bombard the town if order were not restored.[78]

The parallel with Falmouth breaks down at this point, for Machias threw its support behind the radicals. Perhaps the *Margaretta*'s size and armament, a mere sloop with four guns, were too insignificant to induce a sense of awe. Probably the fact that the radical leaders, Benjamin Foster, Jeremiah O'Brien, and George Stillman, were prominent residents, not outside agitators like Thompson, made a difference. Finally, residents of Machias may well have regarded Ichabod Jones in the same light as the townspeople of Scarborough viewed Richard King, as an arrogant, grasping man who had to be humbled. In any case, where Falmouth faltered, Machias pushed on.

After a brief exchange of small arms fire, both sides prepared for battle the next day. The rebels commandeered one of Jones's sloops and hastily constructed bulwarks out of the stacked lumber. Meantime, two young women, Hannah and Rebecca Weston, from the neighboring settlement of Chandler's River (Jonesborough) became local legends by trekking through sixteen miles of woods to Machias bringing additional supplies of powder and shot for the anticipated conflict.[79]

On the morning of June 12, about forty men armed with a motley assortment of guns, clubs, and pitchforks sailed downriver under command of Jeremiah O'Brien to do battle with the *Margaretta*. A small schooner carrying Benjamin Foster and about twenty men more joined them. Together they caught up with the *Margaretta* as it was trying to reach the open sea. Clumsy sailing had cost the Britisher its booms and gaffs and precious time spent in seizing replacements from another vessel. The Americans came alongside, boarded, and in the ensuing melee the British commander received a mortal wound. Deprived of leadership, the British crew quickly surrendered.[80]

The seizure of the *Margaretta* was an astonishing achievement, the sort of coup Samuel Thompson had dreamed of at Georgetown and Falmouth. But once the exhilaration subsided, the same fears of retribution that unnerved Falmouth beset Machias. There was no turning back now, however. In desperation, Machias men surprised and took two more of His Majesty's vessels, the schooner *Diligent* and its tender, which had put in at the mouth of the Machias River on hearing rumors of the strange doings there.[81] The rebels converted the prize vessels into a little squadron for the defense of Machias, but it would have availed little against the revenge intended by the British authorities at Boston had Lieutenant Henry Mowat carried out his orders. As it was, hapless Falmouth did penance for the sins of Machias.

The increasing number of warlike incidents in Maine and along the New England coast proved embarrassing to Vice Admiral Samuel Graves, who commanded the Royal Navy's North American squadron. His initial policy of moderation quite obviously had made no positive impact on the provincials, and so the elderly admiral resorted to the opposite extreme of enforced pacification. Graves's plan was simply to make an example of several of the more rebellious seaport towns by subjecting them to naval bombardment. The Admiralty Board in England provided Graves with unexpected support by ordering him to take vigorous action against all towns in open rebellion.[82] To carry out the task, he selected Lieutenant Henry Mowat. "My Design," wrote Graves to Mowat, "is to chastize Marblehead, Salem, Newbury Port, Cape Anne Harbour, Portsmouth, Ipswich, Saco, Falmouth in Casco Bay, and particularly Mechias where the *Margaretta* was taken, the Officer commanding her killed, and the People made Prisoners, and where the *Diligent* Schooner was seized and the Officers and Crew carried Prisoners up the Country, and where preparations I am informed are now making to invade the Province of Nova Scotia."[83] With the exception of Saco, all the towns Graves marked for destruction had been scenes of major disturbances. Why he included Saco is not clear, but his orders left no doubt that Machias, for its past conduct and future intentions, particularly merited retribution. The irony was that Falmouth, where the recent violence was the work of radicals from the interior, had to bear the brunt of it all.

The four-vessel flotilla began its eastward cruise on October 8, 1775. One after another, it bypassed the towns fated for destruction. In some cases the towns were too scattered for effective bombardment; in others the wind direction was wrong for entering the harbor. Adverse winds finally forced Mowat's vessels to shelter for several days in Townshend Bay (Boothbay Harbor), by which time the squadron had passed eastward of every designated town except Machias, which now was probably Mowat's objective.[84] The weather conditions saved Machias, but they exposed Falmouth to destruction.

When Mowat's squadron appeared in Falmouth Harbor on October 16, residents assumed the British were searching for provisions and so dispatched most of the militia to the numerous islands to protect livestock grazing there. When the town learned that Mowat commanded the flotilla, the inhabitants relaxed, confident that their town stood high in the lieutenant's favor for helping him escape the clutches of Samuel Thompson.[85] Mowat quickly disabused them of that idea with a proclamation accusing Falmouth of "premeditated attacks" on the "best of sovereigns" and of "unpardonable Rebellion."[86] Mowat allowed the people two hours to evacuate the town, after which he would carry out his orders and commence firing. As initial shock gave way to hysteria, a three-man committee finally persuaded Mowat to relent to the extent that, if the town would surrender its stock of firearms, Mowat would request Admiral Graves to verify his orders, thereby giving the admiral a chance to change his mind. As it was late in the day, Mowat agreed to accept only a token number of arms that night; early the next day the townsmen would vote on whether to surrender all their remaining arms in the slender hope that Graves might spare their town. The new deadline was nine o'clock the next morning.[87]

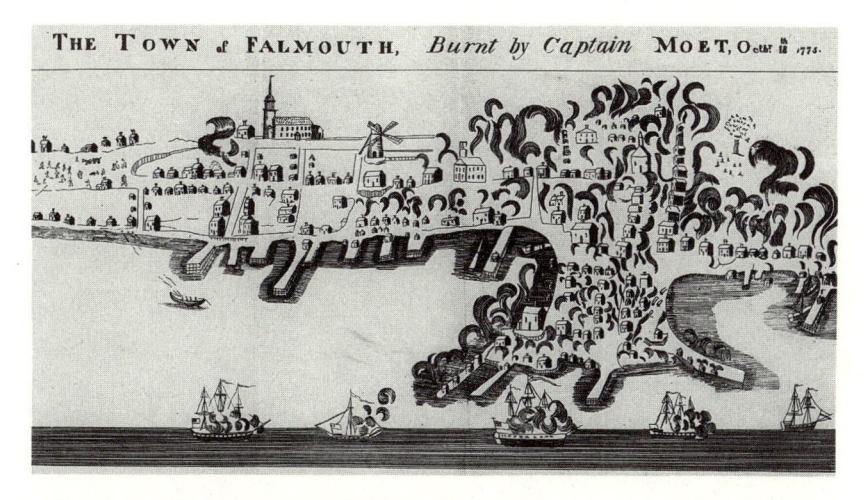

THE TOWN of FALMOUTH, *Burnt by Captain* MOET, Octbr ii 1775.

7. Courtesy of Maine Historical Society.

During the night, Falmouth was a scene of vast confusion. Residents, convinced that the town would be destroyed, desperately tried to save their possessions; however, there were not enough carts, wagons, wheelbarrows, horses, oxen, or hours in the night. By morning, refugees and their belongings still jammed the streets. Adding to the confusion, militia from the nearby towns began filtering into Falmouth once again. The purpose of their presence was never very clear, but the result was to preclude any sort of "deal" with the British. In so chaotic an atmosphere, the town never did hold its scheduled meeting to consider Mowat's offer. On the morning of October 18, half an hour after the deadline, Mowat's fleet began its bombardment. The cannonading lasted until 6:00 P.M., and then the squadron sailed away, leaving behind 130 houses destroyed, along with the Anglican church, the new courthouse, the fire station, and the public library. Thirteen vessels had been at anchor in Falmouth Harbor; Mowat took two and sank the rest.[88]

The militia detachments made no effort to defend the town or even to resist a British landing party, which torched several prominent buildings to speed up the process of destruction. Instead, the visiting militiamen risked life and limb during the bombardment looting the houses and possessions of Falmouth's refugees. The Reverend Jacob Bailey, in Falmouth at the time, reported with outrage that a "multitude of villains were purloining . . . goods and carrying them into the country beyond the reach of justice. . . . The country people," he continued, "were

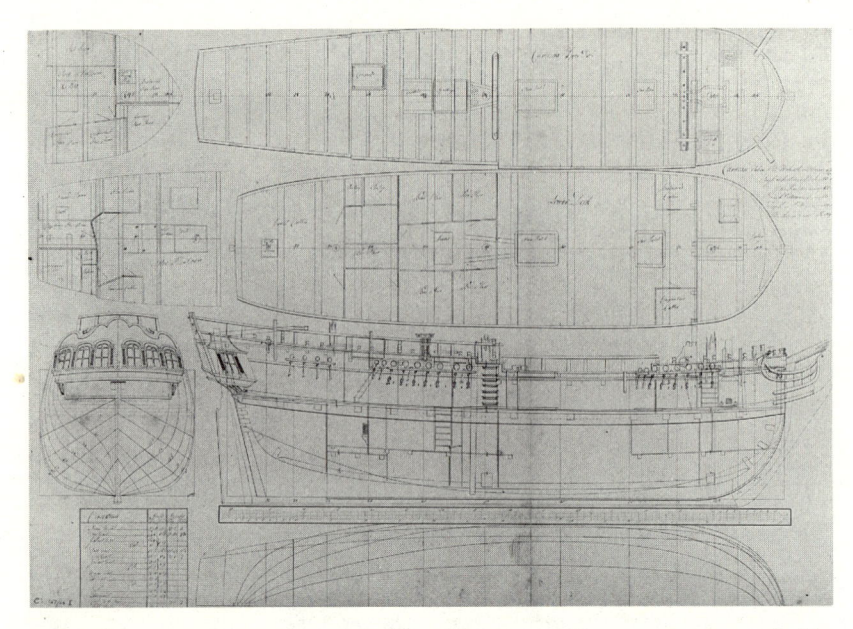

8. Profile of the hull and cross sections of the H.M.S. *Canceaux*, commanded by Lieutenant Henry Mowat in the burning of Falmouth. Courtesy of the National Maritime Museum, Greenwich, London, England.

hardly restrained from destroying those houses that escaped the general devastation. A most surprising instance of perfidious baseness and human cruelty."[89] Although such an account from an avowed Tory might arouse skepticism, Whig sources substantiate the accusation of looting by the backcountry militia. The preamble to a bill enacted by the Massachusetts General Court on February 8, 1776, clearly summarized what occurred: "Whereas, at the time of the late fire, by which the greater part of the Town of Falmouth . . . was destroyed by vessels belonging to the British navy, many persons took and carried away from the owners large quantities of goods, under color of saving them for the use of the owners . . . etc. etc."[90] According to the act, possessors had until April 1, 1776, to surrender the plundered goods to the selectmen of their respective towns or else be treated as possessing stolen property.

Militiamen from Gorham, in particular, seemed to have played a prominent part in the pillaging of their helpless neighbor. Undoubtedly other towns were also involved, but Gorham alone called a special town meeting for October 30, 1775, for a single purpose, "to propose & pursue such measures as may effectively preserve the honor & reputation of said Town notwithstanding the rapine & unjust & cruel treatment of [by] some individuals of the Town aforesaid of the goods and effects of the late sufferers in the awful Conflagration at Falmouth."[91] The voters of Gorham condemned the conduct of any persons, inhabitants of Gorham or not, who carried away property from Falmouth "with a design to convert them to their own use, or to deprive the right Owners of any such goods or furniture."[92]

Burned, looted, its population dispersed as refugees, the leading town in Maine had shared the fate of Scarborough's Richard King. The plight of several hundred homeless families at the onset of winter elicited sympathy and charity from nearby towns and from the General Court, but nevertheless there existed strong sentiment that Falmouth had gotten what it deserved for its pusillanimous conduct in the face of the enemy. Falmouth's representative, Jedediah Preble, complained because "so many members of the honourable [General] Court . . . should be prejudiced against this town for not throwing up a bulwark the night preceding the conflagration."[93] Too forward in rebellion for the British, too backward to satisfy radical Whigs in the interior, Falmouth suffered the penalties of moderates in the polarizing situation.

From the Whig point of view, the punishment inflicted on Falmouth actually had a salutary effect on the rugged few who continued to occupy that blackened spot. Scarcely had the ashes cooled, only several weeks later, than another British man-of-war entered the harbor looking for provisions. Although the ship's commander seized hostages and warned the citizens against any hostile action, the populace, reinforced with militia, retaliated by seizing hostages of their own and by spending a frantic night erecting earthworks. Such a display of martial ardor convinced the British commander he had little to gain at Falmouth, and he sailed away after releasing his hostages.[94] Falmouth, purified by fire, was now on the road to political redemption. But those who bore the brunt of radical zeal in Falmouth and in towns beyond must surely have pondered the cost of their salvation.

THREE

Protective Insignificance

Falmouth's agony was only one detail in an unfolding crisis that had begun at Lexington and Concord on April 19, 1775. As news of the fighting reached Maine, Falmouth's Tory merchant, Thomas Coulson, was challenging the town's Whigs over the Continental Association. By the time Samuel Thompson sought to resolve the stalemate by seizing Lieutenant Mowat, an American army, raised by the aroused towns of New England — including those in Maine — surrounded the British in Boston. War had begun. Precisely six months after the initial clash at Lexington and Concord, the British burned Falmouth. More than anything else, that event brought home to Maine in the most vivid terms the full consequences of resisting imperial authority. Falmouth's fate accentuated the vulnerability of the three eastern counties.

In desperation, Maine towns, isolated, exposed, and fearful, appealed to the revolutionary government in Massachusetts for direction and military assistance in defending not simply a long, accessible coastline against the Royal Navy but also the interior frontier from expected Indian attack. To the harried Provincial Congress, however, the defense of Maine became just one more concern among the crises, confusions, and controversies surrounding the early war effort. Left largely to their own devices and lacking confidence in their resources, Maine communities sought security through their own insignificance. As one resident of Falmouth grimly expressed it, "perhaps the insignificance of this place will be its security. Indeed we have no other."[1]

The military crises enveloping Maine at the northern extremity of the rebellion differed little from those besetting other exposed, isolated border regions. For communities on Long Island Sound, in the Mohawk valley, in the Carolinas and especially Georgia, the war consisted of frequent alarms, lightning raids, and efforts at precarious neutrality. The War for Independence, for border regions from Maine to Georgia, was a nasty and prolonged struggle for survival.

I

Most towns in western Maine heard about the fighting at Lexington and Concord by April 20. On that date, the Reverend Thomas Smith of Falmouth recorded in his diary, "The country is all in alarm everywhere, sending soldiers to Boston. A civil war is now commenced."[2] A resident in the town of Lebanon wrote on the same day, "Squaly good news this Morn. 4 o'Clock AM news of ye Regulars fighting." The "Squaly good news" also unleashed wild rumors that the British had landed and were fighting around Kittery. Several days later reports reached Pownalborough that 1,000 British troops were marauding their way up the Kennebec valley.[3] Here and there militias mustered to meet the imaginary enemy and to harass suspected Tories, but most towns quickly sent off detachments of militia to join the American army forming at Cambridge amid vast confusion.

The militia formed the basic military organization throughout all the provinces and especially in those, like Massachusetts, with an extended frontier and a long tradition of frontier warfare. Virtually all white, adult men were enlisted in one of two types of militia organization, train bands or alarm lists. The former included all able-bodied males sixteen to fifty years of age, who had to provide themselves with suitable military equipment, train regularly, and have one-quarter of their number ready to march at a moment's notice for any emergency. These were the units that marched off first to Cambridge. Exempt from this requirement were civil officers, college students, teachers, deep-sea captains, and preachers, most of whom were included in the less rigorous alarm list along with the older men of the community between the ages of fifty and sixty-five. Militia companies elected their own officers, though the Provincial Congress gradually assumed the authority, once exercised by the royal governor and his council, to appoint staff and field officers for each county and regiment.[4] Elected or appointed, officers were usually members of the provincial elite for whom military command served as one more symbol of prestige.

On April 23, 1775, the Provincial Congress issued a call to raise an army of 13,600 men as rapidly as possible and sent out recruiting orders in wholesale fashion. Many towns had not waited for such orders but sent men off to Cambridge as soon as they had received news of the fighting. The town of York dispatched sixty men on April 20, the alarm having come only the evening before. Militia from Biddeford, Scarborough, and Falmouth quickly followed. As the news worked its way eastward, the more distant towns responded in similar fashion. Indeed, the military response was so rapid and so universal that it threatened to get out of control. Provincial leaders pleaded with the more distant detachments to return home until some sort of order could be created out of the throngs of armed men converging on Cambridge.[5]

Young Henry Sewall in Falmouth experienced the confusion firsthand. On hearing the "bloody news," he joined a militia company to march for Cambridge. After two days on the road, they received word to return. Back in Falmouth, Sewall reenlisted in a company of volunteers, but there was uncertainty not only whether the company should join the army at Cambridge or stay to defend Falmouth but whether Falmouth should be defended at all. Sewall noted that some residents, perhaps in light of what so recently occurred at Lexington and Concord, feared that defending Falmouth would require collecting military stores in a depot or magazine. The very presence of such a supply would give Falmouth a dangerous prominence, and it "will expose us greatly: — and [British General Thomas] Gage having notice of it will send forces to destroy it."[6] Majority opinion favored some sort of military response, but confusion existed over the command of the forces, as well as their purpose. The captain who was raising the troops had received his commission from Colonel Edmund Phinney of Gorham, who as yet had no authority to issue commissions or enlistment orders since he himself had not yet received his commission from the Provincial Congress.[7]

Falmouth's Committee of Correspondence confirmed the sense of confusion and uncertainty. In the same letter to the Provincial Congress complaining about Samuel Thompson's outrageous behavior, the committee described the current recruiting scene:

> We are also concerned lest a deal of confusion should arise from a number of our men in the country possessing themselves of the enlisting papers lately printed, some calling themselves Colonels, some Majors, appointing their own officers, Adjutants, Chaplains,

Chirurgeons, etc., etc., without having, as we can learn, any written orders for so doing; for they seem to contend already who shall be chief officers, and they are uncertain whether the men they enlist are to be stationed here for defence, or march to Cambridge to make up the Standing Army.[8]

In due time, Colonel Phinney received his commission, but so too did two other officers, each of whom had orders to enlist what was meant to be a single regiment. A potentially divisive dispute over the command dissolved when one of the officers voluntarily resigned his commission and the other accepted second-in-command under Phinney. Half of the regiment led by Phinney then marched off to Cambridge, while the remainder stayed behind to defend Falmouth.[9] So tranquil a resolution to the problems of command was unusual; confusion, quarrels, and personal jealousies hampered the military effort throughout the province as leaders competed over military titles and tactics.

The defense of Maine assumed new importance after October 18, 1775, when the British so clearly demonstrated at Falmouth what might befall any seacoast town. The coastal communities of southern Maine, expecting Mowat's fleet momentarily, hastened to prepare their defenses. Kittery and Portsmouth stretched a log boom across their common harbor and hurriedly constructed batteries. Meanwhile, the militia leaders from Kittery, York, and Wells met to coordinate their defense plans. Falmouth and its neighboring towns were equally nervous that the British might reappear in force to occupy the region. A convention of delegates from towns in Cumberland and even York County met to organize defensive measures and to seek help. The convention appealed to General George Washington, now at Cambridge commanding the army there, and to the Provincial Congress. Neither was very receptive; Washington could spare no military aid, although he did order Colonel Edmund Phinney to return to offer advice on the defense of Falmouth. The Provincial Congress, overwhelmed by details concerning the new army and the siege of Boston, rejected the convention's proposal to garrison Falmouth with 1,000 troops to be paid by the state. Instead, it voted to raise garrisons of fifty men each for all the exposed towns in the coastal counties of Massachusetts and Maine. For Falmouth, however, Congress resolved to raise a garrison of only 400 men.[10]

Samuel Freeman and James Sullivan, spokesmen for the Cumberland convention, held a far higher estimate of Falmouth's military importance. Freeman wrote to General Washington in an attempt to enlist his services in lobbying the state into more vigorous action on Falmouth's behalf. Through an aide-de-camp, the general tartly replied that he fully approved of the steps taken and that if anything more needed to be done to defend the area it was up to the inhabitants to provide it.[11] Sullivan had no better luck with the Provincial Congress, where Falmouth still possessed a tainted reputation for its failure to uphold the Association and resist Mowat. The state government did send some cannon and ammunition to Falmouth once the British had evacuated Boston on March 17, 1776. The cannon were defective, however, and, in any case, of little value for a militia that, in Sullivan's estimation, were too few and too divided in leadership to offer effective resistance to the enemy.[12]

For Cumberland County, at least, conditions did not improve even after the Provincial Congress moved to regularize the state militia and its command structure early in 1776. Militia appointments for Lincoln and York counties seemed to cause no serious distress, but in Cumberland County the selection produced consternation. Named as brigadier general, the leading militia officer for the entire county, was none other than Falmouth's old nemesis, Samuel Thompson of Brunswick.[13]

The precise details of Thompson's appointment are obscure, but after "Thompson's War" in Falmouth and his earlier intrusion into Georgetown, he had a growing reputation as an activist in the patriot cause that transcended his own town of Brunswick. An event in 1779 illustrates the nature of Thompson's support and helps to explain why the legislature not only defeated a motion censuring him for his unauthorized activities in Falmouth but replaced it with an expression of approval and then appointed him brigadier general for Cumberland County. In 1779 leaders in Falmouth orchestrated a movement to remove Thompson from his military command on grounds of incompetence and suggested to the General Court an entirely new slate of officers for the county militia. Falmouth's coup failed owing to the successful opposition from a bloc of towns that included only two coastal communities, Harpswell and Cape Elizabeth. The majority of the pro-Thompson communities were small interior political and economic satellites to Falmouth, their entrepôt and shire town: Windham, Gray, Bakerstown (Poland and Minot), and of course Gorham and Brunswick.[14] It is this bloc of chiefly small inland towns that found in Thompson a physical embodiment of their sectional resentments and political aspirations.

To conservative Whigs in Falmouth, giving such authority to a man like Thompson was like setting the wolf to guard the sheep. Furthermore, he totally lacked the traditional qualifications for military command. James Sullivan, an ambitious, Harvard-educated lawyer who before the war had been king's attorney in York County, wanted the position himself. He summarized the social basis of hostility to Thompson by declaring him deficient in education, character, property, and family background. Troops and officers alike, he warned, would refuse to serve under such a person. Indeed, he went on, the gentlemen of Cumberland County were complaining that in such an appointment they were more abused by the General Court than by Parliament.[15] In effect, innkeeper and mob leader Samuel Thompson had bypassed his social superiors in the race for military titles.

More was at stake than military prestige; Thompson's personal style and concept of military leadership contrasted sharply with those of Sullivan and other Whig leaders. At a review of his brigade in the fall of 1776, Brigadier General Samuel Thompson addressed his men, saying that he had heard some of his officers and his men were against him and that unless he could rule in their hearts he would not rule over them. He then demanded a vote of confidence, and, according to the newspaper report, not a single officer and only one soldier — very bold or very foolish — voted against him. Thus inspired, the brigadier general treated his audience to one of his typically flamboyant patriotic orations. He expounded on the glorious cause in which they were all embarked and the honor of dying for the rights of the people rather than submitting to tyranny. In urging his men upon the steady course of discipline, Thompson asked of them one favor, "that was, if he in the Day of Battle gave Back[,] Slay me, said he, for it will be just, and the Man that does must expect the same." At this, the countenance of the men "looked Noble and Cheerful and made a Warlike appearance."[16]

Trite and ostentatious this harangue may sound, yet the highest-ranking officer in the county was declaring that the revolution in which they were equally concerned was more than a mere break from Britain. When Thompson declared that officers ought not lead except by popular support, by a vote of confidence, he reaffirmed democratic principles even in the military and, at least by implication, rejected traditional hierarchical authority everywhere. For Thompson, brigadier general of Cumberland County, the revolution was a democratic social revolution as well as a political one.

By contrast, James Sullivan reveals a much different view. In a letter to the Massachusetts council criticizing the election of militia officers by their men, Sullivan transcended the military issue to which he was ostensibly referring when he wrote, "for such is the state of human nature, that people will not be obedient to power derived immediately from themselves; and as all power is, or ought to be, derived from the people, it would always be well to have a certain *depositum*, where it shall be lodged by the people, and from whence it may be taken by their officers."[17] Sullivan, who would eventually become Democratic-Republican governor of Massachusetts, had little sympathy with democracy. Whether political or military, it smacked of anarchy, and only the refining of popular authority through recognized social leaders could provide society with sufficient direction and discipline.

In effect, the squabble over Thompson's military appointment indicates a continuation of the simmering, unresolved debate over the nature of the Revolution, which had worried Whig leaders from the very start of opposition to Britain. Thompson was emerging as spokesman and symbol for the more radical, democratic goals of the Revolution, expressed most emphatically — although not exclusively — by the small, struggling, less commercial communities of the interior.

Dismay over Thompson's appointment did not unify those gentlemen who received subordinate commissions. The Reverend Samuel Deane summarized relations among the officers in the county's first militia regiment: "[Colonel John] Waite will not serve under Thompson, nor [Lieutenant Colonel Peter] Noyes under Waite, nor [Major William] Frost under Noyes. Our militia are in a pretty situation to expect an invasion. Neither officer'd, equipt, nor disciplined."[18]

II

Even when harmony prevailed within the command, faulty communications and long distances hampered effective action. Ideally, the militia supplied troops to meet any local emergency while providing a regular source of trained manpower for the state or for the Continental Army. The General Court normally called upon the brigadier general in each county of the state for a particular quota of troops. The brigadier generals allocated the quota among the colonels of the county regiments who, in turn, ordered each of their captains to detach the appropriate number of troops from their respective companies. Lincoln County's Brigadier General Charles Cushing revealed how the system worked in practice.

On June 23, 1778, the Massachusetts council resolved to raise a certain number of troops and sent orders to the county brigadiers to detach the required quotas. The orders reached Cushing after the time limit for raising the troops had come and gone. Furthermore, he pointed out, even had the soldiers been produced on schedule, the orders omitted the place to which they were to be sent. In addition, copying and transmitting the council resolve to colonels and captains throughout the county consumed yet more time. Some militia companies produced their quotas very readily, but others had great difficulty because of the scarcity of men, many of whom had been "drawn away by the western Towns who have sent down & enticed them by offering large bounties." Therefore, in response to the council resolve of June 23, Cushing, writing about one month later, stated he had a return of troops from only one colonel, although he had repeated his orders to the others.[19] The militia system did work after a fashion, but at best it was slow, awkward, and inefficient.

Given sufficient time and warning, the militia could provide effective local defense. The militia at Machias, aided by the timely presence of Indian visitors, thwarted a British attack in 1777. When the British moved on up the coast to Boothbay and Wiscasset, they were again turned back by an aroused militia. At Boothbay, the British lost so many of their landing party as prisoners to the local militia that they agreed to depart in exchange for the release of the men.[20] Wiscasset was an even greater humiliation.

On a foggy September night in 1777, Commodore Sir George Collier, in the frigate H.M.S. *Rainbow*, sent a landing party up the Sheepscot River to capture a French ship loading a valuable cargo of masts — the very masts seized from British mast agent Edward Parry at Georgetown in 1775. The British easily gained possession of the vessel only to discover that the sails had been taken ashore as a precaution against just such an eventuality. Once alerted, the local militiamen laid siege to the immobile ship with the British raiders aboard. Their predicament forced Collier to sail his frigate up the river to secure by negotiation what he could not gain by force. He found unexpected support from a neutralist faction among the local population, which, with "jisuitical Smoothness," sought to persuade the militia to surrender the ship and the masts as a means of getting rid of the British without more fighting. The rebels, however, refused to make a deal; Collier had to extricate his raiding party and withdraw under fire as best he could. By this time, the entire Third Regiment of Lincoln County lined the shore, and Collier escaped to sea only by surrendering his prisoners as well as a schooner he had captured earlier.[21]

British raids on Machias, Boothbay, and Wiscasset were unusual in that they were relatively slow, deliberate, even clumsy, maneuvers requiring several days to complete. This allowed the militia time to gather and to prepare defensive measures. More typical was the visit of the British to Naskeag [Brooklin] on the eastern side of Penobscot Bay. In late July 1778, two British armed sloops suddenly appeared, one of them commanded by Charles Callahan, a Tory refugee from Pownalborough. A landing party of sixty men easily brushed away the several defenders, burned their homes and barns, and then either carried off or destroyed the livestock. After exchanging some prisoners, the raiders continued their way up Eggemoggin Reach, plundering settlements and seizing fishing craft as they went.[22]

The Naskeag raid offers a good example of the problems of relying on the militia for defense. Isolated Naskeag received no military support until assistance arrived from Deer Isle the day after the raid. In the majority of cases, the British attacks were of this type, lightning swift, unexpected, devastating, and over before any help could arrive. Colonel John Allan, commanding the forces at Machias, wrote that the coastal residents actually feared the large British warships, such as Collier's *Rainbow*, less than the smaller ones. These little sloops and schooners, "vultures," Allan called them, went everywhere; no vessel or settlement was insignificant enough to be spared.[23]

Even if a timely warning permitted, Maine's primitive economy might prevent the militia from responding to an alarm. Colonel William Jones, whose Lincoln County militia saw action against Collier at Wiscasset, pointed out that the scarcity of food at home prevented many of his men from carrying their own supplies, and thus they had to be fed at the expense of others. Furthermore, the more frequently the militia responded to alarms, the less able was the countryside to support itself, for military activity usually occurred at a time when most men normally would be home planting, haying, or harvesting. Jones pointed out, for example, that during the summer of 1777 British cruisers, both large and small, had been uncommonly active and disruptive along the coast at

Townshend Harbor, Pemaquid, and Sheepscot. Responding to these real emergencies, noted Jones,

> added to the continual terror that obliges the people in the most expos'd parts to keep watch by night even when no enemy is to be seen, have greatly harris'd the Melitia of said regiment & if continued Much longer, threatens to reduce them to extremity that must cut of [off] the possibility of their serving their country, or providing Sustinance for themselves & their families.[24]

A spokesman at Boothbay tried to explain to the General Court the cyclical nature of the problem. The coastal towns were unable to resist the British raiders without military support from the inland communities. The interior towns, however, were so impoverished that they could not send their militias unless the coastal towns provisioned them, and the coastal towns were probably worse off than those of the interior. The situation was equally bad at Machias, where just prior to the British attack in 1777 Colonel Benjamin Foster declared the county was so destitute of food that, except for a few Minutemen, the militia could not leave their families to gather at Machias. Those few who came in tended to desert and had to be brought back by force.[25]

The militia system assumed a level of economic productivity that could provide the surplus necessary to maintain only semiproductive citizen-soldiers. Given an area like Maine, especially its easternmost county where the war was strangling a primitive economy, such a surplus did not exist. The militia became increasingly immobile and ineffective beyond its immediate home locality. The problem was not limited to Lincoln County, although it was most acute there. As early as 1775, James Sullivan foresaw exactly the same situation for the western counties. To the provincial council he argued that if the militia were called up and, if they should obey, the region had no means of supporting such a number of men. The scarcity of provisions was such that if the enemy ever gained a foothold in Falmouth they could control the entire area simply by manipulating the food supply.

> As provisions for our sustenance cannot be raised here, we must come to them [the British] for bread; and where there is no army, or command, the slaughter of a few persons will bring many to submission. This observation I take to be founded in human nature; and it is in vain for people to talk of dying rather than submitting,

for when we are famished, overpowered, or disarmed, we must submit, and are criminal in not doing it.[26]

Colonel William Jones expressed the sentiment of all three counties of Maine when he pleaded that the General Court "no longer be deaf to their Just complaints nor abandon this part of the State helpless unprotected orphan to the will of men that threaten ere-long to make it all their own, or leave it in ruins."[27]

The Massachusetts government finally acknowledged the problem to the extent of paying militiamen on continuous duty and providing a garrison for Machias. That town was not only a crucially important frontier post against the British in Nova Scotia but equally vital as a center of influence over the neighboring Indians. In September 1777 the General Court resolved to supply the town with cannon and a defensive force of 300 volunteers recruited from Lincoln County for three months' duty, after which winter weather would eliminate the need for a garrison.

Despite an enlistment bounty of three pounds, which was later doubled, and the promise of pay equal to Continental forces, recruiting went slowly. Inflation destroyed the financial incentive for military service. The Committee of Safety at Machias explained to the provincial council that "a Soldier gits but about one Bushell and a half of Corn for a months pay [and] this has grately discouraged the people on the whole Shoare from Entering into the Service." Under such circumstances, explained a recruiting officer, the inhabitants found it necessary "to tarry at home to take Care of their distressed Familys, the incouridgement given being so small, as not to be any ways equal to Supporting themselves, much less affording any Relief to their Familys." Those few who did enlist discovered the command was so destitute of supplies and clothing that their colonel, John Allan, occasionally had to equip them with provisions intended for the Indians.[28] The militia was of little help to the volunteer garrison defending Machias; militiamen resisted the call to active service when it involved garrison duty and constructing fortifications. Indeed, the militia insisted on their "right" to respond only to military emergencies. John Allan was therefore more dismayed than relieved when cannon and military stores finally arrived from Boston. "We have at present but very few men," he complained, "which gives me much Concern when I Consider the large Property Deposited here, for fear the Enemy should suddenly pop in and Distroy it."[29]

Boothbay experienced a similar situation. Like Machias, it had requested and received from the General Court several cannon and authorization to raise fifty men in state pay to serve as a garrison. Recruits simply could not be found, however, and the town fathers discovered that the military stores, far from being a deterrent to the enemy, had become "a proper bait, by which our enemies have been induced to pay a degree of attention to this place which it is probable might otherwise have been directed to posts of greater importance."[30] To save the cannon and themselves, the people of Boothbay conveyed the guns deep into the woods out of reach of the marauding enemy, where they would be of no use to anyone. Boothbay, too, sought the security of its own insignificance.

It was natural for the towns of Maine, small, isolated, and vulnerable, to express their insecurity in outbursts of anger and frustration aimed at the government of Massachusetts. The Reverend James Lyon in Machias accused the General Court of thinking that the eastern region was costing more than it was worth and that the best policy was "to neglect it utterly, & suffer it to sink." In Boothbay, Pastor John Murray bitterly observed that "However the Eastern Country may seem neglected by the General Court, it appears to be considered as of no small importance to the enemy of America[.] [H]ow little soever it is concerned in Governmental matters, its inhabitants suppose themselves entitled to the protection of Government in common with other parts of the State."[31]

No inhabitant of Maine seemed to regard the militia as an adequate defense. A modern historian, John Shy, emphasized recently that the militia's major value was not so much military as political. The very existence of an indigenous body of armed men served to bind the loyalty of the population to the patriot cause wherever the British army was not in physical occupation.[32] In Maine, for example, during the summer of 1775, the Lincoln County militia around Penobscot Bay terrorized Tories, seized vessels suspected of trading with the British at Boston, and burned old Fort Pownal at the mouth of the Penobscot River lest it fall into British hands.[33] In like manner, Samuel Thompson's militia at Falmouth forced Tories to flee and lured the British into massive retaliation, sharply polarizing a wavering population. Yet, valid as Shy's observation may be in retrospect, it is important to note that contemporaries viewed the militia as a military, not a political, instrument. From the standpoint of protecting Maine from the British, the militia inspired no confidence.

An effective naval force cruising the coast would have reduced the burden for protection on the militia by hindering the operations of the British naval forces from Nova Scotia. Enemy vessels not only raided coastal communities but captured local shipping as well. In the summer of 1776, for example, the British sloop *Viper* took five fishing vessels off Machias and two more near Gouldsborough.[34] Privately armed vessels from Nova Scotia and British cruisers, occasionally reinforced by larger vessels from the British navy, took a heavy toll of shipping off the Maine coast where they operated without opposition.

After repeated complaints and petitions from downeast communities requesting naval protection, Massachusetts in 1777 arranged to have two Continental frigates, *Boston* and *Hancock*, cruise the eastern coast accompanied by a fleet of armed state vessels. The operation was supposed to sweep the seas clear of British raiders, and, in fact, several enemy vessels were taken, but the enterprise ended in disaster. The state vessels soon disappeared in search of more profitable ventures of their own, and the two frigates ran into a British squadron. After brief resistance, the *Hancock* surrendered, and the *Boston* ignominiously fled to the safety of Wiscasset and then to Boston Harbor.[35] Although the General Court did recommend more vigorous use of the Massachusetts navy to patrol the eastern coast, no significant action was forthcoming; Maine's coastal communities and shipping remained at the mercy of the enemy.

III

Despite Maine's lack of military aggressiveness, during each of the first three years of the war, from 1775 to 1777, the region served as a base for campaigns that invaded British territory to the north. Significantly, the inspiration, leadership, and personnel for such enterprises came from those outside Maine — unconcerned with Maine's preoccupation with obscurity. The first and most famous was Benedict Arnold's ill-fated expedition against Quebec, designed to bring French Canada into the American coalition of rebellious states. Leading a thousand volunteers from the Continental Army besieging Boston, Arnold set out by sea on September 19, 1775, sailed along the Maine coast and into the Kennebec River. At Georgetown, some twenty recruits joined the expedition, and upstream at Gardinerstown the little army transferred into

200 bateaux, which had been rushed to completion in local shipyards. Heavy, awkward, hastily constructed of green wood and designed for use on the lower Kennebec, such craft were poorly suited for the rapids, falls, and portages the army encountered in its struggle across Maine's wilderness.[36] The army's route followed the Kennebec and then cut west and north, across ponds and lakes, through swamps and over hills, and finally to the Chaudière River, which brought them to the Saint Lawrence, 350 miles from the Maine coast. Six hundred and seventy-five men survived exhaustion, starvation, the terrors of a hurricane, and the temptation to desert; on November 8 they stood on the far side of the Saint Lawrence looking across at their objective. Another expedition from the west, led by General Richard Montgomery, reinforced Arnold's little army, and together they assaulted Fortress Quebec on the night of December 30.

A swirling snowstorm helped to obscure the two columns of desperate men who dashed toward the city gates. The British were prepared, however, having been warned by a deserter. Almost at once the attackers lost both commanders: Montgomery was killed outright, and Arnold had to be carried from the field with a serious leg wound. Dispirited and confused, the troops could not retain their momentum. They faltered, milled about, and then the survivors either retreated or surrendered. A hundred of their number lay dead on the barricades; 400 more were taken prisoner. Arnold, convalescing from his wound, resumed the siege, and Congress reinforced him with several thousand more men. It was a futile exercise, however. The French Canadians did not flock to the standard of Liberty; they remained safely noncommitted. In the spring of 1776, British reinforcements sailed up the ice-free Saint Lawrence and drove the demoralized invaders westward up the river, eventually all the way back to Fort Ticonderoga in New York.[37] Overall, Arnold's expedition made little impact on Maine, which merely represented territory to be crossed en route to the objective. Quebec was not a major concern for Maine, and few of its residents participated in the campaign. Arnold's march is remembered today chiefly as an example of inspired leadership and heroic endurance, all the more poignant in the awareness of its futility.

Events in Nova Scotia proved to be a more serious threat to Maine's protective insignificance. The town of Machias in eastern Maine became a haven for Nova Scotians who had fled their homes because of sympathy for the American cause. From their sanctuary in Maine, these refugees tried to liberate Nova Scotia from British "tyranny" by arousing rebellion within the province while invading it from without. Jonathan Eddy and John Allan were two such individuals. Both were landowners, representatives to the provincial assembly, and men of standing in Nova Scotia's Cumberland County. Allan, in addition, was a justice of the peace, sheriff, clerk of the sessions and the supreme courts. Eddy, like many other Nova Scotians, was a New Englander from Massachusetts. Allan had emigrated from Scotland to Nova Scotia as a child but had been educated in New England. Both men demonstrated a powerful ideological commitment to the American cause, yet in Nova Scotia neither was able to convert his personal convictions into effective political action.[38] Sympathy for the American cause did exist in Halifax and in the western counties of Sunbury and Cumberland, but the dissidents were geographically isolated and politically fragmented by royal governors who kept a tight rein over the assembly and local government. In Nova Scotia these institutions never became forums for rallying dissidents as in the rebellious provinces to the south.[39]

Failing in their efforts within Nova Scotia, Eddy and Allan sought direct help from the provinces already in rebellion. Early in 1776, Eddy met with General George Washington at Cambridge and then with the Continental Congress in Philadelphia. His proposal for a seaborne invasion of Nova Scotia, coming so soon after the failure of the expedition against Quebec, met a cool reception in both places. In fact, Washington had already rejected a similar scheme submitted by radical Whigs in Machias, on the grounds that it required control of the sea, which Americans lacked, and that since Nova Scotia possessed little value and posed no threat, "to attack *them* therefore is a Measure of Conquest rather than Defence." Eddy had somewhat better luck when he presented his case to the state of Massachusetts. The General Court approved an expedition against Fort Cumberland at the head of the Bay of Fundy but refused to do more than to promise some provisions and military supplies.[40] At the most, Massachusetts legitimized Eddy's own efforts to raise a military force; the state did not commit itself to provide troops or reinforcements or to undertake a military operation of any kind.

Back in Machias, Eddy began to recruit for the expedition during the early autumn of 1776. The town's leading radicals heartily endorsed the plan, especially their spokesman, the Reverend James Lyon, who had served a parish in Nova Scotia at Onslow before coming to Machias.[41] The local population, however, did not share their pastor's enthusiasm for military ventures, and only twenty-eight enlisted. Undaunted, Eddy set sail for his objective on August 13, stopping frequently along the way to recruit troops from among American sympathizers in western Nova Scotia. Scattered groups joined from around Passamaquoddy Bay and along the Saint John River; sixteen Indians also agreed to accompany the expedition. With a grand total of seventy-two men in open whaleboats and canoes, the expedition set off late in October on the final leg of its journey to seize Fort Cumberland and to raise the standard of revolution in Nova Scotia. Eddy undoubtedly expected his invasion to precipitate a general uprising which, in turn, would convince Massachusetts to assist the enterprise with arms and men. His expectations were doomed from the start.

Too small and too poorly conceived to win much support either in Maine or in Nova Scotia, Eddy's invasion confronted those it sought to liberate with a bitter dilemma. Either they threw in their lot with this motley group of Nova Scotian expatriates and Indians and ran the risk of unsuccessful revolution, or they remained loyal to the crown at the hazard of being plundered by the intruders. In the end, most inhabitants chose the unheroic but pragmatic path of neutrality. Few responded to Eddy's demands for support, but Colonel Joseph Gorham, defending Fort Cumberland, pointedly observed that the residents were equally reluctant to aid him.[42]

Nonetheless, Fort Cumberland remained safely in British hands. The invaders did succeed in capturing an outpost and its twelve-man garrison, which induced some Acadian Frenchmen to join the expedition. They also seized a British sloop aground on the tidal flats below the fort loaded with provisions worth 5,000 pounds sterling. This was the last rebel success. Although Eddy's force had increased to 180 men, a hundred of them were needed to guard prisoners and man outposts. Consequently, Eddy had about eighty men available when he ceremoniously demanded that Colonel Gorham surrender the fort. The British commander accurately assessed his opposition and suggested instead that Eddy surrender to him. Eddy soon discovered that his little army was inadequate to capture the fort either by persuasion or by force. On the night of November 12, a rebel assault against the fort failed, with the loss of one Indian wounded; so did a plan to set fire to some of the fort's buildings and then to attack through the confusion and the smoke. The siege ended abruptly when British reinforcements from Halifax surprised Eddy's army of liberation with a dawn attack on November 31. Eddy led the survivors to Maugerville, a settlement on the Saint John, where he renewed his futile appeals to Massachusetts for men and money with which to resume the campaign.[43]

British retribution added to the number of Nova Scotian refugees at Machias who continually schemed to return home with a victorious army. There was no end to the cyclical pattern; Massachusetts refused to support a movement that could not sustain itself in an area that had little practical value. The revolutionary movement in Nova Scotia, however, could go nowhere without the promise of large-scale outside assistance. While these conditions prevailed, neither the rebels in Massachusetts nor the dissidents in Nova Scotia were willing to take the necessary risks demanded by the other.

John Allan's experience reconfirmed this stalemate when he tried to launch his own invasion of Nova Scotia in 1777. The Continental Congress gave Allan a far more sympathetic hearing than it had given to Jonathan Eddy the year before. At Allan's urging, Congress authorized Massachusetts to raise an expedition of 3,000 men, at Continental expense, to seize Fort Cumberland and then proceed to Halifax to destroy the Royal Navy's dockyard facilities there. In addition, Congress appointed John Allan to the position of Continental superintendent for the eastern Indians with the rank of colonel in the Continental Army. This virtually unknown Nova Scotian refugee was to serve as official representative of the United States to the Passamaquoddy and Saint John, or Malecite, Indians, to bring them into the American orbit and to counter British influence among them (Congress considered the Penobscots, located safely inside Maine, as wards of Massachusetts). Although a newcomer to the American scene, John Allan had achieved a stunning success — political and personal — in his negotiations with Congress.[44]

The grand plan approved by Congress got a decidedly lukewarm response from the Massachusetts government. At most, the General Court agreed to bestow a commission as colonel on John Allan with authority to raise a single regiment from eastern Maine to occupy the Saint John River valley. Even so, this scaled-down enterprise would still extend American hegemony over the Indians, deprive the British of the use of the river as a means of communication with Quebec, and rally discontented Nova Scotians who, in that area, had been highly vocal in their sympathy for the Revolution.[45] Destruction of the dockyards at Halifax would have to wait.

Downeast there was even less enthusiasm for the scheme than in the state government. Not even John Allan's boundless energy and the promise of Continental pay could overcome the reluctance of the young men in Lincoln and Cumberland counties to enlist. Recruitment was nowhere complete when Allan received word that the British were planning a similar campaign to consolidate their control over the Saint John region. Indeed, a British sloop had already reconnoitered the river, and its mere presence was sufficient to induce the settlers there unanimously to reaffirm their loyalty to the crown. In a desperate effort to forestall British occupation, Allan set out for the Saint John at the end of May. In much the same manner as Eddy before him, Allan led an advance party of some forty men, including Indians, in whaleboats and canoes.[46] The main force would come later, but until then it was vital to delay the British expedition. Allan was not misled by the inhabitants' warm welcome and protestations of support for the American cause. He informed the General Court that, "For fear of a second Eddy's Affair," he planned to act on the defensive and avoid alienating the local people by forcing them to take sides.[47] A realist, Allan knew that popular allegiance tended to follow rather than precede a test of strength.

In that test of strength the British once again proved to be the stronger. Although Allan received an additional forty men from Machias, his main force never arrived. The Americans were unable to do more than delay the British landing when the expedition appeared on June 23. Superior in number, the British troops put the Americans to flight up the river into the interior. The remnants of Allan's force managed to return to Machias only in early August, after a long, arduous retreat overland along waterways and portages known only to their Indian guides.[48] The white population of the Saint John now remained passively under British control for the remainder of the war. The British consolidated their presence by constructing a military post, Fort Howe, near the mouth of the river from which they hoped to influence the inhabitants, both Indian and white.

The Indians, however, were not so easily controlled. Possibly to insure their survival as a people regardless of which side won, they divided.

One group of Malecites under Pierre Tomma accepted British hegemony. Despite British military superiority, another large group of Malecites decided to leave their traditional habitations and to place themselves under American protection. Jammed into twenty-seven canoes and led by Chief Ambrose Saint Aubin, the Malecites escorted the defeated Americans all the way to Machias where the Indians clearly intended to resettle. Such a display of support for the American cause, especially at this moment, surprised even John Allan. "It is incredible," he wrote, "what difficulties the Indians undergo in this troublesome time, where so many families are obliged to fly with precipitation rather than become friends to the Tyrant of Britain, some backing their aged parents, others their maimed and decrepid brethren, the old women leading the young children, mothers carrying infants, together with great loads of baggage."[49] Certainly, the Indians feared no retribution from the British, who were as eager as the Americans to purchase their friendship. But to the Indians, the Americans in defeat must have appeared more pliable and more congenial neighbors than the victorious British, whom the Indians had regarded as their traditional enemies for a century and a half.

To British authorities in Nova Scotia, Machias had now become a serious threat to their security. No longer was it an obscure lumber village at the end of civilization. It had now become the rendezvous for political refugees from Nova Scotia, who issued repeated calls for revolution in their home province and twice had tried to invade it. Moreover, one of those refugees, John Allan, appeared to have had disconcerting success in securing the friendship of the Indians. Rumors of yet another attack from Machias prompted the British to launch a counterattack during the summer of 1777.

Machias received warning in time to prepare. Under the direction of Colonel Jonathan Eddy, the defenders stretched a log boom across the Machias River and protected it with a small battery. Farther upstream, they erected several redoubts overlooking the river equipped with cannon from privateers in the harbor. Unwittingly, the Americans benefited from irreconcilable personal differences dividing the British command. Commodore Sir George Collier ordered his fleet to sail for Machias leaving his bitter enemy, Major General Eyre Massey, and the army behind in Nova Scotia.[50] Collier arrived at the mouth of the Machias River on August 13 with three large men-of-war accompanied by a brig and a sloop. Using his marines as infantry, Collier ordered them into the brig and the sloop, which small boats then towed up the Machias River. Under cover of a dense fog, the marines landed, silenced the battery, cut the boom, and burned several buildings. The little flotilla then proceeded upriver toward Machias itself, but although it got within striking distance, the expected onslaught never came. "To the Great surprise and Astonishment of every one[,] in Less than half an Hour after Coming to an Anchor, The Brig & Sloop Both Gote underway without firing a Gun toward the Houses & with greatest precipitation possible having Eleven Boats towing, made down the River against the Tide of flood [sic]."[51]

The only explanation of why the British broke off their attack comes from John Allan, who wrote that the British, confident of success after overcoming initial resistance downriver, were surprised by the fortifications at Machias and feared they were being drawn into a trap.[52] Equally unexpected must have been the presence of Indians who suddenly joined the defenders. John Allan had invited a large number of Penobscot, Passamaquoddy, and Malecite Indians to a conference at Machias to explain away his humiliating defeat on the Saint John. The British attack interrupted the meeting, and not only did the Indians witness the British withdrawal, but some forty to fifty even participated in the action, firing from the shore upon the boat crews desperately trying to move their vessels downstream against the incoming tide.[53] The Indians' "hideous yells" contributed to the British confusion and panic as they tried to run the gauntlet of an aroused countryside. Twice the brig ran aground, a helpless target for every gun the militia and their newfound Indian allies could fire. The defenders even trundled a light cannon through the woods, although its caliber was too small to disable the British vessels. A heavy rain quite literally dampened the pursuit while a land breeze hastened the retreat, so that the British managed to extricate themselves from the hornets' nest they had stirred up.

Accounts of the battle and of the casualties differ wildly. Sir George Collier, in his official report of the action, claimed a significant victory, which forestalled yet another rebel invasion of Nova Scotia at the cost of only three British dead.[54] American estimates of British casualties vary from forty to a hundred, with only one American killed and one wounded. "I suppose," exulted John Allan, "not an action during the War Except Bunker Hill there was such a slaughter."[55]

John Allan's journal for Sunday, August 17, 1777, reflects the sense of euphoria that overspread Machias as the British sailed away from the scene of their humiliation. "All is quiet, and peace seems to have regained her dominion on this late invaded land, and fear left every timerous soul, the soldiers rejoicing in their success, recounting the perils they had escaped, and how the fugitive enemy fled before them, the savages exulting in the share they had in this glorious repulse."[56]

IV

The role of the Indians in the American retreat from the Saint John and in the defense of Machias makes it appear that they were becoming firmly attached to the American cause. Such was not the case, for the Indians, like many of the white settlers in the region, tended to follow the dictates of self-interest, and self-interest required that they be firmly attached to neither side. As individuals, Indians were free to do as they pleased, and some did serve in the American army. As organized tribes, however, the Indians tried to stay aloof from formal connections with either the British or the Americans and to play off one against the other as they bid for Indian friendship. The Micmacs in Nova Scotia and the Penobscots in Maine had the fewest options owing to their geographic locations, but they did not tamely submit. Both tribes resisted efforts by the belligerents to enlist their young men. To John Allan, the Micmac leaders declared, "we want not to molest any but be in Friendship with all." To Allan's question as to which side the Micmacs would support, the Indians replied, "When we see a sufficient Power in this Country we will tell you what we will do. . . . we know we must submit to the strongest Power."[57] The Micmacs eventually yielded to British hegemony, but not before they exerted their independence by sending representatives to offer the Massachusetts provincial council a force of 500 warriors in exchange for provisions, arms, ammunition, and the services of a Catholic priest — a proposal that must have been largely ceremonial in nature.[58]

The Penobscots made no comparable gestures to the British, yet the possibility that they might do so enabled them to extract concessions from the Massachusetts Provincial Congress. The Penobscots for years had been complaining to an unresponsive General Court about the lack of definite boundaries for their lands, beyond which white settlement should not go. The war brought new grievances in that hostilities disrupted the flow of goods to the mouth of the Penobscot River where the Penobscots had formerly traded. The Massachusetts government moved quickly to respond to these complaints. Samuel Freeman, secretary to the Provincial Congress, reflected its prevailing view when he wrote to his father in Falmouth, "I can't help thinking but that they [Indians] should be well treated, justice done them respecting their land, etc., by which they now and forever [can] be secured to the interest of the country."[59] When Chief Orono and his associates traveled to Watertown to negotiate with the Provincial Congress, they received a warm welcome. Congress dispatched a carriage in which to convey the Penobscot dignitaries in style over the last part of their journey. Congress also passed a skillfully worded resolve prohibiting white intrusion into the tract claimed by the Penobscots. The resolve merely excluded settlement from the area that the Indians claimed, without passing judgment on the validity of that claim. To the Penobscots, however, the resolve was a recognition of their exclusive right to the land in question, a difference of interpretation that would be important at the end of the war. Congress also reassured the Penobscots that it would reopen a truck house, or trading post, in their region and in the meantime authorized provisions to be distributed at once.[60] The Penobscots expressed their support for the American cause but deftly turned aside Congress's suggestion that a company of Penobscot warriors join the American army. Instead, the Indians volunteered their services in "cruising the woods" and guarding the approaches from the north.[61]

As valuable as was the friendship of the Penobscots, yet more so was the good will of the Malecites and Passamaquoddies who straddled the ill-defined boundary between Maine and Nova Scotia. Their support was the prize in a bitter diplomatic duel between two Nova Scotians, refugee John Allan, the Continental superintendent for the eastern Indians, and his British counterpart, Michael Francklin, wealthy merchant and former lieutenant governor of Nova Scotia.[62] Both men had the benefit of long experience with the eastern Indians, but Francklin had the initial advantage of relying on a preexisting government that was financially solvent and could provide him with quantities of relatively inexpensive British manufactured goods for trade. When all else failed, Francklin could fall back upon his own considerable fortune to pay for the goods and services his diplomacy required. For a short while,

Francklin possessed the ultimate weapon in winning Indian support, an Acadian French Catholic priest to hear confessions and to offer the sacraments.

In 1778, when Michael Francklin called the Indians to attend a great conference at Fort Howe, promising presents, provisions, and even a priest, the Indians could not resist. John Allan watched in helpless frustration as Malecites, Passamaquoddies, and even some Penobscots joined the Micmacs in recognizing British suzerainty. The Indians took an oath never to engage in activities injurious to the British king, to divulge all schemes they might hear that were hostile to his interests, and finally, never to return to the vicinity of Machias, the source of American influence. To symbolize their separation from the Americans, the Indians surrendered their American presents and even treasured letters and medals from General George Washington.[63] It was a stinging diplomatic defeat for John Allan; yet it is significant that Francklin was unable to arouse the Indians to hostile action against the Americans. Despite the strong British military presence at Fort Howe and all the gifts and ceremony, both secular and religious, Francklin could obtain from the Indians only a promise to refrain from engaging in hostilities against the British—something they had no intention of doing in the first place. It is no wonder that the governor of Nova Scotia sought the aid of Canadian Indians in a futile effort to arouse those in Nova Scotia to more warlike activity.[64]

Before long the pledges given at the Fort Howe conference grew dim, and the Indians returned to Machias and to John Allan once more. In competing for their elusive loyalty, Allan had certain advantages of his own, the foremost of which was his unique personality. He was totally and honestly committed to the American cause, yet he dealt with the Indians not merely as pawns in a power struggle but as people with whom he had a deep sympathy and understanding. Not for politics alone did Allan devote himself to protecting Indians from unscrupulous traders and fraudulent land deals. The Indians showed their affection for Allan by attending him personally in such numbers as to hamper his official and even his domestic life.[65]

The American-French treaty of 1778 provided Allan with another formidable advantage over his British rival. The eastern Indians were still highly sensitive to French influence, and the treaty was a powerful argument to attract those who remained uncommitted. When Allan learned of the treaty, he dispatched several Indians to spread the news among the tribes. Beginning in 1778, groups of Indians, even from the generally pro-British Micmacs, traveled to Boston and to Rhode Island to view firsthand the forces of France assisting the American cause. From the French fleet, Allan obtained French-speaking Catholic priests to minister to the Indians, thereby ending the British monopoly in that sphere.[66] Even British authorities acknowledged the importance of the French treaty in strengthening the Indians' attachment to the rebel cause. Pierre Tomma, chief of the pro-British Malecite band, clearly swayed by the French alliance, left the British-controlled Saint John region to place himself and his people under Allan's protection at Machias. To Allan, Chief Tomma declared, "I am now come & left all I have, and depend on you for our Subsistence for something to Eat, & to keep our backs Warm. . . . I am now Come to obey you in any thing for the Good of America & the [king] of France you may order."[67]

Despite the importance of treaties, religion, and personalities, the truck house, or trading post, was the chief tool by which Americans and British competed for Indian friendship. All the Indians were dependent on trade for guns and ammunition, as well as items such as clothing, knives, cooking utensils, and even food. Massachusetts maintained a truck house on the Saint John River until the British destroyed it in 1777, another on the Penobscot, and the most important one of all, at Machias. Here the Malecites from the Saint John and the Passamaquoddy, some of the Micmacs, and eventually even the Penobscots came to trade and some to settle under John Allan's paternalistic care.

To supply the needs of so many Indians during wartime was a difficult task at best; at times it was impossible. In 1777, for example, a list of goods needed at Machias included 200 bushels of corn, 60 bushels of salt, 200 gallons of rum, the same amount of molasses, 6 barrels of pork, 200 pounds of hog fat, 1,000 pounds of bread, 100 pounds of gunpowder, 400 pounds of musket balls, as well as various kinds of cloth, ribbon, hats, hatchets, knives, beads, and medals.[68] The Continental Congress reimbursed Massachusetts the cost of provisioning the "foreign" Indians, but a wartime economy and enemy control of the sea meant that many items cost 1,500 to 1,800 percent above their sterling price, a situation "Such as must make every honest Inclined person to Shudder who has the management of Public business."[69] When the supply failed, Allan was at his wits' end to find what the Indians required. In one emergency, he commandeered the goods of a private merchant, to whom the General Court eventually had to pay 3,000 pounds in damages and court costs. At other times, to assist the Indians Allan borrowed from the provisions meant for the troops defending Machias.[70] That Massachusetts even tried to satisfy Allan's insatiable demands indicates how important the state government considered his activity.

Allan regarded trade with the Indians as a vital means of diplomatic influence. To be effective, the Indian trade had to be a government monopoly conducted through government truck houses. Only in this manner could Allan insure fair treatment for the native population, who were continuously exploited by private traders. In addition, Allan hoped that the sale in Europe of furs and skins, which the Indians exchanged for provisions, would offset much of the cost of running the truck house.[71] Private traders therefore not only jeopardized good relations with the Indians but also deprived the government of a valuable source of income. On paper it all made good sense; in practice Allan found it impossible to enforce. Despite laws prohibiting private trade with the Indians, and despite Allan's public appeals explaining the reasons for the restrictions, illegal trade persisted.

One of the most notable offenders was Justice of the Peace Stephen Jones, nephew and former agent of Machias's leading citizen, Ichabod. Allan accused Jones of trading bad rum to the Indians for stolen goods. Although Allan instituted legal proceedings against Jones, he had less satisfaction than the Indians who obtained more and better rum by ransacking Jones's store. Jones's prestige and knowledge of legal intricacies enabled him to escape Allan's charges unscathed.[72] Private traders, grumbled Allan, had little to fear from the law. The Indians could be equally difficult to deal with. They had a fatal attraction to rum, for which they traded even their food rations from the truck house, secure in the knowledge that they could obtain more merely on the threat of going over to the British.[73]

Courted by both sides, the eastern Indians could hardly escape a growing awareness of their own self-importance. While the war lasted, they made the most of their unique role as wavering neutrals. John Allan and Michael Francklin both vainly sought exclusive control over the Indians. They both failed, but nevertheless, in this diplomatic warfare, everyone emerged a winner: The Indians managed to avoid a formal commitment to either side and benefited from presents and provisions from both. Indian neutrality, furthermore, spared British and Americans alike from the horrors and expense of frontier warfare for which they both were unprepared. For the Americans in particular, the mere presence of Indians who settled around Machias was a far more effective deterrent to British attack than the militia that was so doubtful a means of local defense.

V

Formal military activity of any kind attracted few of Maine's inhabitants. Indians and whites alike much preferred a profitable neutrality or military insignificance to the discipline, dangers, and uncertainties of combat. On the other hand, the opportunity to plunder a defenseless enemy in an informal kind of warfare called privateering proved almost irresistible. Those engaged in privateering could combine patriotism with quick profit by capitalizing on their maritime skills. A privateer was a privately owned, armed vessel authorized by the government to cruise against the enemy. The object of the cruise was not to engage in hostilities with other armed vessels — there was no profit in that — but rather to capture enemy merchantmen and send them into a friendly port under prize crews. After a maritime court had declared the seizure legal, the captured vessel and its cargo could be sold to benefit the privateer's owners and crew. Officers and crew of the captured vessel might be ransomed or exchanged for prisoners held by the enemy.

There were risks, but the lure of quick profit attracted New Englanders in such swarms that they interfered with each other's activities in the waters off Nova Scotia and in the Gulf of Saint Lawrence. By the end of 1776, they had seized almost 350 British vessels and sacked numerous towns along the Nova Scotian coast.[74] In an effort to regulate the rapacious activities of its privateers, Massachusetts required owners to post bonds to answer for any complaints and forbade privateers to plunder above the high water mark. As a final resort, the Massachusetts government even permitted residents of Nova Scotia to sue in the courts of Massachusetts to recover property or damages from privateersmen who had acted illegally.[75]

Among Maine privateersmen several achieved distinction. Jeremiah O'Brien of Machias was perhaps the most active. He first won fame for his part in seizing the *Margaretta* in June 1775 and then several other British vessels. The prizes became a small squadron under O'Brien's command to protect Machias from the enemy. They were not, strictly speaking, privateers but rather the nucleus of a state navy, commissioned and financed by the Massachusetts government. After the state discharged the fleet in October 1776, O'Brien set out on his own and commanded successively the schooner *Resolution*, ten swivels; the ship *Hannibal*, twenty-four guns; and the privateer schooner *Tiger*. While commanding the *Hannibal*, O'Brien pursued a British merchant fleet into the waters off New York where his own vessel was captured by the British. O'Brien endured six months aboard the notorious prison ship *Jersey* before being transferred to Mill Prison in England. From here he engineered a daring escape and managed to reach France and then return to Maine where he resumed his privateering career. John O'Brien, Jeremiah's brother, was equally vigorous as a privateersman, commanding the brigantine *Adventure*, six guns; the ten-gun schooner *Hibernia*; the cutter *Salamander*; and the twelve-gun ship *Cyrus*.[76]

One of Maine's most successful and colorful privateersmen, in both name and deed, was Agreen Crabtree. He left Attleborough, Massachusetts, where he had been a housewright and settled in the town of Sullivan on Frenchman's Bay in Maine as a mariner and fisherman.[77] When the war broke out, Crabtree, like many other New Englanders, converted his schooner, the *Molly and Hannah*, into a privateer. After an initial cruise on which he took several prizes, Crabtree legalized his activities by obtaining a commission and then descended upon the unprotected Nova Scotian port of Liverpool. Although the town sympathized with the American Revolution, its Whiggish attitudes did not save it; Crabtree netted five vessels in this one swoop. He first seized a well-armed ship of 500 tons, trained its guns upon a brig loaded for England, and took the brig as well. Crabtree then stripped the ship and loaded all valuables aboard the brig, which set out for home with a prize crew aboard. Before following in the *Molly and Hannah*, Crabtree picked up three smaller vessels, two schooners and a sloop. The newspaper account of this affair reported that two of the prizes had reached port safely, but the valuable brig was overdue and might have been retaken by the British navy.[78]

Unlike some privateers who differed only slightly from pirates, Crabtree seemed to mix patriotism with his plundering. In 1777 he brought his vessel to the defense of Machias against the British attack led by

Collier, and later he delighted John Allan by sacking the British truck house near the mouth of the Saint John River. Since it was located well above high water mark, Allan had some qualms about the legality of Crabtree's action but none whatsoever about its efficacy. "I cannot say how far this was Legal for a Privetier," he wrote, "But I am Extreemly Glad it was Done, and am sure Crabtree would not have Done it, if he tho't it not for the Best." Occasionally, Crabtree assisted in disrupting illegal trade with the enemy. One of his captures was none other than Nathan Jones, brother of Ichabod, who, without a permit, was bound for Passamaquoddy in western Nova Scotia.[79] Later Crabtree assisted the inhabitants of Frenchman's Bay, saving them from a marauding American privateersman who had discovered that his own helpless countrymen could be as tempting a target as helpless enemies.[80]

In contrast to privateersmen like O'Brien and Crabtree with heavy investments in relatively large vessels, big crews, and expensive armaments, there were many more humble operations. In 1776 some would-be privateersmen from Falmouth sailed out against British shipping in a small sloop armed with a single cannon and one swivel gun—and were themselves immediately captured. Another group from Falmouth had better luck. Although they could obtain only four cannon for a vessel equipped for twenty, and for lack of boarding pikes had to fix scythe blades to poles, they nonetheless quickly captured a rich prize of eighteen guns.[81] More humble yet were the efforts of thirteen men in an open boat who sailed from Falmouth and sent back three prizes in two days.[82]

These desperate "economy" ventures in privateering could be the most rapacious of all. John Allan was unremitting in his denunciations of these "small Privatiers" and called attention to their "horred Crimes" and "Voricious Dispositions." He warned they were as dangerous to the subjects of the United States as to the British. They "Defy all Authority," and frequently their so-called commissions—if they had any at all—were nothing but old documents they themselves had altered or, even worse, simply letters of recommendation. Allan cited the example of one group that had just returned in two whaleboats from a "privateering" cruise into Minas Basin where they indiscriminately plundered the population and seized a vessel. The commander's commission, grumbled Allan, writing in August 1778, had been issued in 1775 prior to the Declaration of Independence. The officer had scratched out the word "Colonies" and written in "States," altered the signatures, and simply ignored the fact that the commission had been issued for a schooner rather than for a mere whaleboat. Nonetheless, the privateersman was brazen enough to assert the commission had come to him in this fashion from the government.[83] Whaleboat privateering was probably the most nasty aspect of a dirty business. It was a "nickels and dimes" sort of warfare in which the common people with the least to spare suffered the most. The boats tied up each night in a convenient creek or inlet and moved by stealth in the day, looting those too weak to defend themselves and avoiding those who could.[84] At the same time, however, there was a crude sort of democracy about privateering whereby, in contrast to service in the army or the navy, virtually anyone who could obtain arms and a vessel of any kind could engage in a patriotic plundering of the enemy.

For defense, the Nova Scotians relied on their own militia and the British navy. The Nova Scotian militia, however, was no more effective than that in Maine, and, during the first years of the war especially, the Royal Navy, its resources stretched thin, could offer little protection. When the war began, the British navy in American waters consisted of only thirty armed vessels, and many of these were required to serve the army and to do convoy duty.[85] The defense of Nova Scotia by sea initially rested with several small armed sloops, *Viper, Gage,* and *Howe.* These few lightly armed vessels could not stem the onslaught of privateers out of New England, but they did reduce somewhat the effects of privateering by sometimes recapturing prizes taken by American cruisers and by carrying the war to the American coast, frequently aided by Nova Scotian privateers.

Nonetheless, in the early years of the war, Nova Scotia suffered from American privateering quite as much as did Maine from raids by the British. Only Halifax escaped direct attack, and even here American privateers lay in wait just outside the harbor. Almost at will they sailed up the Bay of Fundy, into Minas Basin and Cobequid Bay, around Cape Breton, Saint John Island, and Newfoundland; no place was safe from their destructive attention.

The plight of Liverpool is illustrative. After Crabtree's ruinous raid, the town acquired two cannon and a garrison of fifteen as protection. Nevertheless, American privateersmen cut out a schooner in broad daylight in October 1776. In the following spring, they stole even the cannon, although British authorities later recovered them. During the fall, privateers took another schooner, and in 1778 they raided the local store. Later, still another group systematically sacked the entire town and then seized a vessel in which to carry home their plunder.[86] At this rate, New Englanders did not need to invade Nova Scotia; it was more valuable as enemy territory to be looted.

The raids so disrupted the Nova Scotian economy that prices for food skyrocketed as privateers established a virtual blockade of the province. Nova Scotia became ever more dependent on Britain for food and for whatever protection it did receive, for by itself it was prostrate. The Nova Scotian legislature acknowledged that fact by retiring the guard ship in the Bay of Fundy as a useless expense. The General Court of Massachusetts also recognized the plight of its "enemy" neighbor by permitting some Nova Scotians, friendly to the American cause, to trade with Massachusetts. Such politically inspired generosity, however, could not help many.[87]

So desperate were conditions that eighty-two inhabitants in the town of Yarmouth petitioned their governor at the end of 1775 that they be allowed "to be Neuter" in the war. The petitioners assured the governor that they had no desire to aid the American cause. "It is self-preservation, and that only which drives us at this time to make our Request." They pointed out that many of them had come from New England originally, had family there, and were torn between "natural affection to our nearest relations and good Faith and Friendship to our King and Country." Furthermore, they were in no condition to defend themselves, being "Few in number, and those few Scattered up and down the Woods. Arms we are but poorly Accoutred with, Ammunition we have none."[88]

Yarmouth's pleas went unanswered, and Nova Scotia continued to be plundered almost at will by Yankees, many from Maine, whose rapacious ferocity as privateersmen contrasted sharply with their incapacity to protect their own communities from similar attack by the enemy. Like Nova Scotia, Massachusetts never did devise an effective defense for its coastal frontier. Before the war was over, communities in Maine would echo the plea from Yarmouth "to be Neuter" in a war where insignificance, far from being a source of protection, became an invitation to attack. Bad as things were for Maine, they would get worse. On June 17, 1779, a British expeditionary force appeared at the mouth of the Penobscot River. From this point on, the nature of the war downeast underwent a dramatic transformation.

FOUR

Crisis on the Penobscot

The British force that sailed into Penobscot Bay in mid-June 1779 was no mere raiding party. A frigate, an armed brig, and three sloops-of-war convoyed several transports carrying 700 British troops from the Seventy-fourth and Eighty-second regiments.[1] Their commander, Brigadier General Francis McLean, had orders to establish a permanent base on the east side of Penobscot Bay. The place he selected is now the town of Castine but was then called Majabigwaduce, or Bagaduce for short. On rising ground at the center of the Bagaduce Peninsula, the British began the construction of Fort George. The British occupation had momentous ramifications for Massachusetts and its easternmost counties. Massachusetts mounted a major expedition to dislodge the enemy but suffered a disaster so complete as to leave the state bankrupt, virtually defenseless, and more divided than ever. The British at Bagaduce, having defied the best efforts of the rebels, became a rallying point for loyalists from Maine and Massachusetts who hitherto had no alternative but passivity or flight. Stimulated by the British presence, many chose to stay and fight, and in doing so they transformed the Revolution in Maine into a bitter civil war. British operations in Maine closely resembled those in the South where, beginning in late 1779, the British initiated a strategy of invasion and occupation.

I

The British decision to establish a military base on Penobscot Bay evolved from a complex series of personal, political, and strategic considerations spanning the Atlantic. Long before the Revolution, settlers on lands east of Penobscot Bay had been trying without success to obtain royal confirmation for their grants from a government fearful of losing valuable sources of naval timber.[2] With the coming of the Revolution, some of these landowners schemed for a British occupation as a means of securing title confirmation. Not all of them were actual settlers; some were wealthy speculators, such as Dr. John Calef and John Nutting, who were active participants in negotiations with British officials. Calef and Nutting were both residents of the Boston area but held substantial investments in land around Penobscot Bay. Calef had already served as an agent for downeast propertyholders before the Revolution, traveling all the way to England to lobby unsuccessfully for royal approval of land titles. He took up residence at Bagaduce just before the outbreak of fighting and from there transmitted to influential acquaintances in England proposals for establishing in Maine a separate loyalist government centered on Penobscot Bay.[3] Calef's suggestions reached the office of the secretary of state for colonial affairs where they found unexpected support from a similar scheme submitted independently by a Boston building contractor, John Nutting.

As a builder, Nutting had acquired extensive tracts of timberland along the Penobscot for use in his business. When the British occupied Boston, they hired him to supervise the construction of fortifications and barracks. Like many other Boston loyalists, Nutting accompanied the army when, in March of 1776, it evacuated Boston and moved to Halifax. There he resumed his former occupation but somehow managed to obtain the appointment as messenger to carry to England the official account of Collier's "victory" at Machias. In England Nutting made the most of his opportunity by ingratiating himself with William Knox, the secretary to Lord George Germain, newly appointed secretary of state for colonial affairs. Knox, himself a loyalist refugee from Georgia, was highly receptive to plans for uniting American loyalists in the British cause. During the summer of 1778, Knox and Nutting roughed out a draft proposal for a loyalist province in Maine, which they appropriately named New Ireland, located as it was between New England and Nova Scotia, or New Scotland.[4]

Knox's superior, Lord George Germain, approved of the suggestion for several reasons. Most immediately, he was aware of the impoverished condition of many loyalists and the financial drain their support placed on the British treasury. A permanent settlement such as New

Ireland would provide loyalist refugees with an independent means of subsistence. In the process, the new settlers could readily produce masts, for which the British navy was desperate. Furthermore, a loyalist settlement at Penobscot would help protect Nova Scotia from New England privateers while providing the British with a convenient base from which to harass the New England coast. Finally, in 1778, with France in the war and Spain threatening to follow, the possibility existed that the war might soon cease on the principle of *uti possidetis*, the mutual possession of territory presently occupied. If so, control of Penobscot Bay would provide Britain with a powerful claim to all the territory between the Penobscot and Nova Scotia, if not all of Maine.[5]

Even if the war did not end so diplomatically, the Penobscot scheme would merge nicely into a broad strategic plan by which Britain hoped finally to end the Revolution on its own terms. Starting in December 1778 with the occupation of Savannah, British military efforts concentrated on regaining control of the southern states with the aid of previously untapped loyalist support assumed to exist there. Step by step the British would move from Georgia to the Chesapeake, aiding and aided by loyalists who would no longer be mere refugees but would be agents in their own political restoration and that of the British Empire. Deprived of income from southern exports of tobacco, indigo, and rice, the Revolution would wither and collapse.[6] The creation of New Ireland in Maine was not crucial to this strategic vision, but it embodied similar assumptions regarding the role of loyalists and would serve to distract New England while British forces were preoccupied in the South.

Even before all the details were worked out, Germain sent orders to General Henry Clinton at New York to establish a post on Penobscot Bay suitable for a permanent settlement. Clinton, in turn, entrusted the task to Brigadier General Francis McLean at Halifax, a veteran of the wars in Europe, and recommended to him the services of a capable navy officer with long experience along the northeast coast, Captain Henry Mowat. The expedition reached its destination on schedule and without incident. The frigate and the brig soon departed, leaving the three sloops-of-war under Mowat's command to protect the transports and the British beachhead from rebel counterattack.

There was no armed resistance to the British occupation; the local militia caved in without a shot. Militia colonels Josiah Brewer and Jonathan Buck readily yielded to General McLean's demands that they surrender their regiments. Buck not only complied, he even sent to the British general his entire muster lists with an ingratiating note addressed to "the Noble General McLean," explaining he would have attended the general personally but was regrettably indisposed. Colonel Josiah Brewer also chose not to appear and sent his brother to carry out the humiliating formalities.[7]

Some inhabitants fled westward, but most remained, cautiously friendly to the newcomers. General McLean immediately issued a proclamation promising general amnesty to all who took an oath of allegiance to the king. Those who did so within eight days were promised permission to fish unmolested, assured of legal title to their lands, and guaranteed physical protection from the rebels. Food, land, and protection had a powerful appeal to settlers whose lives, precarious at best, had been badly disrupted by war. Some 500 settlers came in to take the oath, some from as far away as Union River and Deer Isle. A few even actively assisted the British. Dr. John Calef accepted the positions of surgeon and chaplain to the garrison and overseer for all civilians, and a former Boston merchant trading with Bagaduce, Nathan Phillips, received a captain's commission and the task of enlisting and training a loyalist militia. John Perkins, another prominent landholder, and about 100 more civilians voluntarily labored on the fort, helping to prepare for the anticipated rebel assault.[8]

The General Court of Massachusetts heard the shocking news of the British occupation in a rapid succession of alarms from Georgetown, Pownalborough, Falmouth, and Machias. On June 24, while the reports were still pouring in, the state resolved to send its own expedition to drive out the enemy without waiting for help from Continental forces. A fleet made up of state vessels, as well as ones privately owned, was to be readied in the astonishingly unrealistic time of six days. As it was, it took almost a month to acquire the necessary vessels, crews, troops, supplies, and equipment. State agents scoured the countryside for small arms, cannon, powder, and shot. In addition, the expedition required axes and shovels for trenching, field kitchen equipment such as kettles and bowls, and enough flour, pork, beef, rice, peas, molasses, rum, soap, and vinegar to feed and cleanse an army of 1,500 men for several weeks at least.[9]

To encourage voluntary participation by shipowners, the government agreed to insure all private vessels, reimburse all expenses, and to give up its share of any prize money. Owners eagerly responded to what appeared to be a profitable enterprise. Elias Haskett Derby of Salem, whose privateering ventures eventually made him a fortune, contributed a large privateer and then received permission to send along yet another that had not been ready for sea when the fleet sailed.[10] Most of the fleet consisted of privately owned vessels—both transports and privateers—hired, insured, and equipped at state expense. The government of Massachusetts contributed three armed state vessels of its own, and New Hampshire one. The Continental Navy Board sent along two small vessels and the powerful new frigate *Warren*, thirty-two guns, under Commodore Dudley Saltonstall. As the fleet prepared to depart, eager speculators in Boston competed with one another to purchase shares of the anticipated plunder from crews of the vessels in the fleet.[11] Then, on July 19, twenty transports accompanied by nineteen armed vessels sailed for Penobscot Bay.

Those who supplied the blood and sinew for this enterprise were far less eager to participate than the insured shipowners and merchant speculators. To man the fleet, the state resorted to impressment. The sheriffs of Essex and Suffolk counties received orders to guard the ferries and exits from seaport towns and to detain all mariners and marines for service with the fleet, although with the warning "to avoid any abuse or injury being offered to the persons who may be the subjects of Impressment."[12]

To create an army, the General Court ordered 1,500 men to be detached from the county militias closest to the scene of action: 600 each from Cumberland and Lincoln counties, 300 from York. But proximity to the British menace did not evoke popular enthusiasm for the expedition. Indeed, recruiting proceeded with even less efficiency than usual. Owing to recent drafts for the Continental Army, recruits were already scarce, and communities throughout Maine had difficulty meeting these new quotas. On the basis of later comments by officers of the expedition, those who were detached from their militias and sent as soldiers were the "expendables," those the communities needed the least—young boys, old men, and those normally unfit for military service. One officer described them as "Boys, old Men and Invalids; if they belong'd to the Train Band or Alarm List they were Soldiers, whether they could carry a Gun, walk a mile without Crutches, or only Compos Mentis sufficient to keep themselves out of Fire and Water."[13]

So unflattering a description comes from officers eager to excuse themselves from what had turned into a major military disaster; little wonder they blamed their troops. Yet, even if the recruits were inexperienced, infirm, and incompetent, they were wise enough to know that, without additional training and without the aid of the Continental Army, they were to be sent immediately against entrenched British regulars. Many protested in the only way they knew, by fleeing into the woods. Some returned out of fear, others by force. Cumberland County's Brigadier General Samuel Thompson vowed he would make the county "too hot to hold" for those who tried to escape their obligation. Even so, when the expeditionary force met for its first and only military review at Townshend (Boothbay), it still lacked over 500 men. The review also demonstrated that the army was not merely deficient in numbers but, as the troops well knew, lacked discipline, adequate arms, and the knowledge of how to use them. Even their officers appeared ignorant of the most basic military maneuvers.[14]

To make matters worse, following the custom of the time, the General Court divided the command of the expedition. Brigadier General Solomon Lovell headed the army. A farmer from Weymouth, Massachusetts, Lovell was locally prominent as a representative to the state assembly and as a militia officer. He had seen limited service in the French and Indian War; during the Revolution he had served at the siege of Boston and by 1778 was brigadier of Massachusetts troops in the Rhode Island campaign. At the time he received command of the Penobscot expedition, he had a reputation as a popular, steady, capable officer. His orders instructed him to "promote the Greatest Harmoney, peace and concord between the land and Sea Forces" and to "consult with the Commander of the fleet that the Naval Force may Cooperate with the troops under your command in Endeavoring to Captivate Kill or Destroy the whole force of the Enemy there both by Sea & Land."[15]

The commodore of the fleet with whom General Lovell had to cooperate was Dudley Saltonstall, commander of the Continental frigate *Warren*. Saltonstall, from Connecticut, was one of the few "foreigners" to participate in this Massachusetts expedition. He owed his naval commission to the influence of his politically powerful brother-in-law, Silas Deane, and his naval career already had been checkered and tempestuous. Whereas Lovell was personable and obliging, Saltonstall, in the words of one critic, was "willful & unaccommodating," a man upon whose shoulders "The command of a Fleet did not set easy . . . tho' he could fight a very good Battle in a single Ship."[16] Saltonstall's orders were identical to Lovell's, but to expect him to promote "Harmoney, peace and concord between the land and Sea Forces" was to expect the impossible.

II

After the military review at Townshend, the American fleet sailed into Penobscot Bay where a company of Penobscot Indians joined the expedition.[17] On July 25 the American armada dropped anchor off Bagaduce — a fleet so vast its vessels appeared to cover the entire bay. Yet appearances belied reality; every soldier and sailor was acutely aware that the expedition was running an immense risk of being boxed up inside Penobscot Bay by the vastly superior British navy. It was essential for success that the Americans carry out their attack promptly and efficiently. Nonetheless, discord and indecision marred the American operation from the start.

The British defenders, by contrast, had everything to gain through a protracted siege, and they made the most of their meager defenses. Mowat anchored his three vessels so their guns covered the approaches into Bagaduce Harbor and the beach where the Americans were expected to land. The fort itself was far from complete, with only two guns mounted and the walls but four feet high in places. However, the British sailors unloaded the useless off-side guns from their vessels and dragged them up to the fort overlooking the harbor. Reinforced by naval cannon and seamen, the British roughly equaled in number the American army and presented a formidable challenge.[18] To reach the enemy, the American fleet would have to force its way into Bagaduce Harbor bow-first against the raking broadsides of the British warships, face the threat of being fouled by three transports that Mowat had prepared to sail into the American formation, and risk the shot from the fort on the hill. The havoc this might cause to the inexperienced American fleet as it tried to negotiate the intricate channel into Bagaduce Harbor was all too vivid to the cautious American commodore. When a local resident assured him the Americans needed only to sail straight into the harbor and destroy the enemy's defenses in half an hour, Saltonstall snapped, "You seem to be damned knowing about the matter; I'm not going to risk my shipping in that damned hole," and he never did.[19]

Without any clear plan of action, the Americans were clumsy and uncertain. The fleet exchanged shots with the British sloops at long range and to little effect. Early efforts to land troops were equally inauspicious, being thwarted by rough water and high winds. Not until the evening of the twenty-sixth did the Americans experience some success by expelling the British from Nautilus Island just off Bagaduce Peninsula; however, the battery they set up there only caused Mowat to reposition his vessels in a somewhat safer location. Already, some of the naval officers were becoming anxious. In a petition to their commodore, they pointed out the dangers of delay in view of the possibility of enemy reinforcements.[20] General Lovell was finally driven to take a desperate gamble to get his troops ashore somehow. He consented to a landing at the foot of a cliff 100 feet high on the western side of the peninsula, defended at the top by a British detachment. Through the early morning fog of July 28, 400 militia and marines landed on the narrow beach and began to scramble up the face of the bluff. Some of their number remained below to discourage the British defenders at the top with musket fire while the American vessels just offshore raked the top of the cliff with their cannon. The landing boats deliberately returned to the fleet, so the troops had no alternative but to go forward and up. It was a mad, chaotic action lasting only about twenty minutes until the desperate climbers heaved themselves over the edge and drove the defenders back in disarray toward the fort.[21]

This was a crucial moment in the campaign; the way now lay open into the unfinished fort only 600 yards away. The British were demoralized and confused, and General McLean later admitted that he was ready to surrender after making but token resistance to save his reputation.[22] But at this point the attack halted. The Americans too had suffered casualties and were almost as disorganized as the British. The militia could not be trusted in so fluid a situation. By their timidity and inexperience the Americans lost their momentum and momentary advantage; they got near the fort but no nearer to success.

Like the careful amateurs that they were, both Lovell and Saltonstall now resorted to "the book," but they could not agree on which lesson to follow. Lovell did not feel his forces were strong enough for a direct assault on the fort unless the American fleet first engaged the British vessels and prevented their crews from assisting the fort's garrison. Saltonstall, however, adamantly refused to send his fleet into "that damned hole." The army, he insisted, would have to neutralize the fort first. July passed into August, and despite urgent warnings and calls to action from the Massachusetts council and the Navy Board, the two American commanders did nothing but debate their tactical differences in one council of war after another.[23] Each day followed the next in a dreary round of cannonading, casualties, and conferences. With each passing day the British improved their fortifications and the chance that their navy would come to their aid.

Morale in the American camp declined as the siege lengthened. Heavy rains added to the drudgery of digging trenches, constructing gun emplacements, manhandling siege guns into place, only to relocate them again, all the while risking death by enemy fire in a campaign that appeared to be going nowhere. By early August the disintegration of discipline was reaching alarming proportions. A council of war reported that, "many of the Officers being so exceeding slack in their Duty" and the soldiers "so averse to the Service," on any special duty or alarm "one fourth part of the Army are skulked out of the way and conceal'd." General Lovell, despite his optimistic reports to the council in Boston, obviously shared these apprehensions. On August 1 he wrote to the council that his alternatives were "either to continue a regular Siege with volunteer ships that cannot lie here long inactive; and a body of Militia whose domestic affairs cannot admit of their being long from home; or risk the fate of a Storm." He then came to a fateful conclusion: "I think the Enemy cannot be attacked by Storm with any probability of Success — their works being exceedingly strong and our Troops (tho brave) are yet undisciplined."[24] Convinced that he needed more men, Lovell dispatched an urgent request for reinforcements to the council in Boston and even to John Allan in his exposed post at Machias. Although help was soon on the way, the British won the race for reinforcements.

Not only did the British reinforcements arrive first, but the ultimate irony is that they did so just when Lovell and Saltonstall resolved their differences and were in the very act of carrying out a joint assault against the British positions. Without waiting for the reinforcements he had insisted upon, Lovell consented to divide his forces, which he previously had denied he could do, and agreed to occupy a position behind the British fort.[25] This would isolate the fort from Mowat's fleet and enable the American army to attack the fort from two directions at once. For his part, Saltonstall abandoned his insistence that the fort had to be reduced before he entered the harbor. He now agreed to attack Mowat's flotilla while the army engaged the fort. August 12 was the day set, but on the day before, Lovell decided to test the morale of his troops by ordering 600 to muster as though for an immediate assault upon the enemy fort. The army failed the test.

The militiamen plainly showed how they felt about a frontal assault when only 400 reluctantly responded to the call. The regiment from Cumberland County managed with difficulty to raise its quota. The Lincoln County regiment was unable to do so, and that from York had to send so many troops after those who deserted it too was unable to meet its requirement. Lovell did his best to rouse his dispirited troops with a stirring speech wherein he assured them they were destined to succeed not only by force of numbers — a dubious calculation — but "having that Liberal Characteristic 'Sons of Liberty and of Virtue' . . . we must ride triumphant over the rough diabolical Torrent [tyrant?] of Slavery, and the Monsters sent to rivet its Chains." After reminding his men of their obligations to duty, honor, and posterity, he urged "every one submit to his Superior, then we shall have regularity, let each man stand by his Officer, and each Officer animated, press forward to the Object in view."[26]

Lovell's rhetoric failed to convince the rank and file. At this terrifying moment they were realists, uninspired by the myth of the citizen-soldier clad in the invincibility of republican virtue. Lovell sent half of the force forward as skirmishers to draw out the enemy, while the other half were held as reserves. The feint worked only too well; a British detachment sallied out from the fort throwing skirmishers and reserves alike into confusion and then panicked flight. "A General uneasiness took place among the Officers commanding [the] Corps," wrote Lovell afterward, and they "complained that their reputation was at stake to go into the Field with such Men."[27]

Such an accusation might just as well have come from the troops. Except for the seizure of the Bagaduce bluffs, American leadership was notorious for its unprofessional, unsoldierlike conduct. Some of the officers preferred quarters apart from their own men, despite orders to rejoin their units. Colonel of Artillery Paul Revere, who once "spread the alarm," now enjoyed the comparative luxury of quarters aboard the artillery supply vessel in the harbor. Those officers selected to lead the feint against the fort were themselves as timid and confused as their own troops. Indeed, so terrified were they by the prospect of leading an assault, they nullified their own colonel's assignments and drew lots in a grim game wherein losers were leaders. Shortly before what was to have been the Grand Assault several days later, a naval officer walking among the soldiers asked them why they appeared so "dull Sperited & whither they would storm the enemys fort[.] With one consent the answer was with all my hart [just] Give us officers."[28]

A veteran of the expedition later recalled a growing conviction throughout the ranks that leadership so inept had to be intentional, treasonous, and highly placed: "that the old General had agreed to go snacks with the Commodore in whatever they were to have [from the British] for defeating the expedition." Contempt for Lovell and Saltonstall reached such intensity "the General was hissed and hooted at wherever he made his appearance, and the Commodore cursed and execrated by all hands."[29] As fervently as officers wished for reliable troops, so the troops wished for reliable officers in whom they had confidence.

Mutual distrust between officers and men never came to its final test. The Grand Assault had to be postponed for one crucial day while the army regrouped. Then, on Friday, August 13, an inauspicious day, Lovell succeeded in mustering 300 men, one-half of whom, along with fifty marines, managed to take the position behind the British fort, cutting off its naval support. This was the moment for which Commodore Saltonstall had been waiting. The American warships hoisted anchors, but once more the assault failed to materialize. Strange topsails far down Penobscot Bay indicated that what the Americans feared most had occurred; the British relief fleet was at hand.[30]

With an alacrity they had seldom displayed in the campaign, the Americans reembarked their cannon, equipment, and troops so that on the morning of August 14 the British in the fort were astonished to discover the enemy lines were deserted.[31] The tide and a southerly breeze carried the British fleet up the bay: one ship of the line carrying sixty-four guns, commanded by Sir George Collier, followed by four frigates with twenty-four to thirty-two cannon, a sloop and a brig, both armed, soon joined by Mowat's three sloops-of-war. The American fleet lay becalmed, with the armed vessels forming a defensive crescent to protect the transports. The breeze and the British warships reached the American fleet about the same time. Few of the American vessels could hope to match what was coming up the bay toward them; none of them wanted to. Indeed, a council of war aboard the *Warren* had determined

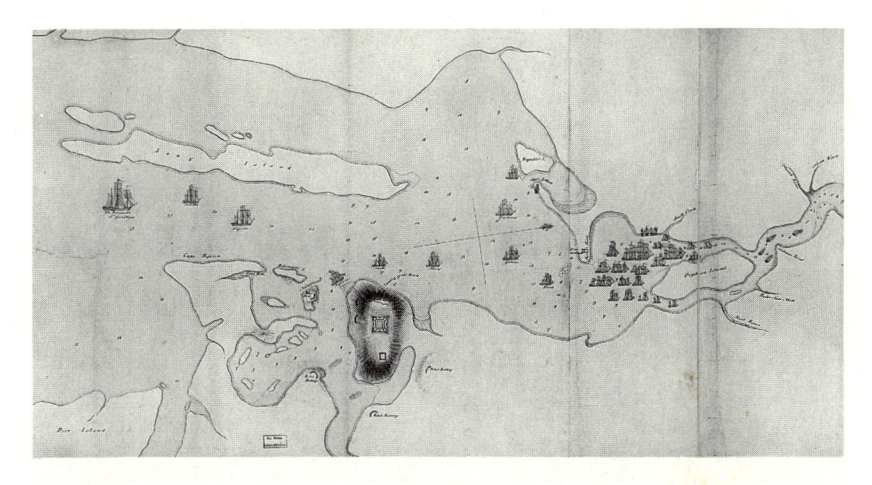

9. "Penobscot River and Bay, with the Operations of the English fleet, under Sir. Geo. Colyer, against the Division of Massachusetts troops operating against Fort Castine, August, 1779." This British map of the American defeat on the Penobscot River shows the American fleet clustered about the mouth of the river, seeking to escape the British squadron under Sir George Collier. Captain Henry Mowat's three vessels, no longer needed to protect Castine, are joining the British fleet. Courtesy of the Library of Congress.

not to engage the enemy but to convoy the supply vessels upriver to some place where a suitable defense could be made. However, no one knew where that location might be, since neither General Lovell nor Commodore Saltonstall had made contingency plans for such an emergency. Lovell, indeed, had refused deliberately to make such preparations for fear of disheartening his men with the idea of defeat. All discipline disintegrated as what began as an orderly retreat degenerated into a rout. As they caught the wind, the American warships went sailing past the slower supply vessels and fled up the Penobscot River. In the words of one British observer, "He was the best fellow who could run and sail the fastest."[32]

What followed was a hideous nightmare for the Americans. Flood tide and a southerly breeze frustrated the few vessels that sought escape around the northerly end of Long Island, or Isleborough, and down the westerly side of the bay. They were either captured or scuttled by their own crews.[33] The same fate befell the rest of the fleet as it sought safety up the Penobscot River. The light wind could not counter the effects of

10. "Destruction of the American Fleet at Penobscot Bay," by Dominic Serres (1722–1793). The British fleet under Sir George Collier pursuing the American expedition up Penobscot Bay, August 14, 1779. Courtesy of the National Maritime Museum, Greenwich, London, England.

the river's current as the tide began to ebb, so that many vessels were in danger of drifting helplessly downstream to the British warships waiting below. Colonel Paul Revere, intent on salvaging his personal baggage, only tardily and with reluctance surrendered his own boat to help rescue the crews. Many commanders simply ran their vessels ashore while the crews and troops rushed to disembark and lose themselves in the comparative safety of the forest, pausing only long enough to set their vessels afire to prevent them from falling into enemy hands. Officers who tried to maneuver their vessels farther upriver and to preserve discipline faced mutiny from panic-stricken crews.[34]

By evening the Penobscot presented a scene out of hell. Towering flames from burning hulks lit up the night sky, leaping with thunderous crescendo when the fires reached the powder magazines. The milling crowds along the shore had won a respite from the British, but now they faced a new danger from their own burning vessels. "When they Blew up," recalled one survivor, "there Shott and Timber flew verey thick up and Down the River." Most of the cannon aboard the burning vessels had been loaded and ready for action, so that when the flames reached the guns they fired indiscriminately. One participant thought he was in as much danger from exploding vessels as he had been before the enemy.[35]

There was no holding the men once they reached shore. Pressed crews, citizen-soldiers, even their officers, considered their enlistments over and that they need stay no longer; the expedition quite clearly was finished. General Lovell himself vanished from the scene, hurrying ninety miles up the river for a two-week visit with the Penobscot Indians. Commodore Saltonstall, who had given no direction so far, could not do it now. Only the army's second-in-command, Brigadier General Peleg Wadsworth, with a few officers tried to rally the troops to make a stand and to save the shipping, guns, and equipment. Seeing the futility of it all, Wadsworth "swang" his pack and headed for Camden. On the way, he salvaged five companies of militia out of the wrecked army, posting them at nearby towns for emergency defense and to boost local morale.[36]

American losses are difficult to establish with any accuracy. Although there is no dispute concerning the destruction of the entire American fleet of some forty vessels, figures on American casualties vary wildly. The army, and presumably most of its records, simply disappeared once ashore. "Our retreat was as badly managed as the whole expedition," wrote a survivor. "Here we were, landed in a wilderness, under no command, those belonging to the ships, unacquainted with the woods, and only knew that a west course would carry us across to Kennebec.... [E]very one shifted for himself. Some got to their homes in two days, while the most of us were six or seven days before we came to an inhabited country. I got through on the seventh day, after keeping a fast of three days." A rather dubious loyalist source reported that the rebels lost 300 men in the retreat alone, during which the survivors treated the inhabitants most shockingly, plundering houses, stealing food, ravishing women, and in some places clashing with the local militia. A modern historian, relying on a contemporary newspaper account, suggests a total of 500 American casualties for the entire campaign. Yet another historian, depending on official sources, cautiously estimates only thirty-three American dead, thirty-two wounded, and four captured.[37] In short, such was the magnitude of disaster, no one could then—or can now—estimate accurately what it cost in American lives.

The cost of the failed expedition in financial terms was a more pressing issue. Shipowners, suppliers, and other creditors of the state immediately began to clamor for payment of debts and compensation for their losses. To maintain its credit, the state had to honor these demands, but for the next fourteen years, while inflation swelled the debt from $1,740,000 to $8,500,000, Massachusetts tried to convince a skeptical Congress that the United States should assume the Penobscot expenses incurred, presumably, in the national interest. Finally, in 1793, as part of a general reassessment of financial relations between the states and the federal government, Congress did accept the bill.[38]

To determine personal responsibility for the Penobscot disaster, the General Court appointed a special Committee of Inquiry. Early in October 1779, after examining many of the officers, the committee submitted its conclusions in a report clearly designed to exonerate the state of Massachusetts and to lay the blame entirely on Commodore Dudley Saltonstall. Ignoring General Lovell's failure to provide an evacuation route for the expedition, as well as his own desertion from the army in its flight up the Penobscot, the committee declared that Lovell had shown "proper Courage and Spirit" and that, had he only received a proper number of troops and adequate support from the navy, he undoubtedly would have defeated the enemy.[39]

Saltonstall was a particularly useful culprit. Since he was from Connecticut, no faction in Massachusetts would rise to his defense, and, furthermore, his Continental commission offered further argument for passing the expense for the failed expedition along to the Continental Congress. The committee, therefore, concluded that Saltonstall's "Want of proper Sperit & Energy" was the "Principal reason" for the failure of the expedition. In general, historians have concurred in the committee's conclusions, and Saltonstall to this day remains the "goat" of Penobscot Bay.[40] He was dismissed from the service, and although he served creditably as commander of a privateer, his reputation never recovered from the Penobscot affair. He was indeed arrogant, contentious, and inept as a fleet commander, yet the failure was not his alone; at the very least he shared responsibility with General Solomon Lovell, whom the committee exonerated with praise.

The Committee of Inquiry also exonerated the army, declaring it deficient only in numbers, not in training, spirit, or discipline — and once again flatly contradicted evidence to the contrary from numerous sources.[41] From the moment the army was raised to the time it disintegrated along the shores of the Penobscot River, it was composed of men who, with good reason, had no desire to serve as soldiers. The troops were only too aware that not only did they lack adequate training but most of their leaders, despite their commissions, were as untrained, inept, and fearful as the men they commanded and offered no inspiration or model of behavior. "Give us officers," the troops had pleaded just before they thought they were to storm the fort.

From the beginning of the campaign to the end, the soldiers' reaction was not to mutiny against incompetent authority but simply to minimize, even nullify, its effects. This they did by avoiding their military obligations, refusing to volunteer, deserting or "skulking" in the woods when drafted for duty, and finally fleeing from the enemy—when they could. By their refusal to follow those who lacked the necessary qualifications for leadership, the rank and file contributed to the fragility of the social fabric, which had so concerned Whig leaders since the very beginning of resistance to Britain. The Committee of Inquiry could not afford to recognize the army's failure of confidence with its social and political implications. Instead, it merely reaffirmed its faith in citizen-soldiers and criticized only their lack of numbers.

III

The failure of Massachusetts to dislodge the British from their midst meant there now existed a rallying point for those who still cherished traditional loyalty to the crown or hostility to Whig leadership. In Maine, the British presence at New Ireland attracted those with strong loyalist convictions who up to now had remained quietly passive or, having fled, wanted to return. During the early years of the war, potential loyalists who remained in their communities had no alternative but to conform to the Whig consensus. Before the British establishment at Bagaduce, the war in Maine was not yet a civil war in that the domestic enemy was unable to fight back. Now, with a vigor sharpened by vengeance, loyalists joined British regulars in plundering coastal settlements, kidnapping local leaders, and enticing inhabitants to reaffirm their allegiance to the king.

A similar situation prevailed in the lower South after the British occupied Savannah and Charleston. Around Savannah, down the Georgia coast, and into the backcountry, people quickly renewed allegiance to the crown. Whig government disappeared, and the militia surrendered as the cause of independence declined. The northward shift of the war into South Carolina stripped Georgia of its organized military forces, both American and British, leaving the region in the hands of armed bands, nominally Tory and Whig, who crisscrossed the state burning, looting, kidnapping, murdering, and even torturing, without restraint. After 1780, when Charleston fell to the British, total civil war and social anarchy engulfed the Carolinas too, so that General Nathaniel Greene, commanding the Continental forces there, noted with astonishment the relentless ferocity with which Tories and Whigs pursued one another. Writes Ronald Hoffman, "No more chaotic a situation can be imagined than that of the Lower South in the years from 1780 to 1783."[42]

Conditions in Maine were only slightly better than in the lower South. The Massachusetts state government did not collapse, but it could do little to protect its easternmost counties because the Penobscot disaster had left the state virtually bankrupt. The Massachusetts Board of War declared that it was "involv'd in difficulties and embarrassments inextricable, and . . . insurmountable," in trying to meet its financial obligations, and in 1781 the state purchasing officer reported that his credit was exhausted and he could no longer obtain provisions without cash. About the same time, the legislature received the disturbing news that the state armories contained no more than 300 firearms. Though the government managed to obtain two small armed vessels to patrol the coast, neither offered much hindrance to enemy privateers. The commander of one declared that his vessel "Sails so amaizing Bad that Every thing I give Chase to will out Sail us." Eventually, the state sold one and exchanged the other for a vessel more suitable to the task, and if the new vessel provided little more protection, at least it was less costly to operate.[43] In 1781 the General Court tried to replenish its armories as well as to protect the Maine coast by offering bounties to American privateers for the capture of enemy cruisers in Maine waters.[44] Despite the inducements, privateersmen continued to prefer easy profit from those who could not fight back.

Without much success, Massachusetts sought outside assistance in protecting the eastern district. The Continental Congress continued to accept the costs of defending Machias, which played a strategic role in Indian affairs, but declined becoming involved in a second expedition against Bagaduce. The idea tempted French commanders in America, but General Washington adamantly opposed the further expenditure of resources on so isolated an objective. Nearby New Hampshire expressed sympathy but noted that it had its own frontiers to defend.[45] Consequently, the defense of Maine had to come from the District's own limited resources.

The burden of meeting the challenge from Bagaduce fell squarely on the citizen-soldiers of Maine, a responsibility that only emphasized the militia's inadequacies. Smoldering feuds in key towns brought defense preparations to a standstill. At Machias, a controversy arose between civilian and military authority. With the enemy to the east in Nova Scotia and to the west at Bagaduce, and with numerous towns resuming their allegiance to the king, Colonel John Allan, the commander at Machias, ordered in the militia to strengthen the town's fortifications and to provide a garrison. Despite the danger of attack, the militia refused to obey. A spokesman boldly informed Allan that "there was No Authority for Calling in the Militia for Such Business" and that to do so was an "Infringment Upon the peoples rights." Authorities jailed one protestor, but although he was soon released, the uproar it caused outweighed any advantage gained by severity. Allan wrote that the controversy "Has Extended the Clamour every where to the Eastward of Penobscut." A year later, Allan was still noting that whenever he called in the militia "Altercations Arises & Inflamed by men of Not the Best Principles for America about the Lawfulness of such things... it Generally Terminates so, as to be no Service or use."[46] Regardless of the danger, Machias townsmen were not about to surrender constitutional scruples to military expediency—but some were willing to surrender Colonel John Allan.

One local leader whom Allan had tried to prosecute for illegal trade with the Indians now sought Allan's removal. Stephen Jones, justice of the peace and chairman of the Machias Committee of Safety, forwarded a series of proposals to the General Court concerning the defense of the town. Included was a recommendation that Allan be relieved of military command, presumably so that he could spend more time in his role as superintendent to the eastern Indians. Allan had his supporters, however. The nearby town of Narraguagus presented a countermemorial stoutly defending his dual role.[47] Although the General Court ignored Jones's scheme and maintained the status quo, Allan was never free from the gnawing fear that enemies were at work trying to undermine his reputation and secure his removal.

The situation in Falmouth was similar to that in Machias. In both places the Penobscot crisis stirred up deep-seated animosities. With the British at Bagaduce, Falmouth remained in constant turmoil, fearing an attack. Responsibility for providing a militia garrison fell to Cumberland County's Brigadier General Samuel Thompson of Brunswick. Falmouth had never forgotten the crisis early in the war when Thompson and his followers had invaded the town to seize the British naval officer, Lieutenant Henry Mowat, an episode that undoubtedly influenced the British to bombard Falmouth in 1775. Now, four years later, when Thompson appeared tardy in providing a garrison, Falmouth's leaders thought they detected a means of finally getting rid of their dangerous antagonist. Led by Falmouth, Committees of Safety, claiming to represent a majority of the towns in Cumberland County, met to compose a scathing indictment of the county militia for the General Court. Under Thompson's command, they declared, the militia was a virtual mob, unarmed, undisciplined, and poorly equipped. Because Brigadier General Thompson, the colonels, and the majors were obviously ignorant of their duty and unfit for public service, the convention presented to the General Court its own slate of officers starting with Major Daniel Ilsley of Falmouth, brother of prominent Enoch Ilsley, in place of Thompson as brigadier general.[48]

In response to this attempted purge, pro-Thompson delegates, chiefly from inland communities like Brunswick, Gorham, Gray, Windham, and Bakerstown (Poland and Minot), held a meeting of their own. Claiming that some of them had been excluded from the previous convention, they asserted that the Cumberland County militia was as well disciplined, equipped, and led as any in the state. They defended Thompson as a "true friend to his Country" and denied that he had discriminated against Falmouth by failing to provide for its defense.[49]

After hearing testimony from both sides, the General Court dismissed all accusations and commended the present militia officers for doing their best under difficult circumstances.[50] Samuel Thompson and his supporters from Falmouth's satellite towns had won yet again in their recurring struggle against their commercial entrepôt.

The General Court assigned the task of putting together a coherent defense from these discordant elements to Brigadier General Peleg Wadsworth, the only American officer to emerge from the Penobscot disaster with an enhanced reputation. In March 1780 Wadsworth was promised 600 troops, to be detached from local militias, and the authority to declare martial law in Lincoln County where the population was showing an alarming tendency to cooperate with the enemy.[51] Wadsworth's plan of defense rested on a highly realistic assessment of local conditions and attitudes. He was aware that most inhabitants were well disposed toward the American cause but that "they are Inhabitants of a new settled Country; thinly scattered over the Wilderness; . . . at a distance from the seat of Government; know but little of what passes there; & small in their own eyes." Wadsworth concluded that most of the settlers would willingly assist any American force offering them some reasonable measure of protection, but failing that, they would readily take an oath of allegiance to Great Britain rather than have their property destroyed.[52]

Wadsworth's measures to restore order and protection in eastern Maine resembled those of American leaders faced with a similar task in the South. He was aware of the political implications of military policy in raising morale and prompting a sense of unity. Toward this end he recommended that the state government cut a road between the Kennebec and Penobscot rivers to facilitate the movement of troops and supplies and to promote a sense of unity among the inhabitants. He also proposed that the government distribute newspapers among the eastern communities to reduce their sense of isolation and defeatism. To neutralize the British at Bagaduce, Wadsworth stationed in the most exposed towns mobile detachments of troops equipped with whaleboats to block enemy raids.[53] At the same time, Wadsworth was willing to employ harsher measures of military and judicial terror to coerce conformity to the patriot cause when necessary.

On April 18, 1780, Wadsworth placed the offshore islands and all Lincoln County settlements within ten miles of the sea under martial law.[54] Few eastern communities were exempt: Lincoln County included the eastern half of Maine, and Wadsworth interpreted "the sea" to include all rivers and inlets navigable by armed vessels. Within the proscribed area, military authorities could arrest any persons of suspect loyalty and subject them to trial by military tribunals without juries, which had the power to impose the death penalty. Effectively enforced, martial law would sever Bagaduce from its mainland sources of information, supplies, and reinforcements.

To isolate Bagaduce by sea, Wadsworth described a line across Pe-

124 Crisis on the Penobscot

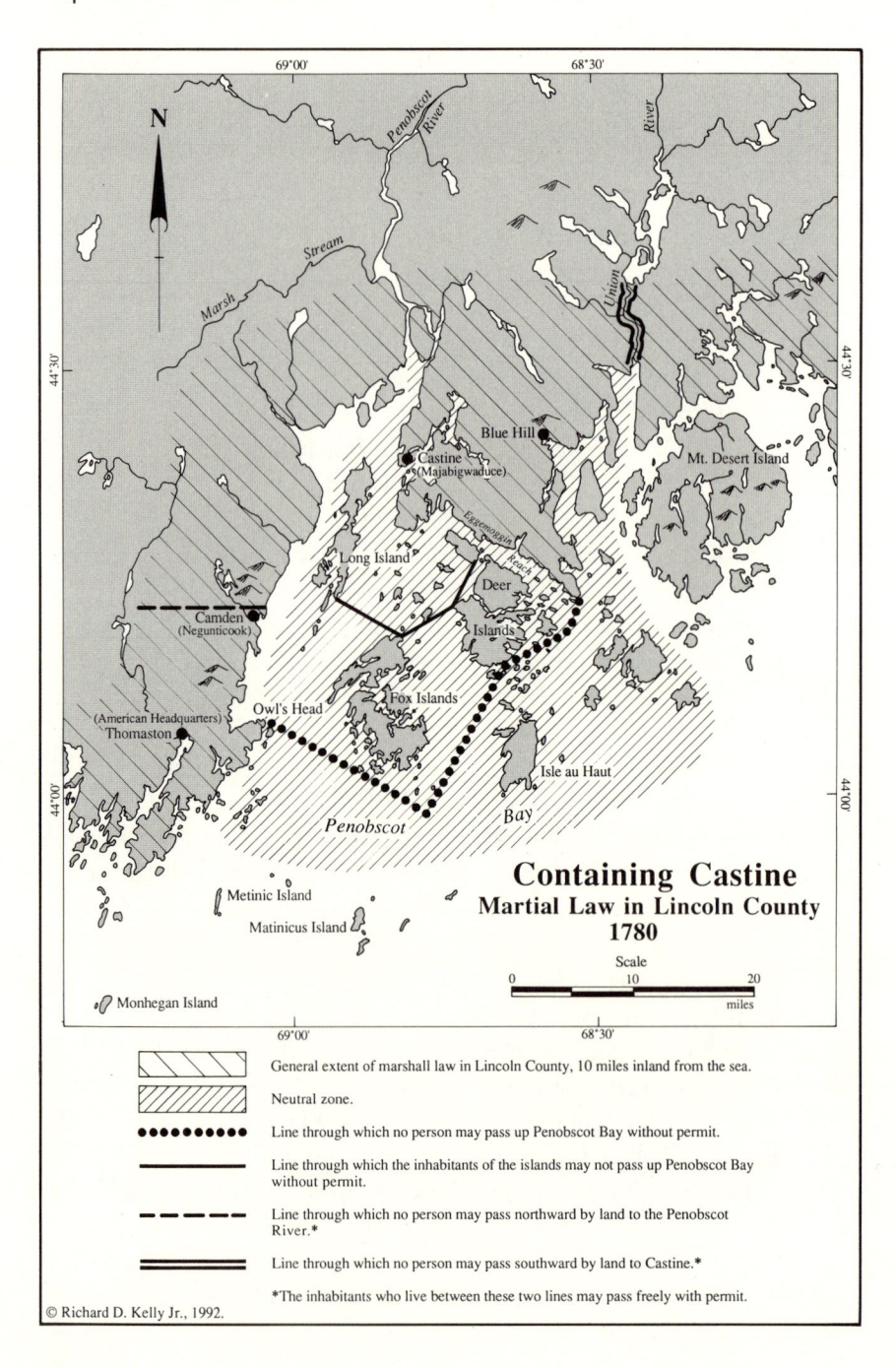

Containing Castine
Martial Law in Lincoln County
1780

General extent of marshall law in Lincoln County, 10 miles inland from the sea.

Neutral zone.

•••••••• Line through which no person may pass up Penobscot Bay without permit.

——— Line through which the inhabitants of the islands may not pass up Penobscot Bay without permit.

– – – – Line through which no person may pass northward by land to the Penobscot River.*

═══════ Line through which no person may pass southward by land to Castine.*

*The inhabitants who live between these two lines may pass freely with permit.

© Richard D. Kelly Jr., 1992.

nobscot Bay, extending from Owl's Head to the southern tip of Vinalhaven, around the outer side of Deer Isle, and to the mainland, beyond which no American vessel could legally proceed (see Fig. 11).[55] However, the residents of the numerous islands in the bay were in a different category. Massachusetts had no effective control in the area. Wadsworth recognized that the defenselessness of the island residents had induced most of them to take the oath to the crown. Consequently, he proclaimed them neutrals, free to travel from island to island, and to and from the mainland, but forbidden to trade with Bagaduce.[56] As neutrals, the islanders were protected from molestation by American forces. They had recourse to Massachusetts courts where they could seek satisfaction from American troops and privateersmen who might occasionally violate their neutrality. In this manner Massachusetts could retain a hold — however precarious — on the loyalties of the islanders despite their oaths of allegiance to the crown and British control of the region.

A curious jurisdictional division gradually evolved in the Penobscot Bay region wherein the British exercised military control, but the state of Massachusetts still provided civil justice. The case of John Bakeman — or Bateman, as he was sometimes called — offers an example of this phenomenon while illustrating the ambiguity of political loyalties even to contemporaries. Long before the British occupation of Bagaduce, Massachusetts authorities received complaints from several leading residents of that area that John Bakeman, the local justice of the peace, was encouraging trade with the enemy. When the government investigated the matter, however, it concluded that, on the contrary, Bakeman was not the villain but the victim of a group who had mobbed his house and assaulted him and his family in retaliation for Bakeman's patriotic efforts to enforce the embargo against the British.

Surprisingly, a committee of justices appointed by the government to investigate the matter further agreed with the complainants that Bakeman was "unsuitable" for the position of justice and ought to be removed. To substantiate their recommendation, the justices forwarded to the Massachusetts General Court a long list of accusations demonstrating that Bakeman was politically and morally unfit for his office.

The British occupation of Bagaduce did not dampen this long-standing feud. Several of Bakeman's leading antagonists, notably Mark Hatch, Joseph Perkins, and Joseph Young, remained at Bagaduce to renew their oaths to the king and even to collaborate with the British, although formerly they had been members of the town's Committee of Safety. Bakeman fled the region, losing considerable property to British confiscation and appealing for vindication to the Massachusetts council. The committee of justices continued to gather evidence concerning the Bakeman affair despite British military presence. But, so contradictory was the testimony, they finally reported in April 1780, "we could not forme aney Judgment who it was that mobed his house, or who did not."

The long saga of John Bakemen does not end even here, for in early 1780 Joseph Young, his chief antagonist, was himself the victim of a riot, despite residing under British military rule near Bagaduce. The rioters sacked his house, abused his family, and plundered his possessions—much like the earlier riot against Bakeman. No evidence connects Bakeman directly to the riot, but he did appear as a hostile witness when Young appealed for redress, significantly enough before Massachusetts, rather than British, authorities. In spite of Young's suspicious conduct with the British, the council allowed him to bring legal action in the courts of Massachusetts against those charged with plundering his house.[57] Massachusetts may have lost military control over the Penobscot region, but it still provided the only civil justice available to the residents, whether or not they had resumed their oath to the crown. Through its legal system, Massachusetts retained recognition and loyalty from inhabitants over whom it had lost control politically, thereby minimizing the effects of British military success.

General Wadsworth's imposition of martial law over areas nominally under American control retained loyalty to the American cause by force rather than persuasion. Martial law apparently lasted only six months, during which time authorities seized and condemned several vessels for trading with the enemy and arrested numerous individuals engaged in treasonous activity.[58] Some had merely disparaged the American cause; others were accused of trading with and conveying information to the enemy at Bagaduce. Several were arrested for acting as guides for British raiding parties. One of them, Jeremiah Baum, became a tragic example to others when authorities hanged him at Thomaston, although he was feeble-minded and hardly responsible for his actions.[59] Most others were merely detained and then released on bond for good behavior. Wadsworth shipped the most dangerous suspects to Boston for more secure confinement than was available in the crumbling jails of Pownalborough or Falmouth.

Martial law, however, proved as unpopular with the revolutionaries as with British sympathizers. The local population regarded martial law as an infringement on their own rights and did their best to nullify it. As John Allan had discovered at Machias, endowing the military with arbitrary power even in the cause of liberty became a form of tyranny. On several occasions, the General Court interfered on behalf of individuals arrested by Wadsworth and also ordered the release of confiscated vessels. Wadsworth, reacting indignantly to the implied criticism, demanded a clarification from the General Court concerning the enforcement of martial law and protested to the governor that his actions, taken only against persons known to be enemies to the American cause, were entirely legal. Yet Wadsworth was not above reproach. On one occasion, he even imprisoned Judge Timothy Langdon for the "treasonous activity" of having issued a writ requiring the return of confiscated property.[60]

The most serious failing with martial law was that it simply did not work. Despite the threat of arbitrary arrest and even the death penalty, British sympathizers continued to assist the enemy and to participate in their devastating raids. A loyalist refugee from Thomaston, for example, led a party to his hometown and returned to Bagaduce in triumph with a loaded vessel as a prize. Because of its location, Camden was especially vulnerable; in the fall of 1779 and then again in 1780, Camden refugees directed British raiders to the town, where they burned houses, barns, and sawmills and carried off livestock.[61] It happened yet again a year later. Guided by two former residents, a detachment of eighty British soldiers from Bagaduce captured Camden's little garrison and its commanding officer without firing a shot. The raiders disarmed the population, destroyed the military structures, and then carried most of the town's military stores back to Bagaduce in captured vessels.[62] Perhaps the most notorious episode occurred in the summer of 1780 when loyalists tried to kidnap Captain Levi Soule at his farm on Broad Cove. They shot him dead when he tried to escape and either wounded or intentionally mutilated Soule's wife when she came to his aid. In at least partial retaliation, Wadsworth inflicted the death penalty on Jeremiah Baum.[63]

The severity of marital law seemed only to inspire the enemy to greater defiance. In 1780 John Jones, a notorious Tory formerly of Pownalborough, had the bravado to return home one night in mid-July.

It was a homecoming the town did not soon forget. Jones led a detachment of British soldiers, who kidnapped the town's leading citizen, Charles Cushing. Cushing, high sheriff and brigadier general of Lincoln County, experienced the humiliation of being captured in his nightshirt without a struggle and being hustled off to captivity at Fort George. He was later paroled and exchanged, but the citizens of Pownalborough could no longer sleep soundly. Several local leaders hired guards, and Cushing himself soon resigned his various offices and permanently left Pownalborough.[64]

Had Wadsworth received the 600 troops promised by the General Court, he might have had more success in enforcing martial law and blunting enemy attacks. Instead, he may have received half that number and virtually no logistical support from an impoverished Massachusetts. In April 1780 he was complaining that only fifty men had arrived, despite his repeated requests to the county brigadiers that they raise their quotas. By the end of May, Wadsworth announced receipt of some 200 men who had been "dropping in by degrees for two Months ... without being reduc'd to order & discipline." For supplies he had camping utensils for only 100 men, ten days' supply of meat, and enough bread to last for two days. When the provisions ran out, the general proposed to set his men to fishing.[65] That would keep them from starving, but only at the expense of their military effectiveness.

But it would not keep them content. By July the troops at Camden had gone hungry long enough. Determined to leave, they "slung their packs," and only with great difficulty could Wadsworth persuade them to remain.[66] By the end of the year, the troops still lacked bread and were "almost unfit for any Duty for want of Clothes," so Wadsworth discharged them early. Now, he observed, "the whole Country on either Side [of] Bagaduce from this Place to Machias, but for the Inhabitants, lays open to the Enemy." In disgust, he requested a discharge from his command, stating that he found himself "quite unequal to the Task, where there are some Intricacies, more perplexities & much Service to be done & ... but very little to do with."[67] However, before Wadsworth could take leave of his command, the British succeeded in capturing not only Captain Daniel Sullivan of Frenchman's Bay, the brother of General John Sullivan, but Brigadier General Peleg Wadsworth himself.

Guided by enemy sympathizers, twenty-five British soldiers surprised the general and his family at Thomaston on a February night in 1781.

The militia guard fled at the first sight of the enemy, but the raiders had their hands full with Wadsworth alone. Armed with a brace of pistols, a blunderbuss, a musket, and a bayonet, he fought off his attackers, wounding three, two of whom soon died. Only when shot through the arm did the general finally yield. His captors hurried him back to Bagaduce where they imprisoned him in Fort George with Major Benjamin Burton, another new captive. When Wadsworth recovered from his wound several months later, the two captives escaped from their prison by cutting through the ceiling, clambering over the walls of the fort, and making their way overland back to safety.[68] But where in Maine was safety? Burton soon departed for Boston, fearing that British sympathizers in his hometown of Cushing might reveal his presence to the enemy.[69] Wadsworth, already having resigned his command prior to being captured, left Maine as well.

Captain Daniel Sullivan, the militia commander at Frenchman's Bay, fell into British hands in much the same way as had Wadsworth and Charles Cushing. Just before dawn in late February 1781, a party from a British privateer surrounded Sullivan's house and took him captive after a brief struggle.[70] In a final effort to escape, Sullivan tried to bribe his guard "with most advantageous offers, such as his daughter to command etc." His offer rejected, Sullivan had to watch in helpless frustration as the British fired his house and that of a neighbor. His one satisfaction lay in the knowledge that the enemy had just missed capturing John Allan, who had left Sullivan's residence only hours before the attack.[71]

IV

John Allan narrowly escaped several British-inspired attempts at capture as he labored among the Indians, trying to restore their confidence in the American cause after the Penobscot defeat. More than ever, the Americans needed Indian support in defending Maine, but the Indians were understandably impressed with British success and distressed at the interruption of their supplies from Massachusetts. After the Penobscot campaign, the state lacked funds with which to obtain provisions for the Indians and the means to transport them. British privateers operating out of Bagaduce made the supply route between Boston and Machias precarious at best. Since the supplies that did get through were a mere fraction of what Allan required, he was forced to extend his personal credit and reduced to becoming "a Pedlar & Hawker, Going myself from place to place to Collect Vegetables in Exchange for Butter."[72]

Despite Allan's frantic efforts, the British appeared to have gained the upper hand in the summer of 1780 when many Indians who had settled around Machias left to attend a British-sponsored gathering at Fort Howe on the Saint John River. News that Malecite Indians were acting as guards for workers cutting masts for the Royal Navy provided another sign of the disturbing new relationship between the Indians and the British.[73] Allan remained reasonably confident the Indians would not attack the Americans, but he believed that the only thing preventing the British from overrunning Maine was their fear of alienating the Indians. If that dread were overcome, warned Allan, there would be no holding the region.[74]

Fortunately for Allan, the powerful French presence in America provided a means of countering British influence. Since the seventeenth century, the eastern Indians had drawn heavily on French culture and support against the English. Now, since France supported the American cause, many Indians looked upon the Revolution with favor, not, however, to the extent of becoming active belligerents. On leaving Machias for the Fort Howe conference, one Malecite assured Allan that "our Language to the Britains is from our Lips only, but when we address the Americans & French its from our hearts."[75] Allan consciously played on Indian fondness for the French and for Catholicism by obtaining the services of priests from French naval units operating off the New England coast. Allan reported that the Indians were delighted with the opportunity to participate in their familiar religious ceremonies and that they expressed "the Greatest Affection for the French, the Connection with whome, much cements their union with us." In another demonstration of support in 1781, the French dispatched a frigate to the eastern waters to show the flag to the inhabitants, both red and white.[76]

To some extent, Allan and his French connection proved too successful. By early 1780 almost 500 Indians had gathered around Machias; all had to be provisioned from the scanty American resources.[77] The difficulty of procuring adequate supplies from Massachusetts threatened to undo Allan's diplomacy. He reported discontent and uneasiness among some of the Indians, who again began drifting back to the Saint John for the more plentiful provisions provided by the British.[78] In the spring of

1782, Allan, "destitute of subsistence," sent a special representative to Boston to plead for supplies. A year later, he personally appeared before the governor and the legislature to beg for support in keeping the Indians from British corruption.[79] Despite their wavering, the eastern Indian tribes remained uncommitted to either side and nonbelligerent throughout the entire war.

In this diplomatic competition, the special triumph of John Allan lay in convincing the Indians that, despite the defeat on the Penobscot, provisions undelivered, and promises unfulfilled, the American cause remained a viable alternative to that of the British, thus enabling the Indians to follow their own neutralist inclinations.[80] It also meant that enough Indians remained in eastern Maine to provide protection for Machias, while the rest of Maine lay open to the enemy.

Militia forces, martial law, and a screen of neutral Indians offered no protection for the scattered communities east of Machias, more isolated and exposed than ever after the Penobscot defeat. Peleg Wadsworth had keenly observed that many of them were distant from the seat of government, ignorant of what went on there, and "small in their own eyes." This sense of inferiority and helplessness gradually undermined commitment to the war. Several years earlier, the town of Yarmouth in Nova Scotia, ravaged by American privateers, had pleaded with its provincial government for a status of neutrality as the only means of survival in a war where the enemy showed no mercy and the government provided no security. Now the towns of eastern Maine, under similar pressures, sought similar relief from their own government — with similar results.

By mid-March 1781, such a proposal was in circulation among some of the eastern Lincoln County towns. John Allan reported that rumors of neutrality were creating confusion and settling communities "much upon The wavering Hand."[81] The proposal came from Francis Shaw, Jr., of Gouldsborough, merchant, colonel of militia, and chairman of the town's Committee of Inspection, Correspondence, and Safety. Shaw claimed to have had a conversation with John Hancock, the new governor of Massachusetts, about conditions downeast and quoted him as saying that, since the state was unable to protect the eastern communities, the inhabitants had an "undoubted Right" to make the best terms possible for the protection of life, family, and property.[82] Shortly after the British had kidnapped Captain Sullivan from Frenchman's Bay, committees from that community and the neighboring towns of Gouldsborough, Narraguagus, and Number Four met to draft a petition requesting that both the British and the state of Massachusetts recognize a condition of neutrality from Penobscot Bay to the Saint Croix River.[83] If this convention sent a proposal to the British at Bagaduce, no copy now exists, but Francis Shaw sent one to Machias with instructions that it be forwarded to several other Lincoln County towns for their approval.

The neutrality argument rested squarely on the familiar Whig premise that government was contractual and conditional, that "Allegiance & protection are Reciprocal" and inseparable. The eastern towns declared that they had suffered more than their share for the common cause and that Massachusetts had been as unsympathetic to their repeated requests for redress as had the British Parliament before the war. Instead of receiving help, the eastern towns had been subjected to plundering and devastation by its foes and to "the addition'l Grievance" of martial law by its friends. The petition therefore concluded that "the Government of Massachusetts (from what cause is totally Immaterial,) have Refused or Neglected to give Protection to us the said Inhabitants in Return for our Allegiance, so that in Justice to our selves, our Familys, & Posterity founded on the Universal Concurrance of Nations we are constrained to Ask of your Excellency & Honours, an Act of Neutrallity."[84] By drawing on revolutionary precedent and by an appeal to accepted Whig political principles, the neutralists justified their attempt to withdraw from the war. It may have seemed like a convincing argument to them, given the prevailing circumstances, but elsewhere it caused a storm of opposition.

Outraged patriotism in Machias, the local "metropolis," brought the neutrality movement to a halt. In a series of resolutions directed to the neighboring towns and to Governor Hancock, a "very full" town meeting expressed its "utmost abhorence" of neutrality. Sweeping aside all theoretical justifications, the meeting accused Francis Shaw, Jr., of having had "private Interest at heart, more than the good of his Country." The Machias townspeople emphasized their own unswerving loyalty to the cause of freedom and declared "that we despise a Neutrality in the present contest, holding as an indisputable truth, those that are not for us, are against us."[85] Led by Stephen Jones, the Machias Committee of Inspection, Correspondence, and Safety drafted an accompanying letter to the resolves that accused Shaw and his counterparts, Nathan Jones of Jonesborough and William Nickells of Narraguagus, of conspiring to restore British control over the region east of Penobscot Bay simply to legalize the illicit trade they already were conducting with the enemy.[86]

From the start, Francis Shaw, Jr., had been concerned that Machias might oppose the neutrality proposal. To Stephen Jones, Shaw had written, "how it may be Receiv'd by your Town I can't Say, (As they are in part Supported) But I dare say it will be Agreed to this way, as we are not, nor cannot be protected."[87] Shaw's distinction is important in explaining Machias's vigorous opposition to neutrality. The war had affected Machias differently than the neighboring towns. Gouldsborough, Jonesborough, Number Four, Narraguagus, and Frenchman's Bay were vulnerably located within easy reach of British privateers. Physically and psychologically, the war had taken a heavy toll upon these isolated settlements — "small in their own eyes," as Wadsworth had described them. To some extent, Machias shared many of the same tribulations, but the war had enhanced that town's importance. Indeed, it became even more important than Pownalborough, the county seat. Machias was the easternmost fortified town in Maine, a haven for Nova Scotian refugees, a staging area for invasions of British-held territory, and most importantly, a bastion against British invasion. As long as Machias held out, the smaller neighboring settlements took strength, and the British could never control the region. Machias could hold out as long as the Indians remained friendly, but their friendship appeared largely dependent on the provisions and diplomacy administered by John Allan at Machias. The town was so strategically important that both Massachusetts and the Continental Congress contributed to its defense. Screened by friendly Indians, supported by state and nation, and situated well up the Machias River beyond easy reach of enemy vessels, Machias understandably assumed an uncompromising attitude toward such trimmers as Shaw, Jones, and Nickells, whose neutrality scheme would undo the town's newfound importance.

The opposition of Machias effectively destroyed the neutralist movement, weakened from the beginning by the reputation of its leaders for illicit trade with the enemy.[88] Neutralism is both elusive and dangerous in a war where morality has become polarized. Enemies at least hold to some principles, erroneous as they may be. Neutrals, however, are open to the charge of being without principles of any kind and of selfishly seeking the best of both sides without risk of personal commitment. As the town of Pleasant River phrased it, "Neither do we Desire to be so

Sneeking as Leave our Friends at the Westerd to Beat the Bush & we to cathch [*sic*] the Hare."[89] Only the state could bestow neutrality without tainting its beneficiaries with self-interest. Wadsworth had managed this for the residents of islands in Penobscot Bay. In this case, neutrality coincided with the best interests of Massachusetts; it provided a subtle means of preserving loyalty where the state had no effective power. On the other hand, the Shaw/Jones/Nickells proposal for neutrality east of the Penobscot worked to their own personal advantage and not to that of the state. When Machias quickly exploited this weakness, the advocates fell away, fearing the accusations of neighbors more than raids by the enemy. Even Francis Shaw, Jr., tried to deny his leading role by claiming merely to be a spokesman for a committee drawn from the offending towns.[90]

Abortive as it may have been, the neutrality movement demonstrated the far-reaching implications of the American defeat on the Penobscot — at least for Maine. What happened on the Penobscot made little impact in the larger scheme of the Revolution. The focus of military action had already shifted to the lower South, there to replicate in surprising detail the character of the war in Maine — and not merely its military aspects. For Mainers, as well as for backcountry settlers in Georgia and the Carolinas, the increasingly ferocious and destructive nature of the war intensified internal divisions, which were social and sectional, political and personal, fragmenting the Revolution. For significant segments of the population, north and south, the ultimate goal was no longer independence but simply survival on any terms possible.

FIVE

A People Divided: The Economic and Social Costs of Revolution

In a conflicted region such as Maine, characterized by a precarious economy and a thinly scattered population, war meant economic and social dislocation accompanied by deepening poverty from which few escaped. Sectional and social rifts widened, and divisions between loyalist and Whig, enhanced by the British at Bagaduce, cut through the already divided society. Maine, as the three easternmost counties of Massachusetts, enjoyed a viable state government, but that government proved incapable of offering effective military or economic aid, especially after 1779. Communities downeast, like those in other border regions, were left to survive largely by their own devices.

I

For Mainers, the single most all-embracing impact of the Revolution was the destruction of their coasting and overseas trade. From Kittery to Machias, seaborne commerce was the lifeblood of the economy. Without trade, the commercial-agricultural towns of York County faced stagnation; communities in Cumberland and especially Lincoln counties faced far worse, for even in the best of times they depended on imported food. By the time war broke out, nonimportation agreements and embargoes had already destroyed Maine's normal rhythm of trade. The port of Boston reopened in March 1776 with the evacuation of the British, but by that time British cruisers made even the coasting trade precarious. Throughout the war some vessels succeeded in reaching France, Spain, the Netherlands, and their island possessions in the West Indies. But as early as the fall of 1775, York reported it had lost half of its oceangoing vessels, and Falmouth lost thirteen merchant vessels all at once when the British burned the town in October of that year. At the end of the war, Falmouth merchants owned only three-quarters of one ship, half a brig, and several small coasters and fishing boats. Spokesmen for Frenchman's Bay complained that in the fall of 1777 all of their coasting vessels had been taken by the enemy. Even small boats scuttling along the bays and inlets were liable to seizure as the settlers at Pleasant River sadly related.[1]

The British post at Bagaduce made a bad situation worse. By 1780 the enemy had seized 80 to 90 percent of the vessels owned in Lincoln County. The selectmen of Pownalborough lamented that "our Vessels are taken, and our Trade wholly destroyed by the Enemy, so that we have but one Coasting Vessel now belonging to this poor Town." Those who still possessed merchant vessels had slight chance of getting them out to sea because enemy men-of-war "snaps up most all the vessels that offers to Pass."[2] Equally dim were any prospects that ships might come to relieve Maine from other places and take away lumber in exchange for cash or provisions.

The Massachusetts government extended a degree of economic relief to certain individuals and less directly to beleaguered coastal communities by permitting a limited and temporary trade with the enemy. It was customary for the General Court to permit refugees and merchants to return to enemy-held territory to settle family and business matters. Francis Shaw, Jr., of Gouldsborough and merchant Richard Codman of Falmouth traveled to Nova Scotia to collect debts, and James Noble Shannon of Machias went there to pay them. Even Abiel Wood, a merchant from Pownalborough with a most dubious reputation for loyalty to the American cause, obtained a permit to transact business in Halifax where his business partner resided.[3] The General Court also welcomed Nova Scotians who performed valuable services to the American cause, such as transporting escaped prisoners home to Massachusetts. Invariably, the grateful government allowed these "enemy" vessels to return under safe-conduct, loaded with provisions. At times, state authorities even permitted the export of food to compensate "known friends of America" in Nova Scotia who were victims of raids by American privateers. In addition, the General Court allowed Nova Scotian merchants to travel to Massachusetts to sue in its courts privateersmen from the state who disregarded legal restraints on their activities.[4]

Inevitably, this licensed traffic with the enemy merged into a flourishing illegal trade. One enterprising merchant obtained a permit to remove his family and possessions from Nova Scotia to Massachusetts. Although he made numerous voyages with "personal effects," his family was still in Nova Scotia three years later. Authorities in Cape Elizabeth seized a vessel supposedly carrying personal property from Nova Scotia when they discovered the license referred to a different vessel sailing under a different master.[5] James Littlefield, master of the sloop *Elizabeth*, also converted a temporary pass into a means of carrying on a regular trade with Nova Scotia. He enjoyed further protection from the fact that his vessel was jointly owned by a merchant in Boston and another in Windsor, Nova Scotia, who provided the *Elizabeth* with a dual set of papers. The subterfuge succeeded until one time when the British navy halted the vessel and retrieved the entire set of American papers, which had failed to sink when thrown overboard. Thanks to Littlefield's powerful connections, a mishap such as that was only a temporary embarrassment, whether it came at the hands of British or American authorities.[6]

Nathan Jones of Gouldsborough discovered a way of trading with the British at Bagaduce by arranging for the "capture" of his loaded vessel. He would then travel to Bagaduce with a permit to ransom his vessel — and to pocket the profits from the sale of its cargo. A loyalist there wryly observed such people coming and going from the mainland every day. "A droll war indeed," he stated. "They come in take the oath and out."[7] A variation of this theme occurred at Machias where a Nova Scotian schooner was brought in as a prize. The master later explained that, instead of turning his vessel over to the admiralty court, local authorities permitted him to ransom his own vessel by purchasing a cargo of lumber. He finally managed to raise the necessary funds, quite literally by selling the shirt from his own back, the buckles from the shoes of a fellow officer, and even the sea stores from the vessel itself.[8] Luckily, it is only a short distance to Nova Scotia.

The flourishing contraband trade disturbed both British and American authorities. Nova Scotia's lieutenant governor grumbled that it was carried on like fair trade in London and added, "I have found all manner of Goods brought here from the old Country constantly purchas'd and sent to the Rebellious Colonies." A similar sentiment prevailed on the American side. Major General Peleg Wadsworth complained about the small craft constantly passing between Maine and Nova Scotia, producing "old permits from [the General] Court, which somewhat embarrasses me." In the vicinity of Bagaduce, the situation was even worse. Wadsworth noted that, despite martial law, "clandestine Traders" continued their activity, pretending to be captured by the British and then getting released to repeat their "treasonable practices." The Cumberland County Court of General Sessions substantiated Wadsworth's complaints in observing the frequency with which people traveled to and from Bagaduce "without leave of any proper authority within this Commonwealth[,] Some with Permits from persons who have no right to grant them to ransom Vessels that have been taken from them—some to trade with the Enemy—and others with an Express design of working for them."[9]

Licensed trade with the enemy annoyed even American privateersmen. All too often, seizures that appeared to be legitimate prizes turned out to be protected by passes from the General Court. One angry privateersman declared to his pass-carrying prize, "By God, you have all got Protections of the Court, and you are all Concerned together."[10] With that he dumped the cargo over the side, expelled the crew, and sailed away with the vessel.

The most inveterate opponent of the "Toleration & Permission given so liberally for people to settle their Business and Remove their Effects from Nova Scotia" was John Allan. He protested that it had "Terminated in an open Trade," and if the General Court continued to wink at the practice, Allan warned, the "Horrors of War will be Endless."[11] Allan had a dual purpose in trying to cut off traffic with the enemy. First, it was impossible for him to dissuade the Indians from trading with the British as long as the Americans did. Furthermore, travelers passing between the lines could easily provide the British with information about the inadequate defenses of Machias, thereby encouraging a British attack. To break up the illegal activities among the traders, Allan arrested several of them and sent to the General Court incriminating information about others. However, his chief antagonists, James Littlefield and Stephen Jones from Machias, Nathan Jones and Francis Shaw, Jr., of Gouldsborough, and William Nickells of Narraguagus all managed to frustrate efforts to stop their trade with the enemy. Allan was more successful in persuading the General Court to tighten its procedures in permitting trade. In 1780 and again in 1782 the state voided all existing passes, requiring merchants to petition anew for trading licenses under more stringent regulations.[12] However, Allan's continuous complaints indicate that the reforms had little practical effect.

Allan expected that his vigorous enforcement of trade regulations would bring down "the Vengeance of the Commercial part of the Eastward upon me." Repeatedly, he accused the "Trading & Leading men" of secretly organizing the lumber trade with the British, of spreading fear and defeatism among the "Commonality," and of trying to undermine his authority. He also seemed to imply that the militia's constitutional scruples against constructing and garrisoning fortifications at Machias arose from intrigue by men whose chief interests were not those of America—the merchants. "The Farming & Common people are as Zealous in the Cause & Determind to Oppose as ever," he wrote, "But those who were Call'd the Leading Man have Turned to Another Object, & Pursue the Paths of the Bane of America ... Makeing Self the Predominant, By which the people in General Knows not which way to Turn or how to Act."[13] In this condemnation of the selfish individualism of merchants, Allan voiced the traditional hostility toward a profession which, driven by the profit motive, appeared to put the welfare of the community and even the nation behind its own.

The merchants had their own spokesman in Nathan Jones. He undoubtedly had much to do with the preparation of a testimonial that appeared in his behalf before the General Court when it investigated his loyalty in 1778. Although the document concerns Jones in particular, it provides an eloquent defense for all who made a living by trade and on whom the welfare of entire communities depended during a time of economic and political chaos. At the outset of the Revolution, Jones's testimonials emphasized that he was engaged in provisioning a large number of people downeast in exchange for their lumber, which he sold. The war brought all this to an end. "And no doubt Coln. Jones with others whose plans were wholly disconcerted[,] all previlidges [sic] cut off[,] a large Family to maintain, and his [financial] Interest in the hands of persons Active to have their debts cancelled[,] surrounded with Enemies ready to take every advantage of the frailties of human Nature ... was greatly frustrated and might possibly drop words unguarded and inconsiderately."

Jones's defense acknowledged that, though he was not blameless, he had aided the American cause by provisioning troops and needy civilians and by serving on the local Committee of Correspondence, Inspection, and Safety. Nevertheless, mobs seized several of his vessels, used them for private gain, and confiscated their cargoes. Who would not complain? Even "Job's patience was nearly exhausted, David cried out under his afflictions, and Sampson was contented to perish in the ruins of the house to be Avenged on the Philistines for his eyes." Surely, then, the General Court could pardon Nathan Jones for an occasional intemperate word or an ill-considered act.[14] And it did. To John Allan's disgust, Jones returned to Gouldsborough a free man, where he resumed "Makeing Self the Predominant" and, not incidentally, helping the downeast communities to survive the war.

Men like Nathan Jones and his merchant colleagues were not hostile to the Revolution, but they had to survive at a time when their normal commercial activities were either cut off or semilegal at best. They were not loyalists, but neither were they committed to a revolutionary struggle for ideals and institutions that destroyed their own fortunes and those of communities depending on them for support. Significantly, Shaw, Jones, and Nickells were prominent in the neutrality movement of 1781, an obvious, if short-term, solution to their own predicament and that of the region as well. But to those like John Allan or other leaders at Machias who, for whatever reasons, were committed to the Revolution, men like Nathan Jones and his fellow merchants were little better than outright loyalists—or Tories, as they were contemptuously called.

II

The destruction of Maine's commerce created a serious food shortage, which no amount of illicit trade could alleviate. Maine depended on its exports for the food it consumed; without trade, famine loomed. As soon as the war began, from Maine the cry went up to the Provincial Congress, "Give us Bread." A petition from the Penobscot area begged Congress to "Compassionate the Case of this Infant Settlement as we are not got to the years of Tillage and raising our own Bread and Clothing." Machias was the most vocal of all in presenting its plight. In May 1775 its petition to the Provincial Congress depicted a dismal situation: a lack of food, mills standing idle, laborers unemployed, an absence of trading vessels, and no hinterland on which to depend. "To you, therefore, honored gentlemen, we humbly apply for relief. You are our last, our only resource.... Pardon our importunity! We cannot take a denial, for, under God, you are all our dependence, and if you neglect us we are ruined. Save, Dr. Sirs, one of your most flourishing settlements from famine & all its horrors."[15]

The pastor at Machias, the Reverend James Lyon, grimly described his living conditions: "my bread is Indian procured with great difficulty, my drink water, my meat moose, & my clothing rags." In the spring of 1778, an Indian agent on the Penobscot reported that he had borrowed corn from the inhabitants to feed the Indians but lacked the means of resupplying those from whom he had borrowed. A year later the situation had not improved, for two vessels loaded with provisions had fallen to the enemy. Frenchman's Bay in 1777 begged leave "to throo our Selves on the marsie of this Honrable Cort for some mony or provishon to Support us throo the winter."[16]

From Deer Isle, Pleasant River, Chandler's River, and Narraguagus the pleas for assistance poured in to the Massachusetts government in ever-increasing numbers.[17] What made the situation yet more alarming, wrote the town of Bristol, was "the reflection that the same want is General from the River of Kennebeck to the most Eastward part of this Province."[18] Throughout the entire war, the memorials and petitions depicted the most distressing conditions in a veritable litany of woe: the collapse of trade, rotting piles of unsold lumber, sawmills silent, men out of work, and families going hungry.

The veracity of these complaints might well be suspect since they were designed to obtain some form of government assistance. Repeatedly, however, private journals, letters, and newspaper accounts verify the grim conditions the petitioners describe. On numerous occasions, the Reverend Thomas Smith of Falmouth recorded in his journal the scarcity of food and the fear of famine. For Parson Jacob Bailey in Pownalborough, famine was stark reality; he described hollow-eyed children and adults, destitute of provisions of any kind, starved into skeletons, digging for clams along the coast.[19] Anxiety over the lack of provisions back home was a frequent theme in the correspondence between a Continental soldier and his mother in Falmouth. A soldier from York expressed his concern about the loss of so many vessels to the enemy and the stagnation this would cause in the town's economy. A resident of the upper Kennebec recalled that during the war "We only breathed & did not live, for weeks many families did not eat, a mouthful of bread."[20] Self-interested the petitions may have been, yet they appear to give an all-too-accurate picture of the time.

Fishing might have alleviated the want to some extent, but fishing boats were as vulnerable as any other kind of vessel. From the shore, townsmen of York watched helplessly while a British privateer took several of their coasting and fishing craft, and Jonathan Sayward noted that "our fishery is greatly distrest and like to be Broke up by the king's vessels & Privateers."[21] If it were too dangerous to go to sea fishing, perhaps the fish could be enticed closer to shore. Several interior towns of Cumberland County petitioned the General Court to require the owners of dams on the Presumpscot River to open fish runs so that people in the interior might benefit from the fishing. Since the cod followed the small fish inshore, the petitioners argued, land-bound inhabitants would benefit, for "our Fishing Craft by Reason of Brittish Cruisers are in these years confined to narrow Limits." From Bristol, Newcastle, and Thomaston came further reports substantiating the collapse of the fishing business.[22]

With commerce and fishing badly disrupted by the enemy, a logical alternative would be to expand agriculture and grow what Maine had imported formerly. There was no lack of effort to increase food production; yet Maine still could not supply its own needs. In addition, in many sections of Maine poor weather conditions hampered production. Eastern Maine experienced a severe drought during the fall harvest of 1774, which helped to account for the scarcity of grain in 1775. Southwestern Maine enjoyed a flourishing year in 1777, but the next brought more drought. "People fear a famine," wrote the Reverend Thomas Smith in 1778. "The Indian corn curls and is like to come to nothing, and there is no prospect of any potatoes nor turnips, . . . Lord have Mercy upon us."[23] Timely rainfall prevented famine, but scarcities persisted. A severe winter struck in 1778–1779, and several people froze to death; bread in Falmouth was scarce and "monstrous dear." But then came January and February of 1780, the most extreme winter experienced for generations. Casco Bay and Penobscot Bay froze over as far as the eye could see. The intense cold and then four feet of snow halted all movement. With spring and summer came another period of drought — and forest fires so extensive that all over New England smoke and windblown ash turned the sun blood red, literally transforming the day of

May 19 into apocalyptic night.[24] Such weather simply did not permit an expansion of agricultural production sufficient to relieve the need for food that suddenly developed with the Revolution and the ruin of the region's commerce.

A scarcity of labor created yet another hindrance to expanded agricultural output. The war drew men from the hayfield to the battlefield, for both were warm-weather activities. As a petition from Machias pointed out, the need to guard against enemy attacks in the summer prevented "our Carrying on our farming business it being much neglected in its proper season occation'd by the peoples being on duty[.] . . . The same calamity to a degree has hapned to the Inhabitants in the other Settlements upon the Shoare who has been Repeatedly called upon duty, particularly in the midst of hay time & harvest & has reduc'd them to many difficultys for the Nessessarys of life this winter."[25]

The disruption in the normal source of labor may explain why some individuals, like John Schaffers of Waldoboro, petitioned to hire several "Hessian," or German, prisoners of war as "servants." The wording of Schaffers's application to the General Court suggests that the practice was not unusual and that he was not alone in making the request. Prisoners, if they consented, received "reasonable wages" and subsistence from their employers and thereby relieved the government of their support. Hessian prisoners might have come from the British army under Burgoyne, German units from which had suffered a sharp defeat at Bennington in August 1777. Two months later the entire British army surrendered at Saratoga, confronting American authorities with the problem of how to cope with so many prisoners. Several years later, several companies of German mercenaries served with the British forces at Castine, and a few might have been captured there or deserted later on.[26] In any case, they would merge easily into Waldoboro's German population, and since they were not liable to the military draft or militia duty, they would constitute a valuable form of assistance for those who could pay and feed them.

Another unorthodox solution to the labor problem occurred in Scarborough where a resident returned from Boston in 1777 with the rumor that the General Court had declared all Negro slaves to be free. He promptly hired one of the town's "freed" slaves as a laborer, and the owner had to appeal for redress to the General Court when he discovered the rumor to be false.[27]

III

Drafts of men for military service constituted the most devastating drain on labor that had been employed in raising food at home. "Now for want of labourers lays common Fences Rotten down and a very considerable part of what was once the most valuable lands is intirely dormant," declared a petition from Cape Elizabeth, which sought a reduction in its quota for the army. The General Court assigned each Massachusetts town on the basis of its polls a quota of men to be supplied for military duty with the state, such as manning the defenses at Machias, Camden, and Falmouth, and for service with the Continental Army. Tours of duty varied between three and twelve months for state service and up to three years, or the duration of the war, for the Continental Army. In the initial enthusiasm of the patriotic cause, voluntary enlistments more than met the demand. In 1775 Brunswick sent off one-third of its able-bodied men, and in 1777 Falmouth surpassed its assigned quota.[28] But the burden became more onerous as the war continued. At the request of the Massachusetts council, John Lewis, muster master for Cumberland County, submitted a report showing that as of February 3, 1778, on an average, over 18 percent of adult males per town in Cumberland County were serving in the Continental Army; in the case of Raymondtown, the figure was 30 percent.[29] These figures did not include those in privateering, in the navy, or in state service, and although the report is limited to thirteen towns in one county, it is probably representative for the other two counties in Maine.

To meet quotas in such numbers, towns either had to conscript men out of the local militia or find volunteers. Drafting recruits from the militia soon proved to be too democratic for comfort, and town leaders found it more desirable to fill their quotas through volunteers, using bounties for inducements as patriotism waned. It was an expensive alternative, for bounties rose ever higher as money depreciated and recruits grew more scarce. Eventually, towns simply ran out of men and money. In 1780 Jonathan Sayward noted that in York "Men are not to be had to go into the army. They have more and more an aversion to it than ever." A year later, Scarborough voted a blank check to a town committee to hire men for the army for whatever time they would go, six months, a year, or three years. Arundel offered those who would enlist for three years or the duration 100 acres of land or three pounds per month in addition to military pay, and Vassalborough promised 500 paper dollars per man. Then, in 1781, Pownalborough failed to find recruits for military service on any terms, and Vassalborough simply stopped trying.[30] The sources of manpower, like sources of money, were drying up. Towns were running out of idealists and men poverty-stricken enough to be attracted by the military bounties.

The race for recruits heightened rivalry between towns as wealthier communities tried to hire away men from poorer ones. New Gloucester, Harpswell, and Brunswick complained about the loss of their men to other towns. The newness and poverty of Coxhall and Massabeeseck subjected their young men to tempting bounties offered by their richer neighbors. Fryeburg demanded that the General Court grant it credit for three of its men who enlisted for towns in New Hampshire and one more who was claimed by Cambridge. A single three-year recruit became the object of a legal action between Gorham and Topsfield, both of which claimed credit for him.[31]

The desperate search for recruits brought unexpected benefits to some of Maine's slaves. Several won their freedom by enlisting, once Massachusetts in 1777 overcame the traditional reluctance to arming blacks. Jonathan Sayward's slave, Prince, enlisted without his owner's permission, and, perhaps because Sayward was a Tory, authorities accepted him. Possibly to forestall a similar loss, Sayward sold Cato, another slave, his freedom for $275. Like Prince, Cato signed up as a three-year recruit, probably committing his wages to pay the costs of emancipation. In Falmouth, Parson Smith enlisted his slave, Romeo, in the army for three years, giving him his liberty in exchange for half of his wages as a soldier. A similar arrangement seems to have existed between a slave, Lonnon Rhode, and his owner in Windham. London Atus, the slave of the Reverend James Lyon of Machias, enlisted in the state forces defending the area and later went to sea aboard a privateer. With his share from his prize money, he was able to purchase his freedom and settle in Machias as a free man.[32] In general, the recruitment of blacks was an indication of increasing desperation on the part of owners, on the part of towns seeking recruits, and by the military, which could no longer afford to exclude Negroes from the ranks.

Responding to the difficulties in raising troops, the General Court in 1781 introduced a new procedure for towns that were deficient in meeting their quotas. It authorized town assessors to divide their towns into the number of "classes," or groups of taxpayers, equal to the number of recruits the town had failed to raise. Each class, therefore, was responsible for producing one soldier or submitting to a fine set at 25 percent above the value of the average bounty.[33] The class method of raising troops spread the responsibility more broadly through society than under the old system when it was simply the obligation of a town committee. The General Court thought so highly of the new procedure that a year later it extended classing to all towns, not just the delinquent ones. By this time, however, the war was obviously winding down, and many towns failed to comply. Among those that did was Berwick where, with certain sardonic humor, authorities constituted one class entirely of "Quaquers," who were now personally responsible for raising military recruits despite their religious scruples to the contrary.[34]

Regardless of the means, conscription was seldom popular with those who had to pay the bills or with those who, for whatever reason, had to endure the distance, discipline, threat of disease and death that accompanied military life. Those who paid the bounties and the taxes could protest through petitions and memorials to the General Court; unwilling soldiers often protested with their feet, deserting from the army and strenuously resisting efforts to recapture them. Opposition to military service never reached the massive proportions of the Bagaduce campaign where enlistments fell short by one-third, yet a continuous stream of individuals testified to the unpopularity of military service. It was not difficult for recruits to desert on the march to Boston or while waiting there in barracks that were unguarded and "in a ruinous situation."[35] Deserters often returned home, hid in the woods, and, with popular support, resisted arrest. One was reported in the vicinity of Fryeburg, and several more were around Pownalborough where Timothy Langdon, an attorney for the state, had the difficult task of apprehending them. When Langdon and the sheriff tried to arrest a deserter aboard a vessel in the river, the master warned them that if they came aboard "there would be a dust kicked up," and even the sailors gave three cheers and "Defied us to come on board."[36] Langdon prudently decided against pressing the issue and let the vessel sail unmolested.

Even when apprehended, deserters could be difficult to hold. One persistent fellow, who had already deserted once, fled from authorities as they marched him back to Boston to rejoin the army. It took three men to recapture him; consequently, Langdon decided to return him to Boston by sea and so put him in irons aboard a vessel. The vessel's master, however, took pity on the prisoner and removed the chains, whereupon the fugitive immediately escaped by leaping overboard and swimming his way to freedom. One unusual recruit was discovered to be a deserter from a prior enlistment after he had been arrested for theft. He escaped prosecution on both counts by agreeing to reenlist in the army as a new recruit—provided he surrender his enlistment bounty to compensate the person whose property he stole. The plaintiff was the very justice of the peace before whom the prisoner was arraigned and who initiated this novel arrangement.[37]

Probably no one faced greater difficulties than the dependents whom soldiers left behind. Modern scholars, such as John Shy, James K. Martin, and Mark E. Lender, have indicated that as the war progressed recruits increasingly came from the lower economic levels, and since their pay was low and often in arrears, their dependents back home suffered and often had to rely on public charity—when available.[38] From Falmouth, the widowed mother of William Bayley, a Continental soldier, wrote to her son that two of his brothers had gone to sea on privateers and a third was on a merchant vessel to the West Indies—leaving her without support. "I woul'd in form you," she wrote plaintively, "that the farm Lays common as all my Sons is gon away. I should be glad if you wold come Home or Write to me the Reasons of your not Coming so that I may know what to depend upon." But when his enlistment expired, William did not come home; lacking shoes and money for the journey, he simply reenlisted. The only help William could offer his mother, in addition to an occasional five dollars from his military pay, usually in arrears, was the advice that she sell what she could spare and "Trust in god who is the Husband of the widow and the Father of the Fatherless and is able to Provide for all who trust in Him."[39]

The wife and family of Dennis Lines, a Continental soldier from Pownalborough, experienced hardships yet more severe. A poor Irish Catholic immigrant, Lines enlisted in the service leaving behind a wife and ten children occupying a wretched log house with no foundation, no chimney or window glass. Two of the oldest boys, about sixteen and seventeen, followed their father's example; they escaped their environment by enlisting in the Continental Army for three years or the duration of the war. The three oldest daughters, unmarried, went "into familys for a living," which left five young children at home with their mother substituting on what little could be spared from a soldier's pay. The death of Dennis Lines in the Battle of New York reduced his widow and family to total destitution. In response to her pleas for charity, the town selectmen declared they had none to grant, and so the unfortunate woman, the widow of a soldier and the mother of two more, appealed to the General Court: "I am in the utmost Distress for every comfort of Life, both for Vettels, and cloaths, . . . and without some Speedy helpe & Releaf, my Children & I must Die."[40]

Another soldier's wife and her six children in Newcastle were "drove to the greatest extremity" by the selectmen's refusal to extend aid. Under pressure, the local authorities grudgingly sold the woman a bushel of corn at an exorbitant price, prompting her solicitor to observe, "in short the soldiers wifes in the eastern country suffer so much that should it be known in the army I should not wonder if all who have left families here should desert."[41]

Not all towns were as tightfisted with their public charity as Newcastle and Pownalborough. During the war, Harpswell was able to provide relief and even the services of a physician to its poor from public taxation. Boothbay established supply stations to distribute food and wood to the town's needy. Nonetheless, the poor had to pay for what they received or else offer to the town as security whatever property they owned or, if they had none, their labor.[42] Even where public charity existed for the needy, town authorities, conscious of the need to keep taxes low, granted relief with reluctance and only in extreme cases. Many towns, especially those in the interior, were too poverty-stricken to offer even that.

In addition to military requirements for manpower, there were other war-induced demographic changes straining Maine's resources. These shifts of population were not as obvious as conscription, yet their effects were far-reaching. Eastern Maine, and particularly Machias, became home for Nova Scotian refugees who sympathized with the American Revolution. Although some, such as Jonathan Eddy, John Allan, and Lewis Delesdernier, entered government service, and the Reverend Seth Noble and Dr. William Chaloner probably resumed their respective professions, the two dozen Nova Scotians who had supported Eddy's ill-fated invasion and retreated with him to Machias had to rely on public charity. Eventually, families joined their men in the new location. After the war, Eddy compiled a list of over sixty refugees, most of whom settled in Maine and thereby constituted a heavy drain on an already dislocated economy.[43]

Indians were the largest single group to descend upon Machias. At John Allan's urging, many of the Malecites from the Saint John River settled near Machias in 1777 and were soon joined by shifting numbers of their relatives from the Passamaquoddy region and by some of the more westerly Penobscots. From time to time their numbers swelled to 500 men, women, and children.[44] Although the Continental Congress assumed the expense of supporting the Indians around Machias, actual supplies, when they arrived at all, came through the Massachusetts government. When they failed, Allan had to draw on scanty local resources. A similar situation prevailed on the Penobscot River where the "domestic" Indians within the borders of Massachusetts were supported at state expense. Regardless of who ultimately paid the bills, the burden on local resources was the same. When supplies ran out at the truck house, the local population had to provide. Even when provisions were available, the Indians more than once plundered outlying settlements of their livestock, aware that American authorities would not dare to retaliate for fear of driving the Indians to the British.[45]

Unexpected movements of population affected all of Maine, not just the region around Machias. Comparative population statistics for Maine's three counties are incomplete, especially for Lincoln County, but overall, the number of polls, or white males over sixteen years old, indicates that between 1778 and 1781, when the war was most intense, York County grew at a mere 3 percent, Cumberland at 11 percent, and Lincoln at only 4 percent. Within the District there was considerable movement away from the coast and the threat of enemy attack. Victims of the fire at Falmouth had to be sheltered in neighboring towns. Settlers on the Isles of Shoals dismantled their houses and rafted them over to the mainland to be reassembled in less exposed locations. Many inhabitants to coastal towns, such as those within reach of the British from Nova Scotia or Bagaduce, sought inland sanctuaries. Carpenter Sylvanus Scott of Machias lost his dwelling, barn, livestock, tools of trade, and all his worldly possessions in the British raid of August 1777, leaving him, his wife, and ten children in utmost distress. When Machias authorities laid aside his petition for charity, he resorted to the Massachusetts General Court for financial assistance to "Remove his Family to some part of this State where they shall be more secure from the ravages of the Enemy."[46]

Many of the coastal communities remained virtually static or even lost population. To be sure, York gained forty polls, and even exposed Thomaston added ten; but North Yarmouth increased by only six, and Townshend experienced no growth whatsoever. Wells lost 20 polls, Falmouth 113, Cape Elizabeth declined by 110, and Georgetown by 131. By contrast, few interior towns failed to experience marked growth. In York County, the towns of Lebanon, Sanford, and Coxhall (Lyman), and in Cumberland, towns such as Gorham, Windham, New Gloucester, Pearsontown (Standish), Gray, and Royalsborough (Durham), all confirm this pattern of rapid interior growth; so too do Medumcook, Hallowell, Vassalborough, and Winthrop in Lincoln County.[47] Rising population figures can be deceptive, however. Refugees like Sylvanus Scott and new arrivals to interior communities seldom contributed quickly to the productive capacity of their new locations; indeed, they were more likely to pose a drain on local resources. Sporadic promises by the Massachusetts legislature to reimburse communities for unusual expenses incurred in provisioning refugees and new arrivals could not alleviate the unexpected demands on the locality. Throughout the entire war and throughout the extent of Maine, displaced persons created an unforeseen strain on a food supply limited by depleted manpower, a severe climate, and a dislocated commerce.

IV

Nothing tested commitment and loyalty to the cause quite so severely as price inflation and war taxation. When the war began, the Provincial Congress of Massachusetts was reluctant to test its popularity by taxing for revenue, and so it resorted instead to printing paper money to pay for soldiers, supplies, and the services of government. In the next two years, Massachusetts issued paper worth a face value of over a million and a half dollars. Other states as well as the Continental Congress employed the same expedient. Since their money circulated in Massachusetts too, the value of paper money depreciated to about one-third of its face value by 1777, despite penalties for passing it at a discount. As money depreciated, prices rose correspondingly. The Reverend Thomas Smith in 1778 bemoaned the fact that "creditors don't receive an eighth part of their old debts, nor ministers of their salaries." By the spring of the next year, he remarked that a barrel of flour was worth more than his entire yearly salary; firewood sold for fifty-two dollars a cord, corn fetched thirty-five dollars a bushel, and coffee went for three dollars a pound.[48]

Inevitably, price inflation and currency depreciation increased social tensions between those who seemed to benefit and those who were hurt by the cheap money, the rising prices, and the scarcities. In Pownalborough, Francis Rittal was arrested, fined, and narrowly escaped being mobbed when it became known he had surplus grain to sell for cash but none for paper. North Yarmouth's Committee of Safety reported, "there are Loud Complaints in this Town with Regard to Persons asking exorbitant Prices for the Necessities of Life." An anonymous "Gentleman at Falmouth" echoed these sentiments by blaming the rising price of sugar on rich merchants whom he accused of exporting sugar to Spain and profiting from the artificial scarcity in America. The "Gentleman" doubted if such profiteers were really "Friends to the Country" and hoped the government would prevent "oppression from our own Grandees as well as those of England." One "grandee" who knew how to turn the present situation to his own advantage was old Jedediah Preble, one of Falmouth's most prominent Whig merchants, member of the town's Committee of Correspondence, and a former brigadier general of militia. Preble had borrowed from a fellow merchant 700 pounds sterling and then in 1778 repaid the debt in depreciated paper. The crusty old merchant silenced his creditor's protests by threatening to expose him as an enemy to his country for refusing to accept its paper currency at face value.[49]

Without much success, the government sought to control inflation, first by legislating prices and wages and then by manipulating the currency. In 1776 and again three years later, the General Court passed laws requiring paper money to be accepted at full value. In addition, the legislature established maximum prices for a detailed list of articles and services in an Act to Prevent Monopoly and Oppression. Most Maine towns faithfully posted the official prices and appointed committees to enforce them, but another attempt at price fixing two years later testified to the failure of the policy.[50]

Uncontrollable inflation led both state government and the Continental Congress to undertake a deflationary monetary policy to stabilize currency and prices. A monetary situation that had initially favored debtors and agricultural regions now gradually shifted to the advantage of creditors and commercial interests. In 1777 Massachusetts began to replace its bills of credit with interest-bearing notes. Three years later, the Continental Congress began to withdraw its bills of credit at a ratio of 40:1, substituting a "new emission" money backed by taxes and paying an annual rate of interest. Such action moderated but did not end currency deflation. Early in 1781 Massachusetts withdrew the legal tender provisions for new emission money, and for practical purposes the state reverted to a hard money currency. Specie provided by privateers and by French forces stationed in New England made such a policy possible.[51] No longer could debtors such as Jedediah Preble force their creditors to take payment in cheap or inflated currency for debts contracted when money was more valuable. Now, after 1781, creditors could refuse to accept paper currency and could demand payment in scarce specie for debts contracted when money was more plentiful. Henry Hodge, for example, sold a sloop to Andrew and Robert Reed of Boothbay for 160 pounds in 1777 when paper money was relatively cheap and legal tender. Hodge demanded payment in 1781, by which time he was able to require his debtors pay the full price in specie. In Falmouth Parson Smith observed the altered circumstances in a terse comment: "There is only hard money passing, and little of that." The changing currency situation made it difficult for debtors everywhere, but the rural and interior regions were at a particular disadvantage. What little specie there was tended to gravitate to the commercial centers, creating inequities in the distribution of money for payment of debts and taxes. Serious enough during the war, this situation would become a major grievance in the immediate postwar era.[52]

The state's tax policies aggravated the situation by discriminating against rural and inland areas in general by overvaluing polls and estates in proportion to personal property, such as money at loan, securities, investments in shipping.[53] The District of Maine was at a particular disadvantage since the war had disrupted its economy and many of its lands were new and unproductive. At first there were few complaints about taxes, for the government financed the war by issuing paper. After several years of war, however, protests echoed from one end of the District to the other in the face of increasing taxes and a waning money supply. Jeremiah Powell, president of the Massachusetts council and a resident of North Yarmouth, wrote in sympathy to a correspondent back home, "You certainly have too great a proportion [of taxes] considering the state of the War in that part of the country and the difficulties you labor Under by the great loss of the Lumber trade & yr Vessels etc. Something must be done for you, and that soon I think, what will become of us that has our Interest there I know not, the Taxes will eat up all the real Estate, if not more equally laid on the State."[54]

Towns responded to their plight with increasingly desperate appeals for relief and eventually, in some cases, an outright refusal to raise any funds at all. In 1780 Fryeburg's taxes totaled 44,585 pounds (paper), excluding the "hard money" tax of 108 pounds that was levied that year. This latter assessment was particularly burdensome, and the sheriff of York County complained it was impossible to raise cash even by selling the property of delinquent taxpayers, so lacking in specie were the inhabitants. A petition from Boothbay near the end of the war described the town as "nothing but the wreck of a Community in ruins," without men of military age, without money, and without the necessities of life. For the General Court to make further demands upon the townspeople, declared the petition, would appear "like insulting their miseries" and "will effectually drive them to a State of desperation." In February, March, and May of 1781, the town of Newcastle deliberately voted against raising any funds, and in October the town, "having their communications cut off (in great Measure) by Sea from the western Part of the Cuntry and consequently their trade[,] Voted not to Assess any State Taxes at present," in the hope that the General Court "will not exact it from us." By the time the war came to an end, a number of Maine towns unilaterally refused any longer to raise money. In the words of a petition from Coxhall, "we are allmost Ready to Cry out under the burden of our taxes as the Children of Israel did in Egypt when they were Required to make Brick without Straw."[55]

Confusion over the collection of taxes added to the burden of paying them. Town officials charged with collecting taxes found their jobs immensely complicated by the varying sorts of paper currency: state and Continental, new emission and old, bills of credit and treasury notes, not to mention rapidly changing rates of depreciation and exchange. After 1778 the collection of taxes became yet more complex when the state began to levy taxes in kind, such as shoes, stockings, shirts, blankets, and beef, with each item assigned a monetary value. Then, in 1780, came the "hard money tax." Since the General Court levied new taxes before the previous ones had been received, the collectors were sometimes hard put to know which taxes they were collecting and in what sort of currency. Several officials discovered they had continued accepting old emission currency for taxes after the General Court had declared it "dead." Gorham's collector complained that some people had received news of the new emission before he did and readily paid him their taxes in money they knew to be worthless.[56] This was no light matter; collectors were personally responsible for the sums assigned to them, and it is no wonder that more than one town collector literally fled from the obligations and penalties of the job.

Town treasurers also found that their old informal methods of record keeping were frequently inadequate for complex wartime transactions. A committee examining the financial records for Pownalborough declared it could find no accounts for some years, and for other years only records of money collected but none for money paid. The committee placed the responsibility on faulty bookkeeping or, more precisely, on the lack of a "proper Book" in which to record the town accounts. Vassalborough had a similar problem, but possibly sensing that fiscal confusion had certain advantages, the town meeting refused to authorize the purchase of an accounting book. The finances for the town of Boothbay were so hopelessly tangled that it took a special committee from the General Court to straighten them out.[57] By the end of the war, a number of towns, especially those in the interior and downeast, had simply given up any pretense of keeping an accurate record of taxes and expenses they could not pay or even understand. In short, they simply threw themselves on the mercy of the state.

One indication of the seriousness of the conditions downeast comes from the Massachusetts government itself, which repeatedly sought ways to alleviate the hardship. The General Court, composed of delegates from towns all of which were anxious to escape the burdens of war, nonetheless responded sympathetically to pleas from Maine. The government could not protect the region militarily, but it did the next best thing in offering economic assistance. From the beginning of the war down to 1779, Massachusetts provided aid through shipments of food or sometimes through funds with which to purchase provisions. In response to appeals from Machias, Bristol, and Frenchman's Bay, the General Court persuaded the Continental Congress and the state of Connecticut to relax embargoes on the export of food so that provisions could be shipped downeast. The Provincial Congress also appealed to coastal towns in Massachusetts to supply food to Machias and other

Maine communities, promising credit for any discrepancy between the cost of supplies and the value of lumber, the only article Maine could offer in exchange. Occasionally the government offered aid directly, as when it voted to supply Deer Isle and Frenchman's Bay with pork, beef, molasses, and rice and to take their lumber in payment. To Deer Isle, the state also sent fishing gear to replace what had been lost and worn out. For Lincoln County, the government reduced taxes by one-third during the first year of the war, and during the next year the General Court made two separate loans totaling 1,600 pounds to be apportioned among the towns of Lincoln County for provisions and military stores.[58]

By 1780 Massachusetts, impoverished by the Bagaduce campaign, could no longer afford to provision the downeast communities, and even if it could, the British cruisers from Bagaduce made it impractical. The General Court, however, continued its assistance by repeatedly suspending or abating its continuous demands for men and money. Thomaston obtained a 50 percent reduction in its taxes over a six-month period because its supplies were cut off and it was incapable of raising the money. The towns of Washington, Fryeburg, and Cape Elizabeth secured reductions and tax credits because they had been overvalued; Brunswick and Harpswell received an extension of the time limit for producing their quotas of beef for the Continental Army. Not always was the General Court so sympathetic; it sharply rejected Berwick's petition for a suspension of legal action against delinquent towns until the state paid its own debts to them. More often than not, however, the state was convinced of the need for relief and sought to provide it, as in 1782 when it enacted a stay of execution for nonpayment of taxes against collectors in Maine's three counties because the people there were "greatly embarrass'd in their lumber trade, & have suffer'd greatly in their fishery, in consequence of the Enemy's retaining possession of Penobscot."[59]

V

With taxes in money and men almost unbearable, commerce destroyed, and food scarce, it is little wonder that support for the Revolution was less than universal—and even less so after 1779 with the British at Bagaduce. Yet the differences that distinguish loyalists from revolutionaries were often obscure—and remain so 200 years later. Merchant

Nathan Jones of Gouldsborough and the contentious contestants of Castine, Joseph Young and John Bakeman, along with many others, illustrate the ambiguities surrounding political labels even to contemporaries who felt obligated to distinguish friend from enemy. Ever since the war, historians have tried to analyze the nature of the Revolution by the number and character of those who supported and those who opposed independence.

Questions of number and motivation are easier to pose than to answer owing to the elusiveness of definitions and statistics, and because of differences in regional and local situations. Historian Paul Smith has offered the least controversial estimate in the number of loyalists when he suggests that out of a total white population in America during the years of the Revolution, estimated at 2,590,000, loyalists constituted 20 percent, or about a half-million people. At a 1:4 ratio of adult males to total population, loyalist men numbered about 128,000 out of 647,500 white American males.[60] At best this is a rule of thumb and is unreliable for particular areas and communities where countless variables at different times influenced political affiliation, such as the presence or absence of armed forces belonging to one side or the other, the opportunity for stability and order, the role of local leaders, and family interests.[61]

Two modern scholars, Richard I. Hunt, Jr., and Robert Sloan, who have examined loyalism in Maine, decline even to estimate the size of Maine's loyalist population, preferring instead to emphasize profile and motivation.[62] A third historian, Edward Cass, analyzes loyalism as one phenomenon in the social history of a single Maine town, Pownalborough. Cass identifies thirty active or suspected loyalists, who constitute barely 10 percent of the adult males in the town.[63] In doing so, Cass revises a list of fifty-six loyalists drawn up in 1779 by Anglican parson Jacob Bailey, himself a loyalist and former resident of the town. Cass excluded those on Bailey's list who remained in good standing in the town throughout the war and who served in the government or the military, or who might not have been legal residents. The contrast between the two lists reveals the problems of identification and definition on even the local level. However, if Bailey's enumeration was accurate at the time he drew it up in 1779, it is noteworthy, though not definitive, that in Pownalborough, as well in several other Kennebec River towns Bailey mentions, loyalists numbered 15 to 20 percent of the adult white males, a ratio comparable to that estimated by Paul Smith for the national level.[64]

On the issues of loyalist motivation and profile, probably the most useful general conclusions are those of William Nelson, who links loyalty to the crown with British officials, ideological conservatives, and self-conscious ethnic and religious minorities recently arrived in America.[65] Such characteristics overlap and blend, for all had much to fear from a radical change in the political status quo and therefore looked to Britain for support. For them it was difficult to accept the Whig contention that ministry, Parliament, and king were all engaged in a devious plot to deprive Americans of their fundamental rights or that the only alternatives were independence and a republic. Regional historians Hunt, Sloan, and also Cass tend to agree with Nelson. Cass states that in Pownalborough "typical" loyalists were of English or European birth, of a faith other than Congregationalist, and most likely not farmers. Those loyalists who went to New Ireland, writes Sloan, demonstrate that loyalism represented a cross-section of American society and that, although economics and Whig persecution were obvious and powerful motives, the most important—and unrecorded—cause of loyalism was loyalism itself. Sloan concludes his study by quoting Maine loyalist David Hatfield who, when asked after the war why he had willingly suffered in a losing cause, stated proudly, with tears in his eyes, "For my loyalty, sir!"[66]

In different ways, the two towns of Falmouth and Pownalborough illustrate the complex nature of loyalism in Maine. In contrast to the ideal New England town, these two had a poorly developed sense of community and experienced profound internal divisions. Falmouth, with a prewar population of 3,000, was Maine's metropolis, its chief customs port, and had enjoyed the status of shire town for Cumberland County since 1760. It had attracted a government bureaucracy and a merchant elite, many of whom supported an Anglican church that had only recently split from the local Congregational establishment.[67]

In Falmouth the founding of the Anglican church, the arrival of many government officials, and many merchants who remained loyal all coincided with the decade of tensions preceding the outbreak of the Revolution. Merchant Thomas Coulson, who caused the uproar in 1775 by challenging the Continental Association and thereby inspired Samuel Thompson to "invade" the town, arrived in Falmouth from England only in 1770. He married a local woman, carried her back to England, and returned to Falmouth in 1774 to build the ship that caused all the commotion.[68] Thomas Oxnard and his brother Edward, both merchants, arrived in Falmouth "some years prior to the Revolution." Edward distinguished himself as a lay leader in the new Anglican community. In 1769 Thomas had the misfortune to accept the post of deputy commissioner of customs for Falmouth. From Scotland, Robert Pagan came to Falmouth in 1769 to represent a Scottish mercantile house and enjoyed rapid success as a storekeeper, lumber merchant, and shipbuilder.[69] He married the daughter of Jeremiah Pote, one of Falmouth's leading merchants whose longtime residence in Falmouth belies the pattern of newcomer. Yet Pote, an ideological conservative, had publicly recorded his disapproval of resistance to Parliament in 1774.[70] Pote was connected by marriage to another leading Tory family, the Wyers, who had come to Falmouth from Charlestown in Massachusetts. David Wyer and his son Thomas assumed positions in the customs office, and David, Jr., became a leading lawyer of conservative principles and Pote's son-in-law.[71]

Several government officials arrived in Falmouth just in time to inherit the growing violence against British regulations and those who enforced them. Joseph Domet, deputy comptroller of customs in 1772 replaced Arthur Savage, who had survived in that position since 1765. George Lyde, the collector, received his commission in 1770. William Tyng moved his mercantile business to Falmouth in 1767 when he secured a commission as sheriff for Cumberland County.[72] Even the Reverend John Wiswall, rector of the new Saint Paul's Anglican Church, received his ordination in 1764, much to the consternation of Congregationalists as far away as New York. The fact that Wiswall had once been an ordained Congregational minister made him a particularly worthy object of suspicion to good Whigs.[73]

In general, Falmouth's loyalists tended to be an Anglican minority in a sea of distrustful Congregationalists, newly arrived British officials taking up their posts in the face of growing hostility and a group of prominent merchants still too new to be integrated closely into the community. For them the rising political temper and its increasingly radical implications were matters of deep concern, especially when the personification of that radicalism was none other than Samuel Thompson. The behavior of Thompson and his militiamen in defying established social and political authority seemed only a prelude to what might follow if imperial authority crumbled. Many of Falmouth's loyalists fled the town to the vessels of Coulson and Mowat in the harbor. The few who remained departed after the town was burned later that fall.[74] Many would reappear at Bagaduce once the British consolidated their position in that place.

Pownalborough, the shire town for Lincoln County, was as sharply divided as Falmouth. The town was relatively new, and its prewar population of 1,424 was highly heterogeneous. Ethnic and religious differences between Anglican priest Jacob Bailey and his polyglot congregation of Huguenots, Lutherans, Dutch Reformed Calvinists, and Catholics, on the one hand, and the majority of Massachusetts Congregationalists, on the other, long antedated imperial tensions. However, these distinctions soon took on political overtones as the Whig-Tory polarization among leaders of the Kennebec Company in Boston reached into its town on the Kennebec River. Dr. Silvester Gardiner's High Church Toryism tainted his client, the Reverend Jacob Bailey, and his parishioners.[75] Aligned against Bailey were his former college mates, brothers Charles and William Cushing, Jonathan Bowman, and their clients. The Cushings and Bowman utilized important family, business, and Whig political connections to optimum advantage in their rise to prominence. Charles Cushing became sheriff of Lincoln County as well as colonel of militia; brother William occupied the posts of judge of the peace and of the quorum and judge of probate until 1772 when he returned to Massachusetts to assume a seat on the superior court. Jonathan Bowman, blessed with being a cousin to John Hancock, gorged an almost insatiable appetite for office with those of collector of the excise, register of probate, register of deeds, clerk of the Courts of Sessions and of Common Pleas, justice of the peace, and finally judge of probate when William Cushing relinquished that position.[76] In contrast to Falmouth, officialdom in Pownalborough was avowedly Whig, Congregationalist, and included the local elite. The Anglican community, alien in religion, in cultural background, and at the lower end of the social-economic ladder, could hope for protection only from the British government.

Until the British established their post at Bagaduce, royal authority around Pownalborough was virtually nonexistent, and loyalists had to accept a submissive role. Yet, as long as they remained quiet, they were generally safe from abuse — except for Samuel Thompson's riotous visit in 1774. Indeed, most of Pownalborough's suspected Tories were relatively safe even when they did not remain quiet. Merchant Abiel Wood flaunted his contempt for the authority of the Continental Congress, yet remained at large with a following dubbed a "party" by one annoyed Whig who accused him of actively aiding the enemy. Jonathan Williamson, another outspoken critic of resistance to British authority, suffered the loss of his position as selectman but little more.[77] A special court declared William Gardiner, son of Dr. Silvester Gardiner, "inimically disposed to this & the other United States of America" and packed him off to Boston as "dangerous to the publick Peace & Safety." There, instead of imprisoning him, the authorities dismissed the charges against him, and Gardiner returned home "to enjoy the privileges of a free subject, any judgment of a Special Court of Sessions in the County of Lincoln notwithstanding."[78]

The person in Pownalborough who bore the brunt of Whig pressure to conform was the leader of the Anglican-loyalist community, the Reverend Jacob Bailey. Persistently, but without success, Jonathan Bowman and Charles Cushing directed a movement to force Bailey into breaking his oath to the crown and acknowledging the new source of political authority, the Continental Congress. Mobs broke windows in his home, mutilated his livestock, and threatened him with bodily harm. His tormentors erected a liberty pole outside the very door of his church, defaced the prayer books, and disrupted the services — all to no avail.

The most serious confrontation occurred over Bailey's adamant refusal to read the Declaration of Independence from his pulpit and his insistence on praying for the king.[79] In the fall of 1776, the Committee of Safety, which included both Bowman and Cushing, examined Bailey on the charge of preaching sedition. Bailey ably defended himself by seizing on the issue of political responsibility in a revolutionary era. His argument is the epitome of ideological conservatism based on the inviolability of his oath as subject and priest. Bailey claimed that, having sworn loyalty to his king, he could not read the Declaration of Independence "without offering great Violence to my Conscience and incurring ... the Guilt of Perjury." Should he commit that sin, Bailey pointed out, any succeeding oath, even to the Continental Congress, would be worthless, a mere political convenience without moral obligation.[80]

Bailey's conservative argument, the inviolability of an oath of allegiance as a binding obligation before God, challenged the Whig emphasis on a conditional political authority based on a contractual relationship between ruler and ruled. Sheriff Cushing squirmed uneasily as he forwarded to the General Court at Boston records of Bailey's examination, noting that the priest had insisted that "nothing could Absolve the Subject from their Allegiance let the King['s] Conduct [be] as bad as possible — If this Doctrine be Just," Cushing asked, "what becomes of all the old officers in the United States that have taken the Oaths of Allegiance! Have they all incurred the guilt of Perjury[?]" As sheriff of Lincoln County, originally holding a royal commission, Cushing might well balk at Bailey's conclusion. As though to reassure himself, he went on to declare, "but those Sentiments are erroneous & False & have no foundation in truth & righteousness and I dare Say the Gen'l Court will take care that such Doctrines should not prevail — If they are Connived at the States will be Saped [*sic*] in their Foundation."[81]

Bailey remained at liberty, doggedly praying for the king and carrying on his religious duties as best he could despite threats, interference, and deepening poverty. Finally, in 1778, Massachusetts granted him and his family permission to leave for Nova Scotia where he secured a new parish.[82] From there Bailey corresponded with his former parishioners in Pownalborough and with friends and acquaintances wherever the war scattered them. Typical of most Tory exiles, he boosted his own spirits, as well as theirs, with the conviction that the rebel cause *must* fail, that virtue and right would ultimately triumph with a terrible vengeance in the restoration of British rule. Repeatedly, he cautioned his correspondents never to be seen in arms against the king and to persevere in their loyalism. A better day was sure to come, since human history, he explained, was a constant tension between the forces of good and of evil. Republican government could not endure; it is "destitute of stability, borders upon confusion and anarchy and is distinguished by perpetual struggles between different leaders fired with ambition or glowing with revenge, who alternately labor to subvert each other and agree in nothing but abusing and oppressing their fellow citizens." Soon conditions must improve; virtue will emerge from obscurity and advance "with a cheerful and modest air, insinuating herself into the affections of the succeeding generation."[83]

Just when this millennium would occur was impossible to foretell, but perhaps the establishment of New Ireland was the beginning. Bailey resisted the invitation to seek a parish there, but some of his former congregation from Pownalborough joined loyalists from Falmouth and others from the Boston area in an attempt to make a new beginning at Bagaduce and to hasten the second coming of imperial authority. Dr. John Calef, John Nutting, and Nathan Phillips were all from the Boston environs and immediately accepted official roles at Bagaduce under British rule. From Falmouth came Jeremiah Pote via Nova Scotia and New York; his son-in-law, Robert Pagan, with his two brothers; Thomas Wyer and his elderly father; and Thomas Oxnard. Representing the Pownalborough region were John Jones, Nathaniel Gardiner, and John Carleton, parishioners of Jacob Bailey who, like many from Falmouth, had suffered humiliation and abuse from Samuel Thompson.[84]

At Bagaduce there was also a group of local Tories who had welcomed the British from the very start: prominent landowners like Joseph and John Perkins and their in-law, Mark Hatch; Mathew Lymeburner, a miller; Thomas and Henry Goldthwait, whose father had commanded old Fort Pownal at the mouth of the Penobscot until the rebels burned it in 1775. Altogether, some 200 families expressed their confidence in British protection and their faith in the British constitution to settle or remain in the new royal province.[85]

The costs of loyalty to the crown, heavy as they might be for the heads of families, could be yet more so for their dependents. "The men lead, the wives and children must Tread the hard road," wrote the wife of one Tory family that remained at Bagaduce and later followed the flag to Nova Scotia.[86] That "hard road" entailed more than a move to a friendlier location. If the family head left precipitously to escape a mobbing or arrest, it meant poverty, loneliness, anxiety, and discrimination for those who remained. One can only imagine life for Lydia Twycross; she remained in Pownalborough with her children for most of the war before finding the opportunity to go to England where her husband served in the British navy.[87] Very probably, her treatment at the hands of vengeful Whigs compared with that of John Allan's wife, left behind in Nova Scotia with five children when her husband fled to Machias. According to Allan, the wives of rebel sympathizers were often harassed in the streets and commonly called "Damn'd Rebel Bitches & Whores."[88] Years could pass before families rejoined their menfolk in British-held territory. Loyalist refugees Thomas Wyer and William Tyng, having fled Falmouth at the beginning of the war, could not return for their families until four years later in 1779, aboard a flag-of-truce vessel with prisoners for exchange. More subtle was Martha Oxnard. She demurely played on the connubial compassion of governor and council in a petition to visit her husband, Thomas, at Bagaduce. In noting that for more than four years she "had been deprived of his Society and he of the tender Pledges of their mutual Affection," she offered a plea they could not refuse. Martha Oxnard not only visited her husband for several months but with her three children eventually joined him there permanently. For Elizabeth Stevens, it was a matter of pure survival that she be allowed to join her brother in British-held New York—for she was destitute.[89]

Loyalist wives who remained behind often had the formidable task of trying to defend family property. State law provided that estates of absentee owners who had gone over to the British were liable to seizure and eventual confiscation, and there was no lack of Whigs who would profit from Tory loss. Rebecca Callahan, whose husband was serving aboard a British privateer, was not intimidated by laws, lawyers, and local committees. She defended her family property so vigorously she narrowly escaped going to jail. By the time she left Pownalborough to join her husband in Nova Scotia, however, she managed to salvage only 70 pounds in personal property out of an estate worth over 1,000 pounds.[90] Another Tory refugee, John Carleton, left behind nine children and a wife when he fled Pownalborough for Bagaduce, eventually to die leading a privateering raid. His wife discovered that the chief claimants for the family estate were her own brother and a family "friend."[91]

Mere suspicion of loyalism could bring disaster to the family of a suspect. Clark Linneken, an impoverished fisherman-farmer in Boothbay, left behind a sickly wife and four children when he was jailed on charges of aiding the British. Although the General Court heeded his pleas and ordered his release, local officials refused to comply until Linneken paid legal and maintenance fees totaling 400 pounds. It took yet another resolve from the General Court to get the unfortunate fellow out of jail and back to his suffering family, which had been left to fend for itself during the coldest months of the year. John Allan, the protector of Machias, urged the arrest of not only a certain John Anderson, whose loyalty Allan suspected, but also Anderson's wife, on the grounds that "she is an Intriguing Person & has been always remarkable for Intelligence."[92] Reason enough to imprison such a woman. Another Tory wife ran a similar risk in her gritty, satiric defiance of Colonel Samuel Thompson for harassing her husband, a simple tailor from Topsham:

> There was a man in our town,
> I'll tell you his condition,
> He sold his oxen and his corn,
> And bought him a Commission.
>
> A Commission thus he did obtain,
> But soon he got a coward's name,
> At Bunker ne'er shewed he his face,
> Nor there his country's fame disgrace.
>
> He came one day to the tailor's gate,
> And there his men assemble,
> Who with his needles and his shears,
> He made them all to tremble.
>
> Some said they were all brave men,
> Some said that they could fight, sir,
> But all of them were made to run,
> And that by the tailor's wife, sir.[93]

Equally suspect as sharp-tongued and "Intriguing" women were members of the religious sect called the Society of Friends, or Quakers. Long before trouble erupted between Britain and its colonies, Quakerism had spread to Maine, and it expanded rapidly during the war. By 1768 Falmouth Quakers were sufficiently numerous as to require a meetinghouse forty by thirty-two feet square with a gallery. The 1777 census listed sixty-four Quakers in Falmouth who, by 1781, were forced to enlarge their meetinghouse once again. In many towns Quakers actively resisted public taxation for support of the established church, and by the onset of the Revolution they had won exemption from religious taxation in Windham and Falmouth.[94] Nevertheless, the Falmouth Quakers continued to provoke excitement and controversy by attending Congregational church services, where they ostentatiously refused to remove their hats and tried to proselytize the congregation.[95]

During the war, they aroused even more resentment by refusing to pay war taxes, to serve in the military, and to swear loyalty oaths at a time when military service and oaths were especially important in identifying friends and enemies. Quaker Nathaniel Palmer of Bristol defended his principles in a moving address to the authorities. "If I shuld affairm to Be true to war, he wrote, "then I Shuld make Shipwrack of faith and good Conchance: for Love is that New Command, which I hope I have Received Ritten on my heart — that I Shuld Love one another: But your Law my friends Strikes at the very Scorce and foundation of all my Religeon which is my Life." Palmer declared his abhorrence of both Whigs and Tories as "Revengeful Parties distroying Eaich other," yet he affirmed he was a "true and Reall friend to my Cuntry" and would never assist its enemies. The local authorities and even the General Court remained unconvinced, and Palmer was sentenced to jail. He escaped his fate, however, by fleeing to the British at Bagaduce — thereby appearing to justify Whig skepticism of Quaker pretensions.[96]

Palmer's case was unique only in his flight. Quakers frequently gave witness to their principles by accepting the consequences of their pacificism: social ostracism, distraint of property, even jail. Although Quakers had a reputation among their critics for personally profiting from their own pacifism, they disciplined their own members who attended auctions where confiscated Quaker goods were sold.[97] But to American authorities, intent on separating friend from foe, the religious neutralism of scrupulous Quakers was dangerous to the Revolution; Quakers and loyalists appeared to be one and the same — subversives within American society.

Before the Revolution Maine had been divided between the rich and the poor, between geographical sections, competing towns, and personal rivalries. The war accentuated these divisions and created new issues over taxes and trade, men and money, while creating new lethal divisions between Whigs and Tories in a war which — in Maine at least — appeared to have no end and no victors. Meanwhile, both rebels and loyalists sought to create institutions that embodied their political ideals and justified the pain and suffering of the war.

SIX

State Making and State Breaking

Amid the turmoil of war, Massachusetts, like all the other states, had to construct a new government to replace the revolutionary committees, conventions, and congresses that had filled the void when royal government collapsed. After rejecting one proposed constitution, Massachusetts adopted a second one that, still republican in form and philosophy, left in control the same men of property and education who had directed the Revolution from the start. Cautious, even conservative, as was the Massachusetts republican experiment, it presented a sharp contrast to the constitution the British government drew up for the loyalists who settled the proposed province of New Ireland. The two frames of government, created at almost the same time, reveal how polarized political thought had become in a few short years. Yet neither constitution achieved its intended stability and permanence. British plans for New Ireland collapsed, and not until the war was over and the loyalists moved one more time could they enjoy civil government under the crown. The republican constitution for the Commonwealth of Massachusetts appeared to be more stable; yet, well before the war ended, ominous signs of discontent hinted at the turbulence that would erupt once the euphoria of victory died away.

I

At the opening of the Revolution, it had been easy enough for Americans to denounce the British monarchy as corrupt and despotic and to recommend a republic as an alternative peculiarly suited to American virtue and freedom. It was another thing to create such a government from the ground up. Virtually everyone agreed on a republic as the appropriate form of state government, but unanimity disappeared over every other issue, such as when to create the new government, how to do it, and the form it should take.

Massachusetts' revolutionary leaders, preoccupied by the war, were slow to take up so controversial an issue as creating a government. At the suggestion of the Continental Congress in 1775, the Massachusetts Provincial Congress simply perpetuated as a temporary expedient a modified version of the old royal charter of 1691. The towns elected their deputies as before to the General Court, which then elected the council. In place of the royal governor, the General Court selected a Committee of Safety as a sort of plural executive. After the Declaration of Independence, however, the old charter was an anachronism and of dubious legality since it originally derived from royal authority rather than popular sovereignty.

The impetus for change came from that part of Massachusetts least touched by the war, Worcester, Hampshire, and Berkshire counties. Separation from Britain had stimulated agitation in these western counties for a government more expressive of the popular will than the old royal charter. Maine towns, geographically isolated and engrossed in the immediacy of war, took no part in the movement for constitutional reform. It was the westerners, through newspapers, petitions, conventions, and even by disrupting courts of law, who prodded the rest of the state into action.[1] Finally, in the spring of 1777, the General Court authorized towns throughout Massachusetts to instruct their delegates to the General Court to draft a state constitution, which would then be returned to the towns for ratification. Despite the expanded responsibilities of the General Court, Maine's thirty-seven incorporated towns showed no more inclination to participate than in previous — or later — years. The seventeen towns in Lincoln County, as usual, sent no representatives at all. Seven of the eleven towns in York County sent delegates, but since one of those delegates represented two towns, York had only six representatives present. Cumberland County's nine towns also sent six delegates; but Falmouth exercised its privilege of sending two, so only five towns actually were represented.[2]

The frame of government that the legislature referred to the towns in 1778 was a compromise between the popular, localist aspirations of the western, rural, and underdeveloped regions of Massachusetts and the more elitist, cosmopolitan interests of the commercial regions of the state, especially on the east coast. Rural and less commercial towns generally favored a high degree of local autonomy, a broad franchise, a unicameral legislature, and, if any governor at all, one with little independent power. Commercial towns, with greater social and economic diversity, advocated a more activist government representing property as well as population in a bicameral legislature and, in addition, a powerful governor.[3] To satisfy both positions, the General Court proposed a weak governor presiding over a bicameral legislature. The franchise for the lower house included all taxpaying adult white males, but for the upper house and chief executive, voters had to possess property worth 60 pounds. Officeholders had to own property ranging from 1,000 pounds for the governor to 200 pounds for representatives.[4]

In the spring of 1778, Massachusetts towns overwhelmingly rejected this proposal. For many reasons, the compromise alienated more people than it satisfied, but in addition there was a growing appreciation of a profound political truth that drafting a constitution was too important a task for a mere legislature. Only a convention elected by the people especially for that purpose and for no other could legitimately express the sovereign will of the people in declaring fundamental law.[5]

Maine towns generally concurred with the repudiation of the new constitution, and their responses reflect the political climate of the District just before the trauma of the British occupation of Bagaduce. Overall, the returns from Maine suggest that interest in a new frame of government progressed in an easterly direction, from York to Lincoln County. Twenty-five Maine communities, out of a total of at least seventy-seven towns and plantations in the District, voted on the 1778 constitution: five in York County, eight in Cumberland, and twelve in Lincoln. The percentage of voter participation, based on polls, also increased in the same direction: York County averaged 25 percent, Cumberland 27 percent, and Lincoln 29 percent. A desire for constitutional change followed the same pattern. Not a single town in York County favored the new frame of government. Two towns in Cumberland County voted approval, and four in Lincoln County indicated the proposed plan to be more acceptable than the status quo.[6] Nonetheless, a large majority of Lincoln County towns opposed the constitution, and two of them, Georgetown and Boothbay, expressed their opposition in the most vibrant democratic terms. Among the several reasons Georgetown rejected the new frame of government was that it restricted the franchise to adult taxpayers who were white — and so "a Man being born in Afraca, India, or ancient American or even being much Sun burnt deprived him of having a Vote for Representative."[7] Boothbay did not vote on the constitution as a whole but disapproved of both the method by which it was drawn up and the timing, for the "hurry of war" hindered serious consideration of so important a document. In addition, the sixty-three townspeople present unanimously opposed any institution, such as a senate or council, that limited or "corrected" the more numerous representatives of the people. This lively concern with popular liberties convinced the town to propose eliminating the positions of governor and lieutenant governor. The offices were expensive and "needless in a free State" and, what is worse, potentially "dangerous to the liberties of the People."[8]

Only Gorham, in Cumberland County, matched Boothbay's ardent localism, or distrust of centralized power. This was in the following year, when many towns were instructing their delegates elected to a special convention to draft yet another new constitution. Gorham had been one of the foremost towns in advocating resistance to British imperial measures, a particular critic of Falmouth, which the Gorham militia had sacked as it was being burned by the British. Its rural localism reappeared in 1779 when it advocated a unicameral legislature on the model of the ancient Hebrews or the uncorrupted Roman senate. Like Boothbay, Gorham declared that governors and a council were "not only unnessessary [sic] but inconvenient, and perhaps dangerous," and the town expressed the hope "they will never exist in this state."[9]

Maine's response to the 1778 constitution contains considerable variation. The results reveal, however, that although Maine generally opposed the new plan a desire for constitutional change progressed in a northern and easterly direction, probably because the residents hoped a new government would deal more effectively with the region's isolation and vulnerability. The three most radical protests in Maine against the 1778 constitution had come from two coastal towns in Lincoln County and from one inland town in Cumberland. The data, admittedly scanty, suggest that already an affinity of political interest was evolving between Maine's eastern and interior towns and the westernmost counties of Massachusetts that had initiated the movement for change a year before. The similarities would become more evident and potentially dangerous in the postwar era. For the time being, however, such developments were obscured by the succession of crises brought on by the British occupation of Bagaduce in the spring of 1779.

Problems of defense, internal disorder, and wavering loyalties—American and Indian—and even the hard winter of 1780 preoccupied much of Maine when the newly elected state constitutional convention met in September 1779. Delegates to this new convention were elected by the incorporated towns throughout the state in the same manner as to the General Court. More than ever, the easternmost counties sensed their own isolation and inferiority. By 1780 Maine had fifty-two incorporated towns, only eight of which sent delegates, and they played an insignificant role among the 293 listed in the convention journal.[10] More intimidating than the numbers, which fluctuated widely, was the presence of well-known, articulate leaders, such as the two Adamses, James Bowdoin, Thomas Hancock, Theophilus Parsons, Benjamin Lincoln, and Caleb Strong. Four Maine delegates, two from York County and one each from Cumberland and Lincoln, were named to the convention's drafting committee, as were representatives from every county in the state. All thirty members of the drafting committee deferred to the influence of its most prestigious member, John Adams, who essentially drafted the entire document himself.[11]

Clearly, the state's revolutionary elite dominated the proceedings, and the new frame of government represented the outlook of the eastern commercial centers from which most of them came. In contrast to the legislative supremacy that characterized the earlier constitution, this new one rested squarely on the Old Whig concept of a separation of powers. A powerful governor possessed the authority to make appointments and veto legislation that came for his approval from a bicameral legislature, the upper house of which represented property and the lower house population. An independent judiciary, appointed by the governor and his council, held office during good behavior. Property qualifications for holding elective office were comparable to those in the rejected plan of 1778, but this time the franchise was limited to adult white males having an annual income of three pounds or owning property worth sixty pounds. The document's long preamble guaranteed traditional fundamental rights, including life, liberty, and property, as well as the freedom of religion for all Christians. At the same time, to help preserve and encourage the virtue necessary to maintain a republic, the constitution, in a highly controversial article, empowered the legislature to support divine worship by public taxation.[12] Although the constitution did not mention any specific religious denomination by name, it appears the framers intended to perpetuate the dominant role of the Congregational church.

Popular reaction to the new constitution was complex and difficult to evaluate. Some towns voted on the entire document; others did so article by article but failed to come to an overall conclusion. Still others approved the document conditional to acceptance of proposed amendments. Significantly, the constitutional convention had the task of interpreting these complex responses. Samuel Eliot Morison pointed out over seventy years ago that in tabulating the returns the convention made sure its labors were not in vain. To obtain the necessary two-thirds majority needed to ratify each article of the constitution, the convention counted as favorable all responses that were not explicit rejections and even included as supporting original articles any votes passed in favor of an amendment or for a substitution to the original. Concludes Morison, the convention "deliberately juggled the returns" to secure an efficient government with the appearance of popular support at a time of political, financial, and military crisis.[13] Not by accident, the eastern commercial elite managed to preserve their positions of power in the government, in the judiciary, and in the church as well—more strongly entrenched than ever now with the appearance of popular will. On June 16, 1780, the convention declared the new constitution ratified; on October 25 the new frame of government became effective.[14]

The real significance in the adoption of the Massachusetts constitution of 1780 for historian Stephen Patterson—and for Samuel Eliot Morison too—lies in the success of eastern representatives, by fair means and foul, in frustrating the aspirations of westerners to bring government closer to the people.[15] As to why Maine towns would support such a constitution, Patterson suggests the persuasive influence exercised in the District by the commercial interests of eastern Massachusetts.[16] Such conceivably might have been the case at the convention, but it is difficult to see how these commercial influences could have manipulated deliberations in so many town meetings without a clearly visible political organization, of which there is no evidence whatsoever.

More important in shaping opinion in Maine were conditions in Maine itself that encouraged the acceptance of a strong, effective government. The British now occupied Bagaduce; Lincoln County was under martial law, internally divided and subject to devastating raids that virtually severed the county from the rest of the state. Cumberland County too was unsettled, nervously expecting a British descent upon Falmouth. The inhabitants of York County shared these apprehensions about conditions to the east, convinced that the British intended as their next target the town of York or Portsmouth. Certainly these immediate realities and fears rather than some nebulous eastern commercial influence shaped the response of Maine towns to the constitution of 1780.

In the face of these new concerns, the voting patterns established in 1778 disintegrated in 1780. Fewer towns and fewer people took an interest in the second constitution, and the results show little coherent regional pattern except that, as before, Lincoln County again recorded the highest average participation and York the lowest. A total of only sixteen Maine towns actually voted on the document, seven in York County, four in Cumberland, and five in Lincoln. Several additional towns implied their opposition by simply refusing to vote. Voter participation also declined from an average of 26 percent in 1778 to about 14 percent in 1780.[17] The "radicals" of 1778 were either silent, like Boothbay, or, like Gorham and Georgetown, converts to the more centralized second frame of government.[18] New spokesmen replaced them in 1780, with the most extreme reaction coming from two towns in York County, Buxton and Wells.

These two towns had been unexceptional in 1778. Two years later, however, they alone reflected the dichotomy between the coastal commercial centers and the smaller, precarious communities of the interior and downeast. Buxton, a relatively new town with an assessed tax of 5,320 pounds in 1780, was located just southwest of Gorham.[19] With an intense localism similar to that exhibited earlier by Gorham and Boothbay in 1778, Buxton declared the "Legislative Authority ought not consist of More branches thane [sic] One House" because "the Inconveniency arising in Negatives and Long debates, is more Injurious to the Good People of this State than Errors which may be Committed without Such Separate branches."[20]

In contrast to Buxton's unicameralism, the coastal town of Wells (1780 assessed tax of 15,400 pounds) went to the opposite extreme. Wells approved the second constitution, but in doing so it urged an amendment that would grant the governor an absolute veto over all acts of the legislature. Claiming to speak on behalf of small towns distant from the capital and seldom represented, Wells feared unchecked legislative tyranny far more than executive tyranny. Wells idealized the chief executive as "the Sole Representative of the whole Commonwealth; The Center of Union to all the several parts and members of the political Body; . . . the Guardian of the Constitution and of the Rights and Interests of the whole State." In the governor, every town "shall always have a Representative," one in whom any town, regardless of size, "may claim an equal Interest . . . with the other parts of the State."[21] By idealizing the governor, by setting him above any faction and self-interest, Wells expressed its distrust of representation based on town delegates in the legislature.

These differences underscore the sectional rift in the District, which had been sporadically evident since the start of the war. The reluctance of the coastal commercial centers to escalate anti-imperial agitation into armed rebellion contrasted sharply with the bellicosity of the interior and easterly settlements. This enhanced the lingering distrust with which the smaller, undeveloped towns regarded coastal lawyers and merchants whose modern individualism clashed with the more traditional community-oriented values of the backcountry. Efforts to establish a new state constitution only accentuated these divisions. Virtually everyone believed in a representative form of government, but many interior and easterly towns envisioned a government representing the people alone through their towns in a unicameral legislature. The centers of commercial activity, however, such as York, Falmouth, North Yarmouth, and of course Wells, insisted on a government representing property as well as people in a bicameral legislature presided over by a wise and vigorous executive.

In 1780 preoccupation with the war tended to blur or mute differences in Maine over the constitution. Indeed, relatively few people became directly involved in the matter. Collectively, the combined returns emphasize that a sizable majority of Maine's electorate, 74 to 86 percent, did not care enough to participate in the voting. Distance and bad weather hindered some people from attending meetings, but others were simply too busy fishing, farming, and making a living to be bothered.[22] The return from Biddeford apologized that only ten voters turned out, but rather than despair, such apathy should "quicken to Zeal and Perseverance those who are desirous of Order, Regularity, and good

Subordination." At the bottom of the return was the exhortation, "Ten men may save the city."[23] The worsening military situation surely deterred others. The town of Boothbay, which did take part in the constitutional debate, nevertheless grumbled in 1778 that "the hurry of war did not permit that calm deliberation necessary to form a constitution for a government of perpetual duration." Another community protested that "invasions of the Enemy and the Divisions among ourselves made it improper if not dangerous at this Time to introduce a new mode of government." More frequently, responses from Maine towns reveal a characteristic sense of insecurity, a feeling that may have discouraged consideration of so weighty a matter as a constitution. No one put it so poignantly as the selectman of Blue Hill, who in 1778 forwarded his town's return with the apology, "Sur and if there is Aney thing that we have Ommetted in the Return I would have you Let us know ... for we Are so as it ware Out of the Wourld that we Dont hardley know Wither we Do Rite or Rong But we mean to Do as Well as We Can."[24]

This sense of detachment and inadequacy had deep roots in the communities downeast. About this same time, Brigadier General Peleg Wadsworth, entrusted with the defense of Maine, cogently noted that the towns of the District suffered from feelings of inferiority; being distant from Boston, ignorant of what went on there, they were "small in their own eyes."[25] Self-preservation — economic and military — was a more immediate consideration for most of Maine than the form of a state government to which few towns had ever sent representatives — but on which they were so dependent.

II

While Massachusetts struggled to discover a formula for a stable republican government, British authorities in London were similarly engaged in devising a new form of colonial government for the loyalist province of New Ireland. Like Lincoln County, it too was under martial law, but in time military rule would give way to civilian administration, and promoters of the loyalist colony pushed ahead vigorously with such plans. By 1780 John Calef, one of the primary figures in the scheme, had returned to England to join Lord George Germain, secretary of state for the colonies, and his undersecretary, William Knox, in setting up the new government. Naturally enough, leading loyalists were nominated to the chief positions. Thomas Oliver, former lieutenant governor of Massachusetts, received the commission as governor. The position would have gone to Thomas Hutchinson, the last civilian governor of the Bay Colony, had he not scoffed at the entire scheme as preposterous. Daniel Leonard, another prominent loyalist from Massachusetts, secured the post of chief justice, and Dr. Henry Caner, former rector of King's Chapel in Boston, was slated to become the first American bishop, although tactfully styled a "vicar general." Even John Calef managed to obtain one of the prizes as clerk of the council.[26]

The government in which deserving loyalists were to find employment might readily have assumed the traditional provincial form of royal governor and council appointed by the crown, with an elected assembly. This was the sort of government with which the loyalists were familiar and which the British were seeking to restore in the South.[27]

By contrast, New Ireland's civil constitution revealed an imperial preoccupation with order arising from years of frustration with powerless royal governors and provincial legislatures claiming to be miniature parliaments. The constitution's two most significant features were the absolute power of the British Parliament to legislate and to tax the settlers of New Ireland and the absence of a popularly elected assembly. Every landholder in New Ireland, on receipt of title to his property, had to take an oath recognizing the king-in-Parliament as the supreme legislature for the province. The king's attorney and solicitor general would determine which laws passed by Parliament would apply to the new province, even though the legislation might not specifically mention New Ireland. As for an elected assembly, that touchstone of English liberty, the constitution deferred its authorization until some unspecified time in the future.[28]

Yet an assembly would appear eventually, and so, "To combat the prevailing disposition of the People to Republicanism, and to balance the Democratic Power of the Assembly," the ministry approved the creation of a "distinct Middle Branch of Legislature," a provincial House of Lords, composed of members appointed by the crown for life and on whom the government would bestow various honors and titles. The constitution also provided for a privy council selected by the crown to advise the governor, whose members would also sit in the upper house to strengthen the royal prerogative in the legislature.[29]

The plan for the distribution of land in New Ireland enhanced yet further the conservative nature of the province. The king's ministers agreed that large tracts ought to be awarded to the most "Meritorious" of loyal subjects to "lay the ground of an Aristocratic Power." They, in turn, would lease parcels to tenants as in New York, "which is the only Province in which there is a Tenantry, and was the least inclined to Rebellion."[30] By means of a class of permanent tenants, a powerful landed aristocracy, and an assembly submissive to king and Parliament, British authorities planned their idealized version of provincial government in America. Perhaps it is just as well it was never put to the test of practical experience.

On August 10, 1780, the ministry passed the proposal; the next day, King George approved the document. Despite such prestigious support for the plan, opposition suddenly arose, not from the loyalists in New Ireland who would have to endure such a regime but from the king's own legal officer. The king's attorney general, Alexander Wedderburn, protested that the scheme was illegal and therefore null and void from the start. Years later, William Knox charged that Wedderburn, disappointed at his failure to obtain a peerage, blamed Lord George Germain and so killed the New Ireland proposal that Germain had sponsored.[31]

Regardless of the attorney general's personal motives, his constitutional stand was sound. Lord Germain, the king, and many others assumed that rebellion had destroyed the legal basis of government in America and in Massachusetts in particular. They saw nothing illegal in establishing a new colony on land claimed by Massachusetts under its charter of 1691. Wedderburn, however, argued that, as far as the law of England was concerned, the revolutionary forms of government were invalid, and the true, legal government of Massachusetts was still the old charter of 1691 with the alterations set forth in the Massachusetts Government Act of 1774. That the rebels in the Bay Colony had rendered the legal government inoperative did not deprive it of legality. The legal borders of Massachusetts included Maine, and since in the eyes of the law the legal foundations of the province remained unimpaired despite the fact of rebellion, England had no right to detach land from Massachusetts without due legal process.[32]

Wedderburn's adverse ruling invalidated the fundamental purpose for which the British forces had seized Bagaduce — the creation of a loyalist province. New Ireland had no legal standing to justify its existence. Nevertheless, the British government did nothing to hinder loyalists who sought to settle there and did not abandon the proposal entirely until after the war.[33] While authorities in England bickered over its constitutional basis, loyalists in America, supported by British troops, created New Ireland without a legal foundation.

Denied the advantages of civil government, the settlers of New Ireland had to make the best of military rule. Relations between the loyalist refugees and their military protectors, however, were far from cordial. Neither Brigadier General Francis McLean nor his successor, Lieutenant Colonel John Campbell, trusted the civilians under their jurisdiction. As the Reverend Jacob Bailey had observed, an oath foresworn tainted future ones. Colonel Campbell believed that, despite oaths of allegiance, none of the inhabitants was truly loyal to the crown, and indeed, he complained, they demonstrated their disloyalty by communicating with the rebels and by encouraging British soldiers to desert.[34] Sir George Collier declared, "all the Inhabitants are Rebels who take an Oath to the King to day, and another to the Congress tomorrow."[35] The military treated the civilians harshly, limiting their freedom of movement, accusing them of illegal trade with the enemy, and consequently subjecting them to military courts and draconian punishments.

In many respects, conditions under martial law were the same for the loyalists of New Ireland as for the inhabitants of Lincoln County, upon whom Massachusetts imposed martial law in 1780. Military government, American or British, invariably generated among the civilians tension and hostility over the loss of traditional rights and liberties. For the Americans, however, martial law lasted for only a short time. More significantly, the civilian government of Massachusetts continued to exist and to serve as a source of appeal and as a restraint upon the military—much to the annoyance of Brigadier General Peleg Wadsworth, who wanted a freer hand in dealing with suspects and "traitors."[36] By contrast, British military officials had no such limitations. The military provided the only government, and it was unchecked in the treatment of civilians. Two residents of Waldoboro who tried to return home after a stay at Bagaduce received 1,000 lashes each for trying to desert to the rebels; one of the victims died under the lash.[37] Seventy-year-old Shubal Williams, convicted of encouraging the desertion of a British soldier, received in punishment 500 lashes—and survived as a living testimony to British barbarity.[38] John and Joseph Perkins and Mark Hatch were somewhat more fortunate. They decided they had had enough of British administration, which they had welcomed so cordially in 1779. With their families they left New Ireland for the town of York, whence the Perkinses had come originally. York gave the refugees a decidedly cool welcome, allowing them to remain only on condition that the men demonstrate their loyalty to the American cause by joining the Continental Army as part of York's military quota. On those terms, British military rule seemed less oppressive, so back to Bagaduce they all went. The British officials, however, viewed the returnees as deserters, imprisoned the men, and commenced action to deprive them of their extensive landholdings.[39] Truly among New Ireland's worst enemies were the British themselves.

Not only did the military abuse the very residents they were sent to protect, but they failed to exploit the military potential of their position on Penobscot Bay. To be sure, the British presence did provide relief for Nova Scotia from the plundering raids by Yankee privateers. Yet the respite was brief; after about a year, the privateering raids resumed— better organized and more destructive than ever.[40] Possibly a more tangible benefit from the British occupation of Bagaduce were the masts and naval stores supplied to the British navy. Almost at once, Jeremiah Pote, Robert Pagan, and Thomas Wyer resumed their former activities as timber merchants and began erecting sawmills, cutting timber, and shipping wood and masts to the British at New York.[41]

Except for these relatively minor exceptions, the British never really exploited the advantages of their presence on the Maine coast. They failed to use their success as a means of weakening relations between the rebels and the Indians, nor did the British ever consider seriously expanding westward against Falmouth, York, and Portsmouth, even as a diversion. As the war's center of operations shifted southward to Georgia and the Carolinas, the British-loyalist enclave at Bagaduce became an isolated outpost, largely forgotten except by those condemned by the fate of war to live there as refugees or as a military garrison. Sir George Collier deprecated the place as unsuitable for either a fort or a settlement: "The Face of the whole country is as dreary as can be imagined, & the greatest Part uncleared & fit nor nothing but wild Beasts."[42] Collier, and General Francis McLean as well, urged that the outpost be abandoned in favor of a position on the Saint John River. Their recommendations had no effect on a ministry whose concerns were elsewhere, and so the isolated occupants at Bagaduce were left to make inglorious war on the enemy's fishing boats, his haystacks, his cattle, and, occasionally, the enemy himself—a forlorn testimony to the failed dream of New Ireland.

For the British government the diplomatic advantages of occupying Bagaduce proved to be as elusive as the military ones. The post on the Penobscot did not provide a viable claim to eastern Maine when the peace negotiations commenced in 1782, although this had been one of the several reasons for seizing the region in the first place. In the peace talks at Paris, British negotiator Richard Oswald had instructions from his government that he might give up British-occupied Savannah, Charleston, and New York but Penobscot was "to be alwise kept," as a buffer between Nova Scotia and the rebellious colonies of New England and as a base from which to harass New England shipping if necessary.[43] Two factors softened Britain's stance on Penobscot: the need for a quick peace in order to separate the Americans from their European allies, especially the French, and the determination of John Adams, one of the American negotiators, to see that his native state of Massachusetts did not suffer the loss of its easternmost county.

Adams came to the negotiations at Paris well prepared with a mountain of documents to dispute the British claim to territory west of the Saint Croix River.[44] Overwhelmed, British negotiators agreed to evacuate Bagaduce and to give up claims to eastern Maine. But now more than ever, the British faced the problem of compensating loyalists, since the Penobscot region would no longer provide lands and provincial offices. In exchange for surrendering claims to eastern Maine, the British accepted a face-saving proviso that the American government would recommend that the several states compensate loyalists for their confiscated property. Since the American Congress under the Articles of Confederation had no power to enforce its recommendations upon the states, where feelings against Tories ran high, no one expected concrete results in the near future.[45]

British plans for a loyalist sanctuary carved out of Maine obviously had failed, and well before the United States and Great Britain signed a preliminary peace in November 1782, many loyalist refugees began drifting into western Nova Scotia—unbidden and unwelcomed by the provincial administration, which feared their disruptive influence.[46] For many of the new residents, it was their second or third removal, yet they were determined to remain under the British constitution. In 1784 the

British government acknowledged the situation by creating out of western Nova Scotia a separate province to be called New Brunswick. At last, the long-suffering loyalist refugees had found a sanctuary and a compensation of sorts in land grants and offices in the new government. The provincial constitution for New Brunswick omitted the antirepublican, aristocratic ideology of the one designed for New Ireland. The new frame of government provided for an appointed governor and council with a representative assembly elected by the adult, white, propertyowning males who had been resident for three months in the province.[47] It was the traditional form of provincial government with which the loyalists were familiar, and they immediately resumed, in the words of one historian, a "robust political life."[48] Robust the politics may have been, yet loyalty to the crown remained a distinguishing characteristic of these refugees and former soldiers.

Even in peacetime, however, and in a new location, the loyalists of New Brunswick were not certain they had found a permanent residence. Most of those from Penobscot had moved only as far away as Passamaquoddy Bay where they established the town of Saint Andrews on the east side of what is now the Saint Croix River. For the next fifteen years, the bitter legacy of New Ireland festered on as British and Americans quarreled over whether the British settlement encroached on American soil — as John Allan, in particular, furiously insisted.[49] The dispute arose because the peace negotiators at Paris had no knowledge of the local geography and worked from an imperfect map of the area when designating the Saint Croix River as the boundary line between Maine and Nova Scotia. After the war, neither side could agree on just which of the several rivers flowing into Passamaquoddy Bay was the Saint Croix. If the American claim prevailed, the hapless loyalists of Saint Andrews would have to move yet again to enjoy the security of the British Empire. In their own behalf, the British and their loyalist allies argued that the Saint Croix was really the Schoodic River, the westernmost of the streams emptying into the bay. Tensions rose as each country insisted on the boundaries most satisfying to its national pride and self-interest. In Jay's Treaty of 1794, the two governments finally agreed to submit their differences to a joint commission, which rendered its decision in October 1798. The commission accepted the British contention that the Schoodic River was the Saint Croix, but the decision provided some satisfaction to the Americans by denying the full British claim that the westernmost tributary of the Schoodic was the main river. In a spirit of compromise, the commission declared the main course of the river to flow along its northerly branch rather than the one farther to the west.[50]

Americans grudgingly accepted the decision, but it was especially satisfying to the loyalists of Saint Andrews, who would not need to move again. Several refugee loyalists had served as the British delegation to the joint commission, and one of them, Robert Pagan, formerly of Falmouth, provided the conclusive evidence that the so-called Schoodic was indeed the Saint Croix. While other commissioners were scrutinizing documents and interviewing former peace negotiators, Pagan, with a copy of a seventeenth-century French map in his possession, engaged in some historic archaeology on a small island in the mouth of the Schoodic River.

By the standards of modern archaeology, Pagan's techniques were crude, but they were effective politically. His deposition relates that he unearthed remains of old buildings, such as bricks, mortar, and stone foundations. "In digging with a spade for a few minutes near one of these piles they turned up a metal spoon, a musket ball, a piece of earthen vessel, and a spike nail, all of which bore evidence of having laid a long time under the surface."[51] Pagan's archaeology helped to convince even the American commissioners that this had to be the site of the settlement established in the seventeenth century by the French explorer Sieur de Monts, who had named the river the Saint Croix.[52] The larger boundary issue between Maine and Canada would drag on for more than forty years, but as of 1798 the loyalist refugees of New Ireland could rest secure in their new settlement—and in a new province as well.

III

To Maine, the end of the war came in an equally tentative manner. Throughout most of the country, hostilities subsided after the surrender of Cornwallis and his army at Yorktown in mid-October 1781. In Maine, however, the fear and the fighting persisted until the bitter end. Tremors of anxiety rippled across Maine's backcountry following a raid by Canadian Indians on the town of Sudbury Canada (Bethel), in August of 1781. Taken by surprise, the widely scattered settlers offered no resistance as the Indians plundered several homes, killed and scalped two men, and took three more captive to help carry their spoils back to Canada. In the annals of Indian raids, this was a minor affair in terms of damage and loss of life. The Indians even voluntarily released two additional captives and inflicted no injury on the settlers' women and children. Even the captives made it safely to Canada where they were exchanged and eventually returned home.[53] Yet to those living on the frontier, newly conscious of their vulnerability, the raid appeared to be a prelude of worse to come. Thereafter, until the end of the war, Massachusetts felt obliged to provide the nervous towns with funds to maintain a garrison during the summer months.

The coastal towns were equally anxious, and with good reason. The defenses at Machias were "deplorable," and a convention of towns from Cumberland County, held early in 1783, expressed concern that Lincoln County might soon be unable to hold back the enemy any longer. The convention expressed its hope to the General Court that "a part of the Continental Forces may be spared to defend this northern State to which the attention of the Enemy now seems to be directed."[54] No help arrived, however, for the plight of Maine aroused little sympathy with the war virtually over. In 1782 General Washington himself discouraged the French from undertaking another attack on the British at Penobscot, the risk being simply too great for an objective so insignificant so late in the war.[55] Mainers did experience a brief moment of triumph in 1782 when an armed sloop from Massachusetts slipped into Bagaduce Harbor and under the very guns of Fort George successfully sailed off with a British privateer as a prize.[56] Yet the British continued their depredations unabated. Jonathan Sayward of York and the Reverend Thomas Smith of Falmouth each recorded in their journals for mid-March 1783 that British privateers off their respective towns were still taking their toll of what little shipping survived. "The Little Privateers," wrote Sayward, "are still taking a number of our vessels."[57]

The manner in which the British and their loyalist allies finally evacuated Bagaduce accentuated Maine's sense of isolation. Although American and British representatives signed a preliminary peace treaty on November 30, 1782, and the war officially came to an end on September 3, 1783, the last shipload of loyalists did not depart Penobscot for Nova Scotia until January 15, 1784.[58] In contrast to John Adams's dogged insistence on preserving the territorial integrity of his state, Massachusetts seemed oddly unconcerned with the British intruders. It exerted no pressure upon them to leave, and when they finally did, no state official was on hand to record the departure. Indeed, the Bay State did not even acknowledge the abandoned post until an officer arrived in the spring of 1784 to make an inventory of what little remained.[59] By that time the local residents were rapidly converting to peacetime use the bricks and timbers of the structures the British had not dismantled or burned.

The apparent failure of Massachusetts to exhibit more concern over conditions downeast arose at least in part from a preoccupation with the peace negotiations in Paris. Newspapers and diaries record the progress of news and rumors brought from Europe to Philadelphia, New York, and Boston and then disseminated through the hinterlands. Of special concern to coastal Massachusetts and Maine was the fate of the fisheries, which played so large a part in the state's economy. The Continental Congress initially had instructed its representatives in Paris to protect the right of Americans to continue fishing off Newfoundland and the Banks as they had before the war. Nevertheless, commercial groups in Boston, nervous that their interests might be compromised in the glittering, corrupt atmosphere of Paris, persuaded Falmouth to join in a resolve expressing concern over the matter. On January 7, 1783, the Falmouth town meeting resolved that the town still approved of the original principles for which they took up arms, "the security of our just and natural rights," and that now one of those rights was "the privilege of the fishery." The town then declared that the Continental Congress should instruct the American negotiators "to make the right of the United States to the fishery an indispensable article of treaty, without which a peace should not be concluded."[60]

In John Adams, Massachusetts fishing interests had a champion at the peace negotiations. He was as protective of the fisheries as he was of the state's claim to the Penobscot region, despite the willingness of his colleague, John Jay, to compromise.[61] With persistence and skill he argued on behalf of New England's God-given "right" to share in the eastern fisheries, not as a "liberty" to be allowed—or withdrawn—at the whim of the British government. This was Adams's finest moment, writes historian Richard B. Morris. "Rising to his full five feet seven inches," Adams exclaimed,

> Gentlemen, is there or can there be a clearer right? . . . When God Almighty made the Banks of Newfoundland at three hundred leagues' distance from the people of America and six hundred

leagues' distance from those of France and England, did he not give as good a right to the former as to the latter? If Heaven in the Creation gave a right, it is ours at least as much as yours. If occupation, use, and possession give a right, we have at least as much as you. If war and blood and treasure give a right, ours is as good as yours.[62]

Despite such eloquence, the Americans did have to compromise: The British conceded to the Americans the "Right to take Fish" in the Gulf of Saint Lawrence, off the Grand Banks and the Banks of Newfoundland. In turn, the American negotiators agreed to accept only the "liberty," rather than the "right," to the coastal fishery in British North American waters and the "liberty" to dry and salt their catch on the uninhabited coasts of Newfoundland, Labrador, and nearby islands.[63] Like the ill-defined boundary between Maine and New Brunswick, the equally ill-defined term "liberty" would cause international difficulties in the future, but for the time being, John Adams and his compatriots in Massachusetts and in the District of Maine could take satisfaction in the security of the fishing industry.

Despite the compromises and ambiguities, the treaty was one in which all Americans could take satisfaction. After eight years of grinding warfare, the most powerful nation in the world had been forced to acknowledge the independence of its former colonies as the United States of America with boundaries stretching from Canada to Florida and from the Atlantic to the Mississippi River. "Such an empire there is not in the world," wrote an American to a loyalist friend in exile, "with the different lands and climates to produce everything necessary for life and trade if properly managed.... In short every advantage is granted. There is nothing more or greater could be except the kingdom was given up."[64] Imprecise boundaries, ambivalent terminology, even the vague proviso for compensating loyalists, could not dampen the sense of relief and exhilaration. The Americans and British had come to terms in the preliminary treaty of November 30, 1782, but that agreement did not become binding until France, Spain, the Netherlands, and Britain agreed to the terms ending the European phase of the war. The European belligerents signed their own preliminary treaties on January 20, 1783, leading to a general armistice. On September 3, 1783, all the preliminary treaties, Anglo-American as well as European, became definitive and effective.[65] The war was over.

The Americans did not wait that long to celebrate their own astonishing success. News that Congress finally had approved the preliminary treaty on April 15, 1783, following weeks of rumors and speculation, set off a series of spontaneous festivities. Communities all the way downeast marked the occasion with sermons, salvos from cannon, the ringing of bells, toasts, bonfires, and illuminations. The residents of Falmouth did not wait for official word. At the end of March, a vessel from Boston brought word that a general peace and armistice had been signed in Paris. Then, several days later, a second vessel brought handbills circulating in Boston that proclaimed unofficially the war was over. That was official enough; Samuel Deane noted in his journal on April 4, "Our men had a mad day of rejoicing—firing cannon incessantly from morning to night." Unfortunately, one of the overcharged cannon burst, killing one of the celebrants.[66] Falmouth's spontaneous celebration—and fatality—did not detract from yet another round of festivities on May 1, after the post brought a formal proclamation from Congress announcing the end of hostilities. "Our people," reported Deane, "had a grand rejoicing day," which included the inevitable sermon, a contribution for the poor, and, as before, salutes from thirteen cannon throughout the day.[67] Other towns, such as Gorham and Scarborough, followed suit, firing off their now needless supplies of gunpowder in salutes to their independence.[68] In York, the celebration concluded with the physical destruction of the gun carriages and their wheels—"supposing we should never want them any more," grumbled Jonathan Sayward.[69]

Americans took a certain perverse delight in contemplating the anguish caused by American independence to those still loyal to the crown. The *New-Hampshire Gazette*, for example, carried two accounts guaranteed to feed the spirit of patriotism and revenge. One of the loyalist residents at Bagaduce, who had fled there "with the rest of the mercenary dependents on the Royal Breath," tried to return to his hometown of Townshend (Boothbay) on hearing of the peace. The unforgiving Whigs there, however, seized him, placed a halter around his neck and a crowbar under his crotch, and hosted him aloft to the masthead of a sloop where he dangled from eight o'clock in the evening until noon the next day. The wretched man was then taken down, put in irons, and shipped back to Bagaduce with his family, after signing a paper never to return on pain of death.[70]

The same issue of the New Hampshire paper carried yet another story centered on Penobscot. A certain Captain Charles Stewart, of the

Highland regiment stationed at Penobscot, swore when he heard news of the peace that "his eyes would never see it in print, and that his ears should never hear, [*sic*] it proclaimed." The next morning he was found in his quarters with his throat cut and a razor in his hand and three stab wounds with a dagger in his body — an example, presumably, of patriotic suicide over Britain's national degradation.[71]

The tragic fate of Captain Stewart may not have been an exaggeration, to judge from the response of Pownalborough's former Anglican preacher, Jacob Bailey, now languishing in exile in Nova Scotia. News of American independence severely shocked Bailey's sense of an orderly, righteous universe. "The moment the court of Great Britain announced the independence of America," he wrote, "it gave the strongest sanction to rebellion, treason, injustice, rapine, fraud, perjury, devastation, massacre, and every species of infernal vice and impiety. The devil and the Congress must be stupefied with astonishment at this unexpected decision in their favour." Unable to bring himself to criticize his monarch, Bailey saw George III as deceived by Parliament, betrayed by his own councillors, and bullied by factions into resigning the dignity of his office. "Thou has unhappily renounced that authority with which the creator and monarch of the universe invested thee.... Thou art now the ridicule of France, the contempt of Congress, and the scorn of every republican rascal in America."[72]

Mere prose could not adequately convey Bailey's depth of emotion; to another correspondent, he unburdened himself in verse:

> Adieu, adieu to politicks
> And all the curst infernal tricks
> Of fools and ministers who strive
> To make rebellion live and thrive,
> Who with malignant force unite
> To cherish ill, and crush what's right,
> Who bear down virtue, truth, and reason
> To build up vice, revolt, and treason,
> Who join in wicked combination
> To overthrow a mighty nation
> To expose their king in nakedness
> To the scorn of Lairs [liars] and the Congress.[73]

Americans spared little sympathy for the losers in the struggle for American independence. In the spring of 1783, celebrations of the successful end of the war and visions of a glorious future preoccupied the new nation. Yet Americans could not long ignore profound problems in their new country — disturbing legacies of the Revolution that threatened to bear out Parson Bailey's grim description of republicanism. Early in 1782, high taxes and a disrupted economy caused a series of conventions and renewed unrest in western Massachusetts. The Reverend Samuel Ely took up the crusade for reform of the state's new constitution and of its judicial system in particular. At Northampton, Ely joined a movement to prevent the judges from holding court. With club in hand, he addressed a crowd, declaring, "Come on, my brave boys, we'll go to the woodpile and get clubs enough to knock their Grey Wiggs off and send them out of the World in an Instant."[74] Such direct action, successful against the British imperial government, was intolerable to the Commonwealth of Massachusetts. State authorities arrested, convicted, and imprisoned Ely in the jail at Springfield. Ely had numerous supporters, however, who broke him out of jail, and he fled for safety to Vermont. Here too Ely's penchant for political action led to his arrest and eventual expulsion from the state. Ely came back to Massachusetts where authorities seized him and returned him to jail — this time on an island in Boston Harbor. In confinement he remained until the spring of 1783 when the state finally released him on parole because of declining health. Ely dropped from sight for the next dozen years, but the state was not rid of him so easily; in 1795 he suddenly reappeared in Maine where he became the self-appointed spokesman against the deepening social and economic injustices of the region.[75] Clearly, the Revolution and a written constitution had left unsolved certain profound problems in society. Those who were discontented now could draw on a revolutionary tradition and the mechanisms of conventions, court closings, and violent protest to demand a change in the status quo.

Additional hints of revolutionary change occurred in the journal of York's old conservative, Jonathan Sayward. On April 12, 1782, he recorded, "I have this day heard there is a paper handed about Proposing that the Province of main should be a separate State, etc. setting the reasons therefore."[76]

Americans may have been celebrating the end of the revolutionary war — but the revolution was not over. It had hardly begun.

SEVEN

The Legacy of Revolution

In the spring of 1783 the war was virtually over; Henry Sewall, serving with the Continental Army at Newburgh, New York, wrote to his parents in the town of York, District of Maine, "The great object of our warfare is happily accomplished.... I rejoice most fervently in this great event—I see with unspeakable satisfaction a feeble, but determined country freed from the impending jaws of tyranny, established free, independent, sovereign—an asylum for liberty—'for the poor and oppressed of all nations and religions.'" At the same time, however, Sewall tempered his enthusiasm with the sobering comment that, for those who had served in the military, "the delicious draught [of liberty] is embittered by the poisonous obtrusion of poverty and dependence."[1]

Hard times were not confined to veterans. A short while later, Jonathan Sayward, also of York, struck a similar note when he wrote in his diary, "As a State we are in Miserable Circumstances.... People are so poor, they know not which way to turn ... and some begin to Doubt whether independence will be so great a Blessing as it was at first thought it would be." A writer in Falmouth's newly established *Gazette* concurred by observing, "In the year 1765, this country was roused to support their rights—In the year 1775 we took up arms in defense of our rights and privileges—and now ten years more have rolled on and all is not right yet."[2] In letters, diaries, and newspapers, postwar idealism met the shock of postwar reality, creating in Maine, and indeed throughout New England in general, disillusionment bordering on despair. Despite independence, the "poor and oppressed" still confronted the "jaws of tyranny"—but in different, more virulent form than ever. The threat now came from within.

I

The financial legacy of the war presented the most immediate threat to Mainers. In addition to current state taxes, many communities staggered under debts for military bounties, for the support of soldiers' families, as well as a backlog of unpaid wartime taxes. Worst off were the newer settlements of the interior, virtually isolated from commercial markets and without an agricultural surplus to convert into taxes. Their back taxes per poll, or adult male, unpaid by 1786 averaged £4.3.10 whereas the unpaid back taxes of the wealthiest commercial towns averaged only £0.14.2 for each poll. Waterborough and Standish were the extremes, owing over £16 and £12 per poll, respectively. Thirty-two of the forty settlements that failed to meet the fifth state tax of 1786 were newly settled plantations.[3]

In petitioning the legislature for relief, agricultural settlements pleaded their geographical isolation, their newness, and their unproductive soil. Canaan Plantation declared its inhabitants were so poverty-stricken that they lacked adequate provisions and lived in shelters "Incomparibly worse, than ordinary Stables to the Westward." The selectmen of Shapleigh protested that, if the state were to insist that all financial obligations be paid, their people would be "Striped [sic] of Real and personal Estate." Raymondtown's officers warned that such a financial burden "must inevetably brak Up the Setlemente."[4] Coastal communities were equally vocal in pleading for relief. They continued their wartime litany of woe over the dislocation of the lumber trade, the collapse of the fishing industry, and the physical destruction from the recent war. Yet commercial communities generally had access to resources with which to pay their taxes, proportionately lighter than the more heavily taxed agricultural towns to begin with.[5]

Aggravating the problem of heavy taxes was a lack of money. In part, the scarcity arose from Britain's exclusion of American shipping from its West Indies islands — causing Maine to lose markets for its lumber and fish. An independent United States could no longer enjoy the profits of the British Empire it had fought so hard to leave. The commercial dislocation and the corresponding lack of money intensified conditions for those confronted by taxes and debts. A New Gloucester resident noted, "We are in a very Poor Situation with respect to our Taxes in this quarter for Money is so Scarce here that even in the Sea ports no Country produce will fetch cash at any Rate." Things were no better in York County where money was so scarce that the representatives to the General Court could not find enough to pay their travel expenses to Boston. Those who had borrowed money to purchase land, livestock, or equipment during times when money was cheaper, or more available, now found themselves in a tightening "chain of debt" that extended throughout society.[6] The pitiable fate of widow Anna Card of York offers a chilling example of what might befall any helpless debtor. To satisfy an obligation of slightly over sixty pounds, she lost half-ownership in a two-story dwelling, a quarter-acre of land, two-thirds part ownership of a grist mill, and ten acres of woods, all assessed at one-quarter of their true value. When even that did not satisfy the debt, Widow Card's flinthearted creditor threw her into debtor's prison while piously insisting on the sanctity of private property as guaranteed by the state's new constitution.[7]

The threat of losing property for taxes or of being jailed for debt struck at the very concept of liberty in a society where property ownership conveyed dignity and personal autonomy. Fear and anxiety accentuated the polarization of society that had been increasing during the war. In the newspaper, "A Countryman" accused the trading community of causing the scarcity of money by purchasing "gauze and all manner of colour'd ribands, and such kind of things" from Great Britain. Another writer declared that cash to the amount of "Thousands, and ten thousands are daily transmitted to Europe, in exchange for their superfluities."[8] As a remedy, he proposed legislation to prohibit merchants from importing anything that required cash in payment rather than the products of America. In the manner of the 1760s and 1770s, articles and letters in the newspaper exhorted readers to return to the simple, austere, republican manner of life and to shun the corrupting luxuries from Europe.

Lawyers and courts received a share of the blame. Throughout the state, heated debate arose over proposals to reform the judicial system and to regulate, even eliminate, associations of lawyers because they needlessly complicated and raised the costs of litigation. In 1786 a town meeting in Bristol instructed its representative to the General Court to support a measure to abolish the "order of lawyers," and Pownalborough elected as its representative John Gardiner, a noted critic of the legal system.[9] As respectable a gentleman as Enoch Freeman of Falmouth copied in his almanac an anonymous bit of antilawyer sentiment entitled "Epitaph on an Attorney":

> Here lieth one who often lied before
> but now he lieth here, he lies no more.[10]

With increasing frequency protest took the form of direct action. In October 1784 at Harpswell and two years later at Cape Elizabeth, crowds "riotously" freed livestock that deputy sheriffs had tried to seize for payment of debts. By 1789 in York County, crowd actions against merchants and magistrates, some involving as many as 100 men at a time, had become so numerous as to raise fears of a "combination" or a "General Insurrection."[11]

As grim as conditions appeared in Maine, they were no worse — and were possibly better — than in the rest of New England, for the attraction of cheap land drew a veritable flood of settlers to the region once the war ended. In 1784, 56,000 people resided in Maine; six years later, the number had swelled to 96,500, and by 1800 population topped 150,000.[12] Natural population growth accounts for some of the increase, but emigration from towns in eastern Massachusetts, Cape Cod, and the islands is chiefly responsible. Many of the new settlers were revolutionary war veterans who — often poor to begin with — had been paid in almost worthless Continental or state securities. But in Maine they could occupy and develop a tract of wild land. In the postrevolutionary era, these squatters justified their informal possession of land in the growing conviction that it had been won from the British crown by all and should benefit all, especially those who had fought and suffered in the common cause. Property in land sufficient to maintain one's family and to pass on to one's heirs was an essential attribute of liberty and of republicanism.[13]

In his study of Concord, Massachusetts, Robert Gross points out that in the decade after the Revolution more than half of the Minutemen who had fought to defend their town had deserted it, some to relocate in Maine. One veteran returned to Concord after the war only to serve time in debtor's prison and to lose his property to a loyalist creditor. In the town of Benton (Clinton) in Maine, he made a new start and prospered as a farmer, doctor, tavern keeper, selectman, and finally, justice of the peace. Several others from Concord settled in Barrettstown (Baldwin), an eastern settlement, promoted by another expatriate from Concord who had settled in New Ipswich, New Hampshire, and speculated in Maine lands. From the Massachusetts town of Marshfield, where they owned a single acre of improved land, a pig, a cow, and six sheep, came the Decrow family to Northport in Maine. Like the Concord migrants, the Decrow family so improved its fortunes by moving, that by 1798 the father was able to divide 350 acres among his three sons, the eldest receiving the house and largest share in return for maintaining his parents in their old age. The future was less kind to Joseph Plumb Martin. Having served in the army through the entire war, Martin took up land in Maine near the mouth of the Penobscot River in what became the town of Prospect. By 1818, at age fifty-nine, Martin was destitute, his total property assessed at fifty-two dollars. Age and infirmities left him barely able to support himself, his sickly wife, and five children. Martin scraped out an existence from his veteran's pension of ninety-six dollars a year and from whatever else he could earn as a town official and as an occasional laborer.[14] For poverty-stricken migrants such as these, landed property in Maine held out the promise — and sometimes the reality — of liberty from poverty and security for the future.

The lure of land in postwar Maine also attracted men of wealth and political influence. Reorganized under Whig leadership, the old speculative land companies, such as the Kennebec Proprietors and their old rivals, the Pejepscot Company, the successors of Clarke and Lake, and the Waldo heirs, undertook vigorous measures to reassert control of their respective and overlapping claims to lands in the Androscoggin, Kennebec, and Penobscot river valleys. Alongside the old guard, and in place of the departed loyalists, a new elite was emerging out of the Revolution. Former generals Peleg Wadsworth, Benjamin Lincoln, and Henry Knox acquired large tracts of land on which to base political ambitions and dreams of aristocratic splendor. Wadsworth returned to Maine at the close of the war and purchased 8,000 acres near Hiram, although he settled as a merchant in Falmouth.[15] Knox and Lincoln were more ambitious; Lincoln obtained some 50,000 acres, but his real importance lay in helping to finance the grandiose schemes of his friend Henry Knox. By marriage and by legal manipulation, Knox acquired the old Waldo patent, about a million acres between the Kennebec and Penobscot rivers. After the war, in partnership with William Duer of New York, Knox expanded his holdings by purchasing over two million acres more from Massachusetts. Not content with this, the partners contracted for yet another million acres of state land east of the Penobscot. From Thomaston, where he constructed a magnificent federal-style mansion, the general entertained in a grand manner while overseeing the economic development of his properties. Such schemes, not always successful, nonetheless testify to the exciting visions generated by the availability of land in Maine for those powerful enough to obtain it. "[N]o part of the United States affords such solid grounds of proffit to capitalists, as the District of Maine," exclaimed Knox.[16]

The contest for land revived the old tensions between those, like Knox, who claimed vast stretches of land by virtue of formal government grant and those who claimed it simply by right of occupancy and improvement—a claim now strengthened by revolutionary republican ideology. Squatters on state-owned land could safely ignore the governor's annual threats of eviction and eventually obtain a hundred acres at a nominal price. With private owners it was a different matter, for businessmen viewed their lands as a means of investment for profit. To them squatters appeared as dangerous, uncivilized intruders denying them their profits and threatening the very fabric of orderly, legal society. Proprietors harassed intruders with threats of legal action and forcible removal until they took out leases or else moved on, leaving their improvements behind. Those who accepted leases, however, discovered all too frequently that they were obligated to pay for land that had no clear title in the first place and left them vulnerable to other claimants, "rising like swarms of bees with their surveyors, to take that which they have no right to." Even before the Revolution, settlers and proprietors had been engaged in "a kind of a Warr" waged in the courts and in the woods.[17] Now that the Revolution was over, the contest resumed. As before, the relentless proprietors skillfully manipulated the Massachusetts legislature and the courts in their own behalf. In reaction, the settlers did not resort to violence against their antagonists—at least not at first—but began a movement to found a separate state of Maine with a government more responsive to their plight.

II

The initiative to form a state separate from Massachusetts did not arise from the desperate farmers of the interior or from ideological dissidents. It first emerged from yet another group of genteel promoters seeking political preeminence in a new state rather than economic preeminence by selling land on the frontiers of the old one. The leading separatists were a small group of men prominent in the Falmouth–Gorham area who had played locally important roles during the Revolution: Enoch Ilsley, a Falmouth merchant; Samuel Freeman, professional officeholder and also a Falmouth merchant; and the two ministers of Falmouth's First Parish Church, the Reverend Thomas Smith and his associate, Samuel Deane. Former general Peleg Wadsworth, now settled in Falmouth as a merchant, was a newcomer to the group, as was Thomas Wait, who established in Falmouth the District's first newspaper, the *Falmouth Gazette*, later renamed the *Cumberland Gazette*. Two leading citizens from the town of Gorham were active participants, Stephen Longfellow, Jr., a former resident of Falmouth and now a gentleman farmer, and William Gorham who, as judge of probate, was one of the few state officeholders to support separation. As long as Maine remained a part of Massachusetts, men such as these would enjoy at best only a local importance, overshadowed by such political giants as James Bowdoin, John Hancock, John and Sam Adams, Elbridge Gerry, and others. A separate state of Maine would enable the founders to satisfy their political ambitions in a state of their own without such prestigious competition. In addition, statehood would enhance the importance of the Falmouth region in general and of the town of Falmouth in particular, for Maine's leading seaport could reasonably expect to be the capital of the new state.

The first public reference to separation appeared in the February 5, 1785, issue of the *Falmouth Gazette* where an acrostic significantly referred to rebuilt Falmouth as "the mistress of a rising STATE."

> From th'Ashes of the old, a *Town* appears,
> And Phoenix like, her plumy head she rears;
> Long may she flourish; be from war secure;
> Made rich by commerce and agriculture;
> O're all her foes triumphant; be content
> Under our happy form of government;
> Till (what no doubt will be her prosp'rous fate)
> Herself's the mistress of a rising STATE.[18]

The idea of statehood was far easier to suggest than to carry out. Through much of 1785, the *Gazette* was filled with suggestions as to who should take the initiative and how separation might be achieved.

Finally, in September and early October, the newspaper carried repeated announcements from "a large and respectable Number of persons," urging all who might be interested to gather at the First Parish Meeting House in Falmouth on October 5. The announcement made it clear that the desirability of separation was a foregone conclusion, and the only topic of discussion would be how to obtain the legitimacy of popular support and how to disengage from Massachusetts in a "regular and orderly" manner. From the start, the promoters insisted that separation, like the Revolution itself, be popular yet orderly.[19]

Toward these ends, the thirty persons who attended this first convention composed a circular letter inviting all communities in Maine to send representatives to a second convention to be held at Falmouth in January 1786. At this meeting, delegates approved a list of grievances, which a third convention in September ratified and sent throughout the District with an "Address to the People," urging an expression of support for separation through a referendum. The convention also adopted a petition to the Massachusetts General Court requesting separation but delayed presenting it until the referendum vote came in.[20]

In their petition, circulars, and newspaper essays, proponents of statehood argued that a separate political existence was the only way to rectify the disadvantages of the present union with Massachusetts. The list of grievances approved by the second convention contained the complaint that the District's geographical location made its concerns different from those of Massachusetts. The distance from Boston hampered residents of Maine in conducting their financial and judicial affairs. It was difficult to maintain representatives at such a distance, and this tended to deprive Maine of sufficient political strength to protect its interests. Consequently, the Commonwealth's taxation and legislation failed to make allowance for Maine's relative poverty and its dependence upon imported food and goods. Had the thirteen colonies been allowed to send representatives to Parliament before the Revolution, declared "Impartialis Secundus," their plight would have been analogous to the present condition of Maine; representation in either case was meaningless if people had to submit to the laws and taxes imposed by a "foreign legislature." Since the present political union with Massachusetts failed to provide Maine with advantages proportionate to the rest of the state, "natural and universal justice," derived "from nature, and the principles of self-preservation," dictated a separation.[21]

Separatists needed more than natural law to legitimize their proposal. To justify separation yet further, they ransacked the past to discover — or invent — historical precedents for a territorial state of Maine with powers of self-government. In this fashion, advocates could claim merely to be restoring tradition rather than breaking with it. They found what they were looking for in Charles I's early-seventeenth-century charter to Sir Ferdinando Gorges for the Province of Maine. The *Falmouth Gazette* published the entire charter in three installments, and commentators emphasized the salient points that the proprietor, Gorges, and his heirs and assigns had authority "to make, ordain, and publish, laws[,] ordinances and CONSTITUTIONS" with the assent of the greater part of the freeholders. Later monarchs had abrogated the charter, but their actions were mere political expedients and carried no legal force. Consequently, the District had every reason to resume the historical rights of self-government that it had never surrendered.[22]

So much for theory, but could Maine afford an autonomous government, and did the District possess the necessary experience and talent to rule itself? Advocates of statehood tried to convince the public that Maine could indeed govern itself more effectively and economically than if united with Massachusetts. "Government is a very simple, easy thing," declared the convention's "Address to the People." "Mysteries in politicks are mere absurdities — invented entirely to gratify the ambitions of princes and designing men — to aggrandize those who govern, at the expense of those who are governed."[23] Opponents may have doubted, but proponents were convinced that the District possessed sufficient political skill and expertise for successful self-government — they were, after all, referring to themselves. Such as assumption did much to dampen the potential radicalism in the "Address."

Separatists were confident the District could afford its own government provided it was small and simple, like those in Rhode Island, Connecticut, and New Hampshire.[24] Numerous schemes for economical government appeared in the newspaper, contrasting sharply with that recently established in Massachusetts. Low salaries for public officials not only saved money, argued "Ruricola," but attracted to office those who served for honor alone. Another writer suggested paying officials in local produce and home manufactures rather than in cash — and the fewer officials the better. Maine did not really need a governor, a council, a senate, or a large house of representatives with the usual army of clerks and messengers. One alternative was a legislature of only twenty-seven members, six representatives and three senators from each of Maine's three counties, who together would elect the chief executive. In the interest of frugality and efficiency, "Scribble-Scrabble" suggested that Maine adopt a unicameral legislature of only twenty-one members representing territorial districts rather than towns.[25] Initially, the costs of self-government might be somewhat higher per capita than at present under Massachusetts, but separatists were optimistic that any increase would be offset by the flood of new immigrants attracted to Maine once it was no longer perceived "as an inconsiderable appendage to the Republic of Massachusetts, or a kind of insignificant Colony to that State."[26]

Despite efforts of the separatists to present their scheme as desirable and reasonable, the issue of separation abruptly took on a more controversial nature in light of events in western Massachusetts. Rumblings of social and economic discontent had persisted in Hampshire, Berkshire, and Worcester counties ever since 1782. At that time Samuel Ely had stirred up crowds to close the county courts as a protest against taxes and the expensive, arbitrary judicial system. The postwar depression of 1785–1786 heightened the discontent, and in town and county conventions protestors in the western counties complained anew over the courts, extortionate taxes, the scarcity of money, and the costliness of a government located in far-off Boston. The *Falmouth Gazette* carried detailed accounts of the unrest and then of the ensuing violence as angry farmers again closed courts and even resorted to armed rebellion under Daniel Shays, Luke Day, and Job Shattuck. During the winter of 1786–1787, General Benjamin Lincoln came out of retirement to lead a hastily recruited state militia, which easily dispersed the rebels.[27] However, the shock waves of open rebellion against the Massachusetts Commonwealth extended throughout the entire country. In Maine, Shays' Rebellion profoundly affected the movement for statehood.

Against such a background, the separation of Maine from Massachusetts assumed a much more radical aspect than the promoters ever intended. The coincidence in timing between the two movements and the common use of conventions to express popular grievances framed in revolutionary rhetoric were embarrassing enough to the genteel leaders of separation. Even more damaging to the separatists' image, however, were those who became their most ardent supporters—the impoverished, angry farmers of Maine's interior. In the western counties of

Massachusetts, such people supported Shays' Rebellion; in Maine, however, disgruntled rural settlers viewed the possibility of statehood as an alternative to violence; but their advocacy of separation brought to the cause the unwelcome whiff of radicalism. Even worse for the separatist leaders, with their obsession for order and respectability, was the vigorous support of Samuel Thompson.

The former brigadier general was no poverty-stricken farmer, but during the war his flamboyant populism had won him a widespread following and a reputation as a dangerous radical in the eyes of Whig leaders. Since the war's end, Thompson had moved his residence from Brunswick across the river to Topsham where he continued his upwardly mobile career, operating a ferry, investing in land and mill sites, and getting elected to the state legislature — as well as to the separation conventions held in Falmouth. Joining Thompson as another outspoken supporter of separation was William Widgery, a self-trained lawyer from New Gloucester, an inland agricultural community like Topsham. One observer quite accurately summed up the separatist movement with the comment that "the whole matter is set on foot & carried by people who either expect places in the New government or persons call'd squatters (of which there are many in these parts of considerable influence)."[28] It was an unstable and short-lived political union.

The composition of separatist conventions took on an increasingly ominous significance in light of Shays' Rebellion. In the January 1786 convention, for example, only four towns from York sent representatives and a mere six from Cumberland County.[29] The most populous, wealthiest areas of the District, containing the leading merchants, lawyers, and officeholders, either opposed separation or were apathetic to it. On the other hand, Lincoln County, notorious for squatter unrest, had representation from ten towns. To the leading separatists, the warning signs were all too clear. Indeed, one of them later described his fellow delegates from the interior with almost hysterical exaggeration as imbued with the sentiments of "genuine insurgents," who "did not hesitate to speak of the senate and the attorney-general as grievances" and sought relief through paper money and legal tender acts.[30]

Conservative separatists were determined to keep control of the proceedings, and they succeeded in defeating a motion that voting should be by town rather than head. The interior towns would have controlled the convention had such a motion passed. As it was, the southern coastal towns with their more numerous delegates easily outvoted the interior towns, whose poverty and isolation limited them to single or even combined delegates.[31] In this manner, the more conservative members of the convention controlled the proceedings and shaped the decisions.

The results were so temperate as to be anticlimactic. The two conventions in 1786 did, indeed, submit to the towns the referendum on separation and the "Appeal to the People," which assured Mainers that "Mysteries in politicks" were merely the inventions of scheming men to justify their monopoly of power. Such measures, however, failed to strike much of a spark; the referendum returns supported separation by a two-to-one margin, but only one-third of Maine's incorporated towns responded. The conservative influence was more evident in the list of grievances and petition to the General Court that the conventions produced. The grievances contained no demands for paper money or stay laws, no revolutionary statement of rights to self-government; instead, the conventions emphasized only the physical difficulties arising from Maine's isolated location. Distance from Massachusetts made administration of justice and political representation awkward and expensive and made taxation discriminatory. Even if Maine received additional representation, the problems arising from a disadvantageous location would persist; the only solution was a separate state. The petition to the General Court was equally restrained; it merely reiterated the list of grievances and humbly requested a separation from Massachusetts, promising an equitable division of public lands and public debt.[32]

Restrained and respectful the petition might have been, yet conservative members of the convention pushed through a motion to withhold it for the present, "as the commonwealth in general is at this time in a perplexed state, and this convention being unwilling to do anything that shall seem to lay any greater burthen on the General Court." Newspaper editor Thomas Wait, an early supporter of separation, agreed to the delay. In his own newspaper, he mused, "Will it not be cruel, in the present distressed situation of the Commonwealth to perplex government with a request of this kind?"[33]

The more radical element did not give up without a struggle. Shays' Rebellion offered precisely the necessary leverage to extract concessions from the legislature. They argued that now, if ever, was the "golden opportunity" to present the petition: "the legislature are now distracted with care and trouble; if we apply to them at this time, they will not dare to refuse our request; and if they do, we can drive them into compliance, by threatening to join in the insurrection." When one of the Portland delegates remonstrated against such a plan of action, he was told he was "out of his senses."[34]

The convention finally compromised by placing the petition in the hands of a committee with discretionary power to submit it to the General Court when it saw fit. The chairman of the committee was Samuel Thompson. Yet even he could not overcome the forces of moderation and the news of rebellion in western Massachusetts. On March 23, 1787, the *Cumberland Gazette* carried a notice that the committee to present the petition on separation to the legislature had decided, "considering the peculiar embarrassments of government, and the alarming and distressed situation of the Western Counties," against submitting the petition at that time.[35] The conservative separatists clearly controlled the actions of the conventions and were determined to keep the movement orderly and peaceable. They managed to do so, but separation became tainted with the charge of radicalism nonetheless.

Opponents of statehood seized upon the movement's timing, techniques, and following to compare it with Shays' Rebellion and to denounce it as revolutionary. Governor James Bowdoin and the General Court expressed the state's official opposition. The governor called separation "a design against the Commonwealth, of very evil tendency." The legislature added that it felt the "danger and impropriety of individuals, or bodies of men, attempting to dismember the state—The social compact solemnly entered into by the people of this Commonwealth, ought, we conceive, to be attended to, and guarded with the utmost care." The town of York declared that since its primary loyalty lay with Massachusetts it would not participate in the separation conventions and that, indeed, conventions of any kind only heightened civil discord. In the summer of 1786, while crowds in Northampton and Worcester were closing courts, a town meeting in Falmouth, now renamed Portland, reconsidered an earlier decision to send delegates to the separatist convention. The town now instructed its delegation to "oppose every measure that might be taken to establish a new Government," for it was not a "proper time" to hold conventions with the western part of the state "but a step from anarchy." Furthermore, "Conventions, at all times, were dangerous things, and always so considered by the General Court."[36]

In newspaper articles the antiseparatists argued that there existed no legitimate way of addressing the people apart from their legislature. In a representative government, declared "A Lad," only the elected representatives embody the people. "Senex" concurred and denounced conventions as "usurpers of the rights of our legislators, strangers and enemies to the constitution." Conventions were unconstitutional and dangerous incitements to violence.[37]

Supporters of conventions and of separation drew on the country's revolutionary tradition to defend their movement and methods. "Scribble-Scrabble" retorted that during the Revolution the British Parliament also had condemned conventions, yet patriotic Americans continued to meet to declare their convictions. Maine had every right to do the same, declared "Solon," for "We can be considered in no light very different from a Colony to the Massachusetts."[38] Furthermore, provisions in the state constitution protecting the right to petition and remonstrate obviously implied a right to hold conventions in which to formulate such means of redress. Another separatist, Thomas Wait, tried to make a distinction between the westerners, who were acting in an "unconstitutional, riotous, not to say treasonable manner," and separatists in Maine, who were moving, with "manly firmness, towards the Grand Object in view, . . . with all that precaution and prudence necessary to ensure the confidence of their constituents, the good will and attention of Government, and Success in the end."[39]

Such arguments defending the respectability and legitimacy of separation made few converts where the cause needed them most—in the District's population centers along the coast. Here the residents were as concerned with preserving valuable commercial connections with the Commonwealth as they were with the taint of Shaysism. York, Wells, Scarborough, and North Yarmouth remained cool to the proposal. Portland, where the movement began, eventually repudiated its own separatists.[40] Few towns, however, were as hostile to the idea of separation as Machias, the easternmost bastion during the war against the British and the neutralists, and now against all those who would separate the District.

The loyalty of Machias to union with Massachusetts had little to do with Shays or with constitutional scruples. It had everything to do with power and prestige. The leaders of Machias envisioned their town as shire town for a new county to be carved out of Lincoln County, an immense jurisdiction that included virtually all of Maine east of the

Kennebec River. Toward that end, Machias became a champion of judicial reform, the sort of reform limited to the extension of courts and counties rather than a reform of the judicial process itself. As early as 1782, spokesmen for Machias were complaining to the government about the inconvenience of attending county court at far-away Pownalborough. As a remedy, they proposed an extension of the registry of deeds and the courts of probate, common pleas, and sessions of the peace as far east as Machias.[41]

These recommendations, however, aroused sharp criticism from nearby towns, such as Gouldsborough, Frenchman's Bay, and Mount Desert, which correctly interpreted them as preliminary to the creation of an expensive new county centered on Machias. A memorial from Mount Desert pointedly observed that the county had not yet recovered from the ravages of the war, "and we think it a little Strang [sic] that People that the other Day was Petitioning for help from the Commonwealth should so Sune Petition for Courts to be Erected here in this Jurisdiction." At a convention of the easternmost towns, several of Machias's wartime antagonists, Francis Shaw, Jr., William Nickells, and Nathan Jones, joined other delegates in remonstrating against the new county.[42]

Machias responded by maligning the patriotism of its leading opponents as men who had cooperated with the British in the recent war and petitioned for neutrality. By contrast, Machias gloried in its own war record as "the means of preserving to this State, all the Country east of Penobscot; for had we not held out against the enemy, or had we come into Mr. Shaw's propos'd plan of Neutrality, all the other settlements as far west as Penobscot, (at least,) would have fell to Britain; and the British Ministry would have had foundation for a demand to the right of Territory aforesaid and the American Ministers at Paris, could have made no Plea against it."[43] Implied in such an argument was the assumption that Machias, having saved Maine from the British, deserved the position of shire town as a reward for its wartime services.

The future importance of Machias depended on union with Massachusetts, not on an independent state of Maine. Machias's leaders, however, were not above using the threat of separation to pressure the Commonwealth. In letters to influential friends in Boston, town leaders urged haste in creating a new county, "more particularly so when the upper part of these Countys are so uneasy and endeavoring to separate from the Commonwealth, the General Court paying a little attention this way at this time will still retain this District in their interest."[44] It is a measure of the General Court's concern that it soon gratified Machias's demands.

III

Separation had to contend with even more than the impact of Shays' Rebellion and opposition from the District's leading coastal communities. The issue of statehood for Maine became enmeshed in the debate over ratification of the federal Constitution. Not only did the debate over the Constitution eclipse the issue of separation, but inexorably, Maine Federalists succeeded in linking Shaysism, implying social disunity, to separation, meaning state disunity, and to antifederalism, national disunity. Strictly speaking, these were separate issues, but they did attract a similar following among those who felt the Revolution was still incomplete and who distrusted distant, strong government. The Federalists made the most of this in political debate.

A conservative member of the separation convention referred to his more radical colleagues as "genuine insurgents." A York County Federalist used the terms "Shaysism" and "antifederalism" interchangeably in describing widespread opposition to the Constitution.[45] Another York Federalist, Judge David Sewall, who had long been denouncing conventions as incipient rebellions, took the final step in blurring all distinctions. Sewall described anti-Federalists as those who favored paper money, canceling the state debt, and as Shaysites who supported a new state of Maine. According to Sewall, many unredeemed Shaysites living in Worcester County hoped that by separating Maine from Massachusetts the central Massachusetts town of Worcester would replace Boston as the capital of the truncated Bay State.[46] Sewall and his Federalist colleagues saw ratification of the Constitution as essential in preserving an orderly, stable republic on both the state and national level. In their minds, anti-Federalists, Shaysites, and separatists assumed each others' attributes and fused into one common threat to that ideal.

The personification of that threat was the delegate to the state ratifying convention from Topsham in the District of Maine, Samuel Thompson. Already notorious for his populist brand of republicanism during the war and for his advocacy of separatism, Thompson epitomized those qualities that stirred such contempt and alarm in Federalists like Judge Sewall. Although poorly educated, Thompson had none of the self-doubts that led one of his fellow delegates from Maine to confess, "I feel my Self So Small on many occations that I all most Scrink into Nothing."[47] Thompson spoke frequently and vigorously against the proposed Constitution, impatiently dismissing the grandiose historical allusions of the better-educated delegates while stressing truths derived from his own personal experience. Occasionally he interrupted debate and more than once had to be called to order by the chair.

Thompson's arguments comprise a classic statement of antifederalism rooted in the conviction that a republic best flourished when it was limited in geographical extent and rested directly in the hands of the electorate. The framers at Philadelphia had exceeded their authority and created a "national consolidation" that would inevitably lead to tyranny. This new plan of government, Thompson argued, placed in the hands of fallible men unlimited national power to legislate, tax, regulate trade, and raise a standing army.[48]

Thompson proposed several means by which to limit such dangerous authority, even suggesting a property qualification for election to office, for, he said, "when men have *nothing to lose*, they have *nothing to fear.*" Annual elections would also serve to restrain bad men in government. Thompson did not draw upon classical Greek or Roman history to illustrate his point; instead, he bluntly declared that only the recent failure of James Bowdoin to win reelection as governor had saved the state from a bloodbath during the time of Shays' Rebellion. Thompson's remarks caused an uproar, for among the convention delegates were not only many Bowdoin supporters but even the former governor himself. Undaunted, Thompson pushed on to advocate yet one more measure by which to check the power of Congress, a national bill of rights, "which shall say, *Thus far shall ye come, and no farther.*"[49]

The ratification process also aroused Thompson's ire. It was too fast and too arbitrary; what would happen, he asked, if three or four states failed to ratify? Would the others use force, and would this not then break up the Union rather than bind it closer? At least, he argued, in Massachusetts the new Constitution ought to have been submitted to the towns rather than to a convention so that people themselves could express their minds. Had that been done, he declared, it would have been clear that public opinion opposed the new government.[50] To Thompson and other anti-Federalists, the proposed government was an illegal and arbitrary assault upon the American republic.

Despite the logic and fervor of their arguments, Thompson and his anti-Federalist allies failed to block ratification. They did, however, force the Federalists to propose ratification with several recommended amendments, thereby making the Constitution somewhat more palatable to its opponents — a technique later followed in many other states. This strategy split the anti-Federalists, so that on February 6, 1788, when the vote for ratification was taken, the Federalists managed a narrow victory of 187 to 168. By four votes, 25 to 21, the Maine delegation supported the majority.[51]

The four-vote difference is misleading, however. At least fourteen eligible towns registered their apathy or disapproval by refusing to send delegates, even though the state agreed to pay travel expenses. In addition, one of the anti-Federalist representatives, Nathaniel Barrell of York, yielded to heavy pressure from Federalist relatives and switched his vote at the last minute.[52] Federalist leaders had good cause to be concerned about the strength of antifederalism in Maine. Had the fourteen towns opposing ratification sent delegates to the convention to join those anti-Federalists already there, the Maine delegation might have voted 24–36 against ratification. Federalists had equally good cause to see the interior communities as the chief source of anti-Federalist strength. Significantly, twenty-one of the twenty-six coastal delegates from Maine supported ratification, whereas sixteen of twenty backcountry representatives opposed it.[53] Antifederalism, although distinct from separatism, had a powerful appeal in the District's interior regions where distrust of authority and grievances over land ran deep.

Most anti-Federalists accepted defeat graciously. New Gloucester's delegate, William Widgery, publicly acknowledged that, although he had fought against the Constitution, he had been overruled by a majority of "wise and understanding men," and he would now "endeavor to sow the seeds of union and peace among the people he represented." Others expressed similar sentiments, but not Samuel Thompson. Angry and bitter, he took no part in the celebration following ratification. Rather than sowing "seeds of union and peace," he threatened to sow discord by stirring up opposition to the Constitution in western Massachusetts where resentments from Shays' Rebellion persisted.[54] Despite Thompson's threats, one of the Federalist leaders interpreted the result of the ratification contest in millennial terms:

> Thompson is roaring about like the old Dragon to devour the *Child now it is born* and breathes forth fire, arrows, and Death, but his Hosts are almost fled & the Inhabitants of this Earth are singing out *now is Salvation come*, the old Serpent is beaten down and anarchy and confusion is rooted out and the republican Angel and his Hosts are proclaiming Peace, wealth, Honor, Liberty, and Independence.[55]

"Old Dragon" Thompson never did go to western Massachusetts to rekindle the fires of rebellion. Instead, he resumed his seat in the General Court as representative from Topsham and tried to rekindle the movement to separate Maine from Massachusetts. In January 1789, the General Court finally took up the petition for separation — the very same petition that the committee, chaired by Thompson, had submitted almost two years before. As a member of the legislature, Thompson could now defend "his" petition and the idea of separation, aided by his old anti-Federalist ally, William Widgery, and other diehards.

The defeat of Shays' Rebellion and of antifederalism meant that the fate of separation was a foregone conclusion; the best that separatists could hope for was to have their petition tabled so that they might take it up again at some later date. Most of the separatist delegates reiterated the old arguments supporting the popularity and justice of statehood for Maine, but Thompson adroitly pointed out that with the inclusion of Maine the state of Massachusetts was simply too large for proper republican administration and the government could do its business more effectively without the three eastern counties. He then tried to turn to his own advantage the ratification of the new federal Constitution he had tried so hard to defeat. Thompson acknowledged that, though he had formerly opposed the change of government, he now accepted it and that under this new Constitution it made sense to separate Maine so the northern states might better counter southern representation in the new national Congress.[56]

On January 22, 1789, Thompson and his allies enjoyed a minor victory. The General Court tabled rather than defeated the petition when it accepted a committee recommendation that "the respectability of the

Eastern Counties demanded so much compliance as that the petition should lay on the files." Separation, for the moment, was all but dead; it expired at what proved to be the last of the Portland conventions in March 1789. Attendance had been dwindling at the previous conventions until at this final one only three delegates arrived — all from Portland. Having elected one of their number president, another one clerk, there was no one to second the motion made by the third to adjourn; the movement came to an end. It would revive and subside several times more before finally reaching fruition in 1820, but for the time being it appeared to be over. Tainted by Shays' Rebellion and by antifederalism, separation lost both its leadership, which waited for a more propitious time to resume the movement, and its backcountry following, which sought other, more radical means to achieve its goals.[57]

The willingness of Massachusetts to redress many of the grievances in the District accelerated the movement's demise. The government first moved to make justice more readily accessible for the isolated residents of Lincoln County. Between 1786 and 1787, the legislature extended the court of probate and registry of deeds to Machias, established sittings of the common pleas and sessions courts as Waldoboro and Hallowell, and set extra terms of the regular courts and a term of the superior court at Pownalborough. In addition, the General Court separated Lincoln County into two additional county jurisdictions, Hancock and Washington. Designated shire town for Washington County, Machias in 1790 finally secured the preeminence it craved.[58]

The creation of two new counties necessitated a series of related changes along with a broad range of remedial legislation to redress the District's complaints. The General Court undertook the wholesale incorporation of communities within the new county jurisdictions so they could levy taxes and elect juries to support the legal system. Not incidentally, incorporation meant increased representation for the District in the state legislature — providing the towns made use of the opportunity. The government also suspended or abated the tax burden for over 30 percent of the towns in Maine and exempted wild lands from taxation for ten years. To alleviate discontent in the interior, the General Court quieted squatters occupying public lands prior to 1784 by granting them title to 100 acres and brought pressure on private land companies to compromise differences with their tenants. The state assumed the expense of laying out roads running from the Kennebec to the Penobscot River and from there to Passamaquoddy Bay and even approved the establishment of a college in the District.[59]

Such reforms removed some of the more immediate sources of discontent among tax-burdened towns and especially among the propertied, more conservative segment of society. The coastal elite and propertied farmers derived the most benefit from the two new counties. They filled the approximately two dozen civil and judicial posts created in each; they are the ones who could anticipate sending sons to the new college, named after one of the District's largest proprietors, James Bowdoin. Along the new roads, the new judges and sheriffs could extend the "civilizing" authority of the state over the "lawless" settlers of the interior. In effect, the reforms of the General Court extended the tangible benefits of continued union with Massachusetts to an expanded local elite, cutting them off from the poorer end of the separatist coalition. Even Samuel Thompson accepted a commission as a justice of the peace for Lincoln County, contributed land to Bowdoin College, and became a member of the college's Board of Overseers.[60] Squatters and frontier farmers grubbing out a precarious existence in isolation, harassed by proprietary agents and court officials, received little. For them the Revolution was still in process. Organized action in a new political world would in time enable dissidents to attain their goals, but first they would attempt to achieve them by more traditional and spontaneous means — violence.

IV

For the next twenty years, impoverished squatters in the backcountry organized secret groups to defend their property — and liberty — from the powerful proprietors backed by the legal authority of the state. These "white Indians" assaulted surveyors, court officials, and proprietary agents — even killing one — and, in addition, burned the houses, barns, and sawmills of their antagonists. A powerful conviction that the Revolution was not yet over and that a new group of Tories had arisen to deny the people the fruits of their victory served to justify such violence.[61]

One of the most notorious of several backcountry spokesmen was the Reverend Samuel Ely, who appeared in Maine after his turbulent failure to reform the courts in western Massachusetts just before Shays' Rebellion. In Maine, Ely rapidly gathered a following among settlers whose hopes and frustrations he articulated in several pamphlets and petitions to the General Court. Ely forcefully challenged the legality of the grants to Henry Knox on the grounds that great proprietary tracts elevating the few above the many were contrary to republican liberty. In a tract entitled *The Deformity of a Hideous Monster Discovered in the Province of Maine, by a Man in the Woods, Looking after Liberty*, Ely argued that poor men were better off under the "despot" King George than now in a "republican" state.

> When we were under the British King we had liberty; but what liberty have we now? Are not the tories far better off than we? . . . We are at present under despots, who take our liberty from us and rule us with as much arbitrary power as despots of Europe. . . . Did we fight for such liberty? . . . We are loth to fight for liberty again, we do not delight in war, but if it must be we will try it once more. . . . The club law is dreadful, but sometimes by it wrongs are rectified.[62]

More imaginative and dramatic were pamphlets by James Shurtleff and Nathan Barlow, who added a powerful mystical element to the protests over the monopoly of wild lands. While in a dreamlike state of mind, both Shurtleff and Barlow were spiritually transported on a tour of heaven and hell; the Goddess of Freedom conducted Shurtleff; Barlow's guide was Christ himself. In both cases the vivid, soul-searing experience raised the struggle over land to cosmic significance. It became a battle between the forces of good and evil wherein squatters' rights and the fate of the American republic merged with the cause of God. Arrayed in opposition were Satan and his minions: the great landed proprietors, the politicians, the elite who gave lip service to republicanism while secretly trying to destroy it.[63] From such a perspective, extremism in defense of liberty was no sin.

Adding moral fervor to backcountry radicalism was a movement Stephen Marini calls the "New Light Stir," an evangelical, millennial, charismatic revival that swept through the backcountry of New England and even Nova Scotia during the Revolution. The New Light Stir filled a religious void that was both physical and spiritual. As early as 1778, there were at least forty towns and plantations in Maine's Lincoln County alone where no orthodox minister had ever settled. After the war, even

Congregationalists resorted to missionary circuit riders in a futile effort to meet the need.[64]

The problem was not merely one of numbers but one of substance and style. Orthodox Calvinism simply failed to meet the emotional and spiritual needs of Maine's rapidly expanding population, especially the culturally heterogeneous backcountry wracked by poverty, the uncertainties of war, and the exhilaration of independence. Instead, Calvinism, as expounded by preachers such as Peter T. Smith of Windham and Thurston Whiting of Warren, became a means of defending the status quo and its vested interests, political and economic.[65]

Both men enjoyed Harvard educations, the patronage of powerful men, and the property of wealthy spouses. Peter Smith's father occupied the prestigious pulpit of Falmouth's First Church, and by marriage the son became the wealthiest landowner in Windham. The Reverend Thurston Whiting had a particular knack of ingratiating himself into the favor of important men. Henry Knox, Maine's great land monopolizer, secured for him a pastorate in the town of Warren after Whiting had been dismissed for scandalous behavior from a church in Newcastle — acquired through the favor of Lincoln County's leading officials, Justice Jonathan Bowman and Sheriff Charles Cushing.

Both Smith and Whiting enjoyed the fellowship of merchants, lawyers, and politicians — and shared their values. Smith's parishioners saw him as a "somewhat arbitrary and dogmatic representative of the squirearchy, a tall portly figure in the cocked hat, tight breeches, and full coat which he wore as a class uniform." Resigning his pulpit in 1790, Smith remained in Windham, readily assuming more secular functions as a justice of the peace, the town representative to the General Court, and agent for the town proprietors.

Farther east, in the town of Warren, Whiting justified Henry Knox's patronage. He openly supported the election of Federalist politicians and preached to disgruntled, disbelieving backcountry squatters sermons on the "charming" nature of a well-regulated, hierarchical society and the need to submit to constituted authority.

In advocating submission to a hierarchical society and its leaders, preachers such as Whiting and Smith were fulfilling a function planned for them by the framers of the Massachusetts constitution. Despite pronouncements of religious freedom, the state constitution provided for the public support of religion — presumably the Congregational church — in the traditional conviction that republican government depended on a moral society. Only a virtuous citizenry could put aside selfish interests to follow the community's corporate good as determined by its political and religious leaders.[66]

Other religious denominations, if they secured official recognition from their respective towns, could apply church taxes to their own support. Such privileged status was not common since it meant less money for the established church, and so most dissenters suffered from practical, if not ideological, discrimination. Typical was the plight of the Baptists in Fryeburg who, in 1790, complained that, so long as they were taxed to support the Congregational minister, they were unable to maintain their own preacher despite their right to do so.[67]

Congregationalists had good reason to fear religious competition that was not confined to the unchurched frontier. Between 1780 and 1800, Baptist congregations in Maine — both Freewill and Separatist — increased from three to seventy-five. In Woolwich, the Baptists split the established Congregational church and attracted so many members that they acquired legal status. The depleted Congregationalists failed to pay their minister his full salary so that he was forced to sue the town for his back pay.[68]

Baptists, in their turn, had reason for concern over the growth of a new religious sect called Shakers. Baptists in particular seemed to be drawn to the Shakers' rapturous experience of God's presence and by the sect's deep sense of spiritual and gender equality. Many others, distressed by a world preoccupied with war and material gain, found solace in Shaker pacifism, their sense of community, and even celibacy. In the decade following the end of the war, Shakers made converts throughout southwestern Maine, especially in Alfred, Gorham, and New Gloucester. So rapidly did Shakers expand that the Freewill Baptists in their 1784 quarterly meeting agreed to hold a day of fasting and prayer, "that God would cut short this delusion and give peace to the churches."[69]

Meanwhile, the steady growth in the number of Quakers continued to worry the orthodox clergy. By the end of the Revolution, the Society of Friends had a membership of about a thousand, gathered into six societies in Maine, chiefly in the urban centers. Even in Portland, a new group of evangelical Quakers appeared whose members, men and women alike, preached to large numbers of people and, in the words of the Reverend Thomas Smith, raised "a sad tumult" over meetings and taxes. More alarming yet from the viewpoint of the establishment were even more radical sects, such as the "come-outers" in Gorham and the "Merry Dancers" of Sanford who attracted many of the returned war veterans. These religious enthusiasts defied conventional social norms by venting their religious excitement in frenzied dancing, trances, odd costumes, and even orgiastic behavior.[70]

Despite such defections from orthodoxy, Congregationalism remained the established religion, denying full equality to dissenters. Conservative courts allowed no significant relief, and although the state did make it easier for minority denominations to apply their taxes to their own preachers, it nonetheless preserved the connection between state and church. To Maine's religious dissenters, many of whom were also backcountry squatters, the only hope of winning both religious and economic democracy was separation from Massachusetts and statehood.

Yet, the traditional nonparty political system failed to provide dissidents with a viable means for attaining their demands. The failure of the first separation movement illustrates that point, and in the immediate postwar environment there was little appearance of change. In the Massachusetts General Court, for example, Maine was as underrepresented as before. The condition of the economy and the cost of sending delegates all the way to Boston still discouraged many towns from exercising their political prerogatives. Between 1782 and 1787, 40 to 82 percent of Maine's delegation was absent from the General Court. When towns did go to the expense of sending representatives, they still selected the lawyers, merchants, and gentlemen farmers who could afford to leave their occupations for long periods of time. At Boston, Maine's delegates continued to protect the status quo, supporting the policies of the commercial centers, which discriminated against the smaller interior settlements on issues of taxation, money, and land.[71]

The recourse for dissenters faced with a nonresponsive political system had always been violence. But not all dissenters accepted that alternative, nor did leaders of the new Commonwealth of Massachusetts — as the fate of Shays' Rebellion indicates. In Maine, backcountry violence was no more successful as a proper response to the threat of powerful proprietors supported by the machinery of state and church. As protest leaders fell silent or went to jail, their followers gradually found salvation in a new political party of opposition within a changing political world.

The Revolution had broadened and deepened political awareness in a society that had been largely nonideological before the war. Prior to the Revolution, most towns met only two or three times a year, unless some local crisis, such as religious dissent, threatened the community consensus. During the war, however, townsmen everywhere had to meet many more times than usual to form committees to correspond, inspect, enforce prices, search out Tories, and enforce measures pertaining to the war. Towns had to evaluate two state and one national constitution, find delegates to attend conventions and congresses, meet to elect governors, senators, and representatives, and eventually participate in national elections as well. The frequency of town meetings marks the increased tempo of political life. The town of Bristol met six and then seven times in 1779 and 1780. During the same period, Brunswick met four and then six times; Scarborough had three, then seven meetings. Gorham summoned its townsmen no less than eleven times in 1777 and fourteen in 1778. Not everyone welcomed the obligations of freedom. In 1780 the only ones attending a town meeting in Bristol to raise clothing for the Continental Army were the selectmen, one clerk, and the constable.[72]

However grudgingly, townsmen not only gathered more frequently than ever before but assigned new duties and filled new offices, while assuming an expanding political function. Towns did not necessarily select new leaders. Statistics compiled by Edward M. Cook, Jr., minimize the revolutionary nature of the new appointments, for towns generally bestowed them on their traditional community leaders. Evidence from Pownalborough, the one Maine town where the political effects of the Revolution have been examined in detail, does not contradict Cook's analysis. Pownalborough, where political leadership was already Whig, experienced at the most a modest democratization in officeholding—meaning that more yeoman farmers, blacksmiths, and innkeepers joined the customary merchants, lawyers, and doctors in sharing local power.[73]

The truly significant political change lies not so much in altered patterns of local officeholding as in the broadening political role assumed by towns during this period. As towns experienced the Revolution, townsmen consciously exercised new powers of popular sovereignty brought on by the war.

With this broadening and deepening of popular political consciousness evolved a changing attitude toward political action. Traditionally, elected leaders determined the good of the community, to which virtuous citizens submitted. Such a concept emphasized the unity of "political truth" and condemned as disruptive political opposition or "factions."[74] In contrast to this corporate political outlook emerged a more individualistic concept of political society as a series of competing groups, from whose clashes and compromises evolved the common good. The best-known exposition of this view occurs in James Madison's "Tenth Federalist," written in defense of the federal Constitution in 1788. Two years earlier, however, as early as April 27, 1786, an article signed by "Scribble-Scrabble" in Portland's *Cumberland Gazette* defended political parties as natural and good in a free society, for as they competed and criticized one another they supported public liberty out of mutual self-interest. "In this manner, by the infinitely wise constitution of nature, is good brought out of evil."[75] Factions, or political parties, were not dangerous to liberty; they were essential for it.

In a changing political climate, Maine's dissenters gravitated to a new party of political opposition. By 1800 the Jeffersonian Republicans provided those who felt excluded from the opportunities of independence with a means of legitimate, organized political action they formerly had lacked. In Maine this included not only backcountry squatters and religious dissidents but a new, vigorous elite for whom the Federalist party had become too limited in both ideology and opportunity. Merchant-lawyer-politicians like John Chandler of Monmouth, John Holmes of Alfred, Albion K. Parris from the town of Paris, William Pitt Preble from Saco, and William King of Bath assumed the leadership of the new party in Maine and, not incidentally, adopted the causes of separation from Massachusetts and separation of church from state.[76] Under the auspices of the new Republican party, Maine's political, economic, and religious dissidents shared a major triumph when, in 1820, the District became a state—a process ably examined by Ronald F. Banks in *Maine Becomes a State* (1970). Statehood, however, was not an end in itself, and as Alan Taylor points out in *Liberty Men and Great Proprietors* (1990), the struggle for liberty continued unabated in the new political arena.

V

For groups without political leverage, the legacy of the Revolution was far more ambiguous. Elite leaders and spokesmen of the Revolution did not view the movement as a means of social reform, indeed, quite the opposite. Lacking political power, or the experience to use it even were the means available, loyalists, blacks, Indians, and women remained passive recipients of whatever fragmentary benefits of independence and republicanism came their way.

Ironically, many leading loyalists returned to Massachusetts with surprising ease to share in the promise of the new republic they had opposed. In 1778 the General Court had proscribed notorious Tories and in the year following passed two confiscation acts, one aimed at specified persons, the other at the general group of absentees who had fled the country. As soon as the war was over, however, loyalists appeared no longer as a threat but as sources of political talent and needed wealth. A new law in 1784 allowed the governor to issue permits for Tories to return and to regain their property if it had not been confiscated and sold. By 1785 all state anti-Tory legislation had been repealed. A writer in the *Cumberland Gazette* reflected the changing attitude by declaring publicly that he would welcome the returnees despite their political views, for their wealth and ability would be valuable assets to Maine if ever it were to become a state.[77]

In such an atmosphere of pragmatic toleration, a number of prominent loyalists, even some who had borne arms for the king, received permission to return to their former homes. The brothers of Sir William Pepperell, Nathaniel and Samuel Sparhawk of Kittery, and the Oxnards of Portland, Thomas and Edward, all came back to resume their roles as merchants. Jonathan Sayward, an acknowledged Tory who spent much of the war confined to his home in York, once again filled offices in town and church. Historian Stephen Patterson points out that the coastal commercial centers were far more lenient in forgiving their old enemies than the less commercial and rural settlements of the interior. Fryeburg, for example, resolved that returning Tories were traitors who ought to be entirely excluded from public office in country and state. Gorham, even more vehemently, voted that anyone who even encouraged the return of any Tory shall be regarded "as an Enemy to these United States and never Suffer'd to hold any office in the Town of Gorham forever after."[78] Despite the town's verbal ferocity, the former sheriff of Cumberland County, William Tyng, resettled in Gorham. Tyng had served in the British army, but his kindness to American prisoners and his sincere Christian character eased his return, as did the fact that he waited ten years after the war ended before coming back.[79]

The experience of John Jones may have had something to do with William Tyng's tactful tardiness in returning. Jones, despite his notoriety for commanding the British raiders who kidnapped Brigadier General Charles Cushing, tried to return "home" to Pownalborough in 1785. A group of citizens forcibly escorted him out of town; but Jones was not to be denied. He eventually returned to resume his former profession as surveyor for the Kennebec Proprietors. In this unpopular role, he defied angry squatters with the same boldness as he had the Sons of Liberty before the war.[80]

In most cases the loyalist returnees or their heirs regained the family property. The government did succeed in confiscating the estates of William Pepperell and Francis Waldo, but the process was long, tortuous, and completed only after the war was over. In numerous other cases, the legal proceedings were so imperfect and so complex that the war was over before they were complete. In such instances former owners could regain possession. Rebecca Callahan, whose husband died in British service, returned to Pownalborough after a sojourn in Nova Scotia and was able to repossess her husband's farm.[81]

Even Silvester Gardiner, the Tory voice of the old Kennebec Proprietors, hoped to come back from English exile to Massachusetts and to his lands in Maine, although his son warned him they had been stripped bare. He got as far as Rhode Island, where he died in 1788.[82] The family lands fell to his two sons, William and John. The first, like Jonathan Sayward, survived the war years in his home at Gardinerstown under suspicion and harassment as a Tory. John, the second son, remained in England and the West Indies during the war where he gained a reputation as a brilliant, eccentric lawyer with radical political leanings. At the war's end he migrated to Massachusetts, and then he too settled on family property in Pownalborough.

In Maine, John Gardiner lived up to his reputation; he actively championed the cause of separation from Massachusetts when that movement revived in the 1790s, and as a representative to the General Court he distinguished himself as a legal reformer. His goal was to simplify the judicial process by eliminating the Old World institutions and practices which he felt were inappropriate to republican equality and simplicity. One measure with which he was identified abolished the law of primogeniture whereby the eldest son inherited a double portion of the parental estate when owners died intestate. Another measure he advocated facilitated the process of breaking an entail, the old feudal restriction requiring property to devolve intact from one generation to the next. The legal fraternity succeeded in blocking several of Gardiner's other efforts to revise the manner of assessing court costs, to reduce the power of bar associations, and to eliminate the complicated and arcane practice of special pleading. Gardiner's conservative opponents must have breathed a sigh of relief on learning in 1793 that "John the Whig" was drowned in the wreck of the vessel carrying him from Pownalborough to Boston.[83]

Certainly the Revolution did much to stimulate antislave sentiment throughout Massachusetts and the District. Slavery was not economically vital, yet it was highly visible. Indeed, in 1783 the Supreme Judicial Court of Massachusetts declared that, since the state constitution proclaimed all men were born free and equal, slavery in Massachusetts was abolished. However, slavery was still a national institution, and repeatedly letters in the *Cumberland Gazette* denounced slavery and the slave trade as a shame to mankind and the ideals of the American republic. Asked one writer, How can we condemn the Algerians for plundering American vessels and holding crews as slaves for ransom when we are no better than they? Another exclaimed, "Blush, Boston — blush!" for the part its merchants played in the slave trade. A long poem entitled "The Negroe's Complaint" included the following stanza:

> Fleecy locks, and black complexion,
>   Cannot forfeit nature's claim;
> Skins may differ, but affection
>   Dwells in black and white the same.[84]

The most dramatic antislavery protest from Maine occurred at the state convention to ratify the federal Constitution. Several of the delegates from the District who opposed the new plan of government included in their criticism its failure to abolish slavery. It was Samuel Thompson, however, who boldly extended the criticism to include the most famous slaveholder of them all. "[S]hall it be said," he declared, "that, after we have established our own independence and freedom, we make *slaves* of others? O! Washington, what a name has he had! How he has immortalized himself! But he holds those in slavery who have as good a right to be free as he has. He is still for self; and, in my opinion, his character has sunk fifty percent."[85]

Throughout Massachusetts and the District, the Revolution heightened popular awareness of the contradictions of slavery in a republic and accelerated slavery's demise. Yet the social and economic condition of former slaves did not necessarily improve with personal freedom. Some simply remained as wage laborers for their former owners, who were now relieved of responsibility for their maintenance and welfare — "modified bondage," in the words of one historian. In Pownalborough, however, Salem, the elderly slave of merchant Abiel Lovejoy, refused to accept his freedom, insisting that in his old age his former owner owed him sustenance for his previous service. In the town of Wells, about a dozen freed blacks established their own community on a piece of land called "Nigger Ridge." Here they maintained a precarious existence by doing odd jobs for the community, making and selling baskets and brooms, raising vegetables, and accepting occasional charity. The significant decline in the number of blacks in York and Wells from fifty-six and thirty-four respectively in 1764 to twenty-six and fifteen in 1790 reveals that some former slaves made use of their new freedom to move. In many instances it was to Portland and other maritime communities where a maturing economy offered the hope of expanded economic opportunities.[86]

Independence provided blacks with ideological and even legal leverage against the institution of slavery, but independence deprived Indians of the advantages they once had enjoyed. During the war, the Penobscots, and especially the Passamaquoddies and Malecites, had used their strategic importance to play British and Americans against each other. After the war, the Indians lost their utility, and peace deprived them of their military significance. The Indians now became a tolerated nuisance, forced to accept whatever terms the victorious Americans wished to impose. Even before the war ended, Massachusetts closed down its truck house on the Kennebec and dismissed the agent. With the end of the war, the state also relieved John Allan of his military responsibilities, and in early 1784 the Continental Congress dismissed him from his superintendency of the eastern Indians and concluded its Indian role in Maine. Almost immediately, the state tried to reopen the old issue of Penobscot Indian land claims in an effort to stimulate white settlement in the area. Surprised and angry, the Penobscots refused to negotiate, at first insisting that in 1775 the Massachusetts Provincial Congress had recognized their claim to lands six miles on both sides of the Penobscot River above the head of tide. Commissioners for the state, however, argued that the government had merely acknowledged the Indians' claim for the time being, without passing judgment on it. By sheer persistence, and by dividing the Indians against themselves, the commissioners obtained a treaty in 1796 whereby the Penobscots gave up almost 190,000 acres, later divided into nine townships, in exchange for an initial supply of ammunition, food, clothing, and rum, to be followed by annual grants of such provisions. Despite government aid, the Penobscots found it increasingly difficult to subsist except by selling off more land and timber rights, thereby reducing yet further their capacity for self-sufficiency. In 1818 they sold to the Commonwealth ten more townships, and by the time Maine joined the union as a separate state the Penobscots were poverty-stricken wards of the new government.[87]

The end of the war left the Passamaquoddy and Malecite Indians in an equally difficult situation. Their lands stretched from eastern Maine into Nova Scotia where the British government was hostile to the Indians who had sympathized with the American cause. Through John Allan, the Passamaquoddies petitioned the General Court for a grant of land in Maine on which to settle in exchange for surrendering their rather shadowy claims to other lands in the District. In response, the state concluded an agreement in 1794 whereby the Passamaquoddy and Malecite tribes gave up whatever claims they had in Maine and received some 23,000 acres along the Saint Croix River at Pine Point and at Indian Township, as well as some islands in the river.[88]

Although they acquired clearly defined lands within a politically friendly environment, Maine's Indians in general appear to be the losers in the Revolution. They suffered through the loss of traditional lands, the loss of mobility, and a humiliating dependence on a government that regarded Indians at best as an obstacle in the path of progress. In his *History of the District of Maine*, published in 1795, James Sullivan, the future attorney general and later governor of Massachusetts, articulated the prevailing view toward the Indian:

> That the whole earth is intended ultimately to be improved, in the highest style to which improvement can be carried by men, is a proposition that no reasonable person will dispute.... Thus, in the general order of the world, the earth is to progress from being a rude mass of matter, till it has reached the highest state of elegance to which the noblest refinement of human reason can bring it. Separated from chaos, it exhibits a barren surface; then becomes an uninhabited and desolate desert; then the habitation of beast, and birds; then the haunts of roaming and unsocial barbarians; then the

dwelling of savage tribes; and finally the high cultivated, and beautifully decorated soil of civilized nations.... If the Savages cannot be incorporated with the emigrants, or become civilized as a nation, it will clearly follow, that they will by degrees be extirpated, and finally cease to exist as a nation.[89]

No one but John Allan spoke on behalf of the Indians after the war was over, and not even he protested the legality of the land transfers. Such treaties were in keeping with the state's time-honored relationship with the tribes. In Massachusetts there were few, if any, who were aware that in 1790 the new federal government had prohibited trade with the Indians and acquisition of their land without government approval. At that time, such legislation appeared applicable only in the western territories where tribes were still independent and sovereign, not where Indians were already under state hegemony. However, almost 200 years later, in an atmosphere more sensitive to the political and ethical issues involved, the Indians of Maine succeeded in obtaining compensation for the illegal loss of land under the federal Trade and Intercourse Act of 1790. In 1980 the Penobscot, Passamaquoddy, and Saint John Indians received an award of $27 million as a trust in addition to $54.5 million more to purchase 300,000 acres of land.[90] Belatedly, and if only partially, the Indians of Maine entered into their revolutionary legacy, whereby they too acquired the means to participate in the country's social and economic potential.

Independence bestowed few direct advantages on American women. Indeed, women shared the same fate as the Indians in that they contributed much to the movement which in turn either ignored or exploited them afterward. During the war, women everywhere had been forced out of their traditional domestic roles to assume responsibilities normally fulfilled by men. The now classic image of Abigail Adams bravely managing family and farm in Braintree, Massachusetts, while husband John conducted governmental business in Philadelphia and France is remarkable only for the personalities involved. Countless other women did the same under far harsher circumstances. Data is scanty on how they survived in the long run; for the short term, however, they quickly learned how to manipulate the political and legal machinery in their own behalf. One of Pownalborough's war widows, Elizabeth Lines, destitute as she was, successfully appealed to the General Court to maintain herself and five small children when the town selectmen refused to help her. In the same town, Lucy, the wife of Francis Rittal and the mother of ten children, also appealed to the General Court on behalf of her husband, jailed under martial law as a suspected loyalist. Her petition, quoting directly from the state's bill of rights, helped to free her sickly husband after nine weeks of confinement. When an American privateer-turned-pirate sacked the Campbell house on Deer Isle, it was not John Campbell but his wife, Mary, who pursued the villains all the way to Falmouth and, despite threats from the crew, sued them in court.[91] Everywhere the hardships of war drew women out of their accustomed domestic roles and, regardless of social station or political loyalties, forced them to assume new and unfamiliar activities as family defenders and providers.

At the end of the war, however, women generally resumed their familiar social functions. The genteel leaders and spokesmen of the Revolution had no intention of altering the traditional social structure, and women, even had they desired it, lacked the political leverage to do so. Historian Joan Hoff Wilson has pointed out that by 1800 women's domestic roles were extolled but their economic and legal privileges were curtailed, their recent revolutionary activity largely ignored, and their political participation discouraged. "For women, the American Revolution was over before it ever began."[92]

The writings of Maine's first novelist, Sally Sayward Barrell Wood, known simply as "Madam Wood," emphasize the importance of maintaining traditional social values in a changing world. Wood was an ardent republican and American nationalist, but as befits the granddaughter of Tory Jonathan Sayward, she was no social revolutionary. Her gothic novels were moralistic and sentimental; through innocence and virtue, Wood's heroines, like miniature republics, must withstand the evils and corruptions of the world that seek their destruction.

Madam Wood lost no opportunity to deplore what she perceived as decay in contemporary morals. When one of her heroines, Amelia, remains true to a loveless marriage, Madam Wood editorializes that the radical English feminist Mary Wollstonecraft would have condemned such a decision as "wanting spirit, and not asserting the rights of her sex." But Wood's Amelia "was not a woman of fashion, nor a woman of spirit. She was an old fashioned wife, and she meant to obey her husband; she meant to do her duty in the strictest sense of the word." In *Dorval; or, The Speculator*, Madam Wood's social message remains unchanged: "A female is never half so lovely, half so engaging or amiable, as when performing her domestic duties, and cheering, with smiles of unaffected good humor, those about her."[93]

Although these triumphs of domestic virtue usually take place in a European setting, Wood clearly embodies American ideals. She disapproves of aristocratic idleness; indeed, Francis Colwort, the hero in *Julia; and the Illuminated Baron*, wins praise for going into trade — a useful occupation. In the process, he travels to the United States, where dwells "a great people whose struggles for liberty have emancipated several millions from tyranny and oppression; who have laws without an arbitrary government and liberty without anarchy and confusion." Yet, despite her vigorous affirmation of republican principles, Madam Wood remained bound by the traditional views of a woman's place in society, no matter how republican that society might be.[94]

The Revolution, however, did create an environment conducive to new ideas — if not action — regarding the role of women in the new republic. Some concepts, such as that of Republican Motherhood, praised women as nurturers of future republican citizens but thereby only strengthened women's traditional domestic functions. Other ideas were more radical, however. As the novels by Madam Wood attest, Mary Wollstonecraft's writings had a profound impact in America's postrevolutionary society. Clergymen and educators, spokesmen for traditional values, professed shock at her suggestions that women should be more than ornamental; that they should be trained to contribute in the fields of medicine, politics, and business and enjoy full political and civil rights along with men. Wollstonecraft's lurid private life made it easy for her detractors to condemn all her ideas as immoral, but she only articulated publicly convictions that many Americans — men as well as women — held privately.[95]

The correspondence of Maine's leading Federalist, George Thatcher of Biddeford, reveals that he was sensitive to women's issues and that he could even appreciate Mary Wollstonecraft, whose writings he had clearly discussed with his wife. From Philadelphia, where he was serving as congressman from Massachusetts, Thatcher wrote to his wife apologizing for his earlier opposition to Wollstonecraft, who had recently died. Having read some of her works, he now termed her "a charming woman — I forgive all her faults, & blot out all her transgressions — Of all the letters I ever read," he wrote, "hers are the most affectionate, & expressive of a heart of good qualities — She was an Angel — but she is no more."[96]

Shortly afterward, Thatcher responded to his wife's query as to why, in addressing his correspondence to her, he insisted on using her maiden name. His response reveals a remarkable awareness of a woman's individuality at a time when she had none apart from that of her father or spouse. "I always thought," wrote Thatcher, "that women when they became wives, should not drop their original names — tis proper to take that of their Husbands, but keep their own —."[97] In these subtle, informal ways, this Harvard-trained, lawyer-politician from Maine demonstrated the elusive change of attitudes and feelings regarding women, not necessarily produced by the Revolution but nurtured in that atmosphere of change.

Broadly speaking, change in the direction of greater freedom was the Revolution's most enduring legacy. Even in Maine, the eastern corner of Massachusetts, the Revolution had fostered a new order based on freedom: freedom from the British Empire; freedom of Maine from Massachusetts; the liberty to participate in the political process, to be free from bondage, free from the state church, and to have equal opportunity to exploit the country's resources — especially its land. In the words of army veteran Henry Sewall, America was becoming "an asylum for liberty."[98]

Even more unsettling was the waning of the ancient ideal of an ethical community linking the disparate elements of life into one comprehensive whole under common moral values. Differing visions of the Revolution and the rise of political parties illustrate the change. So too do the words of Judge William Lithgow, "By thus seeking our own peace and happiness, we shall contribute our share towards maintaining the Commonwealth in strength and splendor."[99] Already weakened prior to the Revolution, the old communal ideal gave way to a new ethical individualism in the postwar era as Americans vigorously grappled with the reality of a pluralistic society, of individual freedom and open competition. Maine and the new republic were embarked on the most revolutionary of tasks, that of building a new community based on the conviction that individuals must be free to develop their own potential and to follow the dictates of their own self-interest. The continuing efforts to harmonize the needs of the community with those of the individual have provided a creative tension throughout American history, so that in one sense the Revolution will never be "finished" so long as its elusive ideals and principles endure to inspire and to beckon.

ABBREVIATIONS

AHR	*American Historical Review*
Am. Arch.	*American Archives*
BHM	*Bangor Historical Magazine*
BG	*Boston Gazette*
CAR	*Report on the Canadian Archives*
CG	*Cumberland Gazette*
CMeHS	*Collections of the Maine Historical Society*
CPMeHS	*Collections and Proceedings of the Maine Historical Society*
DAB	*Dictionary of American Biography*
DCB	*Dictionary of Canadian Biography*
Doc. Hist. Me.	*Documentary History of the State of Maine*
FG	*Falmouth Gazette*
LC	Library of Congress
MaHS	Massachusetts Historical Society
MaSA	Massachusetts State Archives
MeHGR	*Maine Historical and Genealogical Recorder*
MeHS	Maine Historical Society
MeHSN	*Maine Historical Society Newsletter*
MeHSQ	*Maine Historical Society Quarterly*
MeSA	Maine State Archives
NDAR	*Naval Documents of the American Revolution*
NEQ	*New England Quarterly*
NHG	*New-Hampshire Gazette*
PANS	Public Archives of Nova Scotia
WMQ	*William and Mary Quarterly*

NOTES

ONE *Maine*

1. William D. Williamson, *The History of the State of Maine, from its first Discovery A.D. 1620, to the Separation, A.D. 1820*, 2 vols. (Hallowell, Me.: Glazier, Masters, 1832; reprint ed., Freeport, Me.: Cumberland Press, n.d.), 2:9–20; Charles E. Clark, *The Eastern Frontier: The Settlement of Northern New England, 1610–1763* (New York: Alfred A. Knopf, 1970), p. 64.
2. Richard I. Hunt, Jr., "British-American Rivalry for the Support of the Indians of Maine and Nova Scotia, 1775–1783" (M.A. thesis, University of Maine at Orono, 1973), pp. 24–25, 34–37.
3. Address of Penobscot Chiefs to Gov. Sir Francis Bernard, July 26, 1769, *Documentary History of the State of Maine*, ed. James P. Baxter, 24 vols. (Portland: Maine Historical Society, 1869–1916), 24:159 (hereafter cited as *Doc. Hist. Me.*).
4. Hunt, "British-American Rivalry," pp. 25–30.
5. Journal of Rev. David Little, of Wells, during his Mission at Penobscot from July 1, 1774, to October 10, 1774, p. 103, transcript copy in John E. Godfrey Collection, Misc. Box 7/1, Maine Historical Society (MeHS).
6. Evarts B. Greene and Virginia D. Harrington, comps., *American Population before the Federal Census of 1790* (New York: Columbia University Press, 1932; reprint ed., Gloucester, Mass.: Peter Smith, 1966), pp. 36–40; Stanley B. Attwood, *The Length and Breadth of Maine* (Augusta, Me.: Kennebec Journal, 1946; reprint ed., Orono: University of Maine Press, 1974), pp. 21–22.
7. Clark, *Eastern Frontier*, pp. 177–179, 352–355; Benjamin W. Labaree, *Colonial Massachusetts: A History* (Millwood, N.Y.: KTO Press, 1979), pp. 148–152; Robert A. Gross, *The Minutemen and Their World* (New York: Hill and Wang, 1976), pp. 76–88.
8. Clark, *Eastern Frontier*, pp. 210–219, 352.
9. Gordon E. Kershaw, *The Kennebeck Proprietors, 1749–1775: Gentlemen of Large Property & Judicious Men* (Somersworth, N.H.: New Hampshire Publishing and Maine Historical Society, 1975), pp. xiv, 37.

10 Ibid., pp. 122–141, 183.
11 Ibid., pp. 63, 64–74; Clark, *Eastern Frontier*, pp. 175–176; Labaree, *Colonial Massachusetts*, p. 202; Richard Hofstadter, *America in 1750: A Social Portrait* (New York: Alfred A. Knopf, 1971; reprint ed., New York: Vintage Books, 1973), pp. 22–26.
12 Colonial Statistics, Series Z20: Percent Distribution of the White Population, by Nationality, 1790, in *The Statistical History of the United States from Colonial Times to the Present* (Stamford, Conn.: Fairfield Publishers, n.d.), p. 756.
13 Petition from Machias to the General Court, June 18, 1787, *Doc. Hist. Me.*, 21:367–368; John Ahlin, *Maine Rubicon: Downeast Settlers during the American Revolution* (Calais, Me.: Calais Advertiser Press, 1966), p. 5; Greene and Harrington, *American Population*, p. 39.
14 Greene and Harrington, *American Population*, pp. 36–38. In 1776 Falmouth's population declined by 757 from the census of 1765 (ibid., p. 30). The decrease probably represents the effects of war and the burning of the town by the British, October 18, 1775.
15 Rev. David Little's Journal, p. 98; William S. Southgate, "The History of Scarborough, from 1633 to 1783," *Collections of the Maine Historical Society (CMeHS)*, 1st ser. 3 (1853): 179; Joseph J. Malone, *Pine Trees and Politics: The Naval Stores and Forest Policy in Colonial New England, 1691–1775* (Seattle: University of Washington Press, 1964), pp. 154–155; Edwin A. Churchill, "Merchants and Commerce in Falmouth (1740–1775)," *Maine Historical Society Newsletter (MeHSN)* 9 (May 1970): 97–99; William H. Rowe, *The Maritime History of Maine* (New York: W. W. Norton, 1948), pp. 34–43; Clarence Day, *History of Maine Agriculture, 1604–1860* (Orono: University of Maine Press, 1954), pp. 38–40; William H. Rowe, *Ancient North Yarmouth and Yarmouth, Maine, 1626–1936: A History* (Yarmouth, Me.: Southworth-Anthoensin Press, 1937), p. 70.
16 Rowe, *Maritime History of Maine*, p. 267; Douglas R. McManis, *Colonial New England: A Historical Geography* (New York: Oxford University Press, 1975), pp. 102–107.
17 Rev. David Little's Journal, p. 105; William Willis, ed., *Journals of the Rev. Thomas Smith and the Rev. Samuel Deane, Pastors of the First Church in Portland: with Notes and Biographical Notices and a Summary History of Portland* (Portland, Me.: Joseph S. Bailey, 1849), pp. 196, 204, 221 (hereafter cited as Willis, *Smith and Deane Journals*).
18 Day, *Maine Agriculture*, chap. 6; Clark, *Eastern Frontier*, pp. 115, 229–235; *American Husbandry*, ed. Harry J. Carman (New York: Columbia University Press, 1939; reprint ed., Port Washington, N.Y.: Kennikat Press, 1964), pp. 35–43; Bettye H. Pruitt, "Agriculture and Society in the Towns of Massachusetts, 1771: A Statistical Analysis" (Ph.D. diss., Boston University, 1981), pp. 7–30, p. 130, table 16, Appendix, maps 4, 5, 7.
19 Clark, *Eastern Frontier*, pp. 264–265, 339–340; "Notices of the Powell Family and Extracts from Manuscripts of T. D. Powell," *CMeHS*, 1st ser. 7 (1876): 235–236; *King v. Town of York*, Records of the York County Court of General Sessions of the Peace, vol. 11, July 1757–July 1776, April Term, 1766, p. 304, Maine State Archives (MeSA).
20 John Adams, *Diary and Autobiography of John Adams*, ed. L. H. Butterfield, 4 vols.

(Cambridge, Mass.: Harvard University Press, 1962), 1:359, 3:281; Joshua Weeks to Jacob Bailey, Marblehead, Mass., May 23, 1768, Transcripts of the Correspondence of Rev. Jacob Bailey, ed. Charles E. Allen, 4 vols., 3:63, Wiscasset Public Library, Wiscasset, Me.; Rev. David Little's Journal, pp. 96, 103.

21 Rowe, *Maritime History of Maine*, pp. 26–28, 39; Churchill, "Merchants and Commerce in Falmouth," pp. 99–100; G. B. Warden, *Boston, 1689–1776* (Boston: Little, Brown, 1970), p. 17.

22 Ahlin, *Maine Rubicon*, p. 8; Stephen Jones, "Autobiography of Stephen Jones (of Machias)," *Sprague's Journal of Maine History* 3 (April 1916): 210–211; Stephen Jones, "Historical Account of Machias," *Maine Historical Society Quarterly (MeHSQ)* 15 (Fall 1975): 48; Clarence A. Day, "Colonel John Allan," typescript, University of Maine at Orono, p. 65; Benjamin Foster to the General Court, June 19, 1776, Massachusetts State Archives (MaSA), 211:62; "Nathan Jones, Robert Gould, and Francis Shaw," *Bangor Historical Magazine (BHM)* 7 (Oct., Nov., Dec. 1891): 67–71.

23 Kershaw, *Kennebeck Proprietors*, pp. 100–104.

24 Robert Sloan, "New Ireland: Loyalists in Eastern Maine during the American Revolution" (Ph.D. diss., Michigan State University, 1971), p. 31; Vernal Hutchinson, *When the Revolution Came: The Story of Old Deer Isle in the Province of Maine During the War for American Independence* (Ellsworth, Me.: Ellsworth American, 1972), p. 24.

25 Churchill, "Merchants and Commerce in Falmouth," pp. 93–102; Journal of Enoch Freeman, MeHS; Richard King Daybooks, 1758–1759, 1766–1768, Massachusetts Historical Society (MaHS), 1772–1774, MeHS; Jonathan Sayward Diaries, 1760–1799, 40 vols., American Antiquarian Society, Worcester, Mass. (microfilm copy), vol. 2, Jan. 21, 1761, as an example; Ephraim Jones's Account Book, William Willis Papers, vol. L, MeHS.

26 Churchill, "Merchants and Commerce in Falmouth," p. 102.

27 Quoted in Alan Taylor, "Liberty-Men and White Indians: Frontier Migration, Popular Protest, and the Pursuit of Property in the Wake of the American Revolution" (Ph.D. diss., Brandeis University, 1986), p. 365.

28 Ibid., pp. 365–366.

29 Jonathan Sayward Diaries, vol. 4, Dec. 24, 1763; see Sayward's similar acknowledgments of divine blessing at the end of each of the forty years recorded—following which he starts each new year with a list of his assets.

30 Churchill, "Merchants and Commerce in Falmouth," pp. 95–96; Clark, *Eastern Frontier*, p. 160; Edwin A. Churchill, "Enoch Freeman, Trader, Citizen, Revolutionary: A Brief Portrait of an Eighteenth-Century Falmouth Merchant," research paper, April 22, 1969, pp. 9–13.

31 Jack P. Greene, "Independence, Improvement, and Authority: Toward a Framework for Understanding the Histor*ies* of the Southern Backcountry during the Era of the American Revolution," in *An Uncivil War: The Southern Backcountry during the American Revolution*, ed. Ronald Hoffman, Thad W. Tate, and Peter J. Albert (Charlottesville: University Press of Virginia, 1985), p. 12.

32 Clark, *Eastern Frontier*, p. 163.

33 Ibid., p. 117; Edward C. Cass, "A Town Comes of Age: Pownalborough, Maine,

1720–1785" (Ph.D. diss., University of Maine at Orono, 1979), pp. 67–68, 85, 100–101 (hereafter cited as Cass, "Pownalborough"); Day, *Maine Agriculture*, pp. 48–49. See also David C. Smith, "Maine's Changing Landscape to 1820," in *Maine in the Early Republic: From Revolution to Statehood*, ed. Charles E. Clark, James S. Leamon, and Karen Bowden (Hanover, N.H.: University Press of New England, 1988).

34 Henry Tufts, *A Narrative of the Life, Adventures, Travels, and Sufferings of Henry Tufts, now residing at Lemington, in the District of Maine: In Substance as Compiled from his Own Mouth* (Dover, N.H.: Samuel Bragg, Jr., 1807); reprinted as *The Autobiography of a Criminal: Henry Tufts*, intro. and ed. Edmund Pearson (New York: Duffield, 1930).

35 *New-Hampshire Gazette* (*NHG*), April 19, 1765.

36 Jackson Turner Main, *The Social Structure of Revolutionary America* (Princeton, N.J.: Princeton University Press, 1965), p. 41; Randolph Stakeman, "Slavery in Colonial Maine," *MeHSQ* 27 (Fall 1987): 64–65; Joseph Williamson, "Slavery in Maine," *CMeHS*, 1st ser. 7 (1876): 214–215; Williamson, *History of Maine*, 2:373; Stakeman, "Slavery in Colonial Maine," pp. 66–68. Note that Williamson gives a total of 332 Negroes in Maine on the basis of the 1764 census; Stakeman, using Williamson's data, gives the total as 322. The correct total of Williamson's figures is 334.

37 Adele E. Plachta, "The Privileged and the Poor: A History of the District of Maine, 1771–1793" (Ph.D. diss., University of Maine at Orono, 1975), pp. 93–99.

38 Ibid., pp. 95, 96, 150.

39 Pruitt, "Agriculture and Society in Massachusetts," Appendix, map 7; Edward M. Cook, Jr., *The Fathers of the Towns: Leadership and Community Structure in Eighteenth-Century New England* (Baltimore, Md.: Johns Hopkins University Press, 1976), p. 68, table 11, p. 168, table 27, p. 208, Appendix 2.

40 Plachta, "The Privileged and the Poor," p. 150.

41 Cass, "Pownalborough," pp. 72, 100–101; Main, *Social Structure*, pp. 130–132.

42 Cass, "Pownalborough" pp. 130–133. A large number of historians have examined local government in colonial New England; among the most useful are Gross, *The Minutemen and Their World*, pp. 10–15; Michael Zuckerman, *Peaceable Kingdoms: New England Towns in the Eighteenth Century* (New York: Alfred A. Knopf, 1970; reprint ed., Vintage Books, 1972), chap. 3; Stephen E. Patterson, *Political Parties in Revolutionary Massachusetts* (Madison: University of Wisconsin Press, 1973), pp. 23–26; Richard D. Brown, *Revolutionary Politics in Massachusetts: The Boston Committee of Correspondence and the Towns, 1772–1774* (Cambridge, Mass.: Harvard University Press, 1970), pp. 4–5; Cook, *Fathers of the Towns*, passim.

43 Stephen A. Marini, "Religious Revolution in the District of Maine, 1780–1820," in Clark, Leamon, and Bowden, *Maine in the Early Republic*, pp. 119–121; An Act to Encourage the Preaching of the Gospel, July 14, 1772, *Doc. Hist. Me.*, 14:185–186.

44 Bristol Town Records, March 20, 1765–May 9, 1776, MeSA; *NHG*, Aug. 15, 1773; Kennebunkport Town Records, March 30, 1764–Aug. 20, 1771, MeSA; Rev. Thurston Whiting to the Town of Newcastle, Newcastle Town Records, May 9, 1776, MeSA.

45 Stephen A. Marini, *Radical Sects of Revolutionary New England* (Cambridge, Mass.: Harvard University Press, 1982), p. 51; John L. Sibley, *Biographical Sketches of Grad-*

uates of Harvard University, and Clifford K. Shipton, *Biographical Sketches of Those Who Attended Harvard College*, 17 vols. (Cambridge: Harvard University Press and Boston: Massachusetts Historical Society, 1873–1975), 6:406–407, 7:201–203, 12:520–522; Henry S. Burrage, *A History of the Baptists in Maine* (Portland, Me.: Marks Printing House, 1904), pp. 29–36; Clark, *Eastern Frontier*, p. 166; William Williamson, "Sketches of the Lives of Early Maine Ministers," *Collections and Proceedings of the Maine Historical Society (CPMeHS)*, 2nd ser. 6 (1895): 184–185; A. G. Vermilye, "Memoir of the Rev. John Murray, First Minister of the Church in Boothbay," *CMeHS*, 1st ser. 6 (1857): 157–163.

46 John D. Cushing, "Notes on Disestablishment in Massachusetts, 1780–1833," *William and Mary Quarterly (WMQ)* 26 (April 1969): 169–172.
47 Marini, *Radical Sects*, pp. 5–6, 36.
48 Memorial of the Associated Ministers of York to the General Court, and the General Court's Answer, July 9–10, 1772, *Doc. Hist. Me.*, 14:182–184.
49 Cook, *Fathers of the Towns*, pp. 207–208, Appendix 2.
50 Nathaniel Thwing, "Records of Lincoln County: Records of Criminal Actions, 1772," MeHS; L. Kinvin Wroth and Hiller B. Zobel, eds., *Legal Papers of John Adams*, 3 vols. (Cambridge, Mass.: Harvard University Press, 1965), 1:xxxix.
51 Wroth and Zobel, *Legal Papers of John Adams*, 1:xxxix–xl.
52 Ibid., 1:xl–xliii; Robert J. Taylor, *Western Massachusetts in the Revolution* (Providence, R.I.: Brown University Press, 1954), p. 27; Joseph Williamson, "The Professional Tours of John Adams in Maine," *CPMeHS*, 2nd ser. 1 (1890): 301–308; William E. Nelson, *The Americanization of the Common Law: The Impact of Legal Change on Massachusetts Society, 1760–1830* (Cambridge, Mass.: Harvard University Press, 1975), pp. 4–5, 48, 63.
53 Petition from Boothbay to the General Court, March 4, 1766, *Doc. Hist. Me.*, 13:440–441; Petitions from the Inhabitants of Broad Bay, Freetown, Muscongus, and Medumcook, Jan. 14, 1767, ibid., 14:14–18; Taylor, *Western Massachusetts*, pp. 30–31.
54 Wroth and Zobel, *Legal Papers of John Adams*, 1:xl; for Adams's legal fees, see ibid., pp. lxix–lxxii; Warden, *Boston*, pp. 154–155.
55 Wroth and Zobel, *Legal Papers of John Adams*, 1:lxxx.
56 Samuel Freeman's article against lawyers, Willis Papers, vol. S, MeHS; William Freeman, "Samuel Freeman, His Life and Services," *CPMeHS*, 2nd ser. 5 (1894): 5–6.
57 Robert E. Brown, *Middle-Class Democracy and the Revolution in Massachusetts, 1691–1780* (Ithaca, N.Y.: Cornell University Press, 1955), pp. 63–64, 68, 55–60. For a survey of the historical debate, see John B. Kirby, "Early American Politics—the Search for Ideology: An Historiographic Analysis and Critique of the Concept of 'Deference,'" *Journal of Politics* 32 (Nov. 1970): 808–838.
58 Brown, *Middle-Class Democracy*, pp. 72–75; Massachusetts, *Journals of the House of Representatives, 1715–1778*, 53 vols. (Boston: Massachusetts Historical Society, 1919–), 42:4, 47:4. For a list of town incorporation dates, see Attwood, *Length and Breadth of Maine*, p. 21; and for statistics on population, see Greene and Harrington, *American Population*, pp. 29–30.

59 John D. Noble, "Messengers from the Wilderness: Maine's Representatives to the Massachusetts General Court, 1760–1819" (Ph.D. diss., University of Maine at Orono, 1975), pp. 182–183; Plachta, "The Privileged and the Poor," pp. 153–155; Cook, *Fathers of the Towns*, p. 54, table 9; George A. Ernst, *New England Miniature: A History of York, Maine* (Freeport, Me.: Bond Wheelwright, 1961), pp. 75, 78; James H. Stark, *The Loyalists of Massachusetts and the Other Side of the Revolution* (Boston: W. B. Clark, 1910), p. 444.

60 Brown, *Revolutionary Politics*, p. 7; Noble, "Messengers from the Wilderness," pp. 63–64, 134; Plachta, "The Privileged and the Poor," p. 166.

61 Noble, "Messengers from the Wilderness," pp. 2, 64, 132, 169–170, 174; Patterson, *Political Parties*, pp. 41–47, 248. See Plachta, "The Privileged and the Poor," chap. 3, and Cook, *Fathers of the Towns*, pp. 151–153, 207–208, Appendix 2.

62 Gordon Wood, "A Note on Mobs in the American Revolution," *WMQ* 23 (Oct. 1966): 635–642; Jesse Lemisch, "Jack Tar in the Streets: Merchant Seamen in the Politics of Revolutionary America," ibid. 25 (July 1968): 371–407; Pauline Maier, "Popular Uprisings and Civil Authority in Eighteenth-Century America," ibid. 27 (Jan. 1970): 3–35; Dirk Hoerder, *Crowd Action in Revolutionary Massachusetts, 1765–1780* (New York: Academic Press, 1977), pp. 37–38, 49, 56, 368.

63 Maier, "Popular Uprisings," pp. 5, 9; Warden, *Boston*, pp. 136–137, 219.

64 Taylor, "Liberty-Men and White Indians," pp. 80–81.

65 Vice Admiral Samuel Graves to Philip Stephens, *Preston*, Boston, April 11, 1775, in *Naval Documents of the American Revolution*, ed. William B. Clark, William J. Morgan, et al., 9 vols. (Washington, D.C.: U.S. Government Printing Office, 1964–), 1:176–177 (hereafter cited as *NDAR*); Magistrates of Cumberland County to Thomas Gage, Falmouth, Feb. 20, 1775, in L. Kinvin Wroth, *Province in Rebellion* (Cambridge, Mass.: Harvard University Press, 1975), doc. 728, pp. 2036–2037.

66 Jonathan Longfellow to Gov. Thomas Hutchinson, Machias, Nov. 8, 1770, *Doc. Hist. Me.*, 14:112–114; *NHG*, Dec. 21, 1770; "Autobiography of Stephen Jones," p. 211. See also Memorial of Machias Inhabitants to Hutchinson, Nov. 9, 1770, and the Report of the Commissioners on Machias, Sept. 12, 1772, *Doc. Hist. Me.*, 14:114–115, 139.

67 John Adams to Abigail Adams, Falmouth, July 7, 1774, in Wroth and Zobel, *Legal Papers of John Adams*, 1:140.

68 John Adams's notes on his address to the jury in *King v. Stuart*, ibid., 1:136–140.

69 Quoted in Bernard Bailyn, *The Ideological Origins of the American Revolution* (Cambridge, Mass.: Harvard University Press, 1967), p. 67.

70 Ibid., pp. 70–76.

71 Enoch Freeman Almanacs, 1729–1793, entry for 1759, Portland Public Library, Portland, Me.

72 Bailyn, *Ideological Origins*, pp. 79–85; Samuel Freeman to his brother, Falmouth, May 31, 1764, Willis Papers, vol. S, MeHS.

73 James A. Henretta and Gregory H. Nobles, *Evolution and Revolution: American Society, 1600–1820* (Lexington, Mass.: D. C. Heath, 1987), pp. 75–78, 139.

74 Malone, *Pine Trees and Politics*, p. 10; Kershaw, *Kennebeck Proprietors*, p. 202; Rowe, *Maritime History of Maine*, p. 35; Wroth and Zobel, *Legal Papers of John Adams*, 2:247.

75 Malone, *Pine Trees and Politics*, pp. 98–100; Wroth and Zobel, *Legal Papers of John Adams*, 2:247–254; William R. Carlton, "New England Masts and the King's Navy," *New England Quarterly (NEQ)* 12 (March 1939): 9–10, and see Malone, *Pine Trees and Politics*, chap. 7; Kershaw, *Kennebeck Proprietors*, chap. 10.
76 Williamson, *History of Maine*, 2:361–362; Ahlin, *Maine Rubicon*, p. 5.
77 Williamson, *History of Maine*, 2:387, 389–390; Gov. Thomas Hutchinson to the General Court, Cambridge, Mass., Sept. 1770, *Doc. Hist. Me.*, 14:103–105; Hutchinson to the General Court, May 30, 1771, ibid., p. 131; Hutchinson to the House of Representatives, June 19, 1771, ibid., pp. 132–134; Hutchinson to the Earl of Hillsborough, Boston, Jan. 31, 1772, ibid., p. 158; Hutchinson to the Earl of Dartmouth, Boston, Nov. 13, 1772, ibid., pp. 187–188.
78 Williamson, *History of Maine*, 2:389; Gov. Thomas Hutchinson to the House of Representatives, June 19, 1771, *Doc. Hist. Me.*, 14:132–134; Thomas Hutchinson, *The History of the Colony and Province of Massachusetts-Bay*, ed. Lawrence S. Mayo, 3 vols. (Cambridge, Mass.: Harvard University Press, 1936), 3:244–245.
79 Thomas Scammell to Gov. Thomas Hutchinson, Portsmouth, N.H., Jan. 2, 1772, *Doc. Hist. Me.*, 14:153–154; Commissioners' Report on Machias to Hutchinson, Sept. 12, 1771, ibid., pp. 137–138, 139–141.
80 Earl of Stirling to Gov. Francis Bernard, Baskenbridge, England, Aug. 10, 1768, ibid., 14:87; Report of a Committee of the General Court, Sept. 7, 1768, ibid., pp. 88–90; Bernard's Proclamation, Sept. 7, 1768, ibid., pp. 90–91.
81 Petition from Boothbay to the King, April 22, 1772, ibid., 14:166–170; Deposition of Samuel McCobb, Oct. 23, 1772, in Francis B. Greene, *History of Boothbay, Southport, and Boothbay Harbor, Maine, 1623–1905* (Portland, Me.: Loring, Short, and Harmon, 1906), pp. 117–119; *NHG*, Sept. 30, 1768; *Boston Gazette (BG)*, Dec. 26, 1768; *NHG*, Dec. 30, 1768.
82 Irving H. King, "The S.P.G. in New England, 1701–1784" (Ph.D. diss., University of Maine at Orono, 1968), p. 203.
83 Ibid., pp. 193–200.
84 Kershaw, *Kennebeck Proprietors*, pp. 240–241.
85 Ibid., pp. 234–236.
86 Ibid., pp. 231–232.
87 Ibid., pp. 237–239; Sibley and Shipton, *Biographical Sketches*, 13:525–530.
88 Kershaw, *Kennebeck Proprietors*, pp. 246–247.
89 Ibid., pp. 240–241; Petition from the Inhabitants of the West Precinct in Pownalborough to the General Court, n.d., *Doc. Hist. Me.*, 15:82–85.
90 Cass, "Pownalborough," pp. 116–125; Kershaw, *Kennebeck Proprietors*, pp. 239–241; Charles E. Allen, "Rev. Jacob Bailey," *CPMeHS*, 2nd ser. 7 (1896): 227–228.
91 Sibley and Shipton, *Biographical Sketches*, 13:529, 681–683.
92 William Willis, *The History of Portland, from Its First Settlement, with Notices of the Neighbouring Towns, and of the Changes of Government in Maine*, 2 vols. (Portland, Me.: Charles Day, 1833), 2:68–71; John C. Perkins, "Some Old Papers Recently Found in the Old Stone Tower of the First Parish Church of Portland," *CPMeHS*, 2nd ser. 6 (1895): 14; Williamson, "Sketches of the Lives of Early Maine Ministers," ibid., pp. 184–186.
93 *BG*, Jan. 14, 1765.

TWO The Revolution Comes to Maine

1. Edmund Morgan and Helen Morgan, *The Stamp Act Crisis: Prologue to Revolution*, rev. ed. (Chapel Hill: University of North Carolina Press, 1962; reprint ed., New York: Collier Books, 1963), pp. 36–37.
2. Ibid., pp. 96–98.
3. Ibid., chap. 8; Pauline Maier, *From Resistance to Revolution: Colonial Radicals and the Development of American Opposition to Britain* (New York: Alfred A. Knopf, 1972; reprint ed., New York: Vintage Books, 1974), pp. 54–60; Warden, *Boston*, pp. 164–168.
4. Falmouth Town Records, Oct. 10, 1765, MeSA; Willis, *Smith and Deane Journals*, pp. 316, 207; Willis, *History of Portland*, 2:126; *NHG*, March 1, 1765.
5. *NHG*, Jan. 31, 1766; Willis, *Smith and Deane Journals*, p. 317; *BG*, Feb. 3, 1766.
6. Willis, *Smith and Deane Journals*, p. 209; *NHG*, May 30, 1766; Willis, *History of Portland*, 2:127 n.
7. Morgan and Morgan, *Stamp Act Crisis*, p. 167; Kershaw, *Kennebeck Proprietors*, pp. 180–185.
8. Willis, *Smith and Deane Journals*, p. 206; *Bennet v. Bryant*, Records of the Cumberland County Inferior Court of Common Pleas, vol. 2, April 1768–Oct. 1772, Oct. Term, 1771, pp. 408–410, MeSA; William Tyng to Gov. Francis Bernard, Falmouth, Aug. 11, 1766, *Doc. Hist. Me.*, 14:84; *NHG*, Aug. 19, 1768.
9. Francis Waldo to Surveyor General, Falmouth, Aug. 11, 1766, *Doc. Hist. Me.*, 14:8–9; Willis, *Smith and Deane Journals*, p. 319; Willis, *History of Portland*, 2:128; *NHG*, Aug. 22, 1766.
10. Quoted in Hiller B. Zobel, *The Boston Massacre* (New York: W. W. Norton, 1970), pp. 50–51; Gov. Francis Bernard's Proclamation, *BG*, Aug. 25, 1766.
11. Deposition of Silas Burbank, June 28, 1773, and John Adams's Minutes of the Review in *King v. Stuart*, in Wroth and Zobel, *Legal Papers of John Adams*, 1:122, 129.
12. Evidence of John Rice et al., "Evidence of Sundry Persons about the Mob," Richard King Papers (microfilm), Rufus King Papers, New-York Historical Society.
13. Wroth and Zobel, *Legal Papers of John Adams*, 1:126.
14. Ibid., pp. 106–107; for recent accounts of the King riot, see Robert Ernst, *Rufus King, American Federalist* (Chapel Hill: University of North Carolina Press, 1968), pp. 7–13; James S. Leamon, "The Stamp Act Crisis in Maine: The Case of Scarborough," *MeHSN* 11 (Winter 1972): 74–93; Hoerder, *Crowd Action in Revolutionary Massachusetts*, pp. 134–138.
15. Oliver M. Dickerson, *The Navigation Acts and the American Revolution* (Philadelphia: University of Pennsylvania Press, 1951), pp. 115–116, 195–197; Warden, *Boston*, pp. 182–183.
16. John Dickinson, "Letters from a Farmer in Pennsylvania (1767–1768)," in *Colonies to Nation, 1763–1789: A Documentary History of the American Revolution*, ed. Jack P. Greene (New York: McGraw-Hill, 1967; reprint ed., New York: W. W. Norton, 1975), pp. 122–133.
17. "Massachusetts Circular Letter (Feb. 11, 1768)," in Greene, *Colonies to Nation*, pp. 134–136; Warden, *Boston*, pp. 187, 189, 194.

18 Jonathan Sayward Diaries, vol. 9, June 8, Dec. 29, 1768; *BG*, Aug. 15, Sept. 19, 1768; York Town Records, Sept. 13, 1768, MeSA.
19 Brown, *Revolutionary Politics*, pp. 29–30.
20 Rowe, *Ancient North Yarmouth*, p. 150; Josiah Pierce, *A History of the Town of Gorham, Maine* (Portland, Me.: Foster and Cushing, Bailey and Noyes, 1862), p. 110; Kennebunkport Town Records, Sept. 16, 1768, Brunswick Town Records, Sept. 22, 1768, Newcastle Town Records, Sept. 21, 1768, all in MeSA.
21 Falmouth Town Records, Dec. 4, 1768, MeSA; *BG*, Dec. 28, 1767, Oct. 16, 1769; *Old Times in North Yarmouth* 2 (1878): 262; Falmouth Boycott Agreement, June 6, 1769, Willis Papers, vol. O, MeHS; *Maine Historical and Genealogical Recorder* (*MeHGR*) 1 (1884): 9; Brown, *Revolutionary Politics*, p. 29.
22 *BG*, June 18, 1770; Willis, *Smith and Deane Journals*, p. 238; Falmouth Agreement, *BG*, July 9, 1770; *NHG*, July 13, 1770.
23 *Freeman v. Child*, Records of the Cumberland County Inferior Court of Common Pleas, vol. 2, April 1768–Oct. 1772, April Term, 1769, pp. 70–71, MeSA.
24 Memorial of Arthur Savage, Nov. 27, 1771, *Doc. Hist. Me.*, 14:147; Willis, *History of Portland*, 2:132–133 n.
25 Memorial of Arthur Savage, *Doc. Hist. Me.*, 14:147.
26 *Brightman v. Veazy*, Records of the Cumberland County Inferior Court of Common Pleas, vol. 2, April 1768–Oct. 1772, April Term, 1772, pp. 494–496, MeSA.
27 Frank W. C. Hersey, "Tar and Feathers: The Adventures of Captain John Malcom," *Publications of the Colonial Society of Massachusetts* 34 (April 1941): 432–437.
28 Quoted in ibid., p. 439. For a recent account of the affair, see Cass, "Pownalborough," pp. 129–130.
29 Warden, *Boston*, pp. 254–264; Brown, *Revolutionary Politics*, pp. 54–57, 67–80, 110–111, 138.
30 Brown, *Revolutionary Politics*, p. 138.
31 Gorham Town Records, Jan. 7, 1773, MeSA; Brown, *Revolutionary Politics*, p. 118; York Town Records, Dec. 28, 1772, MeSA; Falmouth Town Records, Dec. 24, 1772, Jan. 7, 1773, MeSA; Rowe, *Ancient North Yarmouth*, pp. 151–152.
32 Pownalborough Town Records, March 31, 1773, MeSA.
33 Brown, *Revolutionary Politics*, pp. 120–121.
34 Rowe, *Ancient North Yarmouth*, pp. 152–154; York Town Records, Jan. 20, 1774, MeSA.
35 Falmouth Town Records, Feb. 3, 1774, MeSA; *NHG*, March 4, 1774.
36 Gorham Town Records, Jan. 17, 1774, MeSA.
37 Kittery Town Meeting, Dec. 21, 1773, *MeHGR* 1 (1884): 67–68; Gorham Town Records, Jan. 17, 1774, MeSA; York Town Records, Jan. 21, 1774, MeSA.
38 *NHG*, Sept. 30, 1774; *BG*, Oct. 3, 1774.
39 Jonathan Sayward Diaries, vol. 15, Sept. 28, 1774.
40 *NHG*, Feb. 18, May 13, 1774.
41 Wroth, *Province in Rebellion*, pp. 17–18, 39–40, and related documents: Boston Port Act, doc. 4, pp. 44–51; Lord Dartmouth to General Gage, received Aug. 6, 1774, doc. 147, pp. 502–503; Massachusetts Government Act, doc. 148, pp. 506–519.
42 Ibid., pp. 40–41.
43 John Scollay to Arthur Lee, Boston, May 31, 1774, in *American Archives: Consisting of*

a collection of authentick records, state papers, debates, and letters and other notices of publick affairs, the whole forming a documentary history of the origin and progress of the North American colonies . . . , ed. Peter Force, 4th ser., 6 vols. (Washington, D.C.: M. St. Clair Clarke and Peter Force, 1837–1846), 1:369 (hereafter cited as *Am. Arch.*). Reporting on the Port Act, Scollay wrote, "*Lord North* will find out himself, and that very soon, that he overshot his mark. That which he intended should operate against *Boston* only, will affect every town in this Province. The seaport towns will feel the operation of the Act, in a degree as much as *Boston*, *Boston* being the grand engine that gives motion to all the wheels of commerce. This being stopped, it will sensibly affect the whole trade of the Province. All the seaport towns depend on this to take off by far the greatest part of their imports; they cannot send a vessel to sea again after her return from a voyage, till they send her cargo to *Boston* to be sold. In short, all the running cash in the Province centers in this town. To this market all the trading towns repair with their goods to make money of them."

44 Willis, *History of Portland*, 2:140–141 n.; Gorham Town Records, Jan. 7, 1775, MeSA; Berwick Subscription List, July 18, 1774, Misc. Papers, Box 15/2, MeHS; Nathan Goold, "Capt. Johnson Moulton's Company, the First to Leave the District of Maine in the Revolution," *CPMeHS*, 2nd ser. 10 (1899): 302–303; Buxton Town Meeting, June 20, 1774, *Doc. Hist. Me.*, 14:235–236.

45 Enoch Freeman Almanacs, 1729–1793, entry for 1774. Compare John Locke, "The Second Treatise of Government: An Essay Concerning the True Origin, Extent, and End of Civil Government," pp. 476–477, in John Locke, *Two Treatises of Government*, ed. Peter Laslett, rev. ed. (Cambridge: Cambridge University Press, 1960; reprint ed., New York: Mentor Books, 1965).

46 Wroth, *Province in Rebellion*, p. 67; Charles E. Allen, *History of Dresden, Maine, formerly part of the old town of Pownalborough, from its earliest settlement to the year 1900* ([Augusta, Me.: Kennebec Journal], 1931), p. 293.

47 David R. Ordway, untitled, undated research paper on the closing of the courts in York County, 1773–1776, p. 14, original in possession of L. Kinvin Wroth, University of Maine School of Law, Portland; Ernst, *New England Miniature*, p. 77.

48 William B. Jordan, Jr., *A History of Cape Elizabeth, Maine* (Portland, Me.: House of Falmouth, 1965), p. 45.

49 *BG*, Dec. 5, 1774; York County Resolves, *Am. Arch.*, 4th ser., 1:983–984; Declaration of William Tyng, ibid., p. 799; Allen, *Dresden*, p. 293.

50 William Lincoln, ed., *Journals of Each Provincial Congress of Massachusetts in 1774 and 1775* (Boston: Dutton and Wentworth, 1838), pp. 3–15, 359, 12, 14–15, 81, 83, 279; Selectmen of Bowdoinham to the Provincial Congress, July 18, 1775, *Doc. Hist. Me.*, 14:290–291.

51 Wroth, *Province in Rebellion*, pp. 62–63.

52 Cumberland County Resolves, *Am. Arch.*, 4th ser., 1:798–801; York County Resolves, ibid., pp. 983–984.

53 Solemn League and Covenant, June 8, 1774, in Wroth, *Province in Rebellion*, p. 36, doc. 122, pp. 456–459; Brown, *Revolutionary Politics*, pp. 191–192, 200 n.

54 Cook, *Fathers of the Towns*, p. 208, Appendix 2; see also Pruitt, "Agriculture and Society in Massachusetts," p. 68, table 4, Appendix, maps 3 and 7; Plachta, "The Privileged and the Poor," pp. 95–98, tables 23–25.

55 Gorham Town Records, Aug. 31, 1774, MeSA.
56 Southgate, "History of Scarborough," pp. 189–192.
57 Samuel Goodwin to Gov. Thomas Gage, Pownalborough, Aug. 10, 1774, in Wroth, *Province in Rebellion*, doc. 199, pp. 597–598.
58 Abraham Preble to Gov. Thomas Gage, Bowdoinham, Aug. 3, 1774, ibid., doc. 195, pp. 589–590.
59 For background on Samuel Thompson, see Nathan Goold, "General Samuel Thompson of Brunswick and Topsham, Maine," *CMeHS*, 3rd ser. 1 (1904): 423–458; George A. Wheeler and Henry W. Wheeler, *History of Brunswick, Topsham, and Harpswell, Maine* (Boston: Alfred Mudge and Son, 1878), pp. 811–816; Brunswick Town Records, 1760–1780, passim, MeSA; James H. Maguire, ed., "A Critical Edition of Edward Parry's Journal, March 28, 1775, to August 23, 1777" (Ph.D. diss., Indiana University, 1970), p. 4.
60 William S. Bartlet, *The Frontier Missionary: A Memoir of the Life of the Reverend Jacob Bailey* (Boston: Ide and Dutton, 1853; reprint ed., Ann Arbor, Mich.: University Microfilms, 1979), pp. 106, 351; Allen, *Dresden*, pp. 290–293; Henry O. Thayer, "Loyalists of the Kennebec and One of Them—John Carleton," *Sprague's Journal of Maine History* 5 (Feb., March, April 1918): 246; Sloan, "New Ireland: Loyalists in Eastern Maine," p. 93.
61 Allen, *Dresden*, pp. 290–293.
62 Maguire, "Parry's Journal," pp. xviii–xix, 8; Journal of the Provincial Congress of Massachusetts, April 11, 1775, *NDAR*, 1: 176; Dummer Sewall to the President of the Massachusetts Council, Georgetown, May 6, 1775, ibid., pp. 282, 290–291.
63 Maquire, "Parry's Journal," pp. 12–15.
64 Ibid., pp. 16, 19, 22.
65 Enoch Freeman to the Public, Falmouth, April 10, 1775, *Am. Arch.*, 4th ser., 2:311–312; Minutes of the Falmouth Committee of Inspection, March 2–3, 1775, ibid., pp. 312–313; John Waite to John Adams, Falmouth, March 18, 1775, *NDAR*, 1:152.
66 Minutes of the Falmouth Committee of Inspection, March 2, 1775, *Am. Arch.*, 4th ser., 2:312; Gov. Thomas Gage to William Tyng, Boston, March 31, 1775, in Wroth, *Province in Rebellion*, doc. 740, p. 2049.
67 Quoted in Extract of a Letter from the Chairman of the Committee at Falmouth to Samuel Freeman, Falmouth, April 12, 1775, *Am. Arch.*, 4th ser., 2:318.
68 Minutes of the Falmouth Committee of Inspection, March 3, 1775, ibid., p. 313.
69 Enoch Freeman to Samuel Freeman, Falmouth, May 10, ibid., pp. 550–551; Jedediah Preble to the Provincial Congress, Falmouth, May 14, 1775, *Doc. Hist. Me.*, 14:250–253; Deposition of Rev. John Wiswall, Henry Mowatt Papers, MeHS; Rev. John Wiswall to Mr. Hind, Boston, May 30, 1775, John Wiswall Papers, MeHS.
70 Deposition of Rev. John Wiswall, Mowatt Papers, MeHS; Letter from Falmouth to a Gentleman in Watertown, May 11, 1775, *Am. Arch.*, 4th ser., 2:553.
71 Enoch Freeman to Samuel Freeman, Falmouth, May 10, 1775, *Am. Arch.*, 4th ser., 2:550–551.
72 Daniel Tucker, "Capt. Daniel Tucker in the Revolution," *CPMeHS*, 2nd ser. 8 (1897): 231.
73 Letter from Falmouth to a Gentleman in Watertown, May 11, 1775, *Am. Arch.*, 4th ser., 2:553.

74 Ibid., p. 555.
75 Committee of Correspondence of Falmouth to the Committee of Safety, Falmouth, May 15, 1775, ibid., pp. 586–587.
76 Vice Adm. Samuel Graves to Midshipman James Moore, Boston, May 26, 1775, *NDAR*, 1:537–538.
77 Committee of Machias to the Provincial Congress, Machias, June 14, 1775, *Doc. Hist. Me.*, 14:280; Resolution signed by George Stillman, Machias, June 6, 1775, George Stillman Papers, Manuscript Division, Library of Congress (LC).
78 Committee of Machias to the Provincial Congress, Machias, June 14, 1775, *Doc. Hist. Me.*, 14:281; Jones, "Historical Account of Machias," p. 50.
79 George W. Drisko, *The Revolution: The Life of Hannah Weston, with a Brief History of Her Ancestry*, 2nd ed. (Machias, Me.: George A. Parlin, 1903), pp. 54–61. The two young women were rewarded for their services with twelve yards of cloth valued at £2.8 (ibid., p. 61).
80 Nathaniel Godfrey's Report, June 11, 1775, *NDAR*, 1:655–656; Deposition of Jabez Cobb, ibid., pp. 757–758; Committee of Machias to the Provincial Congress, June 14, 1775, *Doc. Hist. Me.*, 14:281–283; Jones, "Historical Account of Machias," pp. 51–52. For comparative accounts of the *Margaretta* affair, see Edwin A. Churchill, "The Historiography of the *Margaretta* Affair; or, How Not to Let the Facts Interfere with a Good Story," *MeHSQ* 15 (Fall 1975): 60–74.
81 Ahlin, *Maine Rubicon*, p. 23.
82 Donald A. Yerxa, "Admiral Samuel Graves and the Falmouth Affair: A Case Study in British Imperial Pacification, 1775" (M.A. thesis, University of Maine at Orono, 1974), pp. 106–107.
83 Vice Adm. Samuel Graves to Lt. Henry Mowat, Boston, Oct. 6, 1775, *NDAR*, 2:324–326.
84 Lt. Henry Mowat to Vice Adm. Samuel Graves, *Canceaux*, Casco Bay, Oct. 19, 1775, ibid., p. 514. Contemporary pictorial representations of the burning of Falmouth inexplicably show five vessels in Mowat's squadron, literary sources indicate only four.
85 Yerxa, "Graves and the Falmouth Affair," p. 117.
86 Quoted in ibid., pp. 118–119; see also Henry Mowat, Commander of His Majesty's Ship *Canceau*, to the People of Falmouth, *Canceau*, Falmouth, Oct. 16, 1775, *Am. Arch.*, 4th ser., 3:1153.
87 Yerxa, "Graves and the Falmouth Affair," pp. 119–120.
88 Ibid., pp. 123–127; Jacob Bailey, "Letter from Rev. Jacob Bailey, in 1775, Describing the Destruction of Falmouth, Maine," *CMeHS*, 1st ser. 5 (1857): 445–447; Enoch Freeman et al., "Account of the Destruction of Falmouth," Falmouth, Jan. 15, 1776, *Am. Arch.*, 4th ser., 3:1172; "A Short Account of the Destruction of the Town of Falmouth," April 23, 1782, *Doc. Hist. Me.*, 20:406–408. These later accounts claim that the militia opposed the British landing party, but contemporary accounts give little indication of this.
89 Bailey, "Letter," p. 449.
90 Massachusetts, *Acts and Resolves, Public and Private, of the Province of Massachusetts Bay, to which are prefixed the Charters of the Province*, 21 vols. (Boston: Wright and Potter, 1869–1922), 5:456–457.

91 Gorham Town Records, Oct. 28, 1775, MeSA.
92 Ibid., Oct. 30, 1775.
93 Jedediah Preble to Samuel Freeman, Falmouth, Jan. 5, 1776, Willis Papers, vol. O, MeHS.
94 Nathan Goold, "Falmouth Neck in the Revolution," *CPMeHS*, 2nd ser. 8 (1897): 150–153.

THREE *Protective Insignificance*

1 Rev. Samuel Deane to Gen. Jedediah Preble, March 21, 1776, Willis Papers, Autograph Letters, MeHS.
2 Willis, *Smith and Deane Journals*, p. 227. In what can only be a back entry, Smith recorded the fighting at Lexington and Concord on the very day it occurred.
3 Isaac Hasey, "Abstracts Relating to the Revolutionary War, from the Diaries of the Rev. Isaac Hasey, First Settled Minister of the First Parish of Lebanon, Maine (1765–1812)," ed. George W. Chamberlain, *CPMeHS*, 2nd ser. 9 (1898): 132; Allen, *Dresden*, pp. 298–299.
4 Massachusetts, *Acts and Resolves*, 5:445–454; Gross, *The Minutemen and Their World*, pp. 70–73; Williamson, *History of Maine*, 2:445.
5 Nathan Goold, "History of Col. Edmund Phinney's 31st Regiment of Foot, the First Regiment Raised in the County of Cumberland in the Revolutionary War" *CPMeHS*, 2nd ser. 7 (1896): 85, 86–87; Williamson, *History of Maine*, 2: 419–420.
6 Henry Sewall to his Parents, Falmouth, April 25, May 25, 1775, Sewall Family Correspondence, Mellen Papers, Hawthorne–Longfellow Library, Bowdoin College, Brunswick, Me.
7 Ibid., May 25, 1775.
8 Committee of Correspondence of Falmouth to the Committee of Safety at Cambridge, Falmouth, May 15, 1775, *Am. Arch.*, 4th ser., 2:587.
9 Col. Jedediah Preble to the Committee of Safety at Cambridge, May 15, 1775, *Doc. Hist. Me.*, 14:253–254; Goold, "Phinney's 31st Regiment," pp. 90–93.
10 Jonathan Sayward Diaries, vol. 16, Oct. 24, 1775; Records of the Committee of Safety for Cumberland County, Nov. 7–8, 1775, *Am. Arch.*, 4th ser., 4:1320–1321; Gen. George Washington to the Committee of Falmouth, Cambridge, Nov. 6, 1775, ibid., 3:1377; Washington to Col. Edmund Phinney, Cambridge, Nov. 6, 1775, ibid.; James Sullivan to the Council, Falmouth, Nov. 7, 1775, ibid., pp. 1397–1398; Wroth, *Province in Rebellion*, p. 129; Willis, *History of Portland*, 2:159.
11 Samuel Freeman to George Washington, Falmouth, Nov. 17, 1775, *Am. Arch.*, 4th ser., 3:1593–1594; Stephen Moylan to Freeman, Cambridge, Nov. 24, 1775, ibid., p. 1666.
12 James Sullivan to the General Court, Nov. 26, 1775, ibid., 4:1318–1319; Sullivan to Samuel Freeman, Biddeford, Jan. 27, 1776, Willis Papers, vol. S, MeHS; in Sullivan to Freeman, Falmouth, Jan. 21, 1776, ibid., Sullivan likens Cumberland County to a sacrificial beast bound by the General Court and laid on the "Alter [*sic*] of destruction"; Goold, "Falmouth Neck," pp. 84, 154; for disputes concerning command, see *Doc. Hist. Me.*, 14:369–387, passim.

13. Goold, "General Samuel Thompson," pp. 452–453; Williamson, *History of Maine*, 2:445.
14. Goold, "General Samuel Thompson," pp. 447–448; see letters from the Provincial Congress censuring Thompson, May 18, 1775, and approving his conduct, June 26, 1775, in Wroth, *Province in Rebellion*, doc. 889, p. 2522, doc. 512, p. 1734; for Falmouth's efforts to unseat Thompson in the General Court, see Jedediah Preble to John Waite, Boston, March 15, 1777, Willis Papers, Autograph Letters, MeHS; Reports from anti- and pro-Thompson conventions to the General Court, Sept. 17, Oct. 21, 1779, *Doc. Hist. Me.*, 17:143–146, 401–402.
15. Sibley and Shipton, *Biographical Sketches*, 15:303. For background on Sullivan, see ibid., pp. 299–322.
16. *BG*, March 17, 1777.
17. James Sullivan to the Council, Falmouth, Nov. 7, 1775, *Am. Arch.*, 4th ser., 3:1398.
18. Rev. Samuel Deane to Gen. Jedediah Preble, March 21, 1776, Willis Papers, Autograph Letters, MeHS.
19. Charles Cushing to the Council, Pownalborough, July 27, 1778, MaSA, 199:361–362.
20. Ahlin, *Maine Rubicon*, chap. 8; Rev. John Murray to Col. John Waite, Boothbay, Aug. 29, 1777, *Doc. Hist. Me.*, 15:185–186; Rev. Jacob Bailey to anon., n.d., Correspondence of Jacob Bailey, 4:70–71.
21. Timothy Parsons to the Board of War, Pownalborough, Sept. 15, 1777, *Doc. Hist. Me.*, 15:206–209; Parsons to Samuel P. Savage, Pownalborough, Feb. 18, 1779, ibid., 16:187–189. For comparison, see Sir George Collier's account of these events in *A Detail of Some Particular Services Performed in America, during the years, 1776, 1777, 1778, and 1779* (New York: Ithiel Town, 1835; reprint ed., Ann Arbor, Mich.: University Microfilms International, 1980), pp. 30–37, 51–63; see also Journal of H.M.S. *Rainbow*, Sept. 9–12, 1777, *NDAR*, 9:910–911.
22. Capt. William Reed to Col. Jonathan Buck, Naskeag, July 30, 1778, *BHM* 2 (March 1887): 183–184; Hutchinson, *When the Revolution Came*, pp. 54–59; *BG*, Aug. 3, 1778.
23. John Allan to the Board of War, Machias, Nov. 2, 1778, MaSA, 288:92.
24. Memorial of a party of Officers & Men of the Third Regiment of Militia in the county of Lincoln to the General Court, Newcastle, Sept. 15, 1777, *Doc. Hist. Me.*, 15:209–210.
25. Rev. John Murray to Jeremiah Powell, Georgetown, June 18, 1779, ibid., 16:291; Col. Benjamin Foster to the Council, Machias, Aug. 8, 1777, ibid., 15:9–10; Journal of John Allan, Sept. 23, 1777, in Frederic Kidder, *Military Operations in Eastern Maine and Nova Scotia during the Revolution, chiefly compiled from the journals and letters of Colonel John Allan, . . .* (Albany, N.Y.: Joel Munsell, 1867; reprint ed., New York: Kraus Reprint, 1971), p. 138.
26. James Sullivan to John Winthrop et al., Falmouth, Nov. 26, 1775, *Am. Arch.*, 4th ser., 4:1320.
27. Memorial of a party of Officers & Men of the Third Regiment of Militia in the county of Lincoln to the General Court, Newcastle, Sept. 15, 1777, *Doc. Hist. Me.*, 15:210.

28 Committee of Machias to the Council, Jan. 24, 1778, ibid., pp. 336–337; Maj. George Stillman to anon., Machias, Aug. 1, 1778, ibid., 16:46; John Allan to Jeremiah Powell, Machias, Oct. 12, 1777, ibid., 15:242–243.

29 John Allan to the Council, Machias, Sept. 22, 1777, ibid., 15:222; Allan to Jeremiah Powell, Machias, Sept. 24, 1779, ibid., 17:177–180; Allan to Powell, Machias, Oct. 12, 1777, ibid., 15:241.

30 Petition of the Committee of Inspection, Correspondence, and Safety for Boothbay to the General Court, June 24, 1778, ibid., 16:35.

31 Rev. James Lyon to the General Court, Machias, Sept. 1776, ibid., 14:379; Rev. John Murray to Jeremiah Powell, Georgetown, June 18, 1779, ibid., 16:289.

32 John Shy, *A People Numerous and Armed: Reflections on the Military Struggle for American Independence* (London: Oxford University Press, 1976), pp. 216–224.

33 Capt. James Cargill to the General Court, Boothbay, Aug. 2, 1775, *NDAR*, 1:1037–1039; Depositions of Rogers Smith, Samuel Hernden, and William Pendleton, MaSA, 230: 462–464.

34 Committee of Machias to the General Court, Machias, July 9, 1776, *Doc. Hist. Me.*, 14:358–359; Francis Shaw to the General Court, Machias, Aug. 28, 1776, ibid., pp. 374–375. For other examples, see *BG*, Dec. 14, 1778; MaSA, 138:435.

35 Gardner W. Allen, *A Naval History of the American Revolution*, 2 vols. (Boston: Houghton Mifflin, 1913; reprint ed., Williamstown, Mass.: Corner House Publishers, 1970), 1:202–216; Collier, *Detail of Some Particular Services*, pp. 18–23; Capt. John Brisbane to Vice Adm. Richard Lord Howe, Halifax, July 9, 1777, *NDAR*, 9:246–247; Capt. Sir George Collier to Philip Stephens, *Rainbow*, Halifax, July 12, 1777, ibid., pp. 269–273. For diagrams of the naval action, see ibid., pp. 989–999.

36 So clumsy and poorly constructed were the Maine-built bateaux that Arnold's troops became increasingly furious with the builders: "Could we then have come within reach of the villains who constructed these crazy things, they would fully have experienced the effects of our vengeance. Avarice or a desire to destroy us—perhaps both—must have been their motives." Quoted in Justin Smith, *Arnold's March from Cambridge to Quebec; a critical study, together with a reprint of Arnold's Journal* (New York: G. Putnam's Sons, 1903), pp. 78–79.

37 Don Higgenbotham, *The War for American Independence: Military Attitudes, Policies, and Practices, 1763–1789* (New York: Macmillan, 1971), pp. 108–115; Smith, *Arnold's March*, passim.

38 For background on John Allan, see Ahlin, *Maine Rubicon*, pp. 61–63; Allen Johnson and Dumas Malone, eds., *Dictionary of American Biography*, 20 vols., 4 supps. (New York: Charles Scribner's Sons, 1928–1974), 1:182–183 (hereafter cited as *DAB*); George Brown et al., eds., *Dictionary of Canadian Biography*, 10 vols. (Toronto: University of Toronto Press, 1966–), 5:15–16 (hereafter cited as *DCB*). I am indebted to Dr. Alice Stewart, Professor Emeritus, History Department, University of Maine at Orono, for sharing with me her research on Allan. For information on Jonathan Eddy, see Ahlin, *Maine Rubicon*, p. 170, n. 47; George A. Rawlyk, *Nova Scotia's Massachusetts: A Study of Massachusetts–Nova Scotia Relations, 1630 to 1784* (Montreal: McGill–Queen's University Press, 1973), pp. 231–233; Joseph W. Por-

ter, "Memoir of Colonel Jonathan Eddy of Eddington, Maine," *BHM* 4 (Sept. 1888): 41–54; *DCB*, 5:295–296.

39 For background on Nova Scotia and the American Revolution, see John B. Brebner, *The Neutral Yankees of Nova Scotia: A Marginal Colony during the Revolutionary Years* (New York: Columbia University Press, 1937), pp. 157–171, chap. 10; Emily P. Weaver, "Nova Scotia and New England during the Revolution," *American Historical Review (AHR)* 10 (Oct. 1904): 52–71; Rawlyk, *Nova Scotia's Massachusetts*, chaps. 12–13; Ahlin, *Maine Rubicon*, pp. 40–41, 154–155.

40 Gen. George Washington to a Committee of the General Court of Massachusetts, Cambridge, Aug. 11, 1775, *NDAR*, 1:1114–1115; Ahlin, *Maine Rubicon*, pp. 39, 50–52; Viola Barnes, "Francis Legge, Governor of Loyalist Nova Scotia, 1773–1776," *NEQ* 4 (July 1931): 434; Brebner, *Neutral Yankees*, pp. 321–322.

41 Ahlin, *Maine Rubicon*, pp. 9, 51, 58.

42 William Tupper to the General Court, Machias, Nov. 27, 1776, *Doc. Hist. Me.*, 14:399; Maj. Gen. Eyre Massey to Lord George Germain, Halifax, Dec. 20, 1776, in *Report on the Canadian Archives, 1894*, ed. Douglas Brymner (Ottawa: S. E. Dawson, 1895), p. 358 (hereafter cited as *CAR*).

43 Jonathan Eddy to the Council, Wangerville, Jan. 5, 1777, *Doc. Hist. Me.*, 15:35–40; see also Journal of Col. Joseph Gorham to Maj. Gen. Eyre Massey, Fort Cumberland, Nov. 4–10, 1776, *CAR, 1894*, pp. 355–357.

44 Resolve of the Continental Congress, Jan. 8, 1777, in *Journals of the Continental Congress, 1774–1789*, ed. Worthington C. Ford et al., 34 vols. (Washington, D.C.: U.S. Government Printing Office, 1904–1937), 7:20–21, 34, 38–39; Rawlyk, *Nova Scotia's Massachusetts*, pp. 241–245.

45 John Allan to John Hancock, Boston, April 2, 1777, John Allan Papers, MaHS; Rawlyk, *Nova Scotia's Massachusetts*, pp. 243–245; Resolves of the Inhabitants on the Saint John, Maugerville, May 14–21, 1776, in Kidder, *Military Operations*, pp. 62–66; Memorial of the Committee of Sunbury, Nova Scotia, to the Massachusetts General Court, Maugerville, Sept. 24, 1776, *Am. Arch.*, 5th ser., 2:785–786.

46 John Allan to the General Court, Machias, May 30, 1777, *Doc. Hist. Me.*, 14:414–416; Proclamation to the Citizens of the Saint John, Saint John River, May 14, 1777, and Reply of the Inhabitants, May 16, 1777, *CAR, 1894*, pp. 369–370; Allan to the General Court, Machias, June 18, 1777, *Doc. Hist. Me.*, 14:427; Ahlin, *Maine Rubicon*, pp. 78–79; Rawlyk, *Nova Scotia's Massachusetts*, p. 245.

47 John Allan to the General Court, Machias, May 30, 1777, *Doc. Hist. Me.*, 14:415.

48 Francis Shaw to the General Court, Machias, July 4, 1777, ibid., 14:439–440; Shaw to the General Court, Gouldsborough, July 15, 1777, ibid., p. 443; Alexander Campbell to Aney Officer Commanding in State or Continental Service, Committees and other friends to America, Number Four, July 13, 1777, ibid., pp. 440–442; Stephen Smith to the General Court, Machias, July 31, 1777, ibid., 15:1–4; Allan's Journal, June 30–Aug. 2, 1777, in Kidder, *Military Operations*, pp. 109–124; Ahlin, *Maine Rubicon*, p. 81.

49 Allan's Journal, July 13, 1777, in Kidder, *Military Operations*, p. 117; see also entries for July 24, July 27, July 28, pp. 121–122.

50 Brebner, *Neutral Yankees*, p. 327; Maj. Gen. Eyre Massey to Gen. William Howe,

Halifax, Nov. 26, 1777, Military Correspondence between the years 1776 and 1784, being transcripts from the papers in the Royal Institution, London, known as the Dorchester Papers, vol. 1, Public Archives of Nova Scotia (PANS); Sir George Collier to Lord George Germain, Aug. 16, 1777, *CAR*, p. 372; for contrast, see Massey to Germain, Halifax, Sept. 20, 1777, ibid.; Massey to Germain, Halifax, June 3, 1778, ibid., pp. 377–378.

51 John Allan to the Council, Machias, Aug. 17, 1777, *Doc. Hist. Me.*, 15:172. See also Allan's Journal, Aug. 11–15, 1777, in Kidder, *Military Operations*, pp. 126–128; Ahlin, *Maine Rubicon*, pp. 86–97.

52 John Allan to the Council, Machias, Aug. 17, 1777, *Doc. Hist. Me.*, 15:174–175.

53 Ibid., pp. 170–171, 175; Hunt, "British-American Rivalry," p. 87; Ahlin, *Maine Rubicon*, pp. 87, 91.

54 Collier, *Detail of Some Particular Services*, pp. 25–28; see also Sir George Collier to Lord George Germain, Machias, Aug. 16, 1777, *CAR, 1894*, p. 372; also see Journal of H.M.S. *Rainbow*, Aug. 13–17, 1777, *NDAR*, 9:757–758.

55 John Allan to the Council, Machias, Aug. 17, 1777, *Doc. Hist. Me.*, 15:179; Allan's Journal, Aug. 13–15, 1777, in Kidder, *Military Operations*, pp. 126–129; Jonathan Eddy to the Council, Machias, Aug. 17, 1777, *Doc. Hist. Me.*, 15:14–15. John Preble to Jedediah Preble, Machias, Aug. 17, 1777, *NDAR*, 9:760, states that a British deserter reported sixty British dead.

56 Allan's Journal, Aug. 17, 1777, in Kidder, *Military Operations*, p. 129.

57 Quoted in John Allan to the Council, Boston, Nov. 21, 1776, ibid., p. 175.

58 James Bowdoin to George Washington, Boston, July 30, 1776, *Doc. Hist. Me.*, 14:363; Ahlin, *Maine Rubicon*, p. 36.

59 Quoted in [Frank Sprague], "Regarding Soldiers of the American Revolution," *Sprague's Journal of Maine History* 6 (Nov., Dec., Jan. 1918–1919): 107.

60 Resolves of June 21 and June 24, 1775, in Lincoln, *Journals of Each Provincial Congress*, pp. 371–372, 392; [Ronald Banks], "Summary of Massachusetts/Penobscot Relations — UPDATE," Aug. 20, 1977, pp. 27–28, Research and Position Papers Relative to the Indian Land Claims Case, Office of the Attorney General for the State of Maine, State House, Augusta, copies in author's possession; Williamson, *History of Maine*, 2:428–429.

61 Thomas Fletcher to the Council, Aug. 16, 1776, *Doc. Hist. Me.*, 14:367–369; Council to Fletcher, Sept. 7, 1776, *Am. Arch.*, 5th ser., 2:230; Petition of Jedediah Preble to the General Court, Sept. 10, 1776, ibid., p. 758; Resolve of the General Court, Sept. 12, 1776, ibid., p. 765.

62 *DCB*, 4:272–275; Ahlin, *Maine Rubicon*, pp. 100–104; Jonathan Eddy to the Council, Machias, Aug. 1, 1777, *Doc. Hist. Me.*, 15:5.

63 Indian Oath, Sept. 24, 1778, Military Correspondence ... Dorchester Papers, vol. 1, PANS; Richard Hughes to Lord George Germain, Halifax, Oct. 12, 1778, *CAR, 1894*, p. 380.

64 Hunt, "British-American Rivalry," pp. 111–112; Michael Francklin to Sir Guy Carleton, Maugerville, July 23, 1777, Transcripts ... from the military papers known as the Haldimand Collection in the British Museum, vol. 2, PANS; Speech of the Ottawas, Hurons, ... to the Malecite, Passamaquoddy, and Micmac Indians,

June 24, 1780; Michael Francklin to Gen. Henry Clinton, Halifax, Aug. 21, 1780, Military Correspondence... Dorchester Papers, vol. 1, PANS.

65 John Allan to Jeremiah Powell, Machias, Nov. 27, 1777, *Doc. Hist. Me.*, 15:296–297.

66 John Allan to the General Court, Machias, May 22, 1778, ibid., 16:14; Allan to the Council, Machias, Oct. 14, 1778, ibid., pp. 110–111; Hunt, "British-American Rivalry," pp. 125, 133, 178; Ahlin, *Maine Rubicon*, p. 118.

67 Michael Francklin to Gen. Henry Clinton, Halifax, Aug. 2, 1779, Military Correspondence... Dorchester Papers, vol. 1, PANS; Hunt, "British-American Rivalry," p. 113; Address of Pierre Tomma, Chief of Saint Johns, Read in Council, Dec. 27, 1779, *Doc. Hist. Me.*, 18:32–34.

68 Invoice of Sundries wanting in the Truck House at Machias, *Doc. Hist. Me.*, 15:130–131; Massachusetts, *Acts and Resolves*, 20:112. See Harald E. L. Prins, "Two George Washington Medals: Missing Links in the Chain of Friendship between the United States and the Wabanaki Confederacy," *The Medal*, no. 7 (Winter 1985).

69 John Allan to [Council?], Machias, Aug. 4, 1778, *Doc. Hist. Me.*, 16:49.

70 Memorial of James Flinn and William Tupper, n.d., ibid., 17:116–118; Resolve of the House, June 21, 1777, ibid., pp. 121–123; Petition of James Avery to the Council, Boston, July 24, 1779, ibid., pp. 135–136; Resolve of the General Court, Sept. 20, 1779, ibid., pp. 147–148; Massachusetts, *Acts and Resolves*, 20:689; John Allan to [Council?], Machias, Aug. 4, 1778, *Doc. Hist. Me.*, 16:52; Allan to [Council?], Machias, Oct. 8, 1778, ibid., p. 99.

71 Proclamation of John Allan, Machias, Sept. 8, 1777, *Doc. Hist. Me.*, 15:194–196; Allan to Jeremiah Powell, Sept. 25, 1777, ibid., p. 231; Allan to John Jay, Boston, April 21, 1779, Allan Papers, MaHS.

72 For information re Stephen Jones, see *Doc. Hist. Me.*, 15:244–269, passim; John Allan to Jeremiah Powell, Machias, Oct. 17, 1778, ibid., 16:74; Allan's Journal, Oct. 15–25, 1777, in Kidder, *Military Operations*, pp. 144–147; Records of the Lincoln County Court of General Sessions of the Peace, June 2, 1778, MeSA.

73 John Allan to the Council, Aukpaque, River Saint John, June 18, 1777, in Kidder *Military Operations*, pp. 192–193; Memorial of Stephen Smith to the Speaker of the House of Representatives, Boston, June 7, 1777, *Doc. Hist. Me.*, 15:109; Allan to the Council, Machias, Nov. 18, 1777, ibid., pp. 286–287; Allan to Council, Machias, Oct. 8, 1778, ibid., 16:106–107.

74 Peter J. Elliott, "The Penobscot Expedition of 1779: A Study in Naval Frustration" (M.A. thesis, University of Maine at Orono, 1974), p. 12; John D. Faibisy, "Privateering and Piracy: The Effects of New England Raiding upon Nova Scotia during the American Revolution, 1775–1783" (Ph.D. diss., University of Massachusetts at Amherst, 1972), pp. 48–49.

75 Octavius T. Howe, "Massachusetts on the Seas in the War of the American Revolution," in *Commonwealth History of Massachusetts, Colony, Province, and State*, ed. Albert B. Hart, 5 vols. (New York: State History Company, 1928–1930), 3:30; Faibisy, "Privateering and Piracy," pp. 53–54, 331; Ahlin, *Maine Rubicon*, p. 70; MaSA, 227:470.

76 John O'Brien, "Exertions of the O'Brien Family at Machias, Maine, in the American Revolution," *CMeHS*, 1st ser. 2 (1847): 248, 242–249; Ahlin, *Maine Rubicon*, pp. 200–204.

77 Records of the Lincoln County Inferior Court of Common Pleas (1761–1768), 1:85, MeSA, refer to "Agreen Crabtree of Attleborough, housewright"; see also "Captain Agreen Crabtree of Sullivan, Me.," *BHM* 8 (Oct., Nov., Dec. 1893): 230–231.
78 *NHG*, Nov. 5, 1776; Faibisy, "Privateering and Piracy," p. 51.
79 John Allan to [Jeremiah Powell], Machias, Nov. 18, 1777, *Doc. Hist. Me.*, 15:287; Allan to [Powell?], Machias, Nov. 19, 1777, ibid., p. 289.
80 Depositions of Moses Hodgkins, Agreen Crabtree, et al., Sept. 16, 1782, ibid., 20:445–463.
81 Willis, *Smith and Deane Journals*, p. 237 n.; Goold, "Falmouth Neck," pp. 84, 155.
82 *BG*, Sept. 7, 1778.
83 John Allan to Jeremiah Powell, Machias, Aug. 17, 1778, *Doc. Hist. Me.*, 16:72–74; Allan to Powell, Machias, May 18, 1779, ibid., p. 257.
84 "John Fairbanks—His Journal," *CPMeHS*, 2nd ser. 6 (1895): 139–144.
85 Elliott, "Penobscot Expedition," p. 9.
86 Brebner, *Neutral Yankees*, pp. 332–334; Simeon Perkins, *Diary of Simeon Perkins, 1766–1789*, ed. Harold A. Innis, D. C. Harvey, and C. Bruce Fergusson, 2 vols. (Toronto: Champlain Society, 1948, 1958), offers a vivid description of the effects of American privateering from the standpoint of a merchant in Liverpool, N.S.
87 Faibisy, "Privateering and Piracy," p. 122; see pp. 69–71, 139–141, for effects of privateering on prices.
88 Inhabitants of Yarmouth, N.S., to Gov. Francis Legge, Dec. 8, 1775, Colonial Correspondence, no. 217, vol. 52, PANS; the author is grateful to Ann K. Leamon for obtaining from PANS a photocopy of the Yarmouth neutrality petition. Brebner, *Neutral Yankees*, pp. 309–310.

FOUR Crisis on the Penobscot

1 Brig. Gen. Francis McLean to Gen. George Clinton, Halifax, May 28, 1779, and McLean to Clinton, June 26, 1779, Magebiguiduce, Penobscot Expedition Papers, British, transcribed for Joseph Williamson, MeHS. Correspondence generously provided by Prof. Alan Taylor, Boston University, indicates the later presence of two companies of German ("Hessian") troops from Brunswick and Anspach-Bayreuth.
2 Ahlin, *Maine Rubicon*, p. 6; Inhabitants of Fox Islands and Deer Isle to John Calef, Oct. 12, 1772, empowering him to present petitions to the king, Historical Manuscripts concerning Maine in the Landsdowne and Dartmouth Collections, MeHS.
3 Sloan, "New Ireland: Loyalists in Eastern Maine," pp. 12–13.
4 Samuel F. Batchelder, *The Life and Surprising Adventures of John Nutting, Cambridge Loyalist, and His Strange Connection with the Penobscot Expedition* (Cambridge, Mass.: Cambridge Historical Society, 1912), pp. 55–75; Sloan, "New Ireland: Loyalists in Eastern Maine," pp. 12–14; Wilbur H. Siebert, *The Exodus of the Loyalists from Penobscot to Passamaquoddy* (Columbus: Ohio State University Press, 1914), pp. 9–10; Leland J. Bellot, *William Knox: The Life and Thought of an Eighteenth-Century Imperialist* (Austin: University of Texas Press, 1977), p. 166.
5 Lord George Germain to Sir Henry Clinton, Whitehall, Sept. 2, 1778, Military

Correspondence... Dorchester Papers, vol. 1, PANS; Germain to Michael Francklin, July 7, 1780, *CAR*, *1894*, p. 389; Germain to Lt. Gov. Richard Hughes, July 7, 1780, ibid.; Elliott, "Penobscot Expedition," pp. 15–21; Bellot, *Knox*, pp. 163–164; Ahlin, *Maine Rubicon*, p. 124.

6 John Shy, "British Strategy for Pacifying the Southern Colonies, 1778–1781," in *The Southern Experience in the American Revolution*, ed. Jeffrey J. Crow and Larry E. Tise (Chapel Hill: University of North Carolina Press, 1978), pp. 158–160.

7 Hutchinson, *When the Revolution Came*, pp. 70, 73.

8 George A. Wheeler, *History of Castine, Penobscot, and Brooksville, Maine* (Bangor, Me.: Burr and Robinson, 1875; reprint ed., New York: Cornwall Press, 1923), pp. 257–259; Elliott, "Penobscot Expedition," pp. 36–37; John Allan to Jeremiah Powell, Machias, July 16, 1779, *Doc. Hist. Me.*, 16:363; Sloan, "New Ireland: Loyalists in Eastern Maine," pp. 41–42; John Calef, ed., *The Siege of Penobscot* (London, 1781; reprint ed., New York: New York Times and Arno Press, 1971), p. 10; Calef's "Journal," in ibid., p. 16.

9 Concurrence of the General Court to a Report of a Joint Committee, June 24, 1779, *Doc. Hist. Me.*, 16:305; Resolve of the Council, July 3, 1779, ibid., pp. 323–324; Orders of the Board of War, July 5, July 7, 1779, ibid., pp. 325, 326–329; Council to Board of War, July 8, 1779, ibid., pp. 337–338, and July 3, 1779, ibid., p. 375.

10 Resolve of the Council, July 3, 1779, ibid., p. 323; Allen, *Naval History*, 2:421–422; Petition of Elias Haskett Derby, July 21, 1779, and Council permission, July 22, 1779, *Doc. Hist. Me.*, 16:389, 391–392.

11 *BG*, Sept. 27, 1779. For a list of vessels, names, types, armaments, and commanders, see Elliott, "Penobscot Expedition," pp. 117–118, who lists twenty-two armed vessels; Allen, *Naval History*, 2:420–421, lists thirty-nine, including "twenty or more transports." In his "Journal," in Calef, *Siege of Penobscot*, p. 32, Calef enumerates thirty-seven vessels lost. John Cayford, *The Penobscot Expedition, being an account of the largest American naval engagement of the Revolutionary War* (Orrington, Me.: C&H Publishers, 1976), pp. 123–124, names a total of forty-five vessels, including those on detached service.

12 Warrants to the Sheriffs of Suffolk and Essex Counties, July 11, 1779, *Doc. Hist. Me.*, 16:384; see also ibid., pp. 348–349, 368, 372–373.

13 Deposition of Jeremiah Hill, Sept. 29, 1779, ibid., 17:263; see also Depositions of Peleg Wadsworth, Sept. 29, 1779, ibid., p. 273, and of Major [William] Todd, Sept. 28, 1779, ibid., p. 296.

14 Thompson quoted in deposition of Jeremiah Hill, Sept. 29, 1779, ibid., pp. 263–264.

15 Solomon Lovell, *The Original Journal of General Solomon Lovell kept during the Penobscot Expedition, 1779*... (Weymouth, Mass.: Weymouth Historical Society, 1881), pp. 23–51; Elliott, "Penobscot Expedition," p. 45; Calef, *Siege of Penobscot*, p. 13; "Letter from General Peleg Wadsworth to William D. Williamson, Hiram, Jan. 1, 1828," *CPMeHS*, 2nd ser. 2 (1891): 157; *Doc. Hist. Me.*, 16:320–321.

16 Elliott, "Penobscot Expedition," pp. 44–45; "Letter from Peleg Wadsworth," p. 157.

17 Nathan Goold, "Colonel Jonathan Mitchell's Cumberland County Regiment,

Bagaduce Expedition," *CPMeHS*, 2nd ser. 10 (1899): 61, 74. J. W. Penny to Nathan Goold, Mechanic Falls, Me., July 15, 1907, lists the names of the Indians and includes relevant documents from Massachusetts Archives, photocopy from Edwin A. Churchill, Curator of Decorative Arts, Maine State Museum, Augusta.

18 Calef's "Journal," in Calef, *Siege of Penobscot*, pp. 17–18, 21–22.
19 Col. John Brewer, "A Short Statement of What Took Place at Majabigwaduce...," pp. 82–83, in John E. Godfrey Collection, Misc. Box 7/1, MeHS.
20 Deposition of Gawen Brown, Sept. 29, 1779, *Doc. Hist. Me.*, 17:325; General Orders, Headquarters, Transport *Sally*, July 27, 1779, ibid., 16:399; Petition of the Lieutenants and Masters of Several armed Vessels, July 27, 1779, ibid., pp. 400–401.
21 Council of War aboard the *Warren*, July 27, 1779, ibid., 16:401–402; Solomon Lovell to Jeremiah Powell, Majabigwaduce, July 28, 1779, ibid., p. 403; Deposition of Major [William] Todd, Sept. 28, 1779, ibid., 17:293; "Letter from Peleg Wadsworth," p. 157. Note that in Solomon Lovell to Jeremiah Powell, Majabigwaduce, Aug. 1, 1779, *Doc. Hist. Me.*, 16:415, the height of the bluff increases to 200 feet, and in his *Journal*, p. 99, Lovell increases the height yet further to 300 feet; see Sloan, "New Ireland: Loyalists in Eastern Maine," p. 11, n. 19.
22 Brewer, "A Short Statement," p. 89, Godfrey Collection, MeHS; William Hutching's Narrative, in Cayford, *Penobscot Expedition*, p. 120.
23 Deposition of Peleg Wadsworth, Sept. 29, 1779, *Doc. Hist. Me.*, 17:277; for an example of the debate, see ibid., 16:426–434.
24 Proceedings of a Council of War, Majabigwaduce, Aug. 11, 1779, ibid., 16:453; Solomon Lovell to Jeremiah Powell, Majabigwaduce, Aug. 1, 1779, ibid., pp. 417–418.
25 Council of War aboard the *Warren*, Majabigwaduce, Aug. 10, 1779, ibid., 16:445–446; see Capt. Hoysteed Hacker to the Army and the Navy, Majabigwaduce, Aug. 8, 1779, ibid., pp. 438–439.
26 Deposition of Jeremiah Hill, Sept. 29, 1779, ibid., 17:265–266; Deposition of Gawen Brown, Sept. 29, 1779, ibid., pp. 327–328; Lovell's speech printed in Orders of the Day for Aug. 12, 1779, ibid., 16:453–454.
27 "A Part of General Lovell's Relation of Facts," n.d., ibid., 17:81.
28 Orders of the Day, Headquarters, Majabigwaduce, July 20, 1779, ibid., 16:411; Deposition of Jeremiah Hill, Sept. 29, 1779, ibid., 17:266; Deposition of Samuel Morris, n.d., ibid., 16:200.
29 Thomas Philbrook, "The Narrative of Thomas Philbrook," in Hope Rider, *Valour Fore & Aft: Being the Adventures of the Continental Sloop "Providence," 1775–1779, Formerly Flagship "Katy" of Rhode Island's Navy* (Annapolis, Md.: Naval Institute Press, 1977), pp. 229–230.
30 Dudley Saltonstall to [Solomon Lovell], Aug. 13, 1779, *Doc. Hist. Me.*, 16:461.
31 Calef's "Journal," in Calef, *Siege of Penobscot*, pp. 29–30.
32 Deposition of Peleg Wadsworth, [Sept. 29, 1779], *Doc. Hist. Me.*, 17:279; "Letter from Peleg Wadsworth," p. 155; Sergeant [William] Lawrence's Journal, Aug. 14, 1779, in Wheeler, *Castine, Penobscot, and Brooksville*, p. 269. For details concerning the flight upriver, see Council of War on board the *Warren*, Aug. 14, 1779, *Doc. Hist. Me.*, 16:470; Peleg Wadsworth to the Council, Thomaston, Aug. 19, 1779, ibid.,

17:28–29; Solomon Lovell to the Council, Townsend, Sept. 3, 1779, ibid., pp. 76–77; "Captain Henry Mowatt's Account," in Calef, *Siege of Penobscot*, pp. 52–53.

33 Calef's "Journal," in Calef, *Siege of Penobscot*, p. 30; Peleg Wadsworth to Jeremiah Powell, Thomaston, Aug. 19, 1779, *Doc. Hist. Me.*, 17:28–29; Deposition of Titus Salter, Sept. 25, 1779, ibid., p. 214; Deposition of William Todd, Sept. 28, 1779, ibid., pp. 296–300; Letter by Commodore Sir George Collier, *Raisonable*, Penobscot Bay, Aug. 20, 1779, in Cayford, *Penobscot Expedition*, pp. 69–70.

34 Peleg Wadsworth to the Council, Thomaston, Aug. 19, 1779, *Doc. Hist. Me.*, 17:29–30; Deposition of John Cathcart, Sept. 24, 1779, ibid., pp. 245–246; Deposition of Samuel McCobb, Sept. 28, 1779, ibid., pp. 260–261. For Col. Paul Revere, see Deposition by Peleg Wadsworth, Sept. 29, 1779, ibid., pp. 275–276, and especially an analysis of his court-martial in Frederick Grant, Jr., "The Court Martial of Paul Revere," *Boston Bar Journal* 21 (May 1977): 5–13.

35 Deposition of George Little, Sept. 25, 1779, *Doc. Hist. Me.*, 17:242; see also Deposition of Waterman Thomas, Sept. 30, 1779, ibid., p. 312; Deposition of Philip Brown, Sept. 29, 1779, ibid., p. 291.

36 Solomon Lovell to the Council, Georgetown, Aug. 28, 1779, ibid., pp. 61–62; Lovell to Council, Georgetown, Sept. 3, 1779, ibid., p. 78; Peleg Wadsworth to Council, Thomaston, Aug. 19, 1779, ibid., p. 30.

37 Philbrook, "Narrative," in Rider, *Valour Fore & Aft*, p. 231; Jacob Bailey to Joshua Weeks, Halifax, Sept. 22, 1779, Correspondence of Jacob Bailey, 3:311–312; William M. Fowler, Jr., *Rebels under Sail: The American Navy during the Revolution* (New York: Charles Scribner's Sons, 1976), p. 117; Howard H. Peckham, ed., *The Toll of Independence: Engagements & Battle Casualties of the American Revolution* (Chicago: University of Chicago Press, 1974), pp. 62–63.

38 Elliott, "Penobscot Expedition," pp. 83–84, 89.

39 Report of the Committee of both Houses, Oct. 7, 1779, *Doc. Hist. Me.*, 17:359.

40 Ibid., p. 358; see Williamson, *History of Maine*, 2:474, 477–478; Ahlin, *Maine Rubicon*, pp. 133–134; Russell Bourne, "The Penobscot Fiasco," *American Heritage* 25 (Oct. 1974): 33, 100. Elliott, "Penobscot Expedition," emphasizes Saltonstall's responsibility while acknowledging extenuating circumstances over which he had no control. The most vigorous defense of the commodore is a series of manuscript research papers by Rear Adm. Colby Chester, each entitled "Commodore Dudley Saltonstall, the Continental Navy, and the Defeat of the Penobscot Bay Expedition," Colby Chester Papers, Manuscript Division, LC. Although these papers are undocumented, they are thoroughly researched and provide a defense of one navy man by another.

41 Report of the Committee of both Houses, Oct. 7, 1779, *Doc. Hist. Me.*, 17:359–360.

42 Ronald Hoffman, "The 'Disaffected' in the Revolutionary South," in *The American Revolution: Explorations in the History of American Radicalism*, ed. Alfred Young (De Kalb, Ill.: Northern Illinois University Press, 1976), p. 292; Kenneth Coleman, *The American Revolution in Georgia, 1763–1789* (Athens: University of Georgia Press, 1958), chap. 8.

43 Board of War to the General Court, n.d., *Doc. Hist. Me.*, 17:351–352; Charles Miller to James Richardson, Feb. 26, 1781, ibid., 19:156–157; Gov. John Hancock's Ad-

dress, March 9, 1781, ibid., p. 181; John Davis to Caleb Davis, June 3, 1781, Caleb Davis Papers, MaHS; see also John Allan to Caleb Davis, June 20, 1781, ibid. For disposal of the vessels, see resolves of the General Court, July 5–6, 1781, *Doc. Hist. Me.*, 19:302–303.

44 Massachusetts, *Acts and Laws of the Commonwealth of Massachusetts*, 13 vols. (Boston: Wright and Potter, 1890–1898), 1:332.

45 Jeremiah Powell to the U.S. Congress, Feb. 9, 1780, *Doc. Hist. Me.*, 18:91; Gen. George Washington to President of the Massachusetts Council, Morristown, April 17, 1780, ibid., pp. 228–230; Elbridge Gerry and others to the Massachusetts Council, Philadelphia, May 20, 1780, ibid., pp. 275–277; Elliott, "Penobscot Expedition," pp. 76–78, 78–79; Washington to Marquis de Vandreuil, Newburgh, Aug. 10, 1782, *Doc. Hist. Me.*, 20:64–67; General Court to Meshech Weare, April 20, 1780, ibid., 18:201–202; Weare to the Massachusetts Council, Exeter, April 28, 1780, ibid., p. 239.

46 John Allan to Jeremiah Powell, Machias, Sept. 24, 1779, ibid., 17:177, 179–180; Allan to John Hancock, Machias, Nov. 2, 1780, MaSA, 230:277.

47 Resolves of the Machias Committee of Safety, Nov. 6, 1779, *Doc. Hist. Me.*, 17:419–420; Committee of Narraguagus to Joseph Wales, Nov. 6, 1779, ibid., p. 421.

48 Convention of the Cumberland County Committee of Safety to the General Court, Sept. 17, 1779, ibid., pp. 143–146. For background on Daniel Ilsley, see Willis, *History of Portland*, 2:297.

49 Pro-Thompson Convention to the General Court, Oct. 21, 1779, *Doc. Hist. Me.*, 17:401–402.

50 Minutes and Report of the Legislative Committee, n.d., John Lewis Papers, Manuscript Division, LC.

51 Resolves of the General Court, March 25, 1780, *Doc. Hist. Me.*, 18:142–143.

52 Peleg Wadsworth to the Council, Falmouth, July 10, 1780, ibid., p. 342.

53 For Wadsworth's initial plan of defense, see "Wadsworth's Opinions," [1780?], and the Council's response, March 23, 1780, MaSA, 226:347–348, 362. See also William Lithgow to the Council, Georgetown, Sept. 13, 1779, *Doc. Hist. Me.*, 17:131–133; Wadsworth to the Council, Thomaston, May 26, 1780, ibid., 18:279–281.

54 Proclamation of Martial Law, April 18, 1780, *Doc. Hist. Me.*, 18:222–224.

55 Ibid., p. 223.

56 Ibid.

57 The following sources document the Bakeman/Bateman affair: Petition of a number of the Inhabitants of Majabigwaduce read before the General Court, Jan. 10, 1776, Report of a committee of both Houses regarding the conduct of John Bakeman, Feb. 5, 1776, and Resolve thereon, Feb. 7, 1776, all in *Am. Arch.*, 4th ser., 4:1257, 1288–1289, 1433–1434; Report of the Justices of the Peace to the General Court, with the list of accusations against Bakeman, June 15, 1776, MaSA, 210:15–19. See also Petition of John Bakeman to the General Assembly, Brunswick, Oct. 27, 1779, *Doc. Hist. Me.*, 17:407–408; Depositions of John Bakeman and other against Joseph Young, March 21–22, 1780, ibid., 18:153–160; William Lithgow to the Council, Georgetown, April 1, 1780, ibid., pp. 180–181; Petition of Joseph Young to the General Court, Boston, April 13, and the Resolve thereon, April 24, 1780,

ibid., pp. 212–213, 224–225. See also Hutchinson, *When the Revolution Came*, p. 116; Richard I. Hunt, Jr., "The Loyalists of Maine" (Ph.D. diss., University of Maine at Orono, 1980), pp. 206–207. Wheeler, *Castine, Penobscot, and Brooksville*, pp. 168–169, describes John Bakeman as a man "much respected for his sound judgment, and the judiciousness of the advice he gave in all matters relating either to individual or town interests."

58 *Stephen Hall v. Timothy Langdon*, Superior Court Records for Cumberland and Lincoln Counties, 1783, file no. 139858, Suffolk County Court House, Boston, and John Allan's proclamation, *Doc. Hist. Me.*, 18:334–335, both limit martial law to six months or Sept. 30, 1780. Peleg Wadsworth to Gov. John Hancock, Thomaston, Dec. 23, 1780, ibid., 19:68–70, deals with cases arising in that time span. Wadsworth to the Council, Falmouth, April 28, Thomaston, May 26, Sept. 14, and to Lt. Joseph McLellan, Hallowell, Fort Weston [*sic*] Sept. 25, 1780, ibid., 18:240, 280, 414–415, 435.

59 Edward K. Gould, *British and Tory Marauders on the Penobscot* (Rockland, Me., 1932), p. 15; "Letter from Peleg Wadsworth," p. 160; Sloan, "New Ireland: Loyalists in Eastern Maine," pp. 101–102.

60 Peleg Wadsworth to the Council, Sept. 14, Sept. 22, Oct. 7, 1780, *Doc. Hist. Me.*, 18:414–415, 432, 459–460; Wadsworth to Gov. John Hancock, Dec. 23, 1780, ibid., 19:68–70; *Timothy Langdon v. Stephen Hall*, June 1782, Records of the Lincoln County Inferior Court of Common Pleas, MeSA; *Hall v. Langdon*, Superior Court Records for Cumberland and Lincoln Counties, 1783, file no. 139858, Suffolk County Court House.

61 Gould, *British and Tory Marauders*, p. 15; John L. Locke, *Sketches of the History of the Town of Camden, Maine, Including Incidental References to the Neighboring Places and Adjacent Waters* (Hallowell, Me.: Masters, Smith, 1859), pp. 32–34.

62 Petition of Jeremiah Colburn to the General Court, May 15, 1781, *Doc. Hist. Me.*, 19:261–262; Hunt, "Loyalists of Maine," p. 242. For a list of damages at Camden, April 29, 1782, see MaSA, 138:435.

63 Sloan, "New Ireland: Loyalists in Eastern Maine," pp. 102, 105; Hunt, "Loyalists of Maine," pp. 227–230; Peleg Wadsworth to the Council, Falmouth, April 28, 1780, *Doc. Hist. Me.*, 18:241; Cyrus Eaton, *History of Thomaston, Rockland, and South Thomaston, Maine, from Their First Exploration, A.D. 1605, with Family Genealogies*, 2 vols. (Hallowell, Me.: Masters, Smith, 1865), 1:139.

64 Peleg Wadsworth to the President of the Council, Falmouth, July 24, Thomaston, Aug. 7, 1780, *Doc. Hist. Me.*, 18:358, 366–367; Cushing Parole, Aug. 31, 1780, ibid., p. 384; John Jones to Jacob Bailey, Sept. 4, 1780, Correspondence of Jacob Bailey, 3:94; Bailey to anon., Sept. 29, [1780?], ibid., 3:338–339; Charles Cushing to Gov. John Hancock, Boston, Feb. 19, 1782, *Doc. Hist. Me.*, 19:416–417.

65 Peleg Wadsworth to the Council, Falmouth, April 28, 1780, *Doc. Hist. Me.*, 18:239–240; Wadsworth to Jeremiah Powell, Falmouth, May 26, 1780, ibid., p. 279.

66 Peleg Wadsworth to the Council, Falmouth, July 14, 1780, ibid., p. 353.

67 Peleg Wadsworth to Gov. John Hancock, Thomaston, Nov. 28, 1780, Jan. 10, 1781, ibid., 19:55, 88.

68 Timothy Dwight, "The Story of General Wadsworth," *MeHSQ* 15 (July 4, 1976):

227–256; *NHG*, March 19, 1781; Joseph Williamson, "Memoir of Col. Benjamin Burton," *CMeHS*, 1st ser. 7 (1876): 328–334.
69 Dwight, "Story of General Wadsworth," pp. 254–255; Williamson, "Col. Benjamin Burton," p. 334.
70 John Allan to Gov. John Hancock, Machias, March 17, 1781, *Doc. Hist. Me.*, 19:187; Memorial of James Sullivan, May 31, 1781, ibid., pp. 271–272; Extract, Log of H.M. Sloop *Allegiance*, Feb. 25, 1781, Public Records Office, London, photocopy provided by Herbert T. Silsby, II.
71 Extract, Log of H.M. Sloop *Allegiance*, Feb. 25, 1781.
72 John Allan to Jeremiah Powell, Machias, Feb. 20, 1780, *Doc. Hist. Me.*, 18:102.
73 John Allan to the President of the Council, Machias, July 12, 1780, ibid., pp. 345–346; Michael Francklin to Lord George Germain, May 4, 1780, *CAR, 1894*, pp. 387, 396.
74 John Allan to the President of the Council, Machias, July 12, 1780, *Doc. Hist. Me.*, 18:346.
75 Conference with the Indians, Passamaquoddy Indian Camps, July 1, 1780, ibid., pp. 338–339.
76 John Allan to Jeremiah Powell, Machias, Jan. 26, 1781, ibid., 19:107; Resolves of the General Court, Nov. 11, 1780, ibid., pp. 43–44; Allan to Gov. John Hancock, on board *La Estra*, Machias, May 9, 1781, ibid., pp. 256–257; Allan to Hancock, Machias, June 16, 1781, ibid., p. 283.
77 Hunt, "British-American Rivalry," p. 147, n. 41; John Allan to Gov. John Hancock, Machias, Oct. 17, 1781, *Doc. Hist. Me.*, 19:355–356.
78 John Allan to Gov. John Hancock, Machias, March 8, 1782, *Doc. Hist. Me.*, 19:437.
79 Memorial of Lewis Frederick Delesdernier, [Spring 1782], ibid., 20:25–27; John Allan to Gov. John Hancock, Machias, April 12, 16, 17, 25, 1783, ibid., pp. 217–222; Hunt, "British-American Rivalry," pp. 159–161.
80 Hunt, "British-American Rivalry," pp. 186–190.
81 John Allan to Gov. John Hancock, Machias, March 17, 1781, *Doc. Hist. Me.*, 19:188.
82 Francis Shaw, Jr., to Stephen Jones, Gouldsborough, March 17, 1781, ibid., pp. 235–236.
83 Francis Shaw, Jr., to the Governor and Council, Boston, May 3, 1781, ibid., pp. 247–248.
84 Francis Shaw, Jr., to the Governor, Council, Senate, and House, n.p., March 17, 1781, ibid., pp. 243–246.
85 Resolves of the Town of Machias, March 29–April 10, 1781, ibid., pp. 236–237.
86 Machias Committee of Correspondence, Inspection, and Safety to Gov. John Hancock, April 10, 1781, ibid., pp. 238–241.
87 Francis Shaw, Jr., to Stephen Jones, Gouldsborough, March 17, 1781, ibid., p. 236.
88 Hunt, "Loyalists of Maine," p. 243. See also Francis Shaw, Jr., to the Governor and Council, Boston, May 3, July 23, 1781, *Doc. Hist. Me.*, 19:247–249, 307–308; Deposition of Jonas Farnsworth, April 11, 1781, ibid., pp. 241–243.
89 Pleasant River Committee of Correspondence to Machias Committee of Correspondence, April 9, 1781, *Doc. Hist. Me.*, 19:191.

90 Francis Shaw, Jr., to the Governor and Council, Boston, May 3, July 23, 1781, ibid., pp. 246–249, 307–308.

FIVE A People Divided

1 Petition of York to the General Court, Sept. 9, 1775, *Doc. Hist. Me.*, 14:305; Donald A. Yerxa, "Graves and the Falmouth Affair," p. 126; Petition of Falmouth to the General Court, April 10, 1782, MaSA, 188:17; Petition of Falmouth to the General Court, April 15, 1782, *Doc. Hist. Me.*, 19:464–465; Petition of Frenchman's Bay to the General Court, Nov. 24, 1777, ibid., 15:293–294; Petition of Pleasant River to the General Court, Jan. 23, 1779, ibid., 16:165–166.

2 Petition of the Towns of Lincoln County to the General Court, Nov. 16, 1779, *Doc. Hist. Me.*, 17:449; Ezra Taylor to the General Court, Pownalborough, Nov. 28, 1780, ibid., 19:59; Memorial from the Selectmen of Pownalborough to the General Court, n.d., ibid., pp. 399–400; Petition of Pleasant River to the General Court, Jan. 23, 1779, ibid., 16:165–166.

3 Petitions of Francis Shaw, Jr., to the General Court, Boston, April 9, April 15, 1779, and the General Court's Approval thereon, April 21, 1779, ibid., 16:214, 226, 233–234; Petition of Richard Codman to the General Court, n.d., and the General Court's Approval thereon, Sept. 8, 1780, ibid., 18:387, 389–390; Petition of James Noble Shannon to the General Court, Machias, Jan. 1, 1779, and the General Court's Approval, Jan. 23, 1779, ibid., 16:149–150, 167; Petition of Abiel Wood to the Council, n.d., and the General Court's Approval thereon, May 13, 1780, ibid., 18:264–265.

4 Howe, "Massachusetts on the Seas," in Hart, *Commonwealth History of Massachusetts*, 3:48; Edmund D. Poole, ed., *Annals of Yarmouth and Barrington in the Revolutionary War* (Yarmouth, N.S.: Lawson Brothers, 1899), pp. 13–16, 32, 34, 51, 62, 63, 75, 96, 129–131; Depositions of Joseph Homer, Seth Barnes, Peter Coffin, 1778, MaSA, 144:185–190; Order of the General Court re Alexander McNutt, Jan. 12, 1780, and relevant papers, ibid., 223:395–398; Resolve of the General Court on a Petition of William Greenwood, Sept. 24, 1782, in Massachusetts, *Acts and Laws*, 1782–1783, p. 270.

5 Howe, "Massachusetts on the Seas," in Hart, *Commonwealth History of Massachusetts*, 3:48; Memorial of George Deake to the General Court, Cape Elizabeth, March 12, 1778, *Doc. Hist. Me.*, 15:388–389.

6 Committee of Correspondence, Inspection, and Safety for Boston to the Council, Boston, Feb. 24, 1778, *Doc. Hist. Me.*, 15:359–360; Depositions of Jeremiah Thompson and Robert Kent, Feb. 24, 1778, ibid., pp. 360–361; Testimony of Amos Sheffield, Jonathan Card, Presentment of James Avery, nos. 52, 53, 56, Feb. 25, 1779, Crown Prosecutions, PANS; Resolves of the General Court, Jan. 5, May 5, 1780, in Massachusetts, *Acts and Resolves*, 21:340, 495; John Allan to Jeremiah Powell, Machias, Sept. 24, 1779, *Doc. Hist. Me.*, 17:181; Allan to the "Respectable Committee of Boston," Machias, Oct. 4, 1779, ibid., pp. 348–349; Allan to the Council, Machias, Oct. 20, 1779, ibid., pp. 398–399; Allan's Instructions, Machias, Oct. 27, 1779, ibid., p. 409.

Notes to A People Divided 251

7. John Allan to the Council, Machias, March 17, 1781, in Kidder, *Military Operations*, p. 291; Allan to Jeremiah Powell, Machias, Jan. 26, 1781, *Doc. Hist. Me.*, 19:110; Deposition of Jonas Farnsworth, April 11, 1781, ibid., pp. 241–242; Perkins, *Diary*, pp. 38–39, 43, 45, 50; Records of the Proceedings of the Court of Vice Admiralty in Nova Scotia, no. 6, 496:301, PANS; John Jones to Jacob Bailey, Fort George, March 11, 1782, Correspondence of Jacob Bailey, 3:96.
8. Case of the Schooner *Rebecca* in Records of the Proceedings of the Court of Vice Admiralty in Nova Scotia, no. 6, 496:301, PANS.
9. Lt. Gov. Eyre Massey to Sir William Howe, Halifax, March 15, 1778, Military Correspondence, vol. 1, PANS; Massey to Lord George Germain, Halifax, March 23, 1778, *CAR, 1894*, p. 376; Peleg Wadsworth to the Council, Falmouth, April 28, 1780, *Doc. Hist. Me.*, 18:242; Wadsworth to Council, Thomaston, Aug. 7, 1780, ibid., pp. 366–367; Records of the Cumberland County Court of General Sessions of the Peace, Oct. 1782, MeSA.
10. Faibisy, "Privateering and Piracy," pp. 131–132.
11. John Allan to the Council, Machias, Nov. 19, 1777, in Kidder, *Military Operations*, p. 244; Allan to Jeremiah Powell, May 18, 1779, *Doc. Hist. Me.*, 16:257.
12. Resolves of the General Court, June 22, 1779, and Nov. 13, 1780, in Massachusetts, *Acts and Resolves*, 21:79, 22:153; *BG*, Feb. 11, 1782; Brebner, *Neutral Yankees*, pp. 315–316.
13. John Allan to [Jeremiah Powell?], Machias, Nov. 15, 1779, in Kidder, *Military Operations*, p. 273; Allan to Powell, Machias, Feb. 20, 1780, *Doc. Hist. Me.*, 18:103–104; Allan to [Gov. John Hancock], Machias, Nov. 2, 1780, ibid., 19:25–26.
14. Petition on behalf of Nathan Jones, Gouldsborough, Oct. 2, 1778, *Doc. Hist. Me.*, 16:88–91. See also Committee of Gouldsborough to the Council on behalf of Nathan Jones, March 25, 1780, MaSA, 176:373–374.
15. Edmund Bridge to the Provincial Congress, Watertown, July 11, 1775, in Allen, *Dresden*, p. 294; Elihu Hews to Joseph Warren, Penobscot River, June 9, 1775, *Doc. Hist. Me.*, 14:272; Petition of Machias to the Provincial Congress, May 25, 1775, in Charles H. Pope, "Machias in the Revolution," *CPMeHS*, 2nd ser. 6 (1895): 125–126.
16. James Lyon to the General Court, Machias, Aug. 5, 1777, *Doc. Hist. Me.*, 15:7; Josiah Brewer to the General Court, Penobscot, April 12, 1778, ibid., pp. 411–412; Petition of Jonathan Lowder to the Council, Penobscot, March 28, 1779, ibid., 16:202–203; Petition of Frenchman's Bay to the General Court, Nov. 24, 1777, ibid., 15:293–294.
17. See, for example, Petition of Pleasant River to the General Court, Jan. 23, 1779, ibid., 16:165–166; undated Petitions from Narraguagus, Chandler's River, and Union River, ibid., pp. 180–183; Williamson, *History of Maine*, 2:426; Hutchinson, *When the Revolution Came*, pp. 3–4; Petition of the inhabitants of Deer Isle and Sedgwick, June 11, 1775, *BHM* 2 (July 1886–June 1887): 103–104.
18. Petition of Bristol to the General Court, July 18, 1775, MaSA, 138:212.
19. Willis, *Smith and Deane Journals*, pp. 226, 240, 241; Bartlet, *Frontier Missionary*, pp. 128–129.
20. See correspondence between William Bayley and Mrs. Jean Bayley, Bayley Papers,

1724–1782, Andrew Hawes Collection, Box 2/15, MeHS; Henry Sewall to Daniel Sewall, New York, April 28, 1782, Sewall Family Correspondence, Mellen Papers, Hawthorne–Longfellow Library, Bowdoin College; William Gardiner to Silvester Gardiner, Boston, May 14, 1783, Silvester Gardiner Papers, Box 1/5, MeHS.

21 Jonathan Sayward Diaries, vol. 22, July 31, 1781, also July 4, July 28, 1781.
22 Petition from the Selectmen of Gorham to the General Court, Oct. 30, 1781, *Doc. Hist. Me.*, 19:365; Petitions to the General Court from Thomaston, Oct. 1780, ibid., 18:445–446, and from Newcastle, May 29, 1782, and Bristol, May 29, 1782, ibid., 20:21–24.
23 Petition of Machias to the Council, May 25, 1776, in Pope, "Machias in the Revolution," p. 125; Willis, *Smith and Deane Journals*, p. 238; see also Petitions to the General Court from Falmouth, Dec. 31, 1778, *Doc. Hist. Me.*, 16:145, and from Pleasant River, Jan. 23, 1779, ibid., p. 165.
24 Willis, *Smith and Deane Journals*, pp. 239–241, 280; Hutchinson, *When the Revolution Came*, pp. 109–111, 121–122; Williamson, *History of Maine*, 2:482–483; *BG*, May 22, 29, 1780. For a discussion of climate and agriculture in the eighteenth century, see David C. Smith et al., "Climate Fluctuations and Agricultural Change in Southern and Central New England, 1765–1880," *MeHSQ* 21 (Spring 1982): 181–182, 185; William R. Baron, "Eighteenth-Century New England Climate Variation and Its Suggested Impact on Society," ibid., pp. 203, 205, 210–211.
25 Committee of Machias to the Council, Jan. 24, 1778, *Doc. Hist. Me.*, 15:334–335.
26 Petition of John Martin Schaffers to the General Court, Waldoboro, Oct. 25, 1777, and the Council Order thereon, ibid., 15:266–267; Affidavit of Samuel Goodwin, Jr., Feb. 21, 1782, ibid., 18:419. I am indebted to Prof. Alan S. Taylor, Boston University, for correspondence regarding the British employment of German troops at Castine.
27 Petition of Joseph Prouty to the General Court, Scarborough, Sept. 10, 1777, ibid., 15:197; Stakeman, "Slavery in Colonial Maine," p. 76.
28 Petition from the selectmen of Cape Elizabeth to the General Court, n.d., *Doc. Hist. Me.*, 19:385; Nathaniel Larrabee to John Lewis, Brunswick, July 30, 1776, Lewis Papers, LC: Petition from Falmouth to the General Court, April 15, 1782, *Doc. Hist. Me.*, 19:464–465.
29 Percentages are my computations; otherwise, the data are from Illsley's and Morton's census return for Cumberland County, Feb. 3, 1778, Lewis Papers, LC. See also Massachusetts, *Acts and Resolves*, 20:272–273, 336–337.

Table 1

Town	Polls	Cont. Army	Percentage
Falmouth	722	139	19.25
Cape Elizabeth	350	76	21.27
North Yarmouth	404	56	13.86
Brunswick	198	33	16.66
Harpswell	198	27	13.63
Royalsborough	57	12	21.05

Scarborough	465	94	20.21
Gorham	338	47	13.90
Pearsontown	78	15	19.23
Windham	93	21	22.58
New Boston	72	11	15.27
New Gloucester	166	25	15.06
Raymondtown	40	12	30.00

30 Jonathan Sayward Diaries, vol. 21, June 22, 1780; Scarborough Town Records, Dec. 11, 1781, Kennebunkport Town Records, Jan. 9, 1781, Vassalborough Town Records, March 9, 1780, Pownalborough Town Records, Feb. and March 1781, and Vassalborough Town Records, May 10, 1781, all in MeSA.

31 Lewis Papers, LC, passim; Petitions to the General Court from Massabeeseck, n.d., and from Coxhall, Sept. 18, 1782, *Doc. Hist. Me.*, 20:84, 87–88; Fryeburg Town Records, Dec. 27, 1781, MeSA; Cumberland County Court of General Sessions, Aug. 29, 1782, *Doc. Hist. Me.*, 20:83.

32 Jonathan Sayward Diaries, vol. 22, March 29, July 3, 1781; Goold, "Falmouth Neck," p. 72; Samuel T. Dole, "Windham's Colored Patriot," *CMeHS*, 3rd ser. 1 (1904): 316; Stakeman, "Slavery in Colonial Maine," p. 75.

33 Massachusetts, *Acts and Laws*, 1:307–309; Assessors of North Yarmouth to John Lewis, March 29, 1782, Lewis Papers, LC; Louis C. Hatch, "Massachusetts in the Continental Forces," in Hart, *Commonwealth History of Massachusetts*, 3:136; Jonathan Smith, "How Massachusetts Raised Her Troops in the Revolution," *Proceedings of the Massachusetts Historical Society* 55 (June 1922): 354–355.

34 Petition of John Hill for the Town of Berwick to the General Court, April 15, 1782, *Doc. Hist. Me.*, 19:466–467.

35 Memorial of Lt. Col. Ezra Badlam to the General Court, Boston, April 10, 1782, ibid., p. 461.

36 Fryeburg Town Records, Dec. 27, 1781, MeSA; Timothy Langdon to Brig. Gen. William Heath, Pownalborough, Aug. 14, 1777, April 6, 1778, William Heath Papers, MaHS, 6:82, 367, 9:171.

37 Timothy Langdon to Brig. Gen. William Heath, Pownalborough, May 22, 1778, Heath Papers, 9:465; Deposition of Jedediah Preble, Jr., Penobscot, Nov. 8, 1777, *Doc. Hist. Me.*, 15:277–278.

38 Shy, *A People Numerous & Armed*, p. 173; James Kirby Martin and Mark Edward Lender, *A Respectable Army: The Military Origins of the Republic, 1763–1789* (Arlington Heights, Ill.: Harlan Davidson, 1982), pp. 89–94.

39 Correspondence between William Bayley and Mrs. Jean Bayley of Falmouth, especially from William, Oct. 30, 1778, and May 5, 1779, and from Jean Bayley, Falmouth, July 12, 1781, Bayley Papers, Hawes Collection, MeHS.

40 Petition of Elizabeth Lines to the General Court, Pownalborough, West Precinct, April 3, 1779, *Doc. Hist. Me.*, 16:207; see also Allen, *Dresden*, pp. 325–326.

41 Petition of Mary Perham to the General Court, Newcastle, June 1779, *Doc. Hist. Me.*, 16:284–285; Timothy Langdon to the General Court, June 19, 1779, ibid., p. 294.

42 Plachta, "The Privileged and the Poor," pp. 73–74.
43 E. C. Royle, "Pioneer, Patriot, and Rebel: Lewis Delesdernier," manuscript, 1972, pp. L9–L11, Pamphlet 383, MeHS; Resolves Relating to Distress at Machias, Nov. 9, 1776, in Massachusetts, *Acts and Resolves*, 19:647–648; John Allan to the Council, Boston, Feb. 25, 1777, in Kidder, *Military Operations*, pp. 180–181; James Avery to the General Court, read April 29, 1778, *Doc. Hist. Me.*, 15:432–433; Allan to the Council, Machias, Oct. 8, 1778, ibid., 16:108; Council to Allan, Boston, Nov. 9, 1778, ibid., p. 126; "Rebels in Nova Scotia during the Revolutionary War," *Maine Historical Magazine* 9 (April, May, June 1894): 64–65.
44 Ahlin, *Maine Rubicon*, pp. 199–200; Hunt, "British-American Rivalry," p. 147, n. 41.
45 Petition of Winslow to the Governor and General Court, Jan. 27, 1781, *Doc. Hist. Me.*, 19:113–116.
46 Greene and Harrington, *American Population*, pp. 36–40; Plachta, "The Privileged and the Poor," pp. 38–40; Petitions of Sylvanus Scott to the Machias Committee of Inspection, Correspondence and Safety, Aug. 15, 1777, and to the General Court, March 7, 1778, *Doc. Hist. Me.*, 15:167–168, 377.
47 Greene and Harrington, *American Population*, pp. 36–40; see also Plachta, "The Privileged and the Poor," pp. 38–39; Samuel T. Dole, "Paul Little, Esq.," *CMeHS*, 3rd ser. 1 (1904): 347; Willis, *Smith and Deane Journals*, pp. 240; Petitions to the General Court from former Inhabitants on the Penobscot River, Sept. 6, 1779, *Doc. Hist. Me.*, 17:88–89, from the Inhabitants of Lincoln County, Boston, Oct. 1, 1779, ibid., pp. 333–338, from Andrew Patterson, Boston, March 2, 1780, ibid., 18:113–114, from Ezra Taylor, Pownalborough, Nov. 28, 1780, ibid., 19:58.
48 William B. Norton, "Paper Currency in Massachusetts during the Revolution," *NEQ* 7 (March 1934): 57; Oscar Handlin and Mary Handlin, "Revolutionary Economic Policy in Massachusetts," *WMQ* 4 (Jan. 1947): 7–8; Willis, *Smith and Deane Journals*, pp. 239, 241.
49 Allen, *Dresden*, p. 326; North Yarmouth Committee of Safety to John Lewis, June 24, 1776, Lewis Papers, LC; Extract of a Letter from a Gentleman at Falmouth, Oct. 15, 1776, *Doc. Hist. Me.*, 14:387; Bartlet, *Frontier Missionary*, p. 357.
50 Davis R. Dewey, "Economic and Commercial Conditions . . .," in Hart, *Commonwealth History of Massachusetts*, 3:345–346; Handlin and Handlin, "Revolutionary Economic Policy," pp. 7–8, 12–13. See Town Records in MeSA for York, March 11, June 30, 1777, Nov. 3, 1779; Fryeburg, April 1777; Vassalborough, July 27, 1779; Kennebunkport, Aug. 9, 1779; Scarborough, Aug. 9, 1779; Pownalborough, Sept. 27, 1779; Bristol, Nov. 19, 1779; Gorham, Dec. 16, 1779. Willis, *History of Portland*, 2:172–173.
51 Dewey, "Economic and Commercial Conditions," in Hart, *Commonwealth History*, pp. 343–353; Norton, "Paper Currency in Massachusetts," pp. 46–49; Taylor, *Western Massachusetts*, pp. 105–108; Patterson, *Political Parties*, pp. 158–161.
52 Petition of Andrew Reed to the General Court, Boothbay, Sept. 10, 1781, *Doc. Hist. Me.*, 19:322–323; Handlin and Handlin, "Revolutionary Economic Policy," pp. 25–26; Willis, *Smith and Deane Journals*, p. 246; Taylor, *Western Massachusetts*, chap. 6, esp. pp. 104–105; David P. Szatmary, *Shays' Rebellion: The Making of an Agrarian Insurrection* (Amherst: University of Massachusetts Press, 1980), chap. 2.

53 Taylor, *Western Massachusetts*, pp. 108, 139; Szatmary, *Shays' Rebellion*, p. 32; Van Beck Hall, *Politics without Parties: Massachusetts, 1780–1791* (Pittsburgh, Pa.: University of Pittsburgh Press, 1972), p. 99.
54 Jeremiah Powell to John Lewis, Boston, Sept. 7, 1780, Lewis Papers, LC.
55 Fryeburg Town Records, Jan. 30, 1781, MeSA; Petition of Col. Edward Grow to the General Court, n.p., Jan. 22, 1782, *Doc. Hist. Me.*, 19:393–394; John Murray to the General Court, Boothbay, Sept. 20, 1781, ibid., pp. 331–334; Newcastle Town Records, Feb. 1, March 13, May 10, Oct. 3, 1781, MeSA; Petition of Coxhall to the General Court, April 20, 1782, *Doc. Hist. Me.*, 19:479.
56 Petition of John Murray to the General Court, Boston, Sept. 25, 1781, *Doc. Hist. Me.*, 19:337–338; Memorial of Ezra Taylor to the General Court, Pownalborough, Oct. 24, 1781, ibid., p. 362; Petition of James Mosher to the General Court, July 23, 1781, ibid., pp. 305–307.
57 Pownalborough Town Records, March 26, 1782, MeSA; Vassalborough Town Records, March 11, 1782, MeSA; Petition of the Selectmen of Boothbay to the General Court, Oct. 25, 1780, *Doc. Hist. Me.*, 19:4–5; Committee of the General Court re Boothbay Accounts, Feb. 9, 1782, ibid., pp. 464–465.
58 Report on the Petition of Thomas Donnell and others, July 8, 1775, *Doc. Hist. Me.*, 14:290; Pope, "Machias in the Revolution," pp. 127–128; Resolve of the Provincial Congress, June 23, 1775, *Doc. Hist. Me.*, 14:284–285; Hutchinson, *When the Revolution Came*, pp. 9–10; Receipt of the Inhabitants of Deer Isle, June 23, 1775, *Doc. Hist. Me.*, 14:285; Resolve of the General Court, Jan. 12, 1778, ibid., 15:323–324; MaSA, 208: 178, 210:87; Committee Report, Sept. 7, 1776, *Doc. Hist. Me.*, 16:378–379.
59 Resolve of the General Court re Thomaston, Nov. 7, 1780, *Doc. Hist. Me.*, 19:37–38; Resolves of the General Court on behalf of Washington, Nov. 24, 1780, ibid., pp. 47–48, on behalf of Cape Elizabeth, Feb. 17, 1780, ibid., p. 87, and on behalf of Brunswick and Harpswell, June 12, 1781, ibid., pp. 280–281; Fryeburg Town Records, March 19, 1781, MeSA; Petition of the Town of Berwick and the Response of the House, June 21, June 23, 1782, *Doc. Hist. Me.*, 19:289–290; Resolves in favor of the Counties of York, Cumberland, and Lincoln, June 27, 29, 1782, ibid., 20:51.
60 Paul H. Smith, "The American Loyalists: Notes on Their Organization and Numerical Strength," *WMQ*, 3rd ser. 25 (April 1968): 269, 270, n. 26.
61 See Rachel N. Klein, "Frontier Planters and the American Revolution: The South Carolina Backcountry, 1775–1782," in Hoffman, Tate, and Albert, *An Uncivil War*, pp. 44–45, 49; Jeffrey J. Crow, "Liberty Men and Loyalists: Disorder and Disaffection in the North Carolina Backcountry," in ibid., p. 168.
62 Hunt, "Loyalists of Maine"; Sloan, "New Ireland: Loyalists in Eastern Maine."
63 Cass, "Pownalborough," pp. 142–145. Cass states that in Pownalborough loyalists and suspected loyalists constituted only 1 percent of heads of families. It is useful to compare the thirty on Cass's list with the number of polls, or white males over sixteen, which totaled 292 in 1778. In this case, the loyalists and suspects amount to about 10 percent of the adult males.
64 Jacob Bailey to Gen. Francis McLean, Halifax, July 10, 1779, quoted in Allen, *Dresden*, pp. 399–401. Bailey's total of 56 loyalists (including adult sons) constitutes

19 percent of the 292 polls for 1778. See also Thayer, "Loyalists of the Kennebec," p. 245. Working from Bailey's lists, Thayer finds the percentage of loyalists among adult males (polls) in other Kennebec towns is 15 to 20 percent, about the same as in Pownalborough.

65 William H. Nelson, *The American Tory* (Boston: Beacon Press, 1964), pp. 85–91.
66 Cass, "Pownalborough," p. 143; Sloan, "New Ireland: Loyalists in Eastern Maine," pp. 157–158.
67 Hunt, "Loyalists of Maine," pp. 100–101, 105.
68 E. Alfred Jones, *The Loyalists of Massachusetts* (London: Saint Catherine's Press, 1930; reprint ed., Baltimore: Genealogical Publishing, 1969), pp. 101–102.
69 Lorenzo Sabine, *Biographical Sketches of Loyalists of the American Revolution*, 2 vols. (Boston: Little, Brown, 1864), 2:138–139; Hunt, "Loyalists of Maine," p. 103; Jones, *Loyalists of Massachusetts*, p. 227; Stark, *Loyalists of Massachusetts*, pp. 464–465; Hunt, "Loyalists of Maine," pp. 103–104.
70 Sabine, *Biographical Sketches*, 2:198–199; Stark, *Loyalists of Massachusetts*, p. 467; Hunt, "Loyalists of Maine," p. 104.
71 Sabine, *Biographical Sketches*, 2:461–463; Stark, *Loyalists of Massachusetts*, pp. 465–466; Hunt, "Loyalists of Maine," p. 103.
72 Jones, *Loyalists of Massachusetts*, pp. 119–120, 255–256; Hunt, "Loyalists of Maine," pp. 106–108, 102; Stark, *Loyalists of Massachusetts*, p. 447; Sabine, *Biographical Sketches*, 2:369–371.
73 Sibley and Shipton, *Biographical Sketches*, 12:520–524; Sabine, *Biographical Sketches*, 2:448–449; Hunt, "Loyalists of Maine," pp. 104–105.
74 Hunt, "Loyalists of Maine," pp. 117–126; Willis, *History of Portland*, 2:149.
75 Kershaw, *Kennebeck Proprietors*, p. 243; Hunt, "Loyalists of Maine," pp. 136–138.
76 Kershaw, *Kennebeck Proprietors*, pp. 165, 243.
77 Timothy Parsons to the Board of War, Pownalborough, Sept. 15, 1777, *Doc. Hist. Me.*, 15:207; Hunt, "Loyalists of Maine," pp. 144–148; Cass, "Pownalborough," pp. 138–140.
78 Records of the Lincoln County Court of General Sessions of the Peace, Sept. 16, 1777, MeSA; Petition of William Gardiner to the General Court, received Oct. 24, 1777, *Doc. Hist. Me.*, 15:264–265; Massachusetts, *Acts and Resolves*, 20:553; Hunt, "Loyalists of Maine," pp. 190–199.
79 Bartlet, *Frontier Missionary*, pp. 106–129, passim; Kershaw, *Kennebeck Proprietors*, pp. 243–251; Hunt, "Loyalists of Maine," pp. 182–187.
80 Jacob Bailey's Defense before the Pownalborough Committee of Safety, Pownalborough, Oct. 28, 1776, *Doc. Hist. Me.*, 14:390–394.
81 Charles Cushing to Samuel Freeman, Pownalborough, Nov. 16, 1776, ibid., pp. 397–398.
82 Kershaw, *Kennebeck Proprietors*, p. 252.
83 Jacob Bailey to Samuel Goodwin, Cornwallis, N.S., n.d., Correspondence of Jacob Bailey, 3:282; Bailey to Nathaniel Bailey, Cornwallis, N.S., Feb. 16, 1780, ibid., p. 325; Bailey to Thomas Robie, Cornwallis, N.S., Feb. 26, 1780, ibid., p. 329; Bailey to Mr. Badger, Cornwallis, N.S., Aug. 1, 1780, ibid., p. 332; Bailey to J. S. Weeks, Cornwallis, N.S., Dec. 8, 1780, ibid., p. 349; Bailey to Thomas Brown, Cornwallis, N.S., Feb. 24, 1780, ibid., p. 328.

84 Sloan, "New Ireland: Loyalists in Eastern Maine," pp. 79–98; Wilbur H. Siebert, "The Exodus of the Loyalists from Penobscot and the Loyalist Settlement at Passamaquoddy," *Collections of the New Brunswick Historical Society* 9 (1914): 493.
85 Sloan, "New Ireland: Loyalists in Eastern Maine," p. 79.
86 Quoted in Walter Snow, comp., *Brooksville, Maine: "A Town of the Bagaduce"* (Blue Hill, Me.: Weekly Packet, 1967), p. 34.
87 Petition of Lydia Twycross to the General Court, Feb. 21, 1782, and Resolve of the General Court thereon, April 1782, *Doc. Hist. Me.*, 19:417–419; Allen, *Dresden*, p. 397.
88 Quoted in Ernest A. Clarke, "Cumberland Planters and the Aftermath of the Attack on Fort Cumberland," in *They Planted Well: New England Planters in Maritime Canada*, ed. Margaret Conrad (Fredericton, N.B.: Acadiensis Press, 1988), p. 49. See also John Allan to Massachusetts Council, Auke Paque, June 24, 1777, and Allan to Council, Machias, Nov. 18, 1777, in Kidder, *Military Operations*, pp. 196, 242–243.
89 Hunt, "Loyalists of Maine," pp. 212–214; Petition of Martha Oxnard to the General Court, Falmouth, n.d., *Doc. Hist. Me.*, 19:313–314; Petition of Elizabeth Stevens to the General Court, Falmouth, n.d., and Resolve of the General Court thereon, Sept. 14, 1781, ibid., pp. 326–327.
90 Hunt, "Loyalists of Maine," pp. 187–188; Allen, *Dresden*, pp. 395–397. For documents re Rebecca Callahan, see *Doc. Hist. Me.*, vol. 15, passim. For Whig plundering of Tory estates, see David E. Maas, "Honest Graft in Revolutionary Massachusetts," *Boston Bar Journal* 23 (Oct. 1979): 7–15.
91 Thayer, "Loyalists of the Kennebec," pp. 258–259. For Carleton, see Sloan, "New Ireland: Loyalist Colony," pp. 96–97.
92 Petitions of Clark Linneken to the General Court, Pownalborough Gaol, Oct. 18, Dec. 9, 1777, *Doc. Hist. Me.*, 15:250–252, 312–313, and the General Court Resolves thereon, Oct. 24, 1777, Feb. 14, 1778, ibid., pp. 265–266, 358; John Allan to the General Court, Machias, May 30, 1777, ibid., 14:417.
93 Quoted in Wheeler and Wheeler, *Brunswick, Topsham, and Harpswell*, pp. 680–681. See also Hunt, "Loyalists of Maine," pp. 150–151.
94 Willis, *History of Portland*, 2:73–74; Falmouth Society of Friends, Men's Monthly Meeting Records, 1751–1788, pp. 34, 68, MeHS; Greene and Harrington, *American Population*, p. 37; Willis, *Smith and Deane Journals*, p. 347 n.; Samuel T. Dole, *Windham in the Past* (Auburn, Me.: Merrill and Webber, 1916), pp. 129–130; Samuel T. Dole, "Extracts from the Old Records of Windham," *CPMeHS*, 2nd ser. 10 (1899): 313–314. By contrast, Bristol refused to clear Quakers from paying ministerial rates; see Bristol Town Records, April 5, 1784, MeSA.
95 Willis, *Smith and Deane Journals*, p. 347.
96 Petition of Nathaniel Palmer, Boston, April 25, 1780, *Doc. Hist. Me.*, 18:233–235; Hunt, "Loyalists of Maine," pp. 221–222.
97 Willis, *History of Portland*, 2:75; Friends Monthly Records, pp. 62, 63, 87, MeHS.

SIX *State Making and State Breaking*

1 Taylor, *Western Massachusetts*, pp. 75–88.
2 Massachusetts, *Journals of the House of Representatives*, 53:4–6.

3 Taylor, *Western Massachusetts*, pp. 88–90, Stephen Patterson, *Political Parties*, p. 182.
4 Patterson, *Political Parties*, p. 188. For the text of the 1778 constitution, see Oscar Handlin and Mary Handlin, eds., *The Popular Sources of Political Authority: Documents on the Massachusetts Constitution of 1780* (Cambridge, Mass.: Harvard University Press, 1966), pp. 190–201.
5 Patterson, *Political Parties*, p. 188; Handlin and Handlin, *Popular Sources*, pp. 22, 202–379; Taylor, *Western Massachusetts*, pp. 88–90; Robert Brown, *Revolutionary Politics*, pp. 239–241.
6 The number of towns and plantations in Maine is from Greene and Harrington, *American Population*, pp. 36–40. Note that this number includes the incorporated and unincorporated communities. Town returns and the number of people voting are from Handlin and Handlin, *Popular Sources*, pp. 202–323, passim. All adult males could vote on the constitution, so I have derived voting percentages by dividing town votes by the number of polls for each town listed in the 1778 census figures in Greene and Harrington, *American Population*, pp. 36–40. Greene and Harrington define a poll as "usually all men above 21"; see "Note on Methods of Calculation," ibid., p. xxiii.

Table 2   *Constitutional Vote, 1778*

Town	Vote	Polls	Percentage	Pro	Con
York County					
York	147	327	44		x
Kittery	64	561	11		x
Wells	118	611	19		x
Pepperell	56	177	32		x
Berwick	148	748	20		x
Mean			25.2		
Cumberland County					
Falmouth	68	669	10		x
Brunswick	78	192	40		x
Cape Eliz.	31	402	8		x
New Glouc.	109	134	81		x
Pearsontown	21	70	30		x
Gorham	55	321	17		x
N. Yarmouth	84	386	22	x	
Scarborough	39	372	10	x	
Mean			27.3		
Lincoln County					
Pownalborough	42	292	14		x
Georgetown	45	386	12		x
Newcastle	...	132	(refused to vote)		x
Winthrop	21	108	19		x
Edgecomb	15	127	12		x

Notes to State Making and State Breaking 259

Vassalborough	26	116	22		x
Bristol	103	234	44		x
Boothbay*	63	179	35		x
Blue Hill†	26	44	59	x	
Deer Isle†	46	116	40	x	
Penobscot†	33	109	30	x	
Wheelersborough	21	...	...	x	
Mean			28.7		

*Identified as Townshend in Greene and Harrington, *American Population*, p. 39.
†Number of polls in 1776.

7   Return of Georgetown, May 25, 1778, in Handlin and Handlin, *Popular Sources*, p. 277.
8   Return of Boothbay, May 20, 1778, ibid., pp. 245–252.
9   Instructions from Gorham, n.d., ibid., pp. 429–430.
10 Samuel Eliot Morison, "The Struggle over the Adoption of the Constitution of Massachusetts, 1780," *Proceedings of the Massachusetts Historical Society* 50 (May 1917): 356, n. 2. See also Massachusetts, *Journal of the Convention for Framing a Constitution of Government for the State of Massachusetts Bay, from the Commencement of their First Session, Sept. 1, 1779, to the Close of their Last Session, June 16, 1780* (Boston: Dutton and Wentworth, 1832), pp. 16–18.
11 Ronald M. Peters, Jr., *The Massachusetts Constitution of 1780: A Social Compact* (Amherst: University of Massachusetts Press, 1978), pp. 23–25.
12 For a full text of the 1780 constitution, see Handlin and Handlin, *Popular Sources*, pp. 441–472.
13 Morison, "Struggle over Adoption," p. 400.
14 Ibid.; see also Patterson, *Political Parties*, pp. 244–246.
15 Patterson, *Political Parties*, p. 247; Morison, "Struggle over Adoption," p. 401. For differing interpretations, see Handlin and Handlin, *Popular Sources*, pp. 24–25, and Peters, *Massachusetts Constitution*, pp. 37–38—both of which minimize east-west polarization over the constitution.
16 Patterson, *Political Parties*, pp. 95, 248–250.
17 Town returns and the number of people voting are from Handlin and Handlin, *Popular Sources*, pp. 627–630, 726–740, 927–930. As before, all adult white males could vote on the constitution (ibid., p. 23), so I have derived voting percentages by dividing town votes by the polls for each town listed in the 1781 census in Greene and Harrington, *American Population*, pp. 37–40. Greene and Harrington define a poll as "usually all men above 21"; see "Note on Methods of Calculation," ibid., p. xxiii.

Table 3   *Constitutional Vote, 1780*

Town	Vote	Polls	Percentage	Pro	Con
York County					
Arundel	...	246	...	x	
Berwick	28	756	4	x	

260   Notes to State Making and State Breaking

Biddeford	10	215	5	x	
Buxton	53	183	29		x
Sanford	...	209	(refused to vote)		x
Wells	74	591	13	x	
Kittery	80	574	14	x	
York	30	567	5	x	
Mean			12		
Cumberland County					
Falmouth	83	556	15	x	
Cape Eliz.	28	292	10	x	
Gorham*	53	363	15	x	
Brunswick	...	206	(refused to vote)		x
New Gloucester	29	156	19	x	
Mean			15		
Lincoln County					
Pownalborough	49	300	16		x
Vassalborough	...	136	...	x	
Thomaston	...	80	(refused to vote)		x
Waldoboro	...	135	(refused to vote)		x
Edgecomb	20	132	15	x	
Newcastle	27	140	19	x	
Georgetown	...	255	...	x	
Mean			17		

*See Gorham Town Records, April 25, May 24, 1780, MeSA. Forty-seven townspeople voted to accept and six to reject the report of the committee on the constitution. The town records do not include the report, but the *Boston Gazette*, June 12, 1780, published a report by a committee of Gorham on the constitution, probably the one noted in the town records. The report is sharply critical of what it calls the constitution's "spiritual tyranny" but comes to no overall conclusion on the document itself.

18 Gorham's conservative shift to support the constitution of 1780 was only temporary. More characteristically, Gorham's representative at the state convention on adoption of the federal Constitution voted against ratification. See Jonathan Elliot, ed., *The Debates of the Several State Conventions on the Adoption of the Federal Constitution . . .*, 2nd ed., 5 vols. (New York: Burt Franklin, n.d., reprinted from 1888 ed.), 2:181.
19 Handlin and Handlin, *Popular Sources*, p. 942.
20 Return of Buxton, May 1780, in ibid., pp. 731–732. Note the ambiguity of this return, typical of many town responses. Buxton apparently rejected the constitution by 49 to 4 on first consideration but then approved it with amendments by what appears to be 37 to 12.
21 Return of Wells, May 22, 1780, in ibid., pp. 734–740.
22 See returns from Edgecomb and Wheelersborough, ibid., pp. 297, 304.

23 Quoted in Morison, "Struggle over Adoption," p. 366, n. 3.
24 Return of Boothbay, May 20, 1778, in Handlin and Handlin, *Popular Sources*, p. 246; Return of Pownalborough, May 18, 1780, in ibid., p. 629; Return of Bluehill Bay, May 28, 1778, in ibid., p. 285.
25 Peleg Wadsworth to the Council, Falmouth, July 10, 1780, *Doc. Hist. Me.*, 18:342.
26 Joseph Williamson, "The Proposed Province of New Ireland," *CMeHS*, 3rd ser. 1 (1904): 150–152; Siebert, "Exodus of the Loyalists from Penobscot and the Loyalist Settlement at Passamaquoddy," p. 487.
27 Coleman, *American Revolution in Georgia*, pp. 147–148.
28 Williamson, "Proposed Province of New Ireland," pp. 148–150.
29 Ibid., pp. 148–149; Bellot, *Knox*, p. 177.
30 Williamson, "Proposed Province of New Ireland," p. 150.
31 Bellot, *Knox*, p. 177; Sloan, "New Ireland: Loyalists in Eastern Maine," pp. 127–128.
32 Bellot, *Knox*, p. 178.
33 Wilbur Siebert, *Exodus of the Loyalists from Penobscot to Passamaquoddy*, p. 18; Joseph Williamson, "The British Occupation of Penobscot during the Revolution," *CPMeHS*, 2nd ser. 1 (1890): 396.
34 Brig. Gen. Francis McLean to Gen. Henry Clinton, Penobscot, Oct. 21, 1779, and Col. John Campbell to Clinton, Penobscot, March 15, 1781, Military Correspondence . . . Dorchester Papers, vol. 1, PANS; Sloan, "New Ireland: Loyalists in Eastern Maine," pp. 82–83.
35 Sir George Collier to Gen. Henry Clinton, Penobscot, Aug. 24, 1779, Penobscot Expedition Papers, British, MeHS.
36 Brig. Gen. Peleg Wadsworth to the Council, Thomaston, Sept. 14, 1780, *Doc. Hist. Me.*, 18:414–415; Wadsworth to Gov. John Hancock, Thomaston, Dec. 23, 1780, ibid., 19:68–70.
37 Sloan, "New Ireland: Loyalists in Eastern Maine," p. 84.
38 Ibid.; "State of the Inhabitants . . .," in Williamson, "Proposed Province of New Ireland," p. 156.
39 Sloan, "New Ireland: Loyalists in Eastern Maine," pp. 84–85; "State of the Inhabitants," in Williamson, "Proposed Province of New Ireland," p. 155.
40 Faibisy, "Privateering and Piracy," pp. 161–163, 177.
41 *NHG*, Aug. 17, 1782, reporting the capture of a loaded British mast ship from Penobscot bound for New York. See also *BG*, Aug. 12, 1782.
42 Sir George Collier to Gen. Henry Clinton, Penobscot, Aug. 24, 1779, Penobscot Expedition Papers, British, MeHS.
43 Richard B. Morris, *The Peacemakers: The Great Powers and American Independence* (New York: Harper and Row, 1965), p. 270; Sloan, "New Ireland: Loyalists in Eastern Maine," p. 126.
44 James H. Hutson, *John Adams and the Diplomacy of the American Revolution* (Lexington: University of Kentucky Press, 1980), pp. 124–126.
45 Morris, *Peacemakers*, pp. 375, 379–380; Sloan, "New Ireland: Loyalists in Eastern Maine," pp. 126–127; William S. MacNutt, *New Brunswick: A History, 1784–1867* (Toronto: Macmillan, 1963; reprint ed., 1984), p. 14.

46 MacNutt, *New Brunswick*, pp. 16–41.
47 Ibid., pp. 42–63.
48 Ibid., p. 63.
49 Ibid., p. 40; Ahlin, *Maine Rubicon*, pp. 149–151; Sloan, "New Ireland: Loyalists in Eastern Maine," pp. 136–137; John Allan to Thomas Mifflin, Boston, Dec. 25, 1783, Allan Papers, MaHS; Message of Gov. James Bowdoin to the General Court, July 7, 1786, *Doc. Hist. Me.*, 21:230–231.
50 Henry S. Burrage, *Maine in the Northeastern Boundary Controversy* (Portland, Me.: Marks Printing House, 1919), pp. 42–67.
51 Robert Pagan's Deposition, July 20, 1797, in Edgar C. Smith, "Our Eastern Boundary: The St. Croix River Controversy," chap. 5 of *Maine: A History*, ed. Louis C. Hatch (New York: American Historical Society, 1919; reprint ed., 3 vols. in 1, Somersworth: New Hampshire Publishing, 1973), pp. 96–97.
52 Ibid., pp. 55–58. For modern archaeological evidence on the settlement of Saint Croix Island, see Jacob W. Gruber, "The French Settlement on St. Croix Island, Maine: Excavations for the National Park Service, 1968–1969." Manuscript deposited with the National Park Service, U.S. Department of the Interior, North Atlantic Region, Boston, 1970; copy through the generosity of Dr. Robert L. Bradley, Maine State Historical Preservation Commission, Augusta.
53 Nathaniel Segar, *A Brief Narrative of the Captivity and Sufferings of Lt. Nathan'l Segar, Taken Prisoner by the Indians and Carried to Canada during the Revolutionary War* (Paris, Me.: Oxford Bookstore, 1825); William B. Lapham, *History of Bethel, Formerly Sudbury Canada, Oxford County, Maine, 1768–1890* (Augusta: Maine Farmer, 1891), pp. 45–61; Sudbere Canada to the General Court, May 29, 1782, *Doc. Hist. Me.*, 20:24–25; Petition of the Inhabitants of Fryeburg and other Towns to the General Court, June 15, 1782, ibid., pp. 41–42; Memorial of the Selectmen of Fryeburg to the General Court, March 1, 1782, ibid., pp. 107–108; Petition of Sudbury Canada, Bridgeton, and Fryeburg to the General Court, n.d., ibid., pp. 332–333.
54 Representation of the Inhabitants of Falmouth to the General Court, Feb. 3, 1783, *Doc. Hist. Me.*, 20:163–164.
55 Sloan, "New Ireland: Loyalists in Eastern Maine," pp. 110–112.
56 Bourne, "The Penobscot Fiasco," pp. 33, 100.
57 Jonathan Sayward Diaries, vol. 23, March 25, 1782; Willis, *Smith and Deane Journals*, p. 247.
58 Sloan, "New Ireland: Loyalists in Eastern Maine," pp. 138–139, but compare the date of the Resolve of the Massachusetts Senate, March 23, 1784, *Doc. Hist. Me.*, 20:334–335.
59 Samuel McCobb to the General Court, May 24, 1784, *Doc. Hist. Me.*, 20:321–323.
60 Willis, *History of Portland*, 2:174.
61 Hutson, *Adams and Diplomacy*, pp. 127–128.
62 Quoted in Morris, *Peacemakers*, p. 377.
63 Ibid., pp. 378–379; see also Article III of the Definitive Treaty, ibid., p. 463.
64 Samuel Goodwin to Jacob Bailey, Pownalborough, Sept. 9, 1783, Correspondence of Jacob Bailey, 3:1–2.

65 Morris, *Peacemakers*, pp. 409–410, 435–436. Congress did not muster the necessary quorum to approve the final treaty until Jan. 14, 1784 (ibid., p. 447).
66 Willis, *Smith and Deane Journals*, pp. 249, 351. See Tucker, "Daniel Tucker in the Revolution," p. 253.
67 Willis, *Smith and Deane Journals*, pp. 249–250.
68 Scarborough Town Records, April 7, 1783, and Gorham Town Records, May 12, 1783, MeSA.
69 Jonathan Sayward Diaries, vol. 24, April 29, 1783.
70 *NHG*, May 10, 1783.
71 Ibid. A modern skeptic might regard it as a case of murder, not suicide.
72 Jacob Bailey to Capt. Gallop, March 3, 1783, Annapolis, N.S., Correspondence of Jacob Bailey, 3:399.
73 Jacob Bailey to H. B. Brown, Annapolis, N.S., March 12, 1783, ibid., 3:401.
74 Quoted in Robert E. Moody, "Samuel Ely: Forerunner of Shays," *NEQ* 5 (Jan. 1932): 109.
75 Ibid., pp. 110–134, passim.
76 Jonathan Sayward Diaries, vol. 23, April 12(?), 1782.

SEVEN *The Legacy of Revolution*

1 Henry Sewall to Henry Sewall, [Sr.], Newburgh, N.Y., June 18, 1783, Sewall Family Correspondence, Mellen Papers, Hawthorne-Longfellow Library, Bowdoin College.
2 Jonathan Sayward Diaries, vol. 26, Jan. 1, 1785; *Falmouth Gazette* (FG), Aug. 20, 1785; name changes to *Cumberland Gazette* (CG) on April 7, 1786.
3 Plachta, "The Privileged and the Poor," pp. 64, 67, 75, 91, 61, 69, 61–62, 72.
4 Memorial of the People of Canaan Plantation to the General Court, Dec. 16, 1786, *Doc. Hist. Me.*, 21:317–319; Petition of Joshua Bracket of Shapleigh to the General Court, Jan. 29, 1787, ibid., pp. 337–338; Petition of Raymondtown to the General Court, Feb. 5, 1787, ibid., pp. 320–321.
5 Plachta, "The Privileged and the Poor," pp. 2, 56, 60.
6 William Widgery to George Thatcher, New Gloucester, Sept. 14, 1788, in William F. Goodwin, ed., "The Thatcher Papers," *Historical Magazine*, 2nd ser. 6 (Nov.–Dec. 1869): 352–353; Jonathan Sayward Diaries, vol. 28, Jan. 1, 1787; Szatmary, *Shays' Rebellion*, pp. 26–36.
7 Documents re Anna Card, *Doc. Hist. Me.*, 22:48–59, passim.
8 Taylor, "Liberty-Men and White Indians," pp. 1–3, 15–16; *FG*, May 28, 1785; *CG*, Nov. 24, 1786; see also *CG*, Dec. 22, 1786.
9 Bristol Town Records, Oct. 3, 1786, MeSA; see also Frederic Grant, Jr., "Benjamin Austin, Jr.'s Struggle with the Lawyers," *Boston Bar Journal* 25 (Sept. 1987): 19–20, and "Observations on the Pernicious Practice of the Law," *American Bar Association Journal* 68 (May 1982): 580–582.
10 Enoch Freeman Almanac, 1785, n.p., Portland Public Library.
11 Taylor, "Liberty-Men and White Indians," p. 372.
12 Banks, *Maine Becomes a State*, p. 5.

13 Taylor, "Liberty-Men and White Indians," pp. 15–16, 50–51.
14 Gross, *The Minutemen and Their World*, pp. 177–179; Taylor, "Liberty-Men and White Indians," pp. 46–52; Joseph Plumb Martin, *Private Yankee Doodle: Being a Narrative of Some of the Adventures, Dangers, and Sufferings of a Revolutionary Soldier*, ed. George E. Scheer (Boston: Little, Brown, 1962), pp. xii–xv.
15 Joyce Butler, "The Wadsworths: A Portland Family," *MeHSQ* 27 (Spring 1988): 4–6.
16 Taylor, "Liberty-Men and White Indians," pp. 290–303; North Callahan, *Henry Knox: General Washington's General* (New York: Rinehart, 1958), pp. 283, 338–350. See also Carolyn S. Parsons, "Bordering on Magnificence: Urban Domestic Planning in the Maine Woods," in Clark, Leamon, and Bowden, *Maine in the Early Republic*, pp. 62–82; Knox quoted in Taylor, "Liberty-Men and White Indians," p. 281.
17 Samuel Ely, *The Deformity of a Hideous Monster Discovered in the Province of Maine, by a Man in the Woods, Looking after Liberty* (Boston, 1797), pp. 6–7, no. 32081 in *Early American Imprints, 1639–1800*, ed. Clifford K. Shipton, American Antiquarian Society, Worcester, Mass.; Alan Taylor, "A Kind of a Warr: The Contest for Land on the Northeastern Frontier, 1750–1820," *WMQ* 46 (Jan. 1984): 3–24.
18 *FG*, Feb. 5, 1785. An entry in the Jonathan Sayward Diaries, vol. 23, makes it appear as though private discussion of separation took place as early as April 12(?), 1782, but the precise dating of the entries is unclear here.
19 *FG*, Sept. 17, 1785.
20 Banks, *Maine Becomes a State*, pp. 13–22; Williamson, *History of Maine*, 2:522–527; Willis, *History of Portland*, 2:250–256.
21 Daniel Davis, "The Proceedings of Two Conventions, Held at Portland, to Consider the Expediency of a Separate Government in the District of Maine," *Collections of the Massachusetts Historical Society* 4 (1795): 36–37; Report of the Second Convention, Held in Falmouth, Jan. 4–5, 1786, in Banks, *Maine Becomes a State*, pp. 209–211; *FG*, July 9, Nov. 5, 1785.
22 *FG*, July 23, 30, Aug. 6, 13, 1785.
23 Davis, "Proceedings of Two Conventions," p. 39; Proceedings of the Third Convention, Held at Portland, Sept. 6, 1786, in Banks, *Maine Becomes a State*, p. 213.
24 *FG*, June 11, 1785.
25 Ibid., June 4, 11, 18, 1785; *CG*, Sept. 28, 1786; *FG*, March 9, 1786; *CG*, May 11, 1786; *FG*, March 23, 1786.
26 *FG*, June 11, 1785.
27 See Szatmary, *Shays' Rebellion*, for the latest examination of this episode.
28 Goold, "General Samuel Thompson," pp. 454, 456–457; Jonas Clark, Jr., to Jonas Clark, Sr., Falmouth, Oct. 17, 1785, Jonas Clark Papers, Manuscript Division, LC.
29 Davis, "Proceedings of Two Conventions," p. 28.
30 Ibid., p. 33.
31 Ibid., p. 29.
32 Banks, *Maine Becomes a State*, p. 23; Davis, "Proceedings of Two Conventions," pp. 36–37, 40.
33 Davis, "Proceedings of Two Conventions," pp. 32–33; *CG*, Feb. 9, 1787.

34 Davis, "Proceedings of Two Conventions," p. 33.
35 *CG*, March 23, 1787.
36 Gov. James Bowdoin's Address to the General Court, Oct. 20, 1785, *Doc. Hist. Me.*, 21:49; *FG*, Dec. 17, Dec. 10, 1785; *CG*, Aug. 31, 1786.
37 *FG*, March 30, 1786; *CG*, Nov. 31, 1786; see also *CG*, Sept. 21, 28, Nov. 24, 1786, Feb. 23, 1787.
38 *FG*, March 16, 1786. See also *FG*, June 11, July 9, 1785, March 2, 23, 1786, and *CG*, Dec. 8, 1786, for references to Maine as a colony to Massachusetts.
39 *CG*, Sept. 14, 1786.
40 Willis, *History of Portland*, 2:254 n.; Banks, *Maine Becomes a State*, pp. 14-15.
41 Petition of the Inhabitants of Machias to the General Court, Dec. 18, 1782, *Doc. Hist. Me.*, 20:302-303.
42 Memorial and Objections of the Inhabitants of Mount Desert, March 18, 1784, ibid., pp. 329-331; Memorial and Objections to the Petition of Machias, Gouldsborough, May 29, 1784, ibid., pp. 335-337; Proceedings of Delegates from Mount Desert and other Places, April 20, 1784, ibid., pp. 343-344; Petition of Francis Shaw to the General Court, Gouldsborough, n.d., ibid., p. 313.
43 Machias Committee of Correspondence to the General Court, May 12, 1784, ibid., pp. 337-341.
44 Stephen Jones and others for the Town of Machias to Caleb Davis, Machias, May 22, 1786, Davis Papers, MaHS; see also Jones et al. to Davis, Dec. 23, 1786, ibid.
45 Davis, "Proceedings of Two Conventions," p. 33; Jeremiah Hill to George Thatcher, n.p., Jan. 1, 1788, in Goodwin, "Thatcher Papers," pp. 260-261.
46 David Sewall to George Thatcher, York, Feb. 11, 1788, in Goodwin, "Thatcher Papers," p. 271.
47 Samuel Nasson to George Thatcher, Sanford, Feb. 26, 1788, ibid., p. 341.
48 Elliot, *Debates in State Conventions*, 2:61, 80, 33-34.
49 Ibid., pp. 35, 15, 80.
50 Ibid., pp. 61, 96.
51 Ibid., pp. 180-181; Samuel B. Harding, *The Contest over the Ratification of the Federal Constitution in the State of Massachusetts* (New York: Longmans, Green, 1896), pp. 99-100.
52 Plachta, "The Privileged and the Poor," pp. 174, 176, 180; Jackson Turner Main, *The Anti-Federalists: Critics of the Constitution, 1781-1788* (Chapel Hill: University of North Carolina Press, 1961; reprint ed., Chicago: Quadrangle Books, 1964), pp. 203-204.
53 Taylor, "Liberty-Men and White Indians," p. 323. Hall, *Politics without Parties*, p. 178, n. 26, points out that ten of eighteen towns attending separation conventions voted against ratification of the federal Constitution, whereas only five of the twenty-one towns voting for ratification sent representatives to the separation conventions. (Hall notes only twenty-one rather than twenty-five Maine towns voting for ratification because of shared and split delegations.)
54 Elliot, *Debates in State Conventions*, 2:182; Jeremiah Hill to George Thatcher, Biddeford, Feb. 28, 1788, and Thomas B. Wait to Thatcher, Portland, Feb. 29, 1788, in Goodwin, "Thatcher Papers," pp. 342-343.

55 Jeremiah Hill to George Thatcher, Biddeford, Feb. 14, 1788, George Thatcher Papers, p. 139, Boston Public Library.
56 *CG*, Jan. 22, 1789.
57 Ibid., Jan. 29, 1789; Banks, *Maine Becomes a State*, p. 24; see Alan Taylor, *Liberty Men and Great Proprietors: The Revolutionary Settlement on the Maine Frontier, 1760–1820* (Chapel Hill: University of North Carolina Press, 1990).
58 Williamson, *History of Maine*, 2:532–533, 548–549; Hall, *Politics without Parties*, pp. 176–177.
59 Williamson, *History of Maine*, 2:532–533; Hall, *Politics without Parties*, p. 169 n.
60 Williamson, *History of Maine*, 2:549 n.; *Fleet's Pocket Almanack and Massachusetts Register* (Boston: T. and J. Fleet, 1791), pp. 114–115; Taylor, "Liberty-Men and White Indians," pp. 495–500; *Fleet's Register*, 1788, p. 99, 1791, p. 112; Louis C. Hatch, *The History of Bowdoin College* (Portland, Me.: Loring, Short, and Harmon, 1927), pp. 7–8. Thompson contributed to the college financially as well when James Bowdoin turned over to the college a note he held from Thompson worth £823.4.5, to be used in support of a chair in mathematics and experimental philosophy (p. 8).
61 Taylor, "Liberty-Men and White Indians," pp. 15–16, chaps. 6–7.
62 Ely, *Deformity of a Hideous Monster*, pp. 12–13, 24. See also Alan Taylor, "The Disciples of Samuel Ely: Settler Resistance against Henry Knox on the Waldo Patent, 1785–1801," *MeHSQ* 26 (Fall 1986): 66–100; Moody, "Samuel Ely."
63 Alan S. Taylor, "Nathan Barlow's Journey: Mysticism and Popular Protest on the Northeast Frontier," in Clark, Leamon, and Bowden, *Maine in the Early Republic*, pp. 103–110.
64 Marini, *Radical Sects*, chap. 3; Memorial of the Ministers and Elders of the First Presbytery at Topsham to the General Court, June 10, 1778, *Doc. Hist. Me.*, 16:229–232; Paul Coffin, "Memoir and Journals of Rev. Paul Coffin: Missionary Tours in Maine, 1796, 1797, 1798, 1800," *CMeHS*, 1st ser. 4 (1856): 301–405; and Rev. Joseph Field, "Journal of my missionary tour into the District of Maine in the summer of 1805," MeHS.
65 For background on Peter T. Smith, see Sibley and Shipton, *Biographical Sketches*, 13:355–359. For Thurston Whiting, see Taylor, *Liberty Men and Great Proprietors*, pp. 151–153.
66 James M. Banner, Jr., *To the Hartford Convention: The Federalists and the Origins of Party Politics in Massachusetts, 1789–1815* (New York: Alfred A. Knopf, 1970), pp. 26–30, 204–215.
67 Petition of the Fryeburg Baptists to the General Court, Sept. 1790, *Doc. Hist. Me.*, 22:396–398.
68 Stephen Marini, "The Religious Revolution in the District of Maine, 1780–1820," in Clark, Leamon, and Bowden, *Maine in the Early Republic*, p. 120; Henry O. Thayer, "Rev. Josiah Winship," *CMeHS*, 3rd ser. 1 (1904): 104–110; Marini, *Radical Sects*, pp. 87–88.
69 Marini, "The Religious Revolution," pp. 120, 131; Marini, *Radical Sects*, pp. 86–96, 99; Edward D. Andrews, *The People Called Shakers: A Search for the Perfect Society* (New York: Oxford University Press, 1953), p. 40.
70 Joseph Williamson, "Religious Denominations in Maine at the Close of the Revolution, from the Papers of Hon. Wm. D. Williamson," *CMeHS*, 1st ser. 7 (1876): 221;

Willis, *Smith and Deane Journals*, pp. 247, 261; Marini, *Radical Sects*, pp. 43–44, 51–54.
71 Plachta, "The Privileged and the Poor," pp. 158–159, 132–139; Noble, "Messengers from the Wilderness," pp. 130, 133–134, 142–143, 170, 174.
72 Town Records for Bristol, Brunswick, Scarborough, and Gorham, MeSA; Bristol Town Records, July 31, 1780, MeSA.
73 Cook, *Fathers of the Towns*, pp. 186–192; Cass, "Pownalborough," pp. 72, 130, 146–147.
74 Banner, *To the Hartford Convention*, p. 28–30, 65–66; William Nisbet Chambers, *Political Parties in a New Nation: The American Experience, 1776–1809* (New York: Oxford University Press, 1963), chap. 1.
75 Douglass G. Adair, "That Politics May Be Reduced to a Science: David Hume, James Madison, and the Tenth Federalist," in *The Reinterpretation of the American Revolution, 1763–1789*, ed. Jack P. Greene (New York: Harper and Row, 1968), pp. 487–503; *CG*, April 27, 1786.
76 Banks, *Maine Becomes a State*, pp. 44–50.
77 An Act Empowering the Governor to Renew the Licenses of Certain Absentees, 1784, *Doc. Hist. Me.*, 20:356–357; Gov. John Hancock to the General Court, March 19, 1784, ibid., p. 376; Hall, *Politics without Parties*, pp. 141–142; Merrill Jensen, *The New Nation: A History of the United States during the Confederation* (New York: Alfred A. Knopf, 1950), pp. 169–170; Jackson T. Main, *The Sovereign States, 1775–1783* (New York: New Viewpoints, 1973), pp. 279–282; *CG*, Oct. 22, 1785.
78 Hunt, "Loyalists of Maine," pp. 262–263, 210; Stephen Patterson, "The Roots of Massachusetts Federalism: Conservative Politics and Political Culture before 1789," in *Sovereign States in an Age of Uncertainty*, ed. Ronald Hoffman and Peter J. Albert (Charlottesville: University Press of Virginia, 1981), p. 45; Fryeburg Town Records, June 16, 1783, MeSA; Gorham Town Records, May 12, 1783, MeSA.
79 Hunt, "Loyalists of Maine," p. 263.
80 Ibid., p. 260; Sabine, *Biographical Sketches*, 2:139–140. Laurel Thatcher Ulrich, *A Midwife's Tale: The Life of Martha Ballard, Based on Her Diary, 1785–1820* (New York: Alfred A. Knopf, 1990), pp. 16–18.
81 Hunt, "Loyalists of Maine," pp. 210–211, 216, 226, 258–259.
82 Kershaw, *Kennebeck Proprietors*, pp. 286–289.
83 Frederic Allen, "Early Lawyers of Lincoln and Kennebec Counties," *CMeHS*, 1st ser. 6 (1859): 48–52; William Willis, *A History of the Law, the Courts, and the Lawyers of Maine, from its first colonization to the early part of the present century* (Portland, Me.: Bailey and Noyes, 1863), pp. 117–122.
84 Arthur Zilversmit, "Quok Walker, Mumbet, and the Abolition of Slavery in Massachusetts," *WMQ* 25 (Oct. 1968): 615, 623–624; *CG*, June 8, June 28, 1787, Nov. 15, 1790.
85 Elliot, *Debates in State Conventions*, 2:107.
86 Stakeman, "Slavery in Colonial Maine," pp. 76–78; Cass, "Pownalborough," pp. 180–181.
87 Hunt, "British-American Rivalry," pp. 176–177, 181–182; Col. Allan's Report on the Indian Tribes, 1793, in Kidder, *Military Operations*, p. 314; "Summary of Massachusetts/Penobscot Relations—*UPDATE*," Aug. 20, 1977, pp. 39–54, 54–60, 69–71; Williamson, *History of Maine*, 2:571–572, 669–671.

268   Notes to The Legacy of Revolution

88 "Survey of Massachusetts' Relationship with the Passamaquoddy Tribe (as of April 20, 1977)," pp. 33–41, typescript in Research and Position Papers Relative to the Indian Land Claims Case, Office of the Attorney General for the State of Maine, Augusta, copy in author's possession.

89 James Sullivan, *History of the District of Maine* (Boston: I. Thomas and E. T. Andrews, 1795; reprint ed., Augusta: Maine State Museum, 1970), pp. 130–131, 138. See also Charles E. Clark, "James Sullivan's History of Maine and the Romance of Statehood," in Clark, Leamon, and Bowden, *Maine in the Early Republic*, pp. 192–193.

90 An Act to Regulate Trade and Intercourse with the Indian Tribes, July 22, 1790, in United States, *Statutes at Large of the United States of America, 1789–1873*, 17 vols. (Boston: Little, Brown, 1845–1873), 1:137–138; Maine Land Claims Act of 1980, in United States, *Statutes at Large of the United States of America*, 109 vols. (Washington, D.C.: U.S. Government Printing Office, 1874–), 94:1785–1797.

91 Petition of Elizabeth Lines to the General Court, Pownalborough, West Precinct, April 3, 1779, *Doc. Hist. Me.*, 16:207; see also Allen, *Dresden*, pp. 325–326; Petitions of Lucy Rittal to Governor and Council, Pownalborough, Oct. 31, 1780, and to Col. Ezra Taylor, Pownalborough, Nov. 11, 1780, *Doc. Hist. Me.*, 19:10–12, 42–43; Hutchinson, *When the Revolution Came*, pp. 154–160.

92 Joan Hoff Wilson, "The Illusion of Change: Women and the American Revolution," in *The American Revolution: Explorations in the History of American Radicalism*, ed. Alfred Young (De Kalb: Northern Illinois University Press, 1976), p. 431.

93 Sally Wood, *Amelia; or, The Influence of Virtue: An Old Man's Story* (n.p.: Oracle Press, n.d.), p. 103, microfilm copy no. 2754, reel W-11, "American Fiction, 1774–1850," based on a bibliography by Lyle H. Wright, Research Publications, New Haven, Conn.; idem, *Dorval; or, The Speculator: A Novel Founded on Recent Facts* (Portsmouth, N.H.: Ledger Press by Nutting and Wheelock, 1801), p. 10, microfilm copy no. 2755, "American Fiction."

94 Sally Wood, *Julia; and the Illuminated Baron: A Novel Founded on Recent Facts, Which Have Transpired in the Course of the Late Revolution of Moral Principles* (Portsmouth, N.H.: United States Oracle Press, 1800), p. 47; no. 2757, "American Fiction"; Helene Koon, "Sally Sayward Barrell Wood," in *American Women Writers: A Critical Reference Guide from Colonial Times to the Present*, ed. Lina Mainiero, 4 vols. (New York: Unger, 1982), 4:452–454.

95 Wilson, "The Illusion of Change," pp. 389–391; Linda K. Kerber, *Women of the Republic: Intellect and Ideology in Revolutionary America* (Chapel Hill: University of North Carolina Press, 1980), pp. 283–288, 222–225, and Ulrich, *A Midwife's Tale*, pp. 76–101; Mary Beth Norton, *Liberty's Daughters: The Revolutionary Experience of American Women, 1750–1800* (Boston: Little, Brown, 1980), pp. 251–253.

96 George Thatcher to Sarah Savage Thatcher, Philadelphia, Jan. 3, 1800, George Thatcher Papers, MaHS.

97 Norton, *Liberty's Daughters*, pp. 45–46; George Thatcher to Sarah Savage Thatcher, Philadelphia, Jan. 22, 1800, Thatcher Papers, MaHS.

98 Henry Sewall to Henry Sewall, [Sr.], Newburgh, N.Y., June 18, 1783, Sewall Family Correspondence, Mellen Papers, Hawthorne–Longfellow Library.

99 Quoted in Plachta, "The Privileged and the Poor," p. 124.

BIBLIOGRAPHY

PRIMARY SOURCES: MANUSCRIPT

American Antiquarian Society, Worcester, Mass.
Jonathan Sayward Diaries, 1760–1799. 40 vols. Microfilm copy

Boston Public Library
George Thatcher Papers

Hawthorne–Longfellow Library, Bowdoin College, Brunswick, Me.
Sewall Family Correspondence, Mellen Papers.

Library of Congress, Washington, D.C.
Jacob Bailey Papers
Jonas Clark Papers
Nathan Dane Papers
John Lewis Papers
Edward Preble Papers
George Stillman Papers
James Sullivan Papers
John White Almanacs

Lincoln County Cultural and Historical Association, Wiscasset, Me.
Goodwin Papers
Johnson Papers

Maine Historical Society, Portland
Berwick, Maine, Subscription List for Support of Boston's Poor, July 18, 1774, Miscellaneous Papers, Box 15/2
Diary of John Bradbury
Rev. Joseph Field. "Journal of my missionary tour into the District of Maine in the summer of 1805"

Journal of Enoch Freeman
Silvester Gardiner Papers
John E. Godfrey Collection
Andrew Hawes Collection
Historical Manuscripts concerning Maine in the Landsdowne and Dartmouth Collections
Kittery, Maine, Miscellaneous Papers
Richard King Daybooks, 1772–1774
Henry Knox Papers, Microfilm reel no. 52, Item no. 87: Thurston Whiting and Benjamin Bracket to Henry Knox, Warren, Sept. 7, 1801
Lewis Family Papers
Diary of Stephen Longfellow, Longfellow Family Papers
Henry Mowatt Papers
Journal of Edward Oxnard
William Patterson Papers
Penobscot Expedition Papers, British and American, transcribed for Joseph Williamson
Samuel Perley Papers
Charles Pierce Papers
Jeremiah Pote to Capt. Wanton Stover, Falmouth, July 2, 1775, Miscellaneous Papers, Box 27/8
Jeremiah Powell Papers
Sewall Family Papers
Society of Friends, Falmouth Monthly Meeting
William Southgate Papers
George Thatcher Papers
Nathaniel Thwing, "Records of Lincoln County: Records of Criminal Actions, 1772"
Williamson Papers
William Willis Papers
John Wiswall Papers

Maine State Archives, Augusta

JUDICIAL RECORDS
Cumberland County Inferior Court of Common Pleas
Cumberland County Court of General Sessions of the Peace
Lincoln County Inferior Court of Common Pleas
Lincoln County Court of General Sessions of the Peace
York County Inferior Court of Common Pleas
York County Court of General Sessions of the Peace

TOWN RECORDS
Biddeford
Bristol
Brunswick
Falmouth
Fryeburg
Georgetown

Gorham
Kennebunkport
Lebanon
Newcastle
Pownalborough
Scarborough
Vassalborough
York

Massachusetts Historical Society, Boston
John Allan Papers
Caleb Davis Papers
Charles P. Greenough Papers
William Heath Papers
Richard King Daybooks, 1758–1768
Solomon Lovell Papers
James Otis Papers
Samuel P. Savage Papers
George Thatcher Papers
Thomas Wait Papers

Massachusetts State Archives, Office of the Secretary of State, State House, Boston

New-York Historical Society, New York
Richard King Papers (microfilm) in the Rufus King Papers

Portland Public Library, Portland
Enoch Freeman Almanacs, 1729–1793

Public Archives of Nova Scotia, Halifax
Colonial Correspondence
Letter Books and Transcripts of Dispatches from Governors
Military Correspondence between the years 1776 and 1784, being transcripts from the papers in the Royal Institution, London, known as the Dorchester Papers. 2 vols.
Papers relating to Crown Prosecutions
Records of the Proceedings of the Court of Vice Admiralty in Nova Scotia, 1749–1813
Transcripts from the Massachusetts Public Records relating to the American Invasion of Nova Scotia, including the papers of Jonathan Eddy and John Allan
Transcripts of Military Correspondence relating to Nova Scotia and Canada, mainly concerned with the period of the American War of Independence
Transcripts obtained from Ottawa, being selections from the military papers known as the Haldimand Collection in the British Museum. 3 vols.

Public Records Office, London
Extract of the log of H.M. Sloop *Allegiance*, Feb. 25, 1781 (photocopy)

Suffolk County Court House, Office of the Clerk of the Supreme Judicial Court for Suffolk County, Boston, Mass.
Court of Vice Admiralty, Province of Massachusetts Bay, 1765–1772, Minute Book
Superior Court Records for Cumberland and Lincoln Counties, 1765–1785
Superior Court Records for York County, 1765–1785

Wiscasset Public Library, Wiscasset, Me.
Transcripts of the Correspondence of Rev. Jacob Bailey. Ed. Charles E. Allen. 4 vols.

PRIMARY SOURCES: PRINTED

Adams, John. *Diary and Autobiography of John Adams.* Ed. L. H. Butterfield. 4 vols. Cambridge, Mass.: Harvard University Press, 1962.

Allis, Frederick S., Jr., ed. "William Bingham's Maine Lands, 1790–1820." *Publications of the Colonial Society of Massachusetts* 36, 37 (Boston: Colonial Society of Massachusetts, 1954).

American Husbandry. Ed. Harry J. Carman. New York: Columbia University Press, 1939. Reprint. Port Washington, N.Y.: Kennikat Press, 1964.

Bailey, Jacob. "Letter from Rev. Jacob Bailey, in 1775, Describing the Destruction of Falmouth, Maine." *Collections of the Maine Historical Society*, 1st ser. 5 (1857): 437–450.

Bartlet, William S. *The Frontier Missionary: A Memoir of the Life of the Reverend Jacob Bailey.* Boston: Ide and Dutton, 1853. Reprint. Ann Arbor, Mich.: University Microfilms, 1979.

Baxter, James P., ed. *Documentary History of the State of Maine.* 24 vols. Portland: Maine Historical Society, 1869–1916.

Brymner, Douglas, ed. *Report on the Canadian Archives for 1894.* Ottawa: S. E. Dawson, 1895.

Burnett, Edmund C., ed. *Letters of Members of the Continental Congress.* 8 vols. Washington, D.C.: Carnegie Institute, 1921–1936.

Calef, John, ed. *The Siege of Penobscot.* London, 1781. Reprint. New York: New York Times and Arno Press, 1971.

Cayford, John. *The Penobscot Expedition, being an account of the largest American naval engagement of the Revolutionary War.* Orrington, Me.: C&H Publishers, 1976.

Clark, William B., William J. Morgan, et al., eds. *Naval Documents of the American Revolution.* 9 vols. Washington, D.C.: U.S. Government Printing Office, 1964–.

Coffin, Paul. "Memoir and Journals of Rev. Paul Coffin: Missionary Tours in Maine, 1796, 1797, 1798, 1800." *Collections of the Maine Historical Society*, 1st ser. 4 (1856): 301–405.

Collier, George. *A Detail of Some Particular Services Performed in America, during the years 1776, 1777, 1778, and 1779.* New York: Ithiel Town, 1835. Reprint. Ann Arbor, Mich.: University Microfilms International, 1980.

Davis, Daniel. "The Proceedings of Two Conventions, Held at Portland, to Consider the Expediency of a Separate Government in the District of Maine." *Collections of the Massachusetts Historical Society* 4 (1795): 25–40.

Dwight, Timothy. *Travels in New England and New York.* Ed. Barbara M. Solomon. 4 vols. Cambridge, Mass.: Harvard University Press, 1968.
Elliot, Jonathan, ed. *Debates in the Several State Conventions on the Adoption of the Federal Constitution, . . . Together with the Journal of the Federal Convention.* 2nd ed. 5 vols. New York: Burt Franklin, n.d.
Ely, Samuel. *The Deformity of a Hideous Monster Discovered in the Province of Maine, by a Man in the Woods, Looking after Liberty.* Boston, 1797. No. 32081 in *Early American Imprints, 1639–1800,* ed. Clifford K. Shipton. American Antiquarian Society, Worcester, Mass.
Fairbanks, John. "John Fairbanks—His Journal." *Collections and Proceedings of the Maine Historical Society,* 2nd ser. 6 (1895): 139–144.
Fleet's Pocket Almanack and Massachusetts Register. Boston: T. and J. Fleet, 1788–1791.
Force, Peter, ed. *American Archives: Consisting of a collection of authentick records, state papers, debates, and letters and other notices of publick affairs, the whole forming a documentary history of the origin and process of the North American colonies . . .* 4th ser., 6 vols.; 5th ser., 2 vols. Washington, D.C.: M. St. Clair Clarke and Peter Force, 1837–1853.
Ford, Worthington C., et al., eds. *Journals of the Continental Congress, 1774–1789.* 34 vols. Washington, D.C.: U.S. Government Printing Office, 1904–1937.
Goodwin, William F., ed. "The Thatcher Papers." *Historical Magazine,* 2nd ser. 6 (Nov.–Dec. 1869): 257–271, 337–353.
Greene, Jack P., ed. *Colonies to Nation, 1763–1789: A Documentary History of the American Revolution.* New York: McGraw-Hill, 1967. Reprint. New York: W. W. Norton, 1975.
Handlin, Oscar, and Mary Handlin, eds. *The Popular Sources of Political Authority: Documents on the Massachusetts Constitution of 1780.* Cambridge, Mass.: Harvard University Press, 1966.
Hasey, Isaac. "Abstracts Relating to the Revolutionary War, from the Diaries of the Rev. Isaac Hasey, First Settled Minister of the First Parish of Lebanon, Maine (1765–1812)." Ed. George W. Chamberlain. *Collections and Proceedings of the Maine Historical Society,* 2nd ser. 9 (1898): 132–136.
Hutchinson, Thomas. *The History of the Colony and Province of Massachusetts-Bay.* Ed. Lawrence S. Mayo. 3 vols. Cambridge, Mass.: Harvard University Press, 1936.
Jones, Stephen. "Autobiography of Stephen Jones (of Machias)." *Sprague's Journal of Maine History* 3 (April 1916): 199–218.
———. "Historical Account of Machias." *Maine Historical Society Quarterly* 15 (Fall 1975): 47–56.
Kidder, Frederic. *Military Operations in Eastern Maine and Nova Scotia during the Revolution, chiefly compiled from the journals and letters of Colonel John Allan, . . .* Albany, N.Y.: Joel Munsell, 1867. Reprint. New York: Kraus Reprint, 1971.
Lincoln, Benjamin. "Observations on the Climate, Soil, and Value of the Eastern Counties in the District of Maine." *Collections of the Massachusetts Historical Society* 4 (1790): 142–153.
Lincoln, William, ed. *Journals of Each Provincial Congress of Massachusetts in 1774 and 1775.* Boston: Dutton and Wentworth, 1838.
Locke, John. *Two Treatises of Government.* Ed. Peter Laslett. Rev. ed. Cambridge: Cambridge University Press, 1960. Reprint. New York: Mentor Books, 1965.

Lovell, Solomon. *The Original Journal of General Solomon Lovell kept during the Penobscot Expedition, 1779, with a sketch of his life by Gilbert Nash.* Weymouth, Mass.: Weymouth Historical Society, 1881.

Martin, Joseph Plumb. *Private Yankee Doodle: Being a Narrative of Some of the Adventures, Dangers, and Sufferings of a Revolutionary Soldier.* Ed. George E. Scheer. Boston: Little, Brown, 1962.

Massachusetts. *Acts and Laws of the Commonwealth of Massachusetts.* 13 vols. Boston: Wright and Potter, 1890–1898.

———. *Acts and Resolves, Public and Private, of the Province of the Massachusetts Bay, to which are prefixed the Charters of the Province.* 21 vols. Boston: Wright and Potter, 1869–1922.

———. *Journal of the Convention for Framing a Constitution of Government for the State of Massachusetts Bay, from the Commencement of their First Session, Sept. 1, 1779, to the Close of their Last Session, June 16, 1780.* Boston: Dutton and Wentworth, 1832.

———. *Journals of the House of Representatives of Massachusetts, 1715–1778.* 53 vols. Boston: Massachusetts Historical Society, 1919–.

———. *Massachusetts Soldiers and Sailors of the Revolutionary War.* 17 vols. Boston: Wright and Potter, 1896–1908.

Patterson, William D., ed. *The Probate Records of Lincoln County, Maine, 1760–1800.* Portland: Maine Genealogical Society, 1895.

Petition of the Inhabitants of Deer Isle and Sedgwick, June 11, 1775. *Bangor Historical Magazine* 2 (July 1886–June 1887): 103–104.

Perkins, Simeon. *Diary of Simeon Perkins, 1766–1789.* Ed. Harold A. Innis, D. C. Harvey, and C. Bruce Fergusson. 2 vols. Toronto: Champlain Society, 1948, 1958.

Philbrook, Thomas. "The Narrative of Thomas Philbrook." In Hope Rider, *Valour Fore & Aft: Being the Adventures of the Continental Sloop "Providence," 1775–1779, Formerly Flagship "Katy" of Rhode Island's Navy.* Annapolis, Md.: Naval Institute Press, 1977.

Poole, Edmund D., ed. *Annals of Yarmouth and Barrington in the Revolutionary War.* Yarmouth, N.S.: Lawson Brothers, 1899.

Reed, Capt. William, to Col. Jonathan Buck, Naskeag, July 30, 1778, *Bangor Historical Magazine* 2 (March 1887): 183–184.

Reidhead, William. "Journal of William Reidhead." *Bangor Historical Magazine* 5 (June 1890): 226–231.

Segar, Nathaniel. *A Brief Narrative of the Captivity and Sufferings of Lt. Nathan'l Segar, Taken Prisoner by the Indians and Carried to Canada during the Revolutionary War.* Paris, Me.: Oxford Bookstore, 1825. Photocopy, Bethel Historical Society, Bethel, Me.

Shurtleff, James. *A Concise Review of the Spirit which seemed to Govern in the time of the American War.* Augusta, Me., 1798. No. 34548 in *Early American Imprints, 1639–1800,* ed. Clifford K. Shipton. American Antiquarian Society, Worcester, Mass.

Sullivan, James. *History of the District of Maine.* Boston: I. Thomas and E. T. Andrews, 1795. Reprint. Augusta: Maine State Museum, 1970.

Taylor, Robert J., ed. *Massachusetts, Colony to Commonwealth: Documents on the Formation of Its Constitution, 1775–1780.* New York: W. W. Norton, 1961.

Thorpe, Francis N., ed. *Federal and State Constitutions, Colonial Charters, and other Organic Laws of the States, Territories, and Colonies now or heretofore forming the United States of America.* 7 vols. Washington, D.C.: U.S. Government Printing Office, 1909.

Tucker, Daniel. "Capt. Daniel Tucker in the Revolution: An autobiographical Sketch, with prefatory remarks by Rev. E. C. Cummings." *Collections and Proceedings of the Maine Historical Society,* 2nd ser. 8 (1897): 225–254.

Tufts, Henry. *A Narrative of the Life, Adventures, Travels, and Sufferings of Henry Tufts, now residing at Lemington, in the District of Maine: In Substance as Compiled from his Own Mouth.* Dover, N.H.: Samuel Bragg, Jr., 1807. Reprinted as *The Autobiography of a Criminal: Henry Tufts,* intro. and ed. Edmund Pearson. New York: Duffield, 1930.

United States. *Statutes at Large of the United States of America, 1789–1873.* 17 vols. Boston: Little, Brown, 1845–1873.

———. *Statutes at Large of the United States of America.* 109 vols. Washington, D.C.: U.S. Government Printing Office, 1894–.

Wadsworth, Peleg. "Letter from General Peleg Wadsworth to William D. Williamson, Hiram, Jan. 1, 1828." *Collections and Proceedings of the Maine Historical Society,* 2nd ser. 2 (1891): 153–162.

Willis, William, ed. *Journals of the Rev. Thomas Smith and the Rev. Samuel Deane, Pastors of the First Church in Portland: with Notes and Biographical Notices and a Summary History of Portland.* Portland, Me.: Joseph S. Bailey, 1849.

Wood, Sally. *Amelia; or The Influence of Virtue: An Old Man's Story.* N.p.: Oracle Press, n.d. microfilm no. 2754, reel W-11, "American Fiction, 1774–1850," based on a bibliography by Lyle H. Wright, Research Publications, New Haven, Conn.

———. *Dorval; or, The Speculator: A Novel Founded on Recent Facts.* Portsmouth, N.H.: Ledger Press by Nutting and Wheelock, 1801. Microfilm no. 2755, reel W-11, "American Fiction, 1774–1850," based on a bibliography by Lyle H. Wright, Research Publications, New Haven, Conn.

———. *Julia; and the Illuminated Baron: A Novel Founded on Recent Facts, Which Have Transpired in the Course of the Late Revolution of Moral Principles in France.* Portsmouth, N.H.: United States Oracle Press, 1800. Microfilm no. 2757, reel W-11, "American Fiction, 1774–1850," based on a bibliography by Lyle H. Wright, Research Publications, New Haven, Conn.

Wroth, L. Kinvin, and Hiller B. Zobel, eds. *Legal Papers of John Adams.* 3 vols. Cambridge, Mass.: Harvard University Press, 1965.

NEWSPAPERS

Boston Chronicle
Boston Gazette
Essex Gazette
Falmouth Gazette (name changes to *Cumberland Gazette*)
New-Hampshire Gazette

RESEARCH AIDS

Attwood, Stanley B. *The Length and Breadth of Maine.* Augusta, Me.: Kennebec Journal, 1946. Reprint. Orono: University of Maine Press, 1974.

Bangor Public Library. *Bibliography of the State of Maine.* Boston: G. K. Hall, 1962.

Banks, Ronald F., comp. *Maine during the Federal and Jeffersonian Period: A Bibliographical Guide*. Portland: Maine Historical Society, 1974.

Chadbourne, Ava H. *Maine Place Names and the Peopling of Its Towns*. Portland, Me.: Bond Wheelwright, 1955.

Churchill, Edwin A. *Maine Communities and the War for Independence: A Guide for the Study of Local Maine History as Related to the American Revolution*. Augusta: Maine State Museum, 1976.

Churchill, Edwin A., and James S. Leamon, eds. "Maine in the Revolution: A Reader's Guide." *Maine Historical Society Quarterly* 15 (Spring 1976): 147–195.

Clark, Charles E., comp. *Maine during the Colonial Period: A Bibliographical Guide*. Portland: Maine Historical Society, 1974.

Felt, Joseph B., ed. "Statistics of Population in Massachusetts." *Collections of the American Statistical Association* 1, pt. 2 (1845): 121–216.

Freidel, Frank, and Richard Showman, eds. *Harvard Guide to American History*. Rev. ed. 2 vols. Cambridge, Mass.: Harvard University Press, 1974.

Greene, Evarts B., and Virginia D. Harrington, comps. *American Population before the Federal Census of 1790*. New York: Columbia University Press, 1932. Reprint. Gloucester, Mass.: Peter Smith, 1966.

Greenleaf, Moses. *A Statistical Survey of the District of Maine*. Boston: Cummings and Hillard, 1816. Enlarged and reprinted as *A Survey of the State of Maine*. Portland, Me.: Shirley and Hyde, 1829.

Hamer, Philip M., ed. *A Guide to Archives and Manuscripts in the United States*. New Haven: Yale University Press, 1961.

Haskell, John D., ed. *Maine: A Bibliography of Its History*. Boston: G. K. Hall, 1977.

Peckham, Howard H., ed. *The Toll of Independence: Engagements & Battle Casualties of the American Revolution*. Chicago: University of Chicago Press, 1974.

Ring, Elizabeth, ed. *A Reference List of Manuscripts Relating to the History of Maine*. 3 vols. Orono: University of Maine Press, 1938.

The Statistical History of the United States from Colonial Times to the Present. Stanford, Conn.: Fairfield Publishers, n.d.

Stewart Alice, comp. "Maine and Her Canadian Neighbors." Typescript draft bibliography in preparation.

Williamson, Joseph, ed. *A Bibliography of the State of Maine from the Earliest Period to 1891*. 2 vols. Portland, Me.: Thurston Printers, 1896.

SECONDARY SOURCES: BOOKS

Ahlin, John H. *Maine Rubicon: Downeast Settlers during the American Revolution*. Calais, Me.: Calais Advertiser Press, 1966.

Alberts, Robert. *The Golden Voyage: The Life and Times of William Bingham, 1752–1804*. Boston: Houghton Mifflin, 1969.

Allen, Charles E. *History of Dresden, Maine, formerly a part of the old town of Pownalborough, from its earliest settlement to the year 1900*. [Augusta, Me.: Kennebec Journal], 1931.

Allen, Gardner W. *A Naval History of the American Revolution*. 2 vols. Boston: Houghton Mifflin, 1913. Reprint. Williamstown, Mass.: Corner House Publishers, 1970.

Andrews, Edward D. *The People Called Shakers: A Search for the Perfect Society*. New York: Oxford University Press, 1953.
Bailyn, Bernard. *The Ideological Origins of the American Revolution*. Cambridge, Mass.: Harvard University Press, 1967.
———. *The Origins of American Politics*. New York: Alfred A. Knopf, 1968. Reprint. Vintage Books, 1970.
Baker, William A. *A Maritime History of Bath, Maine, and the Kennebec River Region*. 2 vols. Bath, Me.: Marine Research Society of Bath, 1973.
Baldwin, Alice M. *The New England Clergy and the American Revolution*. New York: F. Ungar, 1928.
Banks, Charles E. *History of York, Maine*. 2 vols. Boston: Calkins Press, 1931.
Banks, Ronald F. *Maine Becomes a State: The Movement to Separate Maine from Massachusetts, 1785–1820*. Middletown, Conn.: Wesleyan University Press, 1970. Reprint. Somersworth: New Hampshire Publishing and Maine Historical Society, 1973.
Banner, James M., Jr. *To the Hartford Convention: The Federalists and the Origins of Party Politics in Massachusetts, 1789–1815*. New York: Alfred A. Knopf, 1970.
Batchelder, Samuel F. *The Life and Surprising Adventures of John Nutting, Cambridge Loyalist, and His Strange Connection with the Penobscot Expedition*. Cambridge, Mass.: Cambridge Historical Society, 1912.
Bellot, Leland J. *William Knox: The Life and Thought of an Eighteenth-Century Imperialist*. Austin: University of Texas Press, 1977.
Bourne, Edward E. *The History of Wells and Kennebunk*. Portland, Me.: B. Thurston, 1875.
Bradbury, Charles. *History of Kennebunk Port, 1602–1837*. Kennebunk, Me.: James K. Remich, 1837.
Bragdon, Katherine. *The York and Boston Tea Parties*. York, Me.: Society for the Preservation of Historic Landmarks in York County, 1970.
Brebner, John B. *The Neutral Yankees of Nova Scotia: A Marginal Colony during the Revolutionary Years*. New York: Columbia University Press, 1937.
Bridenbaugh, Carl. *Cities in Revolt: Urban Life in America, 1743–1776*. New York: Alfred A. Knopf, 1955.
Brown, George, et al., eds. *Dictionary of Canadian Biography*. 10 vols. Toronto: University of Toronto Press, 1966–.
Brown, Richard D. *Revolutionary Politics in Massachusetts: The Boston Committee of Correspondence and the Towns, 1772–1774*. Cambridge, Mass.: Harvard University Press, 1970.
Brown, Robert E. *Middle-Class Democracy and the Revolution in Massachusetts, 1691–1780*. Ithaca, N.Y.: Cornell University Press, 1955.
Brown, Wallace. *The Good Americans: The Loyalists in the American Revolution*. New York: William Morrow, 1969.
———. *The King's Friends: The Composition and Motives of the American Claimants*. Providence, R.I.: Brown University Press, 1965.
Burrage, Henry S. *A History of the Baptists in Maine*. Portland, Me.: Marks Printing House, 1904.

———. *Maine in the Northeast Boundary Controversy.* Portland, Me.: Marks Printing House, 1919.

Callahan, North. *Henry Knox: General Washington's General.* New York: Rinehart, 1958.

Calneck, W. A., and A. W. Savary. *History of the County of Annapolis.* Toronto: William Briggs, 1897.

Chambers, William Nisbet. *Political Parties in a New Nation: The American Experience, 1776–1809.* New York: Oxford University Press, 1963.

Clark, Calvin M. *History of the Congregational Churches in Maine.* 2 vols. Portland, Me.: Southworth Printers, 1926, 1935.

Clark, Charles E. *The Eastern Frontier: The Settlement of Northern New England, 1610–1763.* New York: Alfred A. Knopf, 1970.

Clark, Charles E., James S. Leamon, and Karen Bowden, eds. *Maine in the Early Republic: From Revolution to Statehood.* Hanover, N.H.: University Press of New England, 1988.

Coleman, Kenneth. *The American Revolution in Georgia, 1763–1789.* Athens: University of Georgia Press, 1958.

———. *Colonial Georgia: A History.* New York: Charles Scribner's Sons, 1976.

Conrad, Margaret, ed. *They Planted Well: New England Planters in Maritime Canada.* Fredericton, N.B.: Acadiensis Press, 1988.

Cook, Edward M., Jr. *The Fathers of the Towns: Leadership and Community Structure in Eighteenth-Century New England.* Baltimore, Md.: Johns Hopkins University Press, 1976.

Crow, Jeffrey J., and Larry E. Tise, eds. *The Southern Experience in the American Revolution.* Chapel Hill: University of North Carolina Press, 1978.

Davis, Harold A. *An International Community on the St. Croix, 1604–1930.* Orono: University of Maine Press, 1950.

Day, Clarence. *History of Maine Agriculture, 1604–1860.* Orono: University of Maine Press, 1954.

Dickerson, Oliver M. *The Navigation Acts and the American Revolution.* Philadelphia: University of Pennsylvania Press, 1951.

Dole, Samuel T. *Windham in the Past.* Auburn, Me.: Merrill and Webber, 1916.

Drisko, George W. *Narrative of the Town of Machias, the Old and the New, the Early and the Late.* Machias, Me.: Press of the Republic, 1904.

———. *The Revolution: The Life of Hannah Weston, with a Brief History of Her Ancestry.* 2nd ed. Machias, Me.: George A. Parlin, 1903.

Eaton, Cyrus. *Annals of the Town of Warren.* Hallowell, Me.: Masters and Livermore, 1877.

———. *History of Thomaston, Rockland, and South Thomaston, Maine, from Their First Exploration, A.D. 1605, with Family Genealogies.* 2 vols. Hallowell, Me.: Masters, Smith, 1865.

Ernst, George. *New England Miniature: A History of York, Maine.* Freeport, Me.: Bond Wheelwright, 1961.

Ernst, Robert. *Rufus King, American Federalist.* Chapel Hill: University of North Carolina Press, 1968.

Folsom, George. *History of Saco and Biddeford.* Saco, Me.: Alex C. Putnam, 1830.

Fowler, William M., Jr. *Rebels under Sail: The American Navy during the Revolution.* New York: Charles Scribner's Sons, 1976.
French, Allan. *The First Year of the American Revolution.* New York: Octagon Books, 1968.
Goold, Nathan. *Windham, Maine, in the War of the Revolution, 1775–1783.* Portland, Me.: W. H. Bryant, 1900.
Gould, Edward K. *British and Tory Marauders on the Penobscot.* Rockland, Me., 1932.
Greene, Francis B. *History of Boothbay, Southport, and Boothbay Harbor, Maine, 1623–1905.* Portland, Me.: Loring, Short, and Harmon, 1906.
Greene, Jack P., ed. *The Reinterpretation of the American Revolution, 1763–1789.* New York: Harper and Row, 1968.
Greenleaf, Jonathan. *Sketches of the Ecclesiastical History of the State of Maine from the earliest settlement to the present time.* Portsmouth, N.H.: Harrison Gray, 1821.
Gross, Robert A. *The Minutemen and Their World.* New York: Hill and Wang, 1976.
Hall, Van Beck. *Politics without Parties: Massachusetts, 1780–1791.* Pittsburgh: University of Pittsburgh Press, 1972.
Handlin, Oscar, and Mary Handlin. *Commonwealth: A Study of the Role of Government in the American Economy: Massachusetts, 1774–1861.* New York: New York University Press, 1947. Revised, Cambridge, Mass.: Harvard University Press, 1969.
Harding, Samuel B. *The Contest over the Ratification of the Federal Constitution in the State of Massachusetts.* New York: Longmans, Green, 1896.
Hart, Albert B., ed. *Commonwealth History of Massachusetts, Colony, Province, and State.* 5 vols. New York: State History Company, 1928–1930.
Hatch, Louis C. *The History of Bowdoin College.* Portland, Me.: Loring, Short, and Harmon, 1927.
———, ed. *Maine: A History.* 3 vols. New York: American Historical Association, 1919. Reprinted as 1 vol. Somersworth: New Hampshire Publishing, 1974.
Henretta, James, and Gregory Nobles. *Evolution and Revolution: American Society, 1600–1820.* Lexington, Mass.: D. C. Heath, 1987.
Higgenbotham, Don. *The War for American Independence: Military Attitudes, Policies, and Practices, 1763–1789.* New York: Macmillan, 1971.
Hoerder, Dirk. *Crowd Action in Revolutionary Massachusetts, 1765–1780.* New York: Academic Press, 1977.
Hoffman, Ronald, Thad W. Tate, and Peter J. Albert, eds. *An Uncivil War: The Southern Backcountry during the American Revolution.* Charlottesville: University Press of Virginia, 1985.
Hofstadter, Richard. *America in 1750: A Social Portrait.* New York: Alfred A. Knopf, 1971. Reprint. New York: Vintage Books, 1973.
Hosmer, George L. *An Historical Sketch of the Town of Deer Isle, Maine.* Boston: Stanley and Usher, 1886.
Hutchinson, Thomas. *History of the Colony and Province of Massachusetts-Bay.* Ed. Lawrence S. Mayo. 3 vols. Cambridge, Mass.: Harvard University Press, 1936.
Hutchinson, Vernal. *When the Revolution Came: The Story of Old Deer Isle in the Province of Maine During the War for American Independence.* Ellsworth, Me.: Ellsworth American, 1972.

Hutson, James H. *John Adams and the Diplomacy of the American Revolution*. Lexington: University of Kentucky Press, 1980.

Jensen, Merrill. *The New Nation: A History of the United States during the Confederation*. New York: Alfred A. Knopf, 1950.

Johnson, Allen, and Dumas Malone, eds. *Dictionary of American Biography*. 20 vols., 4 supps. New York: Charles Scribner's Sons, 1928–1974.

Jones, E. Alfred. *The Loyalists of Massachusetts*. London: Saint Catherine's Press, 1930. Reprint. Baltimore: Genealogical Publishing, 1969.

Jordan, William B., Jr. *A History of Cape Elizabeth, Maine*. Freeport, Me.: House of Falmouth, 1965.

Kerber, Linda K. *Women of the Republic: Intellect and Ideology in Revolutionary America*. Chapel Hill: University of North Carolina Press, 1980.

Kershaw, Gordon E. *The Kennebeck Proprietors, 1749–1775: Gentlemen of Large Property & Judicious Men*. Somersworth, N.H.: New Hampshire Publishing and Maine Historical Society, 1975.

Klein, Rachel N. *Unification of a Slave State: The Rise of the Planter Class in the South Carolina Backcountry, 1760–1808*. Chapel Hill: University of North Carolina Press, 1990.

Koon, Helene. "Sally Sayward Barrell Wood." In *American Women Writers: A Critical Reference Guide from Colonial Times to the Present*, ed. Lina Mainiero, 4:452–454. 4 vols. New York: Unger, 1982.

Labaree, Benjamin W. *Colonial Massachusetts: A History*. Millwood, N.Y.: KTO Press, 1979.

Lapham, William B. *History of Bethel, Formerly Sudbury Canada, Oxford County, Maine, 1768–1890*. Augusta: Maine Farmer, 1891.

Libby, Orin G. *The Geographical Distribution of the Vote . . . on the Federal Constitution, 1787–1788*. University of Wisconsin Series in Economics, Political Science, and History, vol. 1. Madison: University of Wisconsin Press, 1894.

Locke, John L. *Sketches of the History of the Town of Camden, Maine, Including Incidental References to the Neighboring Places and Adjacent Waters*. Hallowell, Me.: Masters, Smith, 1859.

Lockridge, Kenneth. *A New England Town, the First Hundred Years: Dedham, Massachusetts, 1636–1736*. New York: W. W. Norton, 1970.

Maclay, Edgar S. *A History of American Privateers*. New York: Appleton, 1899.

McLellan, Hugh D. *History of Gorham, Maine*. Portland, Me.: Smith and Sale, 1903.

McLoughlin, William G. *New England Dissent, 1630–1833: The Baptists and the Separation of Church and State*. Cambridge, Mass.: Harvard University Press, 1971.

McManis, Douglas R. *Colonial New England: A Historical Geography*. New York: Oxford University Press, 1975.

MacNutt, William S. *New Brunswick: A History, 1784–1867*. Toronto: Macmillan, 1963. Reprint. 1984.

Maier, Pauline. *From Resistance to Revolution: Colonial Radicals and the Development of American Opposition to Britain*. New York: Alfred A. Knopf, 1972. Reprint. New York: Vintage Books, 1974.

Main, Jackson Turner. *The Anti-Federalists: Critics of the Constitution, 1781–1788*. Chapel

Hill: University of North Carolina Press, 1961. Reprint. Chicago: Quadrangle Books, 1964.
———. *Political Parties before the Constitution*. Chapel Hill: University of North Carolina Press, 1973.
———. *The Social Structure of Revolutionary America*. Princeton, N.J.: Princeton University Press, 1965.
———. *The Sovereign States, 1775–1783*. New York: New Viewpoints, 1973.
———. *The Upper House in Revolutionary America, 1763–1788*. Madison: University of Wisconsin Press, 1967.
Malone, Joseph J. *Pine Trees and Politics: The Naval Stores and Forest Policy in Colonial New England, 1691–1775*. Seattle: University of Washington Press, 1964.
Marini, Stephen A. *Radical Sects of Revolutionary New England*. Cambridge, Mass.: Harvard University Press, 1982.
Martin, James Kirby, and Mark Edward Lender. *A Respectable Army: The Military Origins of the Republic, 1763–1789*. Arlington Heights, Ill.: Harlan Davidson, 1982.
Melcher, Marguerite F. *The Shaker Adventure*. Princeton, N.J.: Princeton University Press, 1941.
Morgan, Edmund, and Helen Morgan. *The Stamp Act Crisis: Prologue to Revolution*. Rev. ed. Chapel Hill: University of North Carolina Press, 1962. Reprint. New York: Collier Books, 1963.
Morison, Samuel Eliot. *The Maritime History of Massachusetts, 1783–1860*. Boston: Houghton Mifflin, 1921. Reprint, 1941.
———. *The Story of Mount Desert Island, Maine*. Boston: Little, Brown, 1960.
Morris, Richard B. *The Peacemakers: The Great Powers and American Independence*. New York: Harper and Row, 1965.
Nadelhaft, Jerome J. *The Disorders of War: The Revolution in South Carolina*. Orono: University of Maine Press, 1981.
Nash, Charles E. *The History of Augusta: First Settlements and Early Days as a Town*. Augusta, Me.: Charles E. Nash and Son, 1904.
Nelson, William E. *The Americanization of the Common Law: The Impact of Legal Change on Massachusetts Society, 1760–1830*. Cambridge, Mass.: Harvard University Press, 1975.
Nelson, William H. *The American Tory*. Boston: Beacon Press, 1964.
Newcomer, Lee N. *The Embattled Farmers: A Massachusetts Countryside in the American Revolution*. New York: King's Crown Press, 1953.
North, James W. *The History of Augusta, Maine, from the Earliest Settlement to the Present Time*. Augusta, Me.: Clapp and North, 1870.
Norton, Mary Beth. *The British-Americans: The Loyalist Exiles in England, 1774–1789*. Boston: Little, Brown, 1972.
———. *Liberty's Daughters: The Revolutionary Experience of American Women, 1750–1800*. Boston: Little, Brown, 1980.
Owen, Henry Wilson. *History of Bath, Maine*. Bath, Me.: The Times, 1936.
Patterson, Stephen E. *Political Parties in Revolutionary Massachusetts*. Madison: University of Wisconsin Press, 1973.
———. "The Roots of Massachusetts Federalism: Conservative Politics and Political

Culture before 1789." In *Sovereign States in an Age of Uncertainty*, ed. Ronald Hoffman and Peter J. Albert. Charlottesville: University Press of Virginia, 1981.

Peters, Ronald M., Jr. *The Massachusetts Constitution of 1780: A Social Compact.* Amherst: University of Massachusetts Press, 1978.

Pierce, Josiah. *A History of the Town of Gorham, Maine.* Portland, Me.: Foster and Cushing, Bailey and Noyes, 1862.

Rawlyk, George A. *Nova Scotia's Massachusetts: A Study of Massachusetts–Nova Scotia Relations, 1630–1784.* Montreal: McGill–Queen's University Press, 1973.

Rowe, William H. *Ancient North Yarmouth and Yarmouth, Maine, 1636–1936: A History.* Yarmouth, Me.: Southworth-Anthoensin Press, 1937.

——. *The Maritime History of Maine.* New York: W. W. Norton, 1948.

Sabine, Lorenzo. *Biographical Sketches of Loyalists of the American Revolution.* 2 vols. Boston: Little, Brown, 1864.

Shy, John. *A People Numerous and Armed: Reflections on the Military Struggle for American Independence.* London: Oxford University Press, 1976.

Sibley, John L. *Biographical Sketches of Graduates of Harvard University*, and Clifford K. Shipton, *Biographical Sketches of Those Who Attended Harvard College.* 17 vols. Cambridge: Harvard University Press; and Boston: Massachusetts Historical Society, 1873–1975.

Siebert, Wilbur H. *The Exodus of the Loyalists from Penobscot to Passamaquoddy.* Columbus: Ohio State University Press, 1914.

Smith, Justin. *Arnold's March from Cambridge to Quebec; a critical study, together with a reprint of Arnold's Journal.* New York: G. Putnam's Sons, 1903.

Smith, Thomas L. *History of the Town of Windham.* Portland, Me.: Hoyt and Fogg, 1873.

Snow, Walter, comp. *Brooksville, Maine: "A Town of the Bagaduce."* Blue Hill, Me.: Weekly Packet, 1967.

Stahl, Jasper J. *History of Old Broad Bay and Waldoboro.* 2 vols. Portland, Me.: Bond Wheelwright, 1956.

Stark, James H. *The Loyalists of Massachusetts and the Other Side of the Revolution.* Boston: W. B. Clark, 1910.

Szatmary, David P. *Shays' Rebellion: The Making of an Agrarian Insurrection.* Amherst: University of Massachusetts Press, 1980.

Taylor, Alan. *Liberty Men and Great Proprietors: The Revolutionary Settlement on the Maine Frontier, 1760–1820.* Chapel Hill: University of North Carolina Press, 1990.

Taylor, Robert J. *Western Massachusetts in the Revolution.* Providence, R.I.: Brown University Press, 1954.

Ulrich, Laurel Thatcher. *A Midwife's Tale: The Life of Martha Ballard, Based on Her Diary, 1785–1820.* New York: Alfred A. Knopf, 1990.

Vickery, James B., III. *A History of the Town of Unity, Maine.* Manchester, Me.: Falmouth Publishing House, 1954.

Warden, G. B. *Boston, 1689–1776.* Boston: Little, Brown, 1970.

Wheeler, George A. *Castine, Past and Present.* Boston: Rockwell and Churchill Press, 1896.

——. *History of Castine, Penobscot, and Brooksville, Maine.* Bangor, Me.: Burr and Robinson, 1875. Reprint. Cornwall, N.Y.: Cornwall Press, 1923.

Wheeler, George A., and Henry W. Wheeler. *History of Brunswick, Topsham, and Harpswell, Maine.* Boston: Alfred Mudge and Son, 1878.
Williamson, Joseph. *History of the City of Belfast in the State of Maine from Its First Settlement in 1770 to 1875.* 2 vols. Portland, Me.: Loring, Short, and Harmon, 1877.
Williamson, William D. *The History of the State of Maine, from its first Discovery A.D. 1620, to the Separation, A.D. 1820.* 2 vols. Hallowell, Me.: Glazier, Masters, 1832. Reprint. Freeport, Me.: Cumberland Press, n.d.
Willis, William. *A History of the Law, the Courts, and the Lawyers of Maine, from its first colonization to the early part of the present century.* Portland, Me.: Bailey and Noyes, 1863.
———. *The History of Portland, from Its First Settlement, with Notices of the Neighbouring Towns, and of the Changes of Government in Maine.* 2 vols. Portland, Me.: Charles Day, 1833.
Wroth, L. Kinvin. *Province in Rebellion.* Cambridge, Mass.: Harvard University Press, 1975.
Young, Alfred, ed. *The American Revolution: Explorations in the History of American Radicalism.* De Kalb: Northern Illinois University Press, 1976.
Zobel, Hiller B. *The Boston Massacre.* New York: W. W. Norton, 1970.
Zuckerman, Michael. *Peaceable Kingdoms: New England Towns in the Eighteenth Century.* New York: Alfred A. Knopf, 1970. Reprint. New York: Vintage Books, 1972.

SECONDARY SOURCES: ARTICLES

Allen, Charles E. "Rev. Jacob Bailey." *Collections and Proceedings of the Maine Historical Society,* 2nd ser. 7 (1896): 225-253.
Allen, Frederic. "Early Lawyers of Lincoln and Kennebec Counties." *Collections of the Maine Historical Society,* 1st ser. 6 (1859): 38-81.
Allen, William. "Bingham Land." *Collections of the Maine Historical Society,* 1st ser. 7 (1876): 351-360.
Armstrong, Maurice W. "Religion and Neutrality in Revolutionary Nova Scotia." *New England Quarterly* 19 (March 1946): 50-62.
Ballard, Edward. "The Early History of the Protestant Episcopal Church in the Diocese of Maine." *Collections of the Maine Historical Society,* 1st ser. 6 (1857): 171-202.
Banks, Charles E. "The Destruction of Falmouth in 1775 and the Responsibility Therefore." *Collections and Proceedings of the Maine Historical Society,* 2nd ser. 5 (1894): 408-421.
Barnes, Viola. "Francis Legge, Governor of Loyalist Nova Scotia, 1773-1776." *New England Quarterly* 4 (July 1931): 424-447.
Baron, William R. "Eighteenth-Century New England Climate Variation and Its Suggested Impact on Society." *Maine Historical Society Quarterly* 21 (Spring 1982): 201-219.
Baxter, James P. "A Lost Manuscript." *Collections and Proceedings of the Maine Historical Society,* 2nd ser. 2 (1891): 345-375.
Bourne, Russell. "The Penobscot Fiasco." *American Heritage* 25 (Oct. 1974): 28-33, 100-101.

Brown, Margaret L. "William Bingham, Eighteenth Century Magnate." *Pennsylvania Magazine of History and Biography* 61 (July 1937): 286-324; (Oct. 1937): 387-434.
Burrage, Henry S. "The Attitude of Maine in the North-Eastern Boundary Controversy." *Collections of the Maine Historical Society,* 3rd ser. 1 (1904): 353-368.
Butler, Joyce. "The Wadsworths: A Portland Family." *Maine Historical Society Quarterly* 27 (Spring 1988): 2-19.
"Captain Agreen Crabtree of Sullivan, Me." *Bangor Historical Magazine* 8 (Jan.-Dec. 1893): 230-231.
Carlton, William R. "New England Masts and the King's Navy." *New England Quarterly* 12 (March 1939): 4-18.
Carter, R. Goldthwaite. "Col. Thomas Goldthwait — Was he a Tory?" *Collections and Proceedings of the Maine Historical Society,* 2nd ser. 7 (1896): 23-44, 185-200, 254-275, 362-379.
Chapman, Leonard B. "The Mast Industry of Old Falmouth." *Collections and Proceedings of the Maine Historical Society,* 2nd ser. 7 (1896): 390-404.
Churchill, Edwin A. "The Historiography of the *Margaretta* Affair; or, How Not to Let the Facts Interfere with a Good Story." *Maine Historical Society Quarterly* 15 (Fall 1975): 60-74.
——. "Merchants and Commerce in Falmouth (1740-1775)." *Maine Historical Society Newsletter* 9 (May 1970): 93-104.
Cushing, John D. "Notes on Disestablishment in Massachusetts, 1780-1833." *William and Mary Quarterly* 26 (April 1969): 169-190.
Dole, Samuel T. "Extracts from the Old Records of Windham." *Collections and Proceedings of the Maine Historical Society,* 2nd ser. 10 (1899): 308-320.
——. "The Meeting-House War in New Marblehead." *Collections and Proceedings of the Maine Historical Society,* 2nd ser 10 (1899): 175-185.
——. "Paul Little, Esq." *Collections of the Maine Historical Society,* 3rd ser. 1 (1904): 344-353.
——. "Windham's Colored Patriot." *Collections of the Maine Historical Society,* 3rd ser. 1 (1904): 316-321.
Dwight, Timothy. "The Story of General Wadsworth." *Maine Historical Society Quarterly* 15 (July 4, 1976): 227-256.
Emery, George F. "The Voice of Maine as Heard in the Genesis of Our Nationality." *Collections and Proceedings of the Maine Historical Society,* 2nd ser. 2 (1891): 51-82.
Faibisy, John D. "Penobscot, 1779: The Eye of the Hurricane." *Maine Historical Society* 19 (Fall 1979): 91-117.
Freeman, William. "Samuel Freeman, His Life and Services." *Collections and Proceedings of the Maine Historical Society,* 2nd ser. 5 (1894): 1-32.
Goold, Nathan. "Capt. Johnson Moulton's Company, the First to Leave the District of Maine in the Revolution." *Collections and Proceedings of the Maine Historical Society,* 2nd ser. 10 (1899): 300-308.
——. "Col. Edmund Phinney's 18th Continental Regiment." *Collections and Proceedings of the Maine Historical Society,* 2nd ser. 9 (1898): 45-106.
——. "Col. James Scamman's 30th Regiment of Foot, 1775." *Collections and Proceedings of the Maine Historical Society,* 2nd ser. 10 (1899): 337-402.
——. "Colonel Jonathan Mitchell's Cumberland County Regiment, Bagaduce Expedi-

tion." *Collections and Proceedings of the Maine Historical Society*, 2nd ser. 10 (1899): 52–80, 143–174.

———. "Falmouth Neck in the Revolution." *Collections and Proceedings of the Maine Historical Society*, 2nd ser. 8 (1897): 66–95, 143–169.

———. "General Samuel Thompson of Brunswick and Topsham, Maine." *Collections of the Maine Historical Society*, 3rd ser. 1 (1904): 423–458.

———. "History of Col. Edmund Phinney's 31st Regiment of Foot, the First Regiment Raised in the County of Cumberland in the Revolutionary War." *Collection and Proceedings of the Maine Historical Society*, 2nd ser. 7 (1896): 85–102, 151–185.

Grant, Frederic, Jr. "Benjamin Austin, Jr.'s Struggle with the Lawyers." *Boston Bar Journal* 25 (Sept. 1981): 19–29.

———. "The Court Martial of Paul Revere." *Boston Bar Journal* 21 (May 1977): 5–13.

———. "Observations on the Pernicious Practice of the Law." *American Bar Association Journal* 68 (May 1982): 580–582.

Handlin, Oscar, and Mary Handlin. "Radicals and Conservatives in Massachusetts." *New England Quarterly* 17 (Sept. 1944): 343–355.

———. "Revolutionary Economic Policy in Massachusetts." *William and Mary Quarterly* 4 (Jan. 1947): 3–26.

Harlow, Ralph V. "Economic Conditions in Massachusetts." *Publications of the Colonial Society of Massachusetts* 20 (1918): 163–191.

Henretta, James A. "Families and Farms: Mentalité in Pre-Industrial America." *William and Mary Quarterly* 25 (Jan. 1978): 3–32.

Hersey, Frank W. C. "Tar and Feathers: The Adventures of Captain John Malcom." *Publications of the Colonial Society of Massachusetts* 34 (April 1941): 429–473.

Huston, James A. "The Logistics of Arnold's March to Quebec." *Military Affairs* 32 (Dec. 1968): 110–124.

Jack, D. R. "Robert and Miriam Pagan." *Acadiensis* 2 (Oct. 1902): 279–287.

Jensen, Merrill. "The American Revolution and American Agriculture." *Agricultural History* 43 (Jan. 1969): 107–125.

Kerr, W. B. "The Merchants of Nova Scotia." *Canadian Historical Review* 13 (March 1932): 20–36.

———. "Nova Scotia in the Critical Years, 1775–6." *Dalhousie Review* 12 (April 1932): 97–107.

Kershaw, Gordon E. "A Question of Orthodoxy: Religious Controversy in a Speculative Land Company, 1759–1775." *New England Quarterly* 46 (June 1973): 205–235.

Kirby, John B. "Early American Politics—the Search for Ideology: An Historiographic Analysis and Critique of the Concept of 'Deference.'" *Journal of Politics* 32 (Nov. 1970): 808–838.

Leamon, James S. "The Stamp Act Crisis in Maine: The Case of Scarborough." *Maine Historical Society Newsletter* 11 (Winter 1972, misprinted 1971): 74–93.

Lemisch, Jesse. "Jack Tar in the Streets: Merchant Seamen in the Politics of Revolutionary America." *William and Mary Quarterly* 25 (July 1968): 371–407.

Lockridge, Kenneth A., and Alan Kreider. "The Evolution of Massachusetts Town Government, 1640–1740." *William and Mary Quarterly* 23 (Oct. 1966): 549–574.

Loring, Amasa. "The Four Judges of North Yarmouth." *Collections and Proceedings of the Maine Historical Society*, 2nd ser. 1 (1890): 57–77.

Maier, Pauline. "Popular Uprisings and Civil Authority in Eighteenth-Century America." *William and Mary Quarterly* 27 (Jan. 1970): 3–35.

Maas, David E. "Honest Graft in Revolutionary Massachusetts." *Boston Bar Journal* 23 (Oct. 1979): 7–15.

Moody, Robert E. "Samuel Ely: Forerunner of Shays." *New England Quarterly* 5 (Jan. 1932): 105–134.

Morison, Samuel Eliot. "The Struggle over the Adoption of the Constitution of Massachusetts, 1780." *Proceedings of the Massachusetts Historical Society* 50 (April 1917): 353–411.

Morse, Sidney G. "State or Continental Privateers?" *American Historical Review* 52 (Oct. 1946): 68–73.

"Nathan Jones, Robert Gould, and Francis Shaw." *Bangor Historical Magazine* 7 (Oct., Nov., Dec. 1891): 67–91.

Norton, William B. "Paper Currency in Massachusetts during the Revolution." *New England Quarterly* 7 (March 1934): 43–69.

"Notices of the Powell Family, and Extracts from Manuscripts of T. D. Powell." *Collections of the Maine Historical Society*, 1st ser. 7 (1876): 233–238.

O'Brien, John. "Exertions of the O'Brien Family at Machias, Maine, in the American Revolution." *Collections of the Maine Historical Society*, 1st ser. 2 (1847): 242–249.

Onuf, Peter S. "State-Making in Revolutionary Crisis." *Journal of American History* 67 (March 1981): 797–815.

Packard, John. "John Gardiner, Barrister." *Sprague's Journal of Maine History* 9 (April, May, June 1921): 49–59.

Perkins, John C. "Rev. Thomas Smith, D.D., and His First Parish of Falmouth, Now Portland." *Collections of the Maine Historical Society*, 3rd ser. 1 (1904): 288–315.

———. "Some Old Papers Recently Found in the Stone Tower of the First Parish Church of Portland." *Collections and Proceedings of the Maine Historical Society*, 2nd ser. 6 (1895): 7–36.

Pope, Charles H. "Machias in the Revolution." *Collections and Proceedings of the Maine Historical Society*, 2nd ser. 6 (1895): 121–138.

Porter, Joseph W. "Memoir of Colonel Jonathan Eddy of Eddington, Maine." *Bangor Historical Magazine* 4 (Sept. 1888): 41–54.

Prins, Harald E. L. "Two George Washington Medals: Missing Links in the Chain of Friendship between the United States and the Wabanaki Confederacy." *The Medal*, no. 7 (Winter 1985).

Rand, Edwin. "Maine Privateers in the Revolution." *New England Quarterly* 11 (Dec. 1938): 826–834.

Rawlyk, George A. "The American Revolution and Nova Scotia Reconsidered." *Dalhousie Review* 43 (Autumn 1963): 379–394.

"Rebels in Nova Scotia during the Revolutionary War." *Maine Historical Magazine* 9 (April, May, June 1894): 61–71.

"Regarding Soldiers of the American Revolution." *Sprague's Journal of Maine History* 6 (Nov., Dec., Jan. 1918–1919): 105–112.

Schmeckebier, L. F. "How Maine Became a State." *Collections and Proceedings of the Maine Historical Society*, 2nd ser. 9 (1898): 146–172.

Scott, Kenneth. "Price Control in New England during the Revolution." *New England Quarterly* 19 (Dec. 1946): 453–473.
Sewall, Joseph. "History of Bath." *Collections of the Maine Historical Society*, 1st ser. 2 (1847): 189–228.
Sewall, Rufus K. "A Refuge for Marie Antoinette in Maine." *Collections and Proceedings of the Maine Historical Society*, 2nd ser. 5 (1894): 284–305.
Siebert, Wilbur H. "The Exodus of the Loyalists from Penobscot and the Loyalist Settlement at Passamaquoddy." *Collections of the New Brunswick Historical Society* 9 (1914): 485–525.
Sloan, Robert. "New Ireland: Men in Pursuit of a Forlorn Hope, 1779–1784." *Maine Historical Society Quarterly* 19 (Fall 1979): 73–90.
Smith, David C., et al. "Climate Fluctuations and Agricultural Change in Southern and Central New England, 1765–1880." *Maine Historical Society Quarterly* 21 (Spring 1982): 179–200.
Smith, Jonathan. "How Massachusetts Raised Her Troops in the Revolution." *Proceedings of the Massachusetts Historical Society* 55 (June 1922): 345–370.
Smith, Paul H. "The American Loyalists: Notes on Their Organization and Numerical Strength." *William and Mary Quarterly* 25 (April 1968): 259–277.
Southgate, William S. "The History of Scarborough, from 1633 to 1783." *Collections of the Maine Historical Society*, 1st ser. 3 (1853): 1–237.
Sprague, John F. "Canadian Refugees in Maine and New England during the American Revolution." *Sprague's Journal of Maine History* 12 (Jan.–Mar. 1924): 16–20.
Stakeman, Randolph. "Slavery in Colonial Maine." *Maine Historical Society Quarterly* 27 (Fall 1987): 58–81.
Steiner, Bruce E. "New England Anglicanism—A Genteel Faith?" *William and Mary Quarterly* 27 (Jan. 1970): 122–135.
Stokesbury, James L. "Jonathan Eddy and the Fourteenth Colony." *Down East* 22 (April 1976): 18–22, 25, 27.
Syrett, David. "Town Meeting Politics in Massachusetts, 1776–1786." *William and Mary Quarterly* 21 (July 1964): 352–366.
Talbot, George F. "The Capture of the *Margaretta*: The First Naval Battle of the Revolution." *Collections and Proceedings of the Maine Historical Society*, 2nd ser. 2 (1891): 1–17.
Taylor, Alan. "The Disciples of Samuel Ely: Settler Resistance against Henry Knox on the Waldo Patent, 1785–1801." *Maine Historical Society Quarterly* 26 (Fall 1986): 66–100.
———. "A Kind of a Warr: The Contest for Land on the Northeastern Frontier, 1750–1820." *William and Mary Quarterly* 46 (Jan. 1984): 3–24.
Thayer, Henry O. "Loyalists of the Kennebec and One of Them—John Carleton." *Sprague's Journal of Maine History* 5 (Feb., March, April 1918): 241–262.
———. "Rev. Josiah Winship." *Collections of the Maine Historical Society*, 3rd ser. 1 (1904): 88–115.
Vermilye, A. G. "Memoir of the Rev. John Murray, First Minister of the Church in Boothbay." *Collections of the Maine Historical Society*, 1st ser. 6 (1857): 153–170.
Vroom, James. "The Penobscot Loyalists." *Acadiensis* 3 (July 1903): 172–182.

Weaver, Emily P. "Nova Scotia and New England during the Revolution." *American Historical Review* 10 (Oct. 1904): 52–71.

Whiting, B. J. "Incident at Quantabacook, March, 1764." *New England Quarterly* 20 (June 1947): 169–196.

Williamson, Joseph. "The British Occupation of Penobscot during the Revolution." *Collections and Proceedings of the Maine Historical Society*, 2nd ser. 1 (1890): 389–400.

———. "Capital Trials in Maine before the Separation." *Collections and Proceedings of the Maine Historical Society*, 2nd ser. 1 (1890): 159–172.

———. "The Conduct of Paul Revere in the Penobscot Expedition." *Collections and Proceedings of the Maine Historical Society*, 2nd ser. 3 (1892): 379–392.

———. "General Henry Knox." *Collections and Proceedings of the Maine Historical Society*, 2nd ser. 1 (1890): 1–27.

———. "Memoir of Col. Benjamin Burton." *Collections of the Maine Historical Society*, 1st ser. 7 (1876): 323–336.

———. "Religious Denominations in Maine at the Close of the Revolution, from the Papers of Hon. Wm. D. Williamson." *Collections of the Maine Historical Society*, 1st ser. 7 (1876): 217–230.

———. "Sir John Moore at Castine during the Revolution." *Collections and Proceedings of the Maine Historical Society*, 2nd ser. 2 (1891): 403–410.

———. "Slavery in Maine." *Collections of the Maine Historical Society*, 1st ser. 7 (1876): 207–216.

———. "The Professional Tours of John Adams in Maine." *Collections and Proceedings of the Maine Historical Society*, 2nd ser. 1 (1890): 301–305.

———. "A Proposed New Arrangement of New England in 1764." *Collections of the Maine Historical Society*, 3rd ser. 1 (1904): 339–343.

———. "The Proposed Province of New Ireland." *Collections of the Maine Historical Society*, 1st ser. 7 (1876): 199–206.

———. "The Proposed Province of New Ireland." *Collections of the Maine Historical Society*, 3rd ser. 1 (1904): 147–157.

Williamson, William D. "Sketches of the Lives of Early Maine Ministers." *Collections and Proceedings of the Maine Historical Society*, 2nd ser. 6 (1895): 184–196, 306–320.

———. "Sketches of the Lives of Early Maine Ministers." *Collections and Proceedings of the Maine Historical Society*, 2nd ser. 7 (1896): 44–326.

Wood, Gordon. "A Note on Mobs in the American Revolution." *William and Mary Quarterly* 23 (Oct. 1966): 635–642.

Yerxa, Donald A. "The Burning of Falmouth, 1775: A Case Study in British Imperial Pacification." *Maine Historical Society Quarterly* 14 (Winter 1975): 119–161.

Zilversmit, Arthur. "Quok Walker, Mumbet, and the Abolition of Slavery in Massachusetts." *William and Mary Quarterly* 25 (Oct. 1968): 614–624.

Zuckerman, Michael. "The Social Context of Democracy in Early Massachusetts." *William and Mary Quarterly* 25 (Oct. 1968): 523–544.

SECONDARY SOURCES: UNPUBLISHED

Allan, W. R. "Colonel Allan's Service in the War of the Revolution and His Reward." Paper in possession of Alice Stewart, Professor Emeritus, University of Maine at Orono.

Cass, Edward C. "A Town Comes of Age: Pownalborough, Maine, 1720–1785." Ph.D. dissertation, University of Maine at Orono, 1979.

Chester, Colby M. "Commodore Dudley Saltonstall, the Continental Navy, and the Defeat of the Penobscot Bay Expedition in 1779." Manuscript Division, Library of Congress, Washington, D.C.

Churchill, Edwin A. "Enoch Freeman, Trader, Citizen, Revolutionary: A Brief Portrait of an Eighteenth-Century Falmouth Merchant." April 22, 1969. Typescript research paper in author's possession.

Cowan, Sara J. "Revolutionary Bounty Lands in Maine." M.A. thesis, Columbia University, 1954. Copy at Maine Historical Society, Portland.

Day, Clarence A. "Colonel John Allan." Typescript research paper in possession of Alice Stewart, Professor Emeritus, University of Maine at Orono.

Elliott, Peter J. "The Penobscot Expedition of 1779: A Study in Naval Frustration." M.A. thesis, University of Maine at Orono, 1974.

Faibisy, John D. "Privateering and Piracy: The Effects of New England Raiding upon Nova Scotia during the American Revolution, 1775–1783." Ph.D. dissertation, University of Massachusetts at Amherst, 1972.

Gagne, Michael. "Rural Opposition to the Federal Constitution: The Case History of Sanford, Maine, 1780–1790." Honors thesis, University of Maine at Portland–Gorham, 1972.

Groton, N. "Biographical Sketch of Col. James Cargill, 1722–1813." Typescript copy at Maine Historical Society, Portland.

Hunt, Richard I., Jr. "British-American Rivalry for the Support of the Indians of Maine and Nova Scotia, 1775–1783." M.A. thesis, University of Maine at Orono, 1973.

———. "The Loyalists of Maine." Ph.D. dissertation, University of Maine at Orono, 1980.

King, Irving H. "The S.P.G. in New England, 1701–1784." Ph.D. dissertation, University of Maine at Orono, 1968.

Leeman, Martha. "A History of Woolwich, Maine, from Discovery to 1860." Honors thesis, University of Maine at Orono, 1948. Copy at Maine Historical Society, Portland.

Maguire, James H., ed. "A Critical Edition of Edward Parry's Journal, March 28, 1775, to August 23, 1777." Ph.D. dissertation, Indiana University, 1970.

Maine. Research and Position Papers Relative to the Indian Land Claims Case. Office of the Attorney General for the State of Maine, Augusta. Copies in author's possession.

Mawhinney, Eugene. "A Social History of Machias, Maine, Previous to 1800." M.A. thesis, University of Maine at Orono, 1949. Copy at Maine Historical Society, Portland.

Noble, John D. "Messengers from the Wilderness: Maine's Representatives to the Massachusetts General Court, 1760–1819." Ph.D. dissertation, University of Maine at Orono, 1975.

Ordway, David. Untitled, undated research paper on the closing of the courts in York County, 1773–1776. Original in possession of L. Kinvin Wroth, University of Maine School of Law, Portland.

Plachta, Adele E. "The Privileged and the Poor: A History of the District of Maine, 1771–1793." Ph.D. dissertation, University of Maine at Orono, 1975.

Pruitt, Bettye Hobbs. "Agriculture and Society in the Towns of Massachusetts, 1771: A Statistical Analysis." Ph.D. dissertation, Boston University, 1981.

Ross, Julie. "Jacob Bailey: Portrait of an Anglican Clergyman in 18th Century Nova Scotia." Honors thesis, Dalhousie University, Halifax, 1972. Microfilm copy at the Public Archives of Nova Scotia, Halifax.

Royle, E. C. "Pioneer, Patriot, and Rebel: Lewis Delesdernier." 1972. Pamphlet 383, Maine Historical Society, Portland.

Sloan, Robert. "New Ireland: Loyalists in Eastern Maine during the American Revolution." Ph.D. dissertation, Michigan State University, East Lansing, 1971. Photocopy at the Maine State Museum, Augusta.

Stewart, Alice. "John Allan." Draft article in preparation for the *Dictionary of Canadian Biography*.

Taylor, Alan. "Liberty-Men and White Indians: Frontier Migration, Popular Protest, and the Pursuit of Property in the Wake of the American Revolution." Ph.D. dissertation, Brandeis University, Waltham, Mass., 1986.

Whitmore, Albert A. "Separation of Maine from Massachusetts." M.A. thesis, University of Maine at Orono, 1917.

Wilde, Margaret F. "History of the Public Land Policy of Maine, 1620–1820." M.A. thesis, University of Maine at Orono, 1940.

Yerxa, Donald A. "Admiral Samuel Graves and the Falmouth Affair: A Case Study in British Imperial Pacification, 1775." M.A. thesis, University of Maine at Orono, 1974.

INDEX

Page numbers in italics refer to illustrations or captions; towns are listed under eighteenth-century names (with new names in parentheses).

Act to Prevent Monopoly and Oppression, 151
Adams, Abigail, 220
Adams, John, 12–13, *28*, 30–31, 170, 179, 182, 183–184, 194, 220
Adams, Samuel, 46, 50, 170, 194
Addison. *See* Pleasant River
Administration of Justice Act, 54, 56
Admiralty Board, British, 69
Admiralty courts, 41
Adventure, privateer, 100
Ahlin, John, xiv
Alarm lists, 75, 108. *See also* Militia
Alfred, Shakers at, 211
Algerian captives, 217
Allan, Col. John, 82–98 passim, 112, 129–149 passim, 163–164, 180, 218, 219, 248n.58; wife left in Nova Scotia, 162
American Board of Customs Commissioners, 45, 48, 49
American-French treaty of 1778, 96
Anderson, John, 163
Androscoggin River, Pejepscot Proprietors' settlements on, 7
Anglican church, 22, 33, 35–38, 157, 159
Anspach-Bayreuth, mercenaries from, 243n.1
Antifederalism, 203, 204, 205

Apthorp, Charles, 7
Arbitration, 57
Archaeology and the Canadian boundary, 181, 262n.52
Arnold, Benedict, 86–87
Articles of Confederation, 179
Arundel (Kennebunkport), 21, 46, 144
Assembly, New Ireland's proposed, 175
Association, Continental embargo, 63, 64, 68, 157
Atus, London, 145

Bagaduce, British-occupied, xv, xvi, 106–107, 123–129, 136, 138, 143, 155, 172. *See also* New Ireland
Bailey, Rev. Jacob, 15, 36, 37, 62, 63, 71, 141, 156, 159, 160–162, 177, 248n.58
Bakeman, John, 125–126, 156
Bakerstown, 78, 122
Baldwin. *See* Barrettstown
Banks, Ronald F., xv, 214
Baptists, 22, 35, 211
Barbary pirates, 217
Barlow, Nathan, 209
Barrell, Nathaniel, 205
Barrettstown (Baldwin), 191
Bastardy, 24
Baum, Jeremiah, 126, 127

Index

Bay of Fundy, 102, 103
Bayley, William, 147
Beef, 155
Bennet, William, 42, 44
Bennington, battle of, 143
Benton (Clinton), 191
Berkshire County (Mass.), radicalism in, 167, 197
Bernard, Gov. Francis, 7–8, 43, 45, 46
Berwick, 5, 9, 12, 146
Bethel (N.B.). *See* Sudbury Canada
Bicameral legislature, 168
Biddeford, 5, 76, 173–174
Bills of credit, 152
Blacks: excluded from franchise, 169, 170; in Maine population, 228n.36
Blue Hill votes on 1780 constitution, 174
Board of War (Massachusetts), 120
Boothbay: militia deter attack, 81; opposes 1778 draft of state constitution, 168–169; property distribution at, 20; public charity at, 148; taxes at, 153, 154; vulnerability of, 82, 83, 85. *See also* Townshend
Boston: Committee of Correspondence, 50, 51, 60; Committee of Inspection, 64; as economic center, 13–14; evacuated by British, 105; port closure, 54, 55–56, 135; press gang riot at, 29; as regional market, 13; representation in General Court, 26
Boston, Continental frigate, 86
Boston Gazette, 38, 46, 47, 57
Boundary, Maine-Canada, 180–181, 184
Bounties: for capture of British ships, 120; enlistment, 81, 144, 145, 146, 147, 189; royal, on strategic goods, 39
Bowdoin, James, 7, 37, 170, 194, 200, 204, 208, 266n.60
Bowdoin, William, 7
Bowdoin College, 208, 266n.60
Bowdoinham, 58–59, 62
Bowman, Edward, 17
Bowman, Jonathan, 37, 159, 160, 210
Boycotts, import, 47, 60. *See also* Continental Association
Breaking an entail, 216–217

Brewer, Josiah, 106–107
Bristol, 19, 21, 141, 142, 213, 257n.94
British naval patrols, 82–83
Broad Bay, 8
Brooklin. *See* Naskeag
Brunswick (Germany), mercenaries from, 243n.1
Brunswick (Me.), 6, 19, 46, 60, 61, 78, 122, 144, 155, 213
Buck, Jonathan, 106–107
Burton, Major Benjamin, 129
Buxton, 56, 172, 260n.19

Calef, Dr. John, 105, 107, 162, 175
Callahan, Charles, 82
Callahan, Rebecca, 163, 216
Cambridge encampment, Continental army, 75
Camden, 127, 144
Campbell, Lt.-Col. John, 177, 221
Campbell, Mary, 221
Canaan Plantation, general poverty in, 189
Canceaux, H.M.S., 64–67, 72
Caner, Dr. Henry, 37, 175
Cannon, 78, 84, 85, 92, 93, 102, 110, 185
Cape Breton, privateering off, 102
Cape Elizabeth, 57, 66, 78, 144, 150, 155, 191
Card, Anna, 190
Caribbean islands, trade with, 13, 14, 135, 189
Carleton, John, 162, 163
Cass, Edward, 156, 157
Castine. *See* Bagaduce
Catholicism. *See* Roman Catholicism
Cato, Sayward slave, 145
Chaloner, Dr. William, 148
Chandler, John, 214
Chandler's River (Jonesborough), 13–14, 20, 69, 141
Charters: colonial, and Parliament, 56; Gorges', 196; Massachusetts, of 1691, 3, 58, 167, 176
Chaudiere River, 87
Chester, Rear Adm. Colby, 246n.40

Churches, and social control, 21–23. *See also* Religion; individual sects
Churchill, Edwin, 15
Church of England. *See* Anglican church
Circular letter on Townshend Acts, 45–46
Clarke and Lake successors, 7, 192
Class method of meeting troop quotas, 145
Class system, colonial, 14–19
Clinton, Gov. Henry, 106
Clinton (Me.). *See* Benton
Coastal defense, 86, 103, 144, 182
Coasting trade, 135–136
Cobequid Bay, privateering in, 102
Codman, Richard, 136
Coercive Acts, 56, 59, 63
Coffee, 151
Collier, Commodore Sir George, 81–82, 92–94, 114, *115*, *116*, 177, 178
"Come-outers," 212
Commissions: militia officers', 29, 75–79; privateers', 101–102
Committee of Inquiry into Penobscot disaster, 118–119
Committees of Correspondence: Boston, 50, 51, 60; Falmouth, 67, 76–77
Committees of Inspection: Boston, 64; Falmouth, 64, 65
Committees of Inspection, Correspondence, and Safety: Gouldsborough, 131; Machias, 132–133
Committees of Safety: Bagaduce, 126; Cumberland County, 122; Machias, 84, 121; Massachusetts, 167; North Yarmouth, 151; Pownalborough, 160
Concord (Mass.): battle of, 63, 65, 75, 237 n.2; postwar resettlement from, 191–192
Congregational church, 21–22, 23, 35–37, 159, 171, 210
Congress, American, 179. *See also* Continental Congress
Connecticut, 154, 196
Constitution: federal, 203–205, 265 n.53; Massachusetts state, 167–169, 170–174, 258–259 n.6, 259–260 nn.17, 18

Construction of fortifications, by militia, 84, 121, 139
Continental Army, 75, 155
Continental Association, 63, 64, 68, 157
Continental Congress, 59, 63, 88, 97, 118, 120, 149, 150, 152, 154, 218
Continental Navy, 86
Contraband trade, 136–138
Conventions: county, 59–60, 77, 182; provincial, 46; separatist, 195, 198–199, 207, 265 n.53; state constitutional (1779), 170–171
Cook, Edward M., Jr., 61, 213
Corn, 151
Cornwallis, Lord Charles, 181
Coulson, Thomas, 64, 65, 67, 74, 157–158, 159
"Country rate," 15
County regiments, 78, 80
County taxes, 24
Courthouses, 24, 26
Court of Common Pleas, York County, dissolved, 57
Courts, 23–25, 49–50, 56–57, 125, 126, 138; admiralty, 42. *See also* Judiciary
Coxhall (Lyman), 145, 150, 153
Crabtree, Agreen, 100–101
Credit, financial, 15
Crime, 18
Crowd action. *See* Riots
Cumberland County, 7, 57, 58, 138, 149; conventions, 59, 77, 182; militia, 78–80, 108, 122, 144–145; representation in General Court, 27–28, 167; and state constitution, 168–169, 172
Cumberland Gazette, 194, 200, 214, 215, 217. *See also* *Falmouth Gazette*
Cursing, 24. *See also* Oaths
Cushing, Sheriff Charles, 37, 58, 128, 159, 160, 162, 210
Cushing, Thomas, 46
Cushing, William, 159
Cyrus, privateer, 100

Day, Clarence, 17
Day, Luke, 197
De Monts, Sieur, 181

294 Index

Deane, Rev. Samuel, 22, 80, 185, 194
Deane, Silas, 109
Debt, 24, 40, 151–152, 190–191
Declaration of Independence, 160, 167
Declaratory Act, 42
Decrow family, 192
Deer Isle, 14, 82, 141, 155, 221
Defamation, 24, 48
Deflation, 151–152
Deformity of a Hideous Monster (Ely), 209
Delesdernier, Lewis, 148
Democracy in militia, 79–80
Dependents: Indian, 149; loyalist, 162–164; military, 147–148, 220–221
Derby, Elias Haskett, 108
Deserters: American, 146, 147; from British, 177, 178
Deviants, social, 18
Dickinson, John, 45
Diligent, schooner, 69
Dissenters, religious, 209–212
Dockyard, Royal Navy, at Halifax, 90
Domet, Joseph, 158
Dorval; or, The Speculator (Wood), 221
"Down east," xvii
Dresden. *See* Pownalborough
Dual ship's papers, 137
Duer, William, 192–193
Durham. *See* Royalsborough
Dutch immigrants at Pownalborough, 37
Dutch Reformed Calvinists, 37, 159

East India Company, 51–52, 54
Eddy, Col. Jonathan, 88–90, 92, 148
Elizabeth, sloop, 137
Elliott, Peter J., 246n.40
Ely, Rev. Samuel, 187, 208–209
Emancipation, black: rumored, 143; through enlistment, 145
Enlistments, voluntary, 144, 145
Entail, breaking of, 216–217
Essex County, American impressment in, 108
European trade, Maine's, disrupted by Revolutionary War, 135

Faction, fear of, 214

Falmouth (Portland), 5, 6, 10, 12, 14, 19, 24, 47, 61, 63, 85, 107, 141, 185, 200; Anglicanism at, 22, 37–38; burned by Mowat's flotilla, 70–73, 74, 169, 236nn.84, 88; *Canceaux* incident ("Thompson's War"), 64–67; Committee of Correspondence, 50, 67, 76–77; loyalism in, 157–159; map of, *16*; militia, 76, 78–79, 122, 144; population, 9, 150; privateering from, 101; Quakers at, 164, 211–212; riots at, 29, 42–43, 48; sacked by Gorham militia, 72, 169; and the Stamp Act, 41–42; and state constitution, 167, 173; and the Tea Act, 52, 53–54
Falmouth Gazette, 188, 194–195, 197. See also *Cumberland Gazette*
Farming, 17–18
Federalists, 203
Fines: for fornication, 18; for nonrepresentation in General Court, 27–28; for not meeting troop quota, 145
Fire: Falmouth burned by Mowat's flotilla, 70–73, 74, 169, 236nn.84, 88; forest, general, of May 1780, 142–143
Firewood, 13, 150
Fishing, 10–11, 13, 14, 142, 183–184
Flogging, 18, 177
Flour, 150
Food shortages, 4, 12, 83, 97, 129–130, 140–144, 154–155
Fornication, 18, 24
Fort Cumberland, militia raid on, 88, 89–90
Fort George (Castine), xv, 104, *115*, 182
Fort Halifax, 7
Fort Howe, 91; British-Indian conference at, 96, 130
Fort Pownal, 85, 162
Fort Ticonderoga, Arnold driven back to, 87
Foster, Col. Benjamin, 83
France, 3, 11, 31, 37, 55, 96–97, 130, 135, 182
Franchise, General Court, 26, 168, 169, 170

Francklin, Michael, 95–96, 98
Frankfort, 7
Freedmen, 218
Freeman, Enoch, 14, 15, 16, 18, 31, 48, 64, 66, 190–191
Freeman, Samuel, 32, 77–78, 194
French and Indian War. *See* Seven Years' War
Frenchman's Bay, 101, 131–132, 133, 136, 141, 155
Friends, Religious Society of. *See* Quakers
Frontier settlements, 6, 9
Frost, Major William, 80
Fryeburg, 9, 145, 153, 155, 211, 215
Fur trade, 14, 39

Gage, Gen. Thomas, 58, 76
Gage, sloop, 102
Gardiner, John, 190, 216–217
Gardiner, Nathaniel, 162
Gardiner, Dr. Silvester, 7, 14, 36, 159, 216
Gardiner, William, 160
Gardinerstown (Gardiner), 7, 86
Garrison duty, by militia, 84, 121, 139
General Court, 7, 25–29, 34, 72, 84, 88, 90, 125, 127, 142–155 passim, 207, 212, 215; and Bagaduce expedition, 107–108, 118–119; expenses of delegates to, 27, 190; grants relief to war widows, 220–221; issues passes to occupied territory, 136, 137, 138; and Provincial Congress, 58–59; redresses District's grievances, 206–208; Townshend Acts, circular letter on, 45–46; unresponsive to Penobscots' complaints, 94–95. *See also* Provincial Congress
George III, 160, 176, 186
Georgetown, 6, 36, 62, 63, 86, 107; demographics, 9, 20, 150; mast trade at, 10, 63–64; and state constitution, 168–169, 172
Germain, Lord George, 105–106, 176
Germans: immigrants to Lincoln County, 8, 37; mercenaries, 143, 243 n.1
Gerry, Elbridge, 194
Goldthwait, Thomas and Henry, 162

Gorges, Sir Ferdinando, 196
Gorham, 46, 50, 60, 61, 154, 185, 213, 215
Gorham: demographics, 12, 19, 150; discourages returning Tories, 215; militia, 66, 72, 145, 169; religious dissenters at, 211, 212; and state constitution, 169, 172, 260 n.18; supports Thompson's command of militia, 78, 122; and Tea Act, 52, 53
Gorham, Col. Joseph, 89
Gorham, William, 194
Gould, Robert, 13–14
Gouldsborough, 13, 14, 20, 86, 131–132, 133, 202
Governor, Massachusetts, 167–173
Governor's council: of Massachusetts, 169, 170; of New Ireland, 175
Grand Banks fishery, 11, 183–184
Graves, Vice Admiral Samuel, 67, 69, 70
Gray, 78, 122, 150. *See also* New Boston
Great Awakening, 21, 36
Great Britain, 30–39, 41
Greene, Gen. Nathaniel, 120
Gross, Robert, 191
Guard ship, British, in Fundy Bay, 103
Guerrilla warfare, xvi

Hallowell, Benjamin, 7
Hallowell (Me.), 7, 150
Hampshire County (Mass.), radicalism in, 167, 197
Hancock, John, 15, 47, 132, 159, 194
Hancock, Thomas, 7, 15, 170
Hancock, Continental frigate, 86
Hancock County, 207
Hannibal, Continental ship, 100
Hard money, 15, 151, 152; tax in, 153
Harpswell, 78, 145, 148, 155, 191
Hatch, Louis C., xiv
Hatch, Mark, 125, 162, 177–178
Hatfield, David, 157
"Hessian" mercenaries, 143, 243 n.1
Hibernia, privateer, 100
Hillsborough, earl of, 45, 47–48
History of the District of Maine (Sullivan), xiii–xiv, 219–220

Hodge, Henry, 152
Hoffman, Ronald, 120
Holmes, John, 214
Horses, scarcity of downeast, 13
House of Commons, British, 26
House of Lords, provincial, proposed for New Ireland, 175
House of Representatives, provincial, 58
House ownership, 19
Howe, sloop, 102
Huguenots, 37, 159
Hunt, Richard I., Jr., 156, 157
Hutchinson, Gov. Thomas, 8, 28, 34–35, 41, 42, 175

Ilsley, Enoch, 43, 122, 194
Ilsley, Major Daniel, 122
Immigrants, non-English, 8, 37
Impressment into navy: American, 108; British, 29, 108
Indians, 3–5, 33, 81, 84, 89, 93, 111, 138, 149, 220; as allies, xv, 90, 94–99 passim, 129–131; Fort Howe conference, 96, 130; neutrality of, 91–92, 94–99 passim, 131; postwar condition of, 218–219; provisioning of, 130–131; stage raid on Sudbury Canada, 181–182
Indian Township, 219
Inferior Court of Common Pleas, 24
Inflation, 150–152
Intolerable Acts, 54
Irish immigrants at Pownalborough, 37. *See also* Scots-Irish immigration
Isleborough. *See* Long Island
Isles of Shoals, 149

Jails, 24
Jay's Treaty of 1794, 180
Jeffersonian Republicans, 214
Jersey, British prison ship, 100
Jones, Col. William, 82–84
Jones, Ichabod, 13–14, 16, 29, 67–68, 98
Jones, John, 127–128, 162, 216
Jones, John Coffin, 14
Jones, Nathan, 14, 101, 132, 137, 138, 139–140, 156, 202

Jones, Stephen, 30, 98, 132, 138
Jonesborough, 13–14, 20. *See also* Chandler's River
Jones Plantation, 9
Judiciary, 170, 187, 202, 207, 216–217. *See also* Courts
Julia; and the Illuminated Baron (Wood), 222
Justices of the peace, 21, 23–25

Kennebec Proprietors, 7–8, 14, 34, 36–37, 159, 192
Kennebec River, 7, 87, 218
Kent, Nathaniel, 14
King, Richard, 14, 16, 18, 43–44, 61, 68, 73, 214
King, prayers for, 160
King George's War, 6
King's Highway (U. S. Route 1), decrepitude of, 12
King William's War, 5
Kittery, 5, 9, 12, 53, 77
Knox, Henry, 192–193, 209, 210
Knox, William, 105, 176

Laborers, unskilled, 18
Labor supply, 144–150
Land: colonial government policy, 34–35; distribution at New Ireland, 175–176; grants, 6–8, 105; Indian, 33, 218–220; issues addressed by General Court, 206–207; postwar settlement of, 190–191; wild, exempted from tax, 207
Langdon, Judge Timothy, 127, 146
Law practice, 25–26, 190–191
Lebanon, 150
Legislature: bicameral, 168; New Ireland, proposed, 175; Nova Scotia, 103; unicameral, 172, 173, 197
Lender, Mark E., 147
Leonard, Daniel, 175
"Letters from a Farmer in Pennsylvania" (Dickinson), 45
Lewis, John, 144
Lewiston, 9
Lexington and Concord (Mass.), battles of, 63, 65, 75, 237n.2

Liberty Men and Great Proprietors (Taylor), xiv, 214
Lieutenant governor, 169
Lincoln, Gen. Benjamin, 170, 192, 197
Lincoln County, 7, 59, 155; General Court representation, 27–28, 167; judiciary, 57, 58, 160; under martial law, 123–127, 172, 177, 248n.58; militia, 78, 81, 85, 108; population, 6, 149; and state constitution, 168–169, 172
Lincolnshire Company, 8
Lines, Denis, 147–148
Lines, Elizabeth, 220–221
Linnekin, Clark, 163
Lithgow, Judge William, 223
Litigation, 180–191; fees, 25
Littlefield, James, 137, 138
Liverpool (N.S.) raid, 100, 102–103
Livestock ownership, 13, 19
Locke, John, 56
Log booms: Kittery-Portsmouth, 77; Machias, 92
Longfellow, Stephen, Jr., 29–30, 194
Long Island (Isleborough), 115
Lovejoy, Abiel, and his slave, 218
Lovell, Brig. Gen. Solomon, 109–118 passim
Loyalists, 104, 155–164, 179, 215, 255–256nn.63, 64; harassment of, 61–63, 66, 85; at New Ireland, 105–106, 119; resettled in Nova Scotia, 179–180 (*see also* Refugees: loyalist)
Lumbering, 10, 11, 13–14, 155
Lutherans, 37, 159
Lyde, George, 158
Lyman. *See* Coxhall
Lymeburner, Matthew, 162
Lyon, Rev. James, 18, 85, 89, 141, 145

MacClenachan, William, 36
Machias, 8–13 passim, 19, 70, 84, 86, 97, 107, 120, 129, 137, 148, 149, 207; British raid on, 81, 149; coastal defenses at, 144, 182; Collier's first raid on, 92–93; Committees of Inspection, Correspondence, and Safety, 84, 121, 132–133; considers neutrality, 132–134; embargo forces confrontation at, 67–69; food shortage at, 140–141, 143; and militia, 84, 121, 139; and Nova Scotia invasion attempt, 87–92; riot at, 21, 29–30; separatism at, 201–202; vulnerability of, 82, 83, 85
McLean, Brig. Gen. Francis, 104, 106, 107, 111, 177, 178
McLellan, Hugh, 17
Maine: and Britain, 30–39; historiography, xiii–xiv, xv–xvi; population, 6–9; social stratification of, xv (*see also* Social class); statehood movement, xv, 195–207 (*see also* Separatism)
Maine: A History (Hatch), xiv
Maine Becomes a State (Banks), xv, 214
Maine Rubicon (Ahlin), xiv
Majabigwaduce (Castine), 14. *See also* Bagaduce
Malcolm, Capt. Daniel, 49
Malcolm, John, 49
Malecites, 4, 90–96 passim, 130, 149, 218, 219
Margaretta, H.M.S., 68, 69, 100
Mariner, John, 17
Marini, Stephen, 209
Martial law: in Lincoln County, 122–129, 172, 177, 248n.58; in occupied Bagaduce, 174, 177–181
Martin, James K., 147
Martin, Joseph Plumb, 192
Massabeeseck, 145
Massachusetts: Board of War, 120; Charter of 1691, 3, 58, 167, 176; Committee of Safety, 167; council urges swift action at Bagaduce, 112; fleet destroyed in Penobscot expedition, 115–117; hegemony of, xiii; legislature (*see* General Court; Provincial Congress); monetary policy, 151–152; Navy Board, 112; postwar commission on Indians, 218–219; tax policies, 152–154
Massachusetts Government Act, 54, 56, 176
Massey, Maj. Gen. Eyre, 92
Masts, 10, 14, 33–35, 39, 63–64, 105, 130, 178

298 Index

Medumcook, 150
Mercantilism, 32, 38–39
Mercenaries, German, 143
Merchant class, Maine, 14–17
"Merry Dancers," 212
Micmacs, 4, 94, 96, 97
Military stores, 76, 84, 85, 155. *See also* Naval stores
Militia, 61, 66, 75, 82, 107–109, 122, 128; balks at garrison and construction duty, 84, 121, 139; at burning of Falmouth, 71–73, 236n.88; economic constraints on, 82–84; morale of, 112, 113, 119; officers, 29, 75–81 passim; plunder by, 71–73, 117, 169; recruitment (*see* Recruitment); Tory, 120
Minas Basin, privateering in, 102
Ministers: scarcity of, 23; social status of, 21
Minot. *See* Bakerstown
Missionaries, 23, 36, 210
Molasses, 155
Money, revolutionary, 150–152
Montgomery, Gen. Richard, 87
Moore, Midshipman James, 68, 69
Morale, militia, 112, 113, 119
Morison, Samuel Eliot, 171
Morris, Richard B., 183
Mount Desert, town of, eschews separatism, 202
Mount Desert Island, 8
Mowat, Capt. Henry, 64, 65, 66, 69, 106, 110, 114, *115*, 122, 159, 236n.84
"Murder Act," 54
Murray, Rev. John, 85

Narraguagus, 121, 131–132, 133, 141
Naskeag (Brooklin), 82
Natural Law, 195. *See also* State of nature
Nautilus Island, 111
Naval stores, 39, 178. *See also* Military stores
Navy Board (Mass.), 112
"Negroe's Complaint" (*Cumberland Gazette*), 217
Nelson, William, 157
Neutrality: American petitions for, 103, 131–132, 202; declared for inhabitants of Penobscot Bay, 125; of Indians, 91–92, 94–99 passim, 131; Yarmouth (N.S.) petitions for, 103, 131
New Boston, 7. *See also* Gray
New Brunswick created, 180
Newcastle, 21, 46, 142, 148, 153
"New Emission" money, Continental, 152, 154
Newfoundland, 102, 183–184
New Gloucester, 7, 145, 150, 211
New-Hampshire Gazette, 12, 18, 53, 185
New Hampshire government, as model for separatists, 196
New Ireland, 105–106, 157, 174–181. *See also* Bagaduce
New Lights, 21–22, 209–210
New Marblehead (Windham), 7
"New Song of the Success of 1759" (Freeman), 31
Nickells, William, 132, 138, 140, 202
"Nigger Ridge," Wells, 218
Nobel, Rev. Seth, 148
Nonimportation agreements, prerevolutionary, 47, 60. *See also* Continental Association
Northport, 192
North Yarmouth, 6, 46, 50, 51, 150, 173
Nova Scotia, 14, 102, 103; accepts loyalist refugees, 179–180; attempted invasion of, 87–92; privateering off, 99–103, 106, 131, 136; refugees from, 88, 90
Noyes, Lt. Col. Peter, 80
Number Four, 8, 131–132, 133
Nutting, John, 105, 162

O'Brien, Jeremiah, 29, 68, 69, 99–100
O'Brien, John, 100
Oaths: impious, 24; loyalty, 160–161, 177
Old Lights, 21–22
Oliver, Andrew, 41
Oliver, Thomas, 175
Orono, Chief, 95
Oswald, Richard, 179
Oxnard, Edward, 158, 215
Oxnard, Martha, 163
Oxnard, Thomas, 158, 162, 163, 215

Pagan, Robert, 158, 162, 178, 181
Palmer, Nathaniel, 165
Paper money, 150, 151, 198
Paris peace negotiations, 179, 183, 202
Parliament, 6, 26, 33–34, 42, 45, 52–59 passim, 175, 186
Parris, Albion K., 214
Parry, Edward, 63–64, 81
Parsons, Theophilus, 170
Passamaquoddy Indians, 4, 90–96 passim, 218, 219
Passamaquoddy-Saint John Indians. See Malecites
Patterson, Stephen, 171, 215
Pearsontown, 150. See also Standish
Pejepscot Company, 7, 8, 192
Pemaquid, British naval patrols off, 82–83
Penobscot Bay, 85, 106, 140
Penobscot Indians, 4, 5, 90–96 passim, 110, 149, 218–219, 220
Penobscot River, 7, 97, 115–117, 141
Pepperell, Sir William, 57, 59; brothers of, 215
Pepperellborough, 61. See also Saco
Perkins, John, 107, 162, 177–178
Perkins, Joseph, 125, 162, 177–178
Philadelphia, population of, 32
Phillips, Nathan, 14, 107, 162
Phinney, Col. Edmund, 76, 77
Pine Point, Indian settlement at, 219
Pitts, James, 7
Pittston, 7, 19
Pleasant River (Addison), 133–134, 136, 141
Poland. See Bakerstown
Polly, sloop, 68
Poor, in Maine, 18, 19, 20
Poor law, 24
Population: American colonial, 32; black, 19, 228n.36; Maine, after colonial wars, 6–9; wartime shifts in, 149–150
Pork, 155
Port Act, 54, 55, 234n.43
Portland. See Falmouth
Portsmouth, N.H., defenses against British, 77
Postal service, 12

Pote, Jeremiah, 158, 162, 178
Powell, Jeremiah, 152–153
Pownalborough (Dresden), 7, 9, 14, 20, 24, 50–51, 63, 107, 127–128, 136–151 passim, 154, 160, 213, 221; church strife at, 36–37; judiciary, 24, 57; loyalism in, 156–157, 159–161, 255n.63; and Solemn League and Covenant, 61–62
Pownall, Gov. Thomas, 7
Prayers for the king, 160
Preble, Jedediah, 66, 73, 151, 152
Preble, William Pitt, 214
Presbyterians, 37
Press gang riots, Boston and Falmouth, 29
Presumpscot River fish runs, 142
Price fixing, 151
Primogeniture, 216
Prince, slave of Sayward, 145
Privateering, xv, 99–103, 120, 129, 131, 138, 178, 182
Privy Council of England, 24
Proclamation Line, Appalachian, 6
Profit, 15
Property ownership, 17, 18, 19–20, 170, 190
Prospect, 192
Prostitution, 18
Provincial Congress, 58–59, 63, 76, 74, 95, 140–141, 150, 167, 218. See also General Court
Public office, 23–28 passim, 29

Quakers, 22, 35, 146, 164–165, 211–212, 257n.94
Quartering Act, 54–55
Quebec Act, 55
Quebec expedition, Arnold's, 86–87, 239n.36
Queen Anne's War, 5

Radicalism, backcountry, 167, 197, 208–212
Rainbow, H.M.S., 81–82
Ransom of own vessels, 137
Raymondtown, 9, 189

Recruitment, military, 80–81, 84, 91, 108, 144–146, 252–253 n.29
Reed, Andrew and Robert, 152
Refugees: loyalist, 104, 105–106, 127, 179; from Nova Scotia, 88, 90, 148
Regulator Movement (Carolinas), 25
Religion, 21–23, 35–38, 62, 209–212; freedom of, 170
Resolution, schooner, 100
Revere, Paul, 113, 116
Revolutionary War, xv–xvi; end of, 181–187
Rhode, Lonnon, 145
Rhode Island government, as model for separatists, 196
Rice, Thomas, 49
Rice, relief shipments of, 155
Rights, constitutional, 170, 204
Riots: Boston, 29; Falmouth, 29, 48; Machias, 21, 29–30; Scarborough, 30, 43–44; over Stamp Act, 41–42; Wiscasset, 49; Woolwich, 29; at Young's house in Bagaduce, 126. *See also* "White Indians"
Rittal, Francis, 151, 221
Road-building, 12, 207–208
Roman Catholicism, 3, 37, 55, 130, 159
Romeo, slave of Thomas Smith, 145
Rouse, William, 17
Royalsborough (Durham), 150
Rum, 5, 12, 15, 98

Sabbath breaking, 24
Saco, 5, 12. *See also* Pepperellborough
Safe-conduct, Nova Scotian vessels under, 136
Saint Andrews, N.B., 180
Saint Aubin, Chief Ambrose, 92
Saint Croix River, 179, 180–181; French settlement at, 181, 262 n.52; Indian settlement at Pine Point, 219
Saint George, 6
Saint Georges River, settled by Scots-Irish, 8
Saint John Island, privateering off, 102
Saint John River, 90–91, 97
Saint Lawrence River, 87
Salamander, privateer, 100

Salaries, government, 49–50, 196–197
Saltonstall, Commodore Dudley, 108–118 passim, 246 n.40
Sanford, 12, 150, 212
Saratoga, battle of, 143
Savage, Arthur, 158
Savannah (Ga.), occupied by British, 106, 119–120
Sawmills, 9
Sayward, Jonathan, 14, 16, 18, 28, 45, 46, 142, 144, 145, 182–188 passim, 215, 221, 264 n.18
Scarborough, 5, 6, 14, 19, 30, 46, 61, 66, 76, 143, 144, 185, 213
Schaffers, John, 143
Schoodic River, 180–181
Scollay, John, 234 n.43
Scots-Irish immigration, 8, 37
Scott, Sylvanus, 149, 150
Separatism, 206–207, 264 n.18. *See also* Statehood movement
Seven Years' War, 6
Sewall, Henry, 76, 188, 223
Sewall, Judge David, 203, 204
Shakers, 211
Shannon, James Noble, 136
Shapleigh petitions for tax relief, 189
Shattuck, Job, 197
Shaw, Francis, 13–14
Shaw, Francis, Jr., 14, 132–140 passim, 202
Shays, Daniel, 197
"Shaysism," 203
Shays' Rebellion, 197–205 passim, 212
Sheepscot, British naval patrols, 82–83
Shire towns, 9
Shirley, Gov. William, 7
Shurtleff, James, 209
Shy, John, 85, 147
Sieur de Monts, 181
Slavery, 18–19, 143, 145, 217–218
Sloan, Robert, 156, 157
Smith, Paul, 156, 157
Smith, Peter T., 210
Smith, Rev. Thomas, 18, 38, 42, 75, 141, 142, 150, 152, 182, 194, 211, 237 n.2; enlists his slave, 145

Social class: property and, 17–20; riot and, 29, 30
Society for Propagating Christian Knowledge, 36
Society for the Propagation of the Gospel, 35, 36, 38
Solemn Leagues and Covenants, 60–63
Sons of Liberty: Boston, 41; Scarborough, 44
Soule, Capt. Levi, 127
Sparhawk, Nathaniel and Samuel, 215
Special Court of Sessions, Lincoln County, 160
Specie, 15, 151, 152
Squatters, 191, 193, 198, 208, 212
Stakeman, Randolph, 228n.36
Stamp Act, 40–42
Standish, 189. *See also* Pearsontown
State constitution, Massachusetts, 167–169, 170–174, 258–259n.6, 259–260nn.17, 18
Statehood movement, Maine, xv, 195–207. *See also* Separatism
State of nature, 50–51. *See also* Natural Law
Stevens, Elizabeth, 163
Stewart, Capt. Charles, 185–186
Stiles, Ezra, 23
Stillman, Richard, 68
Strong, Caleb, 170
Sudbury Canada, 181–182
Suffolk County, American impressment in, 108
Sugar, 151
Sullivan, Capt. Daniel, 128, 129
Sullivan, Gen. John, 128
Sullivan, James, xiii–xiv, 77–84 passim, 219–220
Supreme Judicial Court, 24
Swearing. *See* Oaths
Swiss immigrants to Waldoboro, 8
Sylvester (Turner), 9

Taxes: county, 24; General Court grants relief from, 155, 207; postwar, 152–154, 190–191; religious, 22, 164, 171

Taxpayers: "classing" of, and troop quotas, 145–146; and General Court franchise, 169
Taylor, Alan, xiv, 214
Tea Act of 1773, 51–54
Temple, Capt. Robert, 8
Thatcher, George, 222–223
Theft, 24
Third Regiment, Lincoln County, 82
Thomaston, 127, 142, 150, 155
Thompson, Samuel, 62–80 passim, 109, 157–62 passim, 198, 200–208 passim, 217, 266n.60; satirized, 164
Thwing, Nathaniel, 24
Tiger, privateer, 100
Tomma, Pierre, 92, 97
Topsfield (Mass.), 145
Topsham, 6
Tories. *See* Loyalists
Town committees, 59
Town government, 20–21
Town meetings, 51, 213
Townshend (Boothbay), 70, 82–83, 109, 112, 113, 150, 185. *See also* Boothbay
Townshend Acts, 45–49
Trade: with enemy, 136–138; foreign, disrupted, 135; with Indians, private, 98
Trade and Intercourse Act of 1790, 220
Trading post. *See* Truck houses
Train bands, 75, 108. *See also* Militia
Truck houses (trading posts), 4, 95, 97, 98, 101, 218
Tufts, Henry, 18
Turner. *See* Sylvester
Twycross, Lydia, 162
Tyng, Sheriff William, 48, 58, 59, 158, 162–163, 215

Unicameral legislature, 172, 173, 197
Unity, sloop, 68
Universalism, 62

Vassalborough, 7, 144, 145, 150, 154
Veterans, as squatters, 191
Veto, gubernatorial, 170
Viper, sloop, 86, 102

Wadsworth, Brig. Gen. Peleg, 117, 122–138 passim, 174, 177, 192, 194
Wait, Thomas, 199, 201
Waite, Col. John, 80
Waldo, Francis, 216
Waldo, Samuel, 8
Waldoboro, German and Swiss immigration to, 8
Waldo patent, 192
Warren (Me.), Scots-Irish settle near, 8
Warren, Continental frigate, 108
Washington, George, 77–78, 88, 121, 182, 217
Washington (Me.), given tax relief, 155
Washington County created, 207
Waterborough, postwar tax burden, 189
Wedderburn, Alexander, 176
Wells, 5, 9, 77, 150, 172–177
Weston, Hannah and Rebecca, 68–69, 236n.79
Whaleboats, 102, 123
Wheeler, William, 37
"White Indians," 29, 35, 53, 208
Whiting, Thurston, 210
Widgery, William, 198, 205
Williams, Shubal, 177
Williamson, Jonathan, 160
Williamson, Joseph, 228n.36
Williamson, William, xiv
Wilson, Joan Hoff, 221

Windham, 66, 78, 122, 150, 164. *See also* New Marblehead
Winslow, 7
Winthrop, 150
Wiscasset, 10, 49, 63, 81
Wiswall, Rev. John, 38, 65, 158
Wollstonecraft, Mary, 221, 222
Women, postwar, 220–223
Wood, Abiel, 49, 136, 160
Wood, Sally Sayward Barrell, 221–222
Woolwich, 29, 50, 62, 211
Worcester County (Mass.), radicalism in, 167, 197
Writ of review, 25
Wyer, David, 158, 162
Wyer, David, Jr., 158
Wyer, Thomas, 158, 162–163, 178

Yarmouth (N.S.) petitions for neutrality, 103, 131
York, 5, 12, 14, 24, 28, 42, 50, 53, 167, 173, 178, 200; loses vessels to British, 135–136, 141, 142; militia, 76, 77, 144; population change, 9, 150
York County, 57, 149, 153, 191; convention movement, 59, 60; General Court representation, 27–28, 167; militia, 78, 108; and state constitution, 168–169, 172
Yorktown, battle of, 181
Young, Joseph, 125, 126, 156